Women Direct Shakespeare in America

Women Direct Shakespeare in America

Productions from the 1990s

Nancy Taylor

Madison • Teaneck
Fairleigh Dickinson University Press

© 2005 by Rosemont Publishing & Printing Corp.

All rights reserved. Authorization to photocopy items for internal or personal use, or the internal or personal use of specific clients, is granted by the copyright owner, provided that a base fee of $10.00, plus eight cents per page, per copy is paid directly to the Copyright Clearance Center, 222 Rosewood Drive, Danvers, Massachusetts 01923. [0-8386-4049-4/05 $10.00 + 8¢ pp, pc.]

Associated University Presses
2010 Eastpark Boulevard
Cranbury, NJ 08512

The paper used in this publication meets the requirements of the American National Standard for Permanence of Paper for Printed Library Materials Z39.48-1984.

Library of Congress Cataloging-in-Publication Data

Taylor, Nancy, 1962–
    Women direct Shakespeare in America : productions from the1990s / Nancy Taylor.
       p.   cm.
    Includes bibliographical references and index.
    ISBN 0-8386-4049-4 (alk. paper)
    1. Shakespeare, William, 1564–1616—Stage history—United States. 2. Shakespeare, William, 1564–1616—Stage history—1950– 3. Women theatrical producers and directors—United States. 4. Theater—United States—History—20th century. I. Title.
PR3105.T395   2005
792.02′33′0922—dc22
                                      2004015220

PRINTED IN THE UNITED STATES OF AMERICA

Contents

Acknowledgments   7
Introduction   11

             The Directors   33

    Jayme Koszyn   36
    Lisa Wolpe   41
    Tina Packer   49
    Ellen O'Brien   56
    Abigail Adams   60
    Melia Bensussen   65
    Barbara Gaines   71
    JoAnne Akalaitis   77

            The Productions

1. Destruction Wrought by Domestic Violence: Jayme Koszyn and Lisa Wolpe Direct *Romeo and Juliet*   87
2. "How do poor people live?": Tina Packer and Ellen O'Brien Direct *Measure for Measure*   128
3. Whose Gender Is It Anyway?: Abigail Adams and Melia Bensussen Direct *Twelfth Night*   164
4. Once Upon a Time: Barbara Gaines and JoAnne Akalaitis Direct *Cymbeline*   206

Epilogue 239
Notes 242
Bibliography 270
Index 297

Acknowledgments

A BOOK IS NOT BORN WITHOUT LOTS OF HELP ALONG THE WAY. Thanks to Kathy Murphy Anderson and Michael Perlis who were supportive of me in my transition from an English program, where I had hit a dead end, to a theater program, where I really belonged. Thanks to my dissertation committee at Tufts University, Barbara Freedman, Barbara Grossman, Susan Clark, and especially Laurence Senelick, who encouraged me to keep peddling my book until I found the right home for it. Thanks to Bill Worthen who read the introduction and made some helpful comments. *Great* thanks goes to Barbara Hodgdon, who so generously read the entire manuscript and gave me wonderful, detailed feedback. She really helped me turn the dissertation into a book. Donna LaRue has my thanks for being a supportive friend and colleague and for running down some citations at the Tufts library when I would have had to drive two hours to lay my hands on the book. Thanks also to my mom who has provided encouragement throughout the process. Thanks to Harry Keyishian and the reader at Fairleigh Dickinson University Press who believed in the project and the editors at Associated University Presses, Julien Yoseloff, Christine Retz, and Deborah Bloom, who helped ready the book for publication. And thanks to my dear Adam, who came into my life late in this story but helped me celebrate just the same.

I'd also like to thank my students and community members at MacMurray College, where I started my career, who have taught me about directing Shakespeare and who have helped me bring him to life. Thanks also to the encouragement and constructive criticism of my colleagues, especially Jeannie Zeck and Robert Seufert. I look forward to learning more from my students and colleagues at Illinois College. And to my good friend and colleague/mentor John Austin, who has provided enormous support to me as I've started my career, I wouldn't be here without you. I hope many years of directing Shakespeare and studying more of "his" directors, particularly women, lie ahead.

Women Direct Shakespeare in America

Introduction

On a warm day in June 1998, I was sitting with six other acting workshop participants in the front rows of a theater. Prior to arriving, we had been instructed to memorize a Shakespearean monologue that held some significance for us. The instructor was asking the actor onstage if there was anyone in her own life who reminded her of Angelo, particularly considering his relationship with Isabella in the scene from which she had taken her monologue, 2.2 of *Measure for Measure*. The actor looked puzzled. She said she couldn't think of anyone she knew who fit Angelo's role. But what became apparent through the instructor's continued questioning was that for this actor, Angelo was her father, who had begun to rape her when she was nine, a crime that continued until she left home at sixteen. She had tried once to talk to him about it, but he did not really understand the problem, or perhaps deflected the discussion. At any rate, she had not been able to confront him fully. To release the actor's anger, grief, and pain into the monologue, the instructor was using the relatively common method of holding the actor's arms behind her back while she tried to break free so that she encountered physical resistance. It was working well. At a pause, the instructor said something to the effect of, "You shouldn't really be behaving this way. This is not acceptable conduct for women in this society." The actor went limp and suddenly looked worried, confused. The instructor repeated the admonition in a tone of voice that was slightly different from her typical intonation, cueing the actor that she was not speaking those words in her own voice; rather, she was taking on the role of conservative society, a role with which she did not personally identify. The instructor was using her own authority to encourage the actor to resist a damaging cultural authority. In an environment that invited the actor to fight such dictates, she recognized the lies—cultural, familial, and psychological—that had so long constrained her. Although she had been angry before, this recognition released an even deeper core of fury. I will never forget hearing the rage and contempt in her voice, seeing it in her body as she threw herself against the arms of her instructor and cried, "O, it is excellent / To have a giant's strength, but it is tyrannous / To use it like a giant" (2.2.108–10). The actor had chosen to direct her monologue to the only man in our group close to her father's age. I suddenly noticed his large frame shaking as he sobbed silently. In a processing session afterward, he shared with the whole corps of sixty workshop participants that he hoped he would always be and be perceived as a loving and nurturing father.

I witnessed this event during my first week of Shakespeare and Company's month-long intensive actor training program. I was there partly on a scholarly mission of research, having chosen Tina Packer as one of the women directors I would study for this project. However, having trained as an actor but never this intensively, I was also excited by this opportunity to delve into Shakespeare through the craft of acting. Some of the methodologies used in the workshop were feminist (by some arguments), or at least indirectly achieved feminist goals; others did not. But I definitely grappled with my own history, my own subjectivity within that very specific social context, and these explorations fed some of the best acting I have ever done. It reaffirmed my decision to study how women have recently directed Shakespeare in this country.

As a theater professor and artist interested in both the academic study of how Shakespeare's texts are made material in production and the theatrical experience of embodying the text myself or directing actors, I am interested in how other women are interpreting and staging Shakespeare, particularly in the wake of second-wave feminism (1970s) in this country. Even though some women still resist what they understand as feminism, various feminist ideas and activities are widespread throughout American culture. I wonder if women directors' work reveals any common feminist assumptions they share as a result of study; of exposure to other, particularly avant-garde, productions; or of their lived experience in this culture. I wonder about how they represent the female body onstage and how they encourage various ways of seeing.[1] How are their choices potentially constrained by economic or institutional pressures? How do spectators respond to their choices?

This book offers a series of case studies of how eight women have directed Shakespeare on the 1990s American stage. Such an approach allows me to produce and distribute an archival record of their work—"thick descriptions," to use Clifford Geertz's recently cited phrase—albeit filtered through my own ideological lens, which is primarily a composite of various feminisms.[2] And certainly rendering a material production, which begins with a discursive play text, into another discursive text, this book, has its limitations. For the process includes not only viewing the subjectively produced archival records, but also seeing, analyzing, and remembering (or misremembering, as the case may sometimes be). But reproductions are always a step removed from the original, a retelling "with a difference," both because of the process of changing the thisness of performance into the thatness of the texts,[3] and because ideology is always present in our thinking and our viewing. Disavowal of ideology, as I found among some directors, only reveals an unacknowledged ideology. Production choices are, in some senses, always political even though only those resistant to dominant, and therefore naturalized, ideologies will be commonly viewed as such.[4] But I tried to analyze as best I could what sorts of ideologies—whether personal, directorial, "designorial," "actorial," or theatrical—guided the production of meaning in performance. I also tried to separate my own lens from the directors' ideas and to take pleasure in their work as a spectator as well as to study it as a feminist academic writer.

In order to highlight a particular set of concerns central to gender studies and thereby narrow the scope of the project, I have focused primarily on how women directors have interpreted and staged female subjectivity, particularly within romantic or sexual relationships between men and women. I use the term "sex relations" to describe this area because it concerns the relation of male to female. Certainly gender, defined here as cultural ideas about sexual identity, comes into play, but that is an additional layer moving alongside sex relations. I have paired the eight directors and four plays in the project so I can compare two directors' productions of each play: *Romeo and Juliet, Measure for Measure, Twelfth Night,* and *Cymbeline.* The plays I chose span three genres, including two subgenres: tragedy, dark comedy, cross-dressing comedy, and romance. This allows me to examine how the genre affects or fails to affect the directors' difficulty in negotiating between the conventions driving the genre and their own desired impact on the audience. In the democratically feminist vein of choosing both central and marginal subjects, I have selected widely interpreted and performed plays as well as plays receiving less critical and theatrical attention, but all four raise different questions concerning female subjectivity as it functions in potentially erotic relationships between the sexes. In part, the plays were chosen because a number of women I wanted to study had directed them, but I began with a cross-genre framework.

A similar ethic guided my choice of directors for the project, and I have chosen a wide range of women in an attempt to create a relatively broad sampling.[5] Four worked as freelance directors on the productions I am studying, though JoAnne Akalaitis and Melia Bensussen have since taken academic appointments. In addition, Abigail Adams was on a brief hiatus from her position as artistic director of The People's Light and Theatre Company of Malvern, Pennsylvania. Three other directors are also artistic directors of their own companies: Tina Packer, Barbara Gaines, and Lisa Wolpe. Most are teachers as well as directors. Ellen O'Brien was a professor in the Department of Theatre Studies of a small liberal arts college, but she has since taken a position as a consultant for the Shakespeare Theatre in Washington, D.C., and also teaches in the Academy of Classical Acting, an MFA program affiliated with the Shakespeare Theatre and George Washington University. Although researching eight productions does not define trends concerning all women directors of Shakespeare in this country, it at least documents and explores a range of tactics such directors employ as well as offering analysis of the kinds of cultural work in which their productions potentially engage. The directors in this study represent a cross-section of professionally central and marginal, ideologically humanist and postmodern, theatrically realistic and avant-garde. They also cross institutional and geographical boundaries, their works performed for diverse audiences.

I used a wide range of materials when researching these productions. In terms of visual records of the plays, while I saw only two of the eight in the theater (Tina Packer's *Measure for Measure* and Abby Adams's *Twelfth Night*), for four others I viewed a video recording of a performance (Jayme Koszyn's *Romeo and Juliet*, Melia Bensussen's *Twelfth Night*, JoAnne Akalaitis's *Cymbeline*, and Barbara Gaines's *Cymbeline*), and for a fifth I viewed a video of crucial scenes (Lisa Wolpe's *Romeo and Juliet*). For only one (Ellen O'Brien's *Measure for Measure*) did I have to rely purely on production photographs. Attending a live performance (or two) has long been considered the most authentic method of reviewing. Certainly, the spectator is freer to take in any and all elements of the production according to his or her whim or purpose of the moment. The video controls the spectator's viewpoint to varying degrees, imposing a second audiovisual script onto the stage script.[6] Natural sight is generally clearer than a recording through a lens situated at the back of the house, though, depending on the size of the house and the possibility for close-up focus, facial expressions may be rendered more visible by the camera than by the natural eye. Audience response is also usually more discernible when one is part of that audience rather than merely seeing or hearing its responses as recorded on tape. Also missing from the audiovisual script is a sense of the theater building's architecture (though I was able to visit all of the production sites except for Wolpe's) and the contextualizing extratheatrical experiences involved in attending a performance. However, I discovered that use of the videotape was often an asset. Occasionally, while taking notes in the theater, I would hear people laugh, and look up, only to have missed the joke. With the possibility of viewing and reviewing, critical scenes could be analyzed a number of times, first impressions confirmed or revised, and nothing lost to the vagaries of trying to write in the dark (legibly enough to be read later) and watch as simultaneously as possible. The audiovisual script is perhaps the ideal record of staged "kinetic phenomena."[7]

I also made use of more traditional materials: promptbooks, reviews, recent stage history of the plays, material on the directors' other work, material on the institutions they worked for, and production photographs. All of these materials, various kinds of reproductions, bear the marks of their "scribes" and limitations of their medium. Most were also not produced for my consumption as a theater historian and critic. Reviews usually capture only one performance of a given run, written for a specific audience and purpose generally not consonant with mine. Some production photographs do not even cite moments that appear on the stage but rather represent an image the director or public relations manager considered important for archival and publicity purposes. Even promptbooks record the blocking only up until the end of the rehearsal process, which, particularly for long runs, may not remain stable. I did not have access to all of the promptbooks, and I chose not to focus significant attention on cuts. The text is itself a construct whose boundaries change in the transition from literary drama to performance script and also, potentially, throughout the rehearsal process. Any performance is already an adaptation of the text, and cuts in these productions did not produce radical alterations of the play.

One of the most important sources of information was interviews with the directors. The interviews came last in the process because I wanted to come to the performance with only my own preconceptions. Creating an oral history of a production has its own difficulties, however. The mediation of "the real" through someone's spoken narrative of her experience filtered through the lens of ideology, time, and a response constructed for an academic interviewer creates the possibility of a significant divide between objective reality and the momentarily remembered and narrated past. However, this book does not attempt the impossible—to recapture objectively the moments of rehearsal, the developmental trajectory of the director's ideas at the time, or even the production itself. The very process of mediation, concerning both my own subjective view of the materials I was studying and the directors' choices about self-representation are also the subject of this project. Like Charlotte Canning and her work on feminist theaters in the USA, I see these interviews "both as true and as impressions of occurrences . . . as stable accounts of events and as subjective and conflicting memories." The directors and I have constructed "a collective historical subject together," a collection of their experiences in working with Shakespeare in a specific context. The method is obviously collaborative,[8] but the interviews also require the kind of analysis necessary for interpreting any other primary source material. While my discursive rendering of these performances may result to a certain extent in a history of theatrical documents rather than theater history,[9] in combination these various records create a composite archive producing an image of a theatrical happening rich for analysis.

Yet my methods of analysis were complicated in a number of ways. To begin with, some of the women directors' relationships with feminism are marked by qualification, uneasiness, or outright rejection, and so they resist a feminist line of inquiry. Misha Berson interviewed some women theater practitioners in the mid 1990s, and she quotes Irene Lewis, the artistic director of Center Stage: "I think that posing gender questions to women artistic directors diminishes the larger issues we face—those associated with the art reproduced."[10] Lewis resists any suggestion that feminist issues influence her work. Likewise, Deborah Warner declined to be interviewed by Elizabeth Schaefer because she felt the study would create a "regressive and reductive" context for her work.[11] I discovered that very few directors read feminist theory or even literary criticism, but various feminisms have been in the culture so long that some of their ideas have been absorbed and reproduced onstage, much as Freud's ideas have come to play a dominant role in many Americans' consciousness. Not surprisingly, women are more likely than men to direct plays in ways that are responsive to feminist concerns, though it is also true that some male directors create productions that are more feminist than those created by women directors. Feminism developed out of women's experience of a male-dominated society, increasing many people's awareness of how this society has often oppressed women. Whether the women directors I have chosen for the project are consciously feminist or not, and while one consciously resists such a label, their experiences as women in this culture have created worldviews responsive in some ways to feminist concerns, which often find expression in their performance choices. Similarly, Lizbeth Goodman found that although most of the British performance artists she researched considered themselves feminists as long as they could define what feminism meant to them, there were a few exceptions—Emilyn Claid, Mara de Wit, Ann Jellicoe, and Nina Rapi, for example. Most of the artists Goodman interviewed *were* concerned, however, about being *labeled* feminists because of the kinds of prejudices often attached to the term.[12]

The backlash of postfeminism, which in some instances might narrow job opportunities or box office revenue if misunderstood and publicly proclaimed, may push women directors toward a separation between the personal and professional. Goodman cites director Clare Venables, who describes herself as "absolutely a feminist" but not a "feminist artist," even though she believes a feminist philosophy informs her work. Goodman claims the distinction is important to a number of women she interviewed.[13] Similarly, Linda Hart notes that Karen Finley describes her ideology and performance practices as primarily radical and liberal feminist. Even though one may grant that such oppositional positions are common among U.S. feminists and need not be unified, a further contradiction surfaces when analyzing Finley's performances, which "occupy politic-aesthetic spaces that are not easily subsumed under either a liberal or radical feminist agenda."[14] In this work I negotiate among various definitions of feminism, the directors' self-proclaimed viewpoints, my own reading of their productions, and reviewers' readings as well.

Goodman also remarks on the difficulty of *evaluating* women's work in the theater: "For those of us whose job it is to criticize and review theatre, as well as to make it and theorize about it, the issue of sisterly solidarity is a minefield of conflicting values and allegiances."[15] I have sometimes found myself reluctant to criticize these women whose work I admire, who generously gave of their time to assist me in this project, and who are in some ways my mentors. My sentiments echo Geraldine Harris, who also began her work because she was interested in women performance artists: "My pleasure in these works inevitably has to do with a sexed/gendered identification with the practitioners." Harris refused to establish any evaluative model prior to her research, both to avoid appropriating the women's works into the category of feminist theater and to resist the tendency to dictate practice by theory, although she admits to ending up with something like a thesis by the end of her book (*Staging Femininities* [1999]). She used the theories of Judith Butler, Jacques Derrida, and Diane Elam to interrogate three productions by women performance artists, privileging the "relational positionalities" the shows created through encouraging an interplay between dramatic form, authorial intention, and audience interpretation. The audience was actively encouraged to participate in the "process of making meanings." By highlighting the negotiation necessary in the interpretation of a theatrical event resistant to absolutes, the performances produced a "politics of undecidability," which, as a postmodern feminist performance critic, she applauded. But she also allowed the performances to interrogate the internal contradictions in and the provisionality of these academic theories.[16] I have taken a similar approach to this project.

Analyzing these productions within a feminist performance theory framework is itself problematic in some ways. I do not want to suggest that practice should necessarily follow theory, because theatrical practice in particular is often resistant to academic theories. But as a performance critic, I can articulate what kind of cultural work performances might be doing in a way that the performances themselves cannot articulate. Richard Schechner has written recently about the pervasive *de*ductive as opposed to *in*ductive bent to performance studies, calling for new theories to be generated from archival and historical research, from experiencing and describing productions to illuminate them as opposed to applying theory to practice.[17] He also advocates studying mainstream theater.[18] The most cutting-edge work in this field, however, analyzes productions of feminist performance artists, who produce works very different from most productions of Shakespeare. So theories used in that enterprise need to be adapted somewhat to Shakespearean productions and held open to revisions induced by the productions themselves.

Not unlike most feminist critics in this regard, women directors often gravitate toward working with contemporary women-authored plays. However, in *Upstaging Big Daddy: Directing Theater as if Gender and Race Matter,* editors Ellen Donkin and Susan Clement begin their introduction by writing, "Feminist directing must begin with a reassessment of classical drama."[19] When women directors choose to work with Shakespeare's plays, written predominantly by and for men, in which women are underrepresented and often misrepresented, they have the opportunity to undermine the play's patriarchal values so that "the truths of women's lives can unfold and grow."[20] They can encourage spectators to become "resistant readers."

Many of the directors I studied did just this. Gender politics are often featured more prominently in their productions than in the largely male-generated stage traditions for the plays they direct. In general, they seem more conscious of interpersonal relationships, especially those within the family, and the various ways the female body can be experienced and constructed. They portray individual women characters rather than multiple versions of "woman." They represent women's sexuality as complex, integrated into the character's subjectivity, and not dichotomized by the virgin or whore model. They criticize male characters and male-dominated cultural institutions that oppress others. They are more critical of abusive violence and corrupt power.

Yet those of us who view productions of Shakespeare as a potential voice for feminism are in a minority among feminist performance critics. English actor and director Tilda Swinton even advocates returning to all-male productions of Shakespeare.[21] A scholar and performer, Lorraine Helms discusses Elizabethan theatrical practice and the resulting difficulties of women playing Shakespeare today. Because the roles were initially played by boys, who needed to be viewed as different from the men, particularly in soliloquies when the men may not have been onstage or in physical proximity to the boys, the text often uses strategies that may now infantilize or eroticize the women playing those roles.[22] This makes producing Shakespeare in a way that is responsive to feminist concerns all the more challenging, but it also suggests that women directors attracted to Shakespeare are probably less radical ideologically. Still, they can find compelling ways subtly to reach people's consciousness and promote social change for a wider audience than feminist avant-garde theater could reach. Most directors do not aspire to social change, more motivated by theatrical than political concerns. But that does not mean that their productions will not encourage change. And in publicly analyzing the performance text, I am, as Carol Chillington Rutter writes, "reimagining the canon, opening up its supplementary physical, visual, gestural, iconic texts, making more space for the kind of work women do in play."[23] Although my ideologies are not generally Marxist, I do acknowledge, along with many other feminist performance critics, a desire to see theater participate in the cultural work of producing more equitable relations between the sexes and more equitable positions for men and women in society by promoting different ways of seeing. This can lead to different ways of doing.

Ways of seeing can be influenced by staging practices. Especially from the viewpoint of earlier feminist performance critics, a realistic style based on Stanislavsky's value of re-creating "the life of the human spirit" on stage has been seen as encouraging voyeurism and the objectification of women by putting the audience member in a position of authority, a transcendent, objective judge who sees the "truth" from the privileged stance of looking through the fourth wall. Stage realism can also resist historicization and encourage spectators to accept the social conditions presented in the play as inevitable.

The degree to which an individual actor becomes a "woman" once performing a classical role within realistic stage conventions, however, is debatable. Penny Gay notes that the materiality of embodiment is itself a disruptive force to a theoretical reading of "woman" in a play:

> A determined actress (or actor) can disrupt such voyeurism . . . by investing all the textualities of the production (speeches, costume, body language, how she inhabits the stage space and how she relates to the other performers) with her own individual energy; in a sense, by fighting for her role, as the embodiment of a *particular* woman enclosed in a narrative that pretends to be universal.[24]

But Gay's reasonable and practical argument raises an issue beyond the reproduction of apparently fixed social relations and the passivity of women actors and characters encouraged by stage realism. Within the framework of Western representation, the female body has overwhelmingly been coded as the site of male desire. Sue-Ellen Case and Jill Dolan believe that one of the most fundamental theatrical apparatuses for supporting or dismantling patriarchal encodings is acting style, because the style of acting encourages or disrupts the male gaze. Fourth-wall realism in particular contributes to voyeurism and the sexual objectification of actors.

The legacy of the equation between "actresses" and prostitutes is perhaps as old as the acting profession itself, and it has not yet completely disappeared. Some Restoration women actors openly plied both trades. Porn stars and prostitutes are still crossing over into performance art. But in addition to the reinforcement this equation receives from historical material conditions, sexuality is associated with acting both because it is an embodied art and because presenting one's body onstage for the audience's viewing pleasure suggests the possibility that it is a commodity potentially, as Laurence Senelick writes, "vendible in its entirety."[25] Because women have usually been coded in the West as objects of desire and their performance is usually gendered onstage even more pointedly than in everyday life, women's representation in the theater has often been both highly sexualized and essentialized. Lesley Ferris argues that women actors have often been read as nonmimetic, because they merely played themselves on stage, rather than using their artistic talents to create an individual character. Especially in the nineteenth century, "playing themselves" meant being "woman." Men have always enjoyed a separation between their bodies as actors and the characters they played. But it is precisely the woman's body, rather than what it creates, that has often been the primary signifier onstage.[26]

Because "woman" has been coded so strongly as an object, it becomes difficult for women to represent anything else. Dolan sums up the difficulty and suggests alternatives: "Gender is produced by representational processes that inscribe ideology of gender through both psychoanalytic and material means of production. The materialistic feminist project, then, becomes to disrupt the narrative of gender ideology, to denaturalize gender as representation, and to demystify the workings of the genderized representational apparatus itself."[27] So what kind of theater aesthetics adaptable to productions of Shakespeare help to resist women's objectification in the theater? Barbara Freedman argues that, at the very least, women actors need to break their status as purely objects of the male gaze by looking back.[28] Peggy Phelan has also suggested that the economy of representation in which masculine desire progresses from projection to identification to objectification is dependent on the visibility of the actor and a coherent viewpoint for the spectator. She advocates for performers and critics to be active in redesigning the stable positions for theatrical exchange—to upset the traditional arrangement of spectators who pay to watch actors assume characters in a conventional narrative and perform as if the audience did not exist. The female body can begin to be represented truthfully when it is situated *between* bipolar categories of analysis rather than conforming as a matter of fact to stereotypes.[29] Susan Bennett has argued that by parodically citing gender in the theater, we can begin to reveal its performativity, to reveal both the theatrical construction of gender and the cultural construction of gender, which the stage exaggerates, distorts, and codifies in ways that seem "natural" but often serve to support dominant ideologies concerning gender behavior.

The women directors I studied have often used avant-garde techniques in ways that feminist performance critics have adapted to their own purposes. They frequently use direct address; use characters as stagehands performing set changes in full view of the audience; call attention to various theatrical conventions; resist interpretive traditions accumulated through decades of the play's performance history; reveal the constructedness of gender; cast against type, gender, or race; or use a stage image to subvert the apparent meaning of the text. Spectators' own constructions of gender and sex relations may then be challenged in ways that help to resist women's objectification.

But the tendency of male desire to sexualize women onstage is not, in and of itself, the problem. After all, most heterosexual women actors want to attract the men in the audience (at least the ones they consider attractive), and the women in the audience identify with the actor who has the power to attract all the men in the theater, onstage and off. And, potentially, some of the women in the theater too. Even Dolan admits:

> Despite all I know theoretically about the ideological dangers and misuses of performative presence, and its implication in structures of power and authority, I continue to find women's presence onstage seductive.... I'm not ready to give up the intense pleasure I find in a powerful female performer.... Part of the pleasure of women's presence is the direct call it sounds to *my* desire.[30]

A woman actor's subjectivity need not be erased by the male gaze if she chooses the power to attract men as part of her subjectivity. By contrast, Dolan argues that once a woman realizes she is being looked at, she wears the male gaze and her own subjectivity is completely denied.[31] I would argue that the challenge for an actor becomes to remind men of her power and agency and to reveal herself as *more* than a sexual object.[32] In this way, she refuses to be the passive prize of male mastery, thereby promoting a shift from hierarchy to mutuality, from an intrapsychic relationship to an intersubjective relationship. Although theater may in some ways tend to accentuate the culture's sexual objectification of women (though it also encourages the sexual objectification of men), it can still work toward representing women as sexual subjects. In the theater, discursive bodies, which have been theorized as sites of appropriation and subjection, are also theatrical and performative bodies, which although "of" the text, always exceed it.[33] I find Anna Cutler's work particularly illuminating on the subject. She proposes conceiving of the female body in performance as "inevitably inscribed but in the process of change, an unknowable yet potential form which lends itself to . . . possibility."[34]

A potentially powerful approach for women actors involves the fusion of Stanislavskian and Brechtian techniques and the creation of a different form. I am not advocating that either the actor completely submerge herself into her role behind the fourth wall or that she separate herself from her role and "quote" it to the audience. Rather, she invests the character with her own particular life, while showing an awareness that she is acting. She does not break character when she looks at the audience, but instead suggests a character aware of its status *as* character. Her status as an actor at that particular moment is also revealed, but her presence as actor does not replace or judge the character; both actor and character are present, questioning the typical lamination of character and unified subject. The actor includes herself in the performance.[35] When she addresses the audience within her character, she asks for their sympathy and identification, but makes them aware of the request, and thereby gives them the option to choose. Given such a choice, the audience's emotions *and* intellect are more intensely engaged because another human being is communicating directly with them and expects a response.

Gale Edwards's 1995 RSC production of *The Taming of the Shrew* presented some interesting choices that can be read along these lines. Barbara Hodgdon insightfully analyzes the performance in *The Shakespeare Trade: Performances and Appropriations*. At the end of Petruchio's wife-taming speech, Kate, played by Josie Lawrence, appeared seated in a chair behind her husband, and the set's walls closed in to imprison her, yet she was still visible through a window and was watched by different men in the play.³⁶ In this way, the typical representational economy of female object and male voyeur was staged but inscribed with codes that would lead the audience to view such a practice as potentially oppressive. Hodgdon discusses the possible effects of using an unusual connection between speech, sight, and silence: "In a variant of Brecht's 'not . . . but' in which '(s)he who is being shown shows (her)self,' Kate's notorious silence becomes part of the performer's subject, exposing her body as the scene of farcical cultural inscription. Proposing sight as a means of making Kate's silence readable as a counter-narrative, Edwards's staging calls attention to the bridling of the script that, by calling attention to the bridling of her voice, constructs Kate as a partial subject." This view is furthered by Kate's correspondence with the half-nude dummy in the tailor scene (4.3) and the dismembered dress. Sinking down beside the dummy and caressing the ruined masterpiece, herself in an underdress, she silently spoke a "feminine narrative of loss and desire." The image of the two stripped women downstage left provided a searing commentary on the men bantering stage right about how the master will use the mistress' dress.³⁷

In the final scene, Kate's speech functioned as "a performative aria" in a space that became increasingly marked as representational, with Lawrence controlling center stage. Hodgdon remarks on an interesting use of gesture:

> As she speaks of the fragility of women's bodies, her voice softens and her hand slips down her body, eroticizing its sexual difference; for a moment, it looks as though she will pointedly identify "soft conditions" with her crotch, but she stops just short of that. Although her language denotes a submissive body, her gesture, performed *in public* for the eyes of women as well as men, asserts her control of her own body, coopts any desiring looks for herself.³⁸

Lawrence was dressed in a gown whose low-cut neckline and fitted bodice revealed her full breasts. Her body and face fall within normative standards of beauty. By inviting sexual attention and then resisting it, she called attention to issues of sexual viewing and power in the theater.

Finding ways to incorporate such moments into Shakespeare productions can begin by asking the question, "What does this play, this performance, make me that I no longer want to be?"³⁹ A woman director can guide the production toward showing sexual difference without creating rigid oppositions and situating especially women characters' subjectivities between bipolar categories of analysis. She can particularize both the character and actor by foregrounding surprising elements in each one's personality, abilities, or physique, drawing attention to markers other than sex and destabilizing the normative. Within this framework, the construction of gender and the female body becomes more evident. She can reveal the individual as part of larger social formations and historicize different social and gender codes by staging colliding temporalities. She can encourage a female actor to reveal the tension between historical constructions of gender and the self-directed construction of the actor's and her character's own subjectivities, the ways in which she, as the historical actor/subject as well as the historical character, is resistant, or perhaps unfortunately is not resistant, to oppressive gender and sex relation codes. This resistance is best rooted in experiences of oppression as well as pleasure both inside and outside of the staged action and the representational frame. Representation itself needs, in some way, to be the subject of the production. And the spectators need to be aware that they, too, are the potential objects of the actor's gaze. The flow of power is then circular and bilateral rather than unidirectional and unilateral. The pleasures of performing and viewing can fuel each other without degenerating into the oppressions resulting from intrapsychic fantasy and gender code gridlock.

Yet what of this translates to the audience? Even Dolan admits that her attempts to undermine an antipornography play were not successful:

> The conventions of realist spectatorship perpetuate themselves so readily that even a production clearly marked as revisionist was read as real. . . . American spectators in proscenium houses seem so schooled to look for truth that even though our production was highly stylized and disruptive, some spectators, seeing a man dressed as a woman, could only see that as real, and therefore transvestism, not as a layered interpretation of gender as a performed role.[40]

American audiences are so schooled in realism because of their widespread exposure to television and cinema, which rely on this mode of theater almost exclusively and therefore normalize it to the point of excluding meanings potentially generated by more stylized modes of theatrical production. Past readings and past viewings create or fail to create a kind of performance literacy that significantly shapes future ways of seeing. Theatrical constructions—particularly of gender—are perceived sometimes too narrowly by means of naturalized cultural constructions, the very thing the theater production may have been trying to question.

Yet even determining audience perception is often impossible, for reception is never unified and each performance is never exactly the same as any other. In addition to recording and analyzing my own responses, my study of stage reviews multiplied the responses available for analysis, creating at least a sampling of audience interpretations. Scholars and reviewers provide, however, more of an aberrant than median response, "let alone the illusion of a normative one," as Peter Holland writes. I recognize, as he does, that discussion of audience response is a convenient rhetorical fiction, and in the final analysis, my reaction measures myself.[41] However, production analysis is not complete unless it includes some discussion of audience response, however qualified. I discovered that reviewers frequently do not read the directors' choices as feminist. Yet reviewers who are women are much more likely to remark upon such choices than those who are men, and those in academic institutions writing for academic journals are more attuned to potentially feminist choices in production, almost regardless of sex, than those reviewers writing for a more mainstream audience.

Literary and theatrical cultures, however, differ in terms of their "readings" and interpretive thinking, a conflict rooted partially in the desire of each branch of the Shakespeare industry to retain authority over Shakespeare.[42] W. B. Worthen in his book *Shakespeare and the Authority of Performance* (1997) argues that "performance has no intrinsic relation to texts,"[43] that the concern over a performance's fidelity to the text is historically and culturally determined:

> The fact that performance should be held to criteria of *literary* authenticity at all, that theatre should be taken to (re)produce meanings located in the text or in "Shakespeare," is a measure of the theatre's changing historical relation to literature, a relationship specifically characteristic of Anglo-North American Shakespeare production, and specifically characteristic of the modern era.[44]

Perhaps particularly American performance criticism needs to proclaim its independence from literary interpretation, and my own references to literary criticism are brief because the scholarship of literary culture typically does not address performance. Although some crossover is productive, the literary mode of cultural production is largely separate from the performance mode of cultural production.

The production of meaning, then, is influenced by various sites. In asking the women directors about their vision of the play and what they wanted to communicate with various production choices, I cast them as authors whose ideas translated into intentions. This is in some ways unavoidable because as artists, they *are* authors, particularly of the stage action, and they do make choices not arbitrarily but with intention. To a certain extent, their agency as subjects depends on this. Nevertheless, I also recognize—as many of them do—the inability and undesirability to control audience response, to judge meanings somehow "wrong" if they miss or distort or exceed the director's vision. Like Harris's view, mine balances between privileging directorial intention and audience interpretation:

> [C]reating a performance and creating a "reading" are both kinds of production, operating within different yet interconnected discursive fields.... Aside from anything else, these groups are never absolute "opposites" but exist in a relationship of interconnectedness, interdependence and therefore of mutual, shared responsibility for the reproduction of the culture of which they are a part and hence for "real" action in the world.[45]

Directors, authors, and audience members share authority in the creation of meaning.

Meaning is also historically and culturally determined, or perhaps more accurately, made possible or impossible. Choosing the 1990s in America as the time and place to study women directing Shakespeare created a particular kind of contextualization that has not been examined extensively in other studies. In Susan Bassnett's introduction to the section entitled "The Changing Status of Women in Theatre" for *The Routledge Reader in Gender and Performance,* she remarks that despite the surge of energy and activity prompted by the flourishing of the women's movement in the 1970s and the increase in women actors and directors, recent studies in England show that the overwhelming majority of upper administrative positions in theaters are occupied by men. When Schaefer interviewed high-profile English directors for *Ms-Directing Shakespeare: Women Direct Shakespeare,* she learned of the difficulty women have had infiltrating positions of theatrical power in England. Men also receive the largest percentage of Arts Council funding. Part of this is attributable to cuts in funding for the arts across the board, but certainly the visions of many early feminist directors have not been fulfilled.[46]

Were such studies completed in America, the results would probably be similar. However, in the late 1980s, women were hired as artistic directors for a number of American regional theaters, often as the first women to hold those posts. Still a minority, women in positions of power in the American theater nevertheless increased during the last decade of the twentieth century.[47] In her introduction to *Transforming Shakespeare: Contemporary Women's Re-Visions in Literature and Performance* (1999), Marianne Novy remarks that the volume's treatment of English women directors "needs to be supplemented with an awareness of their colleagues around the globe."[48] Women directors' work with Shakespeare in America has received less critical attention, but I also believe that our culture's less formal approach to Shakespearean productions allows for performances that are more flexible and adaptive to various women directors' concerns. In the 1990s, more women directed than in previous decades and became more visible, since some were in higher profile positions.

Defining the work of women directors with Shakespeare in America, however, is largely a futile endeavor. In his book *English Shakespeares: Shakespeare on the English Stage in the 1990s,* Peter Holland claims that "there can be no single definition of English Shakespeare production; this book both witnesses and celebrates its diversity."[49] Although some issues recur in his discussions, it is genuinely impossible to make a definitive statement about English Shakespeares; and if this is true for Shakespeare's own country with a population probably not as diverse as America, it is certainly true for the United States. In his introduction to *Performing America: Cultural Nationalism in American Theatre,* Jeffrey Mason writes:

> In general, we aspired to learn something about the interaction between nationhood, as a way of establishing or articulating an identity for people or culture, and its expression onstage. The reflexive interactions between stage, nation, culture, and constituents, especially in so multifarious a country as the United States, seem dazzlingly complex.[50]

Although it is impossible to characterize American women directors monolithically, comparisons between the directors in this study and other directors of Shakespeare both here and abroad occasionally yield discernible trends.

Initially institutionalized in this country as a founding father, Shakespeare has never been more popular than now. There are 130 Shakespeare theaters or festivals in America.[51] Through the medium of film, especially the enormously successful *Shake-*

speare in Love, he has been further popularized.⁵² But for theater practitioners, intimidation is a more common response than either resistance or embrace. When former RSC voice director Cicely Berry held a workshop in New York with American and British actors in 1996, American actor Cherry Jones remarked, "We have the Method and naturalism at our disposal. What we still lack is the facility with the language. It's not part of our culture," to which Scottish actor George Anton replied, "I can't understand why American actors keep beating themselves up thinking we've got a secret. Shakespeare wrote for people 400 years ago. We aren't those people." Not satisfied, Jones said, "Your people have had 400 years of constant contact with his works, and constant performances."⁵³ Robert Brustein remarked in 1989 that, although the American theater surpassed the British both in its drama and acting, its practitioners still operated under an inferiority complex, which should be ended by a Theatrical Declaration of Independence.⁵⁴ When reviewing Ralph Berry's *On Directing Shakespeare,* he wrote that what was really missing from the book was "the presence of truly radical and unorthodox Shakespeare directors from the Continent."⁵⁵ Although genuinely oppositional, political productions of Shakespeare are difficult to produce in England's post-Thatcherite era, where the largest Shakespeare institutions are subsidized by business and a conservative government.⁵⁶ America's historical development into a democratic superpower that has never been occupied, nor its citizens subjected to severe oppression, influences its artists' interpretation of Shakespeare, and likewise results in generally more conservative productions. J. Ellen Gainor, Mason's coeditor of *Performing America,* sees a postcolonial movement similar to our country's founding moments, where communities are "using the theatre to resist a dominant culture, to question its hegemonic hold, and to disrupt its attempt to define and control representation."⁵⁷ But none of the essays in Gainor and Mason's volume treat productions of Shakespeare. America has been more liberal than England, however, in fostering a less male-dominated hegemony of Shakespeare's directors, perhaps partly because his privileged position is not quite as high in American as in Anglo theater culture. So although women directing Shakespeare on the 1990s American stage may be less radical than their Continental counterparts, at least many of them are working in this area, and their productions often encourage feminist readings.

The first part of the book looks at the directors and gives space to their voices in quotes from my interviews with them. In this section I discuss their primarily theatrical biographies, institutional opportunities and limitations, their working methods, and more general views about producing Shakespeare. My information on their working methods varies widely, largely because even though I used a similar set of questions for all the interviews, the responses I got ranged from half an hour to two hours, and in Packer's case, I had virtually a month of experience with her methods. Rather than unify all the responses to a model of roughly equal length and development, I rendered detail where it was given.

The second part of the book focuses on their visions for the productions and the productions themselves. Chapter 1 analyzes Jayme Koszyn's (1992) and Lisa Wolpe's (1993) productions of *Romeo and Juliet*. As a context for analysis, I look in this chapter at the parallel connection between sex and violence in 1990s American and sixteenth-century Veronian cultures. Both Koszyn and Wolpe recognized and staged this connection, but perhaps even more interesting is their mutual focus on domestic violence as the center of the tragedy.

Chapter 2 discusses Ellen O'Brien's (1991) and Tina Packer's (1996) *Measure for Measure*. This play, Shakespeare's last comedy, is the comedy that shows the closest affinity to tragedy, so it fits nicely into a graduated scale for studying genre from tragedy to romance. Largely because of interpretive problems, *Measure for Measure* is not often produced. It raises difficult questions concerning women's sexual and vocational choices within a male-dominated culture. Both O'Brien and Packer portrayed Isabella sympathetically, a trend that has developed only recently, and they also marked class distinctions within the playworld. But excited by new developments in materialist criticism at the time, O'Brien focused extensively on the power dynamics in the play and the corruption of the ruling class.

Chapter 3 looks at Abigail Adams's (1996) and Melia Bensussen's (1995) productions of *Twelfth Night*. Because *Measure for Measure* is not a cross-dressing comedy, I wanted a lighter comedy that employed a cross-dressing role. Both productions foregrounded gender construction, an issue the play inevitably raises, though Bensussen made it a stronger focus. She also problematized the ending, while Adams's goal was to support the traditional happy-marriage closure of comedy. Both productions were produced by freelance directors for summer Shakespeare festivals, although the North Carolina Shakespeare Festival is somewhat more conservative than the Oregon Shakespeare Festival.

Chapter 4 studies Barbara Gaines's (1989) and JoAnne Akalaitis's (1989) productions of *Cymbeline*. Although these productions were not technically in the 1990s, they were staged within six months of the new decade, so I believe their inclusion is justified. *Cymbeline* is a romance that reveals a seriously tarnished hero whose misogyny is troubling. Both directors chose to present the play as a fairy tale and set it in a distancing frame, although Gaines is primarily a psychologically realistic, humanist director who made Imogen a modern princess in a Renaissance dress and Posthumus her golden prince. By contrast, Akalaitis, who usually works with more avant-garde techniques, created a production that interrogated historical, dramatic, and theatrical conventions. Her intention of revealing a less than golden hero was largely subverted by the actor playing the role.

The wide range of beliefs held and techniques deployed by these directors makes their apparently common impulses all the more remarkable: to create women characters as subjects in their sexual relationships with men or to reveal the problems inherent in playworlds, cultural forces, and theatrical conventions that refuse to grant them this opportunity. At one end of the spectrum, Ellen O'Brien is consciously political in her interpretations and staging practices, and at the other end, Barbara Gaines disavows feminism, believing theater practitioners shouldn't even read critics. Yet each of the directors shows, in different ways, some evidence of feminist ideology in their work. Such productions are capable of stimulating a greater awareness of gender issues within their audiences.

The Directors

During my oral defense of this project when it was a dissertation, one of my examiners told me the story of a woman who was elected to be a judge primarily because of her sex. She rejected the offer because she didn't believe her vagina should qualify her for the position. I was asked if these women qualified for my project because they had vaginas. My answer was "yes and no." Since most of theater history until quite recently has been largely written by men about men's work, I feel that I have a responsibility as a female scholar to balance out the scale, to present what Schafer and others call an alternative history.[1] If both sexes are doing the work, both should be represented. On the other hand, I didn't choose just any random sampling of women directors. Having a vagina was certainly not the only qualification for inclusion in this project. I was looking for experienced, creative, intelligent women with a wide range of backgrounds, approaches, and working environments whose productions were worthy of study regardless of their sex.

Aside from asking questions about the individual production choices, I explored with them their preparation process, how they approached rehearsal, and more broadly, their views on representing women in Shakespeare's plays. I asked if they saw women characters primarily as subjects or victims. Did productions of the plays tend to reinforce the patriarchal values present in the text? How did genre affect the depiction of women? Did women characters seem to be objects of male desire or projections of otherness and, if so, how did they play against this in production? In *Enter the Body: Women and Representation on Shakespeare's Stage,* Rutter argues that "costume in the theatre is the most conspicuously charged material for writing politics of the body,"[2] and I asked about their views on how costumes or lack thereof impacted the way the audience viewed the women as actors and characters. How did their knowledge of historical gender relations impact their approach? Did the plays, in their view, generally support or criticize stereotypical models for gender behavior? I asked them if reading about the play or seeing other productions had influenced their thinking, and how specifically their ideas had taken shape before beginning the rehearsal process. I also asked about what influenced their casting decisions and whether they tended to work more hierarchically or collaboratively. What guided their decisions about textual editing? Did the expectations of their audience or the institution they worked for guide or restrict their artistic choices? Did they consider themselves to be feminist—why or why not? Enjoy getting to know these women who all have interesting things to say about working with Shakespeare in the late-twentieth-century American theater.

Jayme Koszyn

Koszyn has more of a regional rather than a national visibility as a director, yet her ideas for this production were powerful.[3] She earned a BA in English from Princeton, where she studied under Daniel Seltzer, and an MFA in Directing from Boston University. She has spoken throughout North America on dramaturgy and the arts in education. She has also directed a number of education and humanities programs, including the Young Critics' Institute, Drama as Discovery (an NEH program), and the Huntington Theatre Company's Humanities Forum. Recruited to the Brooklyn Academy of Music (BAM) by Harvey Lichtenstein to be the first director of the Education and Humanities Department, from 1995–2001, she conceived and executed all of the programs.

Koszyn has worked extensively with college students both as a teacher and director. At Boston College, Boston University and its Institute, she has taught directing, script analysis, theater history, and dramaturgy. In addition to the two plays she directed for MIT, she has directed productions for Boston University, Brandeis University, Northeastern University, and Emerson College. But Koszyn's work with professional theaters and organizations is even more extensive, and all told, she directed more than fifty productions before going to BAM, many of them for equity theaters. Her work has been nominated for Washington's Helen Hayes Awards, and she has worked with the Handel and Hayden Society, the White River [Vermont] Theater Festival, the Woolley Mammoth [Washington, D.C.] Theater Company, and the Huntington Theatre Company, where her play *The Paradise* premiered. For nine seasons she was the dramaturg for the Huntington Theatre Company. She also served as the president for Literary Managers and Dramaturgs for the Americas from 1996–1998. In many ways, her experience in professional as well as academic theaters working alternately as a teacher and director make her an ideal candidate for directing college theater.

One of my first impetuses for choosing this project came from my discussions with Koszyn about directing, when working for her as a dramaturg on the Huntington Theatre Company's production of *To Kill a Mockingbird*. The director was a man, and Koszyn had told me that I should watch women direct, which raised the question for me, Do women direct differently from men? Authority and hierarchy, inherent in any work situation but especially pointed in directing, are also strongly implicated in cultural constructions of gender, and Koszyn was somewhat overwhelmed by my question about how she handled these areas as a woman director:

> I am a small woman, a petite woman, who's always looked young for her age. I think that my body, the space I take up physically, and the temperament that I project has, at least in the initial phase of every rehearsal with company members I don't know, definitely been part of the exchange, and I don't quite know how. I do have to say that ultimately a director is an authority and has a point of view. I can work very collaboratively, but ultimately my point of view needs to be what drives the production. And it can drive it in a very open, even-handed way. But ain't nothing worse than a production with no point of view. If you subscribe to that, the director is the one with the point of view and the ultimate authority. And if the director is a woman, then it must raise the same kind of questions, obstacles, hurdles, issues that any woman in any position of authority with any point of view that is attempting to be projected in this society would raise. It's an *enormously* important question.
>
> Two years ago I was on a panel at the Ensemble Studio Theatre. A very dear friend of mine had put this symposium together about women writers and women theater artists, and I was the moderator. So I called up all the panelists and I said, "We're going to address in some way or another the question, 'How has being a woman affected your life in the theater?'" And almost without exception, everyone on the panel said, "Oh, haven't we gotten over this question? Haven't we gotten beyond this? This is just so obsolete." And I sat on the panel with my jaw at my knees saying, "Either I'm absolutely from another planet or everyone else is completely in denial." How could you possibly say that being a woman hasn't affected your work, or that it isn't a question we should even address? [4]

As a dramaturg, she has seen male directors' need for dominance played out in unfortunate ways: "I've worked on certain productions as dramaturg where I've seen that there was an imbalance in the quality of the actors specifically related to gender, where women actors who were far superior, experienced, and technically proficient were passed over for less experienced, less strong-minded and strong-willed actors because of the director's particular fears or concerns. And then what ends up happening is an imbalance in the production, where the men are much higher qualified and simply better actors than the women. So what happens is, by extension, the characterizations become imbalanced, and the actual characters lose their strength."

She finds this particularly true in *Hamlet* productions.[5] People tend to blame the writing, but she believes it's more attributable to casting weak actors in the women's roles: "Perpetually, a kind of mediocre actress is cast in the production as Ophelia or Gertrude and then the character disappears, or a very strong-minded, talented actress is cast, but within political dynamics of rehearsal, that person is kind of shut up and pushed aside, and then the integrity of the character is not allowed to be developed."

I asked Koszyn if she ever worried about the objectification of women onstage when they were in revealing costumes or nude: "This is a really good question, and I'm probably tapping into areas of criticism that I've never read but just by instinct I'm aware of because I've dealt with them as a director in rehearsal. I've had real inner struggles about presenting women onstage being victimized. I'm always perplexed and confused about knowing whether, if I present women's victimization onstage, am I further promoting such activity or am I telling it like it is—to lead audiences through a period of self-examination and then hopefully become part of the solution?"

Although she has staged rapes, for instance, in a way that reflected reality and felt right to her, she will not direct Joe Orton plays because she believes the sexualization of women in his plays is rooted in a hatred of the women characters. "As long as men and women are both naked if the story calls for it, rather than the woman always being exposed, I think it's fine."

Koszyn's desire to expose equally both the male and the female body when the dramatic situation naturally requires it is a move in the right direction. But whether it is the result of some innate sexual difference, cultural conditioning, or the representational apparatus, women are still much more easily objectified onstage than men.[6] In addition, the sexual objectification of men onstage is less dangerous because, once leaving the theater, the still largely patriarchal society the female audience members enter prevents them from carrying that objectification from a moment in the theater into their views of and relationships with men in the world. The reverse, however, is clearly not the case. As art historian John Berger suggests, the visual objectification can lead to behavioral objectification: "A naked body has to be seen as an object in order to become a nude. (The sight of it as an object stimulates the use of it as an object.)"[7] Still, such a momentary objectification can be significantly eclipsed by women characters' strong subjectivity in the rest of a production.

Koszyn's goal in working with Shakespeare is to maintain the balance between showing the victimization and the strength of the women characters, a goal she admirably achieved in this production. She undercut attempts at victimization when she could. When Mercutio mocked the nurse (2.4), the latter stared him down and he became embarrassed, his energy dying away. Koszyn also reports that she extensively edited the text so it would more closely fulfill her vision, though she never cut or rearranged lines in response to specifically feminist concerns. Yet she cut a number of the nurse's lines of protest in response to Mercutio's harassment, apparently to give her more power in that scene.

I asked Koszyn about the potential danger of reproducing the patriarchal values imbedded in the plays. Koszyn argues that the plays are not presented as documentaries of their time. Despite the fact that such works will inevitably be informed by the culture that surrounds them, great artists such as Shakespeare found ways to step outside of society and criticize it: "[The mark of greatness in a playwright is his/her ability to] role play in different voices and see things from other people's perspectives, and those perspectives must include women. These playwrights were born of women, and in some cases, like Shakespeare, married to quite strong women, and had, like Shakespeare, quite strong daughters as well."

While this may be something of an overstatement, given our scant evidence of the women in Shakespeare's life, Koszyn believes that some of Shakespeare's women, including Juliet, are some of the "most real women, because of the power of their intentions, that we've ever seen." A society that victimizes women does not deny their ability to become powerful. Then she turned the question around, "Do we have any idea what 'man' is? What's a real man?" In addition, great artists have the power "to generate alternate universes" and "to transform a world." But Koszyn does not limit this artistic power to Shakespeare. In her estimation, concern over reproducing the play's patriarchal values "completely denies the ability, sensibility, and again, the imagination of a woman director to transform those texts." A woman artist's power to transform is a recurrent theme among feminists working with Shakespeare.

Institutional Opportunities and Limitations

As one of the most prestigious science and technology institutions of higher learning in the world, MIT would seem an unlikely place for fostering Shakespeare productions. Quite surprisingly, the literature department has a strong Shakespeare contingent headed by a respected scholar, Peter Donaldson, who has also created the Shakespeare Interactive Archive.[8] In addition, the theater arts department sponsors a Shakespeare Ensemble dedicated to producing a Shakespeare play each semester. They have also hired Tina Packer, artistic director of Shakespeare and Company, to teach and direct. The institution has a fairly strong support network for Shakespeare production. Koszyn's dark vision of *Romeo and Juliet,* which centered on domestic violence and its effects on the external world, surprised and, to some degree, disturbed some audience members, including faculty. But she was given complete artistic freedom, a freedom she might not have enjoyed were she working in a more provincial environment, especially if the producer were worried about box office receipts.

Because MIT does not draw students who are interested in pursuing a theatrical career, the pool of talented, dedicated actors is even smaller than in some other scholastic institutions. Koszyn was very pleased with her Juliet (Monica Gomi) and Mercutio (Ryun Yu), and they were quite good, but I observed that the rest of the cast was not as strong. She did her best with the available students.

A second difficulty arose from the nature of the production itself. Her casting of the play was directed by the desire to create a visual impression of childlike protagonists and an instinct for choosing actors whose backgrounds would give them access to the dynamics the production required of them. Her Juliet was a petite undergraduate who looked young for her age, while Capulet (Orin Tempkin) was a large, imposing graduate student. But her casting really began by choosing a play she thought the company could handle so that the actors would be able to collaborate with her as much as possible. In this sense, her script selection was informed by her collaborative directing style.

Koszyn believes that whatever is happening in the play will be mirrored in the rehearsal process.[9] She believes that a strict division between personal and professional lives is false, that they always significantly overlap, and she pursued this fusion while working on *Romeo and Juliet*. As the cast worked through the play, their own issues about "the home being driven by anger and hatred, about violence, and about trying to escape through love" surfaced. The lack of emotional maturity in the students translated into some projection and emotional tension in rehearsal, which was something of a liability, but Koszyn carefully pushed and protected her actors.

The pivotal scene for her, 3.5, she read as Capulet literally beating up Juliet. She had the entire cast in the room for the rehearsal of that scene because she wanted the whole community to be present. She had carefully prepared for this scene and, as they were working, she checked in with them to make sure they were not going too far with the violence, but they all assured her it needed to go even further. The cathartic experience of the entire cast during that rehearsal left her very shaken and "scared for society." The rehearsal also reaffirmed her belief that her view of this play touched a contemporary nerve. Despite the cast's difficulty in dealing with these issues, their youth, in this case, was primarily an asset because they were so close to the forces driving Koszyn's vision.

Lisa Wolpe

Just a few months after Koszyn's production, on America's opposite coast, Lisa Wolpe codirected *Romeo and Juliet* with Erica Bilder, who was the fight choreographer. Lisa Wolpe is the artistic director of the Los Angeles Women's Shakespeare Company (LAWSC), which she founded in 1993. LAWSC is a nonprofit professional company that employs women not only for all of its actors but also for the rest of the creative and technical staff. Wolpe thinks that by giving all the words to women and allowing their voices to be onstage and in the world, she participates in healing the past wound of women's marginalization in theater and culture. Part of her mission statement reads:

We provide opportunities for collaboration between a multi-racial group of highly accomplished artists who are actors, producers, directors, choreographers, designers and educators. LAWSC contributes to a transformation of the perceptions of women's roles in our society by working to create a deeper, more powerful, unbounded view of women's potential. . . . Our ongoing mission is to provide a creative forum for the exploration of violence, victimization, power, love, race, and gender issues, and to provide positive role models for women and girls.[10]

Although Wolpe's casting is radical, her interpretations of Shakespeare's plays are generally not. Her primary goal is not to be startlingly original or definitive. Of her *Romeo and Juliet,* she said, "It's a fairly traditional production. I didn't push it to any strange new worlds." She does solid work with high production values—talented and well-trained actors and designers working with enough money to produce high-quality work in all the areas of production: "The aesthetic is the greatest possible Shakespeare and also a place where women create everything." But whether she intends to create feminist work or not, her very decision to produce all-women versions of the plays, exploring issues important to women, inevitably impacts her audiences in ways that traditional casting does not.

Wolpe has produced, directed, and performed in most of the company's major productions. She has also worked with Berkeley Repertory Theatre, Arizona Theatre Company, The People's Light and Theatre Company, New Women's Repertory Company [Los Angeles], Shakespeare and Company, and other regional theaters. Wolpe has acted for television and film, as well, and is a freelance producer for corporate events and video projects. She is on the faculty of Shakespeare and Company and the Sedona Shakespeare Institute. She has attracted national attention, and has been interviewed by PBS and CNN. Of all the directors I have interviewed for this project, she is probably the most talented and experienced actor, a woman who consistently works on both sides of the footlights.[11]

Wolpe's somewhat harsh view of the world and her desire generally to depict the real rather than the ideal leads her to see most of the women in Shakespeare's plays as victims. This does not, however, deny their strength, in her view. Their victimization is the story of the journey of their lives rather than who they are. She views Juliet as both strong and a victim, and thinks Shakespeare was criticizing not only Capulet for his tyrannical control, but the society that supported him.

Wolpe produces Shakespeare because she believes he is the best writer she can find. Not only does he tell powerful stories, but he also tells them beautifully and so heightens the experience of hearing such stories. For Wolpe, people are drawn to poetry in times of need, to hear great truths distilled in beautiful forms: "And Shakespeare always delivers that and makes the ordinary extraordinary, brings you to those great questions in the middle of an ordinary day, especially in Los Angeles where people are mostly focused on money or fame, which are both temporal things that really hold very little interest to a questioning mind. Something like this can really change a life."[12] And yet she is willing to cut and rearrange the text if it interferes with what she wants to communicate. In one of her more recent productions, *A Midsummer Night's Dream,* she cut much of the rude commentary by the upper-class characters because she wanted to convey that the experience in the forest had transformed them into better people. Usually, she cuts only for time, which was the principle guiding *Romeo and Juliet,* but she does not allow the text to have more authority than she, and her revisions seem judicious.

Institutional Opportunities and Limitations

Directing for one's own company gives women significant freedoms. Wolpe has developed clear ideas concerning the cultural importance of her work, considering process and product, individual artists and the communities for which they perform. Before founding LAWSC, Wolpe had been working with Kristin Linklater, who had formed the Company of Women [Boston] with Carol Gilligan. Linklater had formerly worked with Tina Packer, and her ideas still form the basis of Packer's approach to Shakespeare. Linklater and Wolpe discussed the possibility of a satellite company. When Company of Women came to Los Angeles and held a workshop at Universal Studios, they found a group of forty-three women interested in learning how to play men. Soon after this, Wolpe assembled a team and produced *Romeo and Juliet,* which opened 18 March 1993.[13]

Like Linklater, Wolpe believes that an actor's natural voice and impulses are released from the body once it is free of blocks normally constraining it.[14] For this reason, learning to act like a man begins with learning what it is like to inhabit a man's body. While aware of the connection between the phallus and a weapon, she also thinks about the vulnerability it gives men to have external genitals and a resulting need to protect them. She encourages the women in her company to reimagine themselves as male, to think about a man's bone structure, physical weight, and relationship to gravity, to observe the way men move. The women often discover this translates into holding their heads higher, broadening their shoulders, and inhabiting the space surrounding them more fully.[15]

The women actors also draw on their own experiences and psyches, the traits they identify as masculine and feminine within each of them. Wolpe usually begins rehearsal with a process developed by Tina Packer called "dropping in," which seeks to draw out an actor's associations with each significant word the character speaks, and to develop a connection between the actor's and the character's histories and, consequently, a connection between their psyches. Wolpe's acting ethic, inherited from Linklater and Packer, encourages the presentation of one's self and life to the audience through the enactment of the role. This encourages an actor to invest the characters she plays with her own particular life. Since Wolpe uses this process at the beginning of rehearsal, the actor does not have to deny her own impulses and experiences as a resource for developing the character, but discovers her capacity to move beyond her own gender and even gender as a category. In Wolpe's promotional video, *A Muse of Fire,* one of the women who sometimes codirects with her, Natsuko Ohama, speaks of her belief that LAWSC's performance of *Romeo and Juliet* revealed "a universal chord of feeling and thought and human experience" because the women actors had transcended gender and allowed the audience to see "a human being, a kind of place before there is male and femaleness."[16] It seems as if Ohama values removing gender, since she espouses staging a mode of existence that is *pre*-gender, as if gender could be escaped altogether.[17] But her liberal humanism means that her philosophy, methods, and desired impact are quite different from those espoused by a materialist feminist approach. When Dolan directs, she plays with stereotypes and tries to create *post*-gender characterization, characterizations that accentuate particular attributes of either gender to stress their construction and performance, both of which are capable of revision. In contrast, Wolpe tries to avoid stereotypes, and rarely works from the outside in or with a feminist agenda concerning character depiction, but focuses on working from the inside out. In her view, she resists society's stereotypes not by caricaturing them, but by showing women as powerful in male roles, as able to say, "No, absolutely not," as able to express rage without taming it, as being powerful enough to speak a command and have it executed, as bending an entire country to their will because they are potentates, as picking up swords and fighting to the death. The conclusion a male reviewer, Elias Stimac, reached when writing about LAWSC's production of *Othello* is the fundamental message she wants to communicate to all of her audiences: "A woman can be whatever she wants to be."[18] Although not particularly realistic even for work in the theater, at least Wolpe presents opportunities for artists and audience members to explore this possibility.

That women are usually not willing to take complete control of a situation and pursue their own wills regardless of resistance is, in Wolpe's opinion, a product of both cultural conditioning and a "womanly" instinct. Like most contemporary feminists, she straddles the fence between nature and nurture when evaluating women's behaviors and impulses. She feels impulses toward being both controlling and nurturing in herself:

> As a woman who runs a company and who is not afraid of those parts of myself that are masculine, I have a pretty good ability to say, "Absolutely, no. I've had enough." But the woman in me makes me try three times in every relationship to make it work, reinvest in the same people, try to be patient, think of God's grace and what's the highest self I can come from, and love everybody up, and just try to make a good situation, and take as much as I can before I tell somebody, "I've had enough"—things that men don't do.

In some ways, Wolpe shows evidence here of cultural feminism in its essentializing polarization of men and women that still places women in the superior position. But later she said, "It would be really lessening my work to start talking about how easy it is to walk a mile in a man's shoes and how women are superior and more complex." She did not fully articulate her integration of this contradiction.

Wolpe believes cultural conditioning is largely responsible for not only gender-specific attitudes, but also actions. In the rehearsal room, for instance, men are less "emotionally responsible" in that they more often act insensitively or throw a chair. Such behavior is generally accepted from men, but when a woman does it, she is labeled "a bitch." Wolpe has observed that to protect their power when attacked, men usually make an aggressive show of strength, while women usually play low status.

Wolpe constructs herself as a lesbian who feels comfortable expressing a broad range of human impulses usually culturally constricted to one gender or the other. She believes, perhaps optimistically, that she acts according to the situation and her immediate need: "I become incredibly tyrannical when I'm producing, directing, and playing Hamlet at the same time. I need immediate results. I need everything I need when I need it. Whereas two months after the show closes when I'm having margueritas at the river with a friend, I'm very easy to negotiate with over what you want to do next." While her creation of this company seems an outgrowth of radical feminism, Wolpe's own values and life embody her conception of androgyny. When interviewed about playing the title role in *Hamlet,* she said, "I don't know if I'm playing a man anymore, or just expressing myself fully."[19] But since Hamlet is in some ways a fairly feminine character, she might not feel the same way about all of Shakespeare's male roles.

The short distance for Wolpe between playing a man and expressing herself, a paradigm her approach to acting encourages in the rest of the company, probably accounts for the frequent commentary by reviewers that, soon into the production, the audience forgets women are playing men. Sometimes male reviewers see her as spoofing sexist male stereotypes, or playing with convention, as in her villainous portrayal of Richard III. Although Philip Brandes's review of *Richard III* for the *Los Angeles Times* was generally complimentary, he commented on Wolpe's "overacting": "It's a good thing Wolpe can't grow a mustache, or she'd be twirling it in every scene."[20] Writing for *Back Stage West,* Paul Birchall praised her deft exposure of male foibles in his review of *A Midsummer Night's Dream.*[21] But Wolpe seeks to avoid stereotypes. She recognizes them in the plays, but finds the human element and seeks to embody that. She says of *Richard III,* "At one level it's melodrama and a morality play—but at a deeper level, it's very real, full of every unloved portion of ourselves. He's hated by his mother, brother, etc., and he gets even."[22] Her play with convention comes purely from putting women in men's roles. Birchall's review reveals the potential gap between directorial intention and audience interpretation. Perhaps the most interesting thing about Brandes's criticism is that he points to the biological difference between men and women, the one gap Wolpe cannot cross, as if needing to protect his territory. Eureka Angelos, another woman actor who plays male roles, finds that male reviewers criticize her depictions as one-dimensional stereotypes while not objecting to women actors who create female stereotypes.[23] Wolpe recognized the character was written as a villain and played this to the hilt, which delighted many reviewers. Tony Tran wrote:

> The best reason to see this *Richard III* is its taut, superb acting. Lisa Wolpe delivers an overwhelming, hypnotic portrayal of the dominating central figure. Her inspiration and energy never flag as she imparts shape and depth to Richard's Machiavellian nature, whether he be carrying out his villainous sexual stratagems . . . or facing a parade of tormenting demons on the eve of the last battle. . . . [E]ven hardened skeptics will be convinced by this brilliant, revelatory staging by the Los Angeles Women's Shakespeare Company. [24]

While male reviewers occasionally point to male stereotypes, women reviewers point to the transformation of the women. Writing for a Los Angeles Japanese daily newspaper, Martha Nakagawa reported: "What you'll witness is not simply women wearing men's clothing cast in non-traditional roles, but rather, the actual transformation of the performer into the role of the character, where gender and race no longer become a distraction."[25] Likewise, *ShowCase Entertainment Magazine* reviewer Madeleine Shaner noted: "After the first few minutes of disbelief at the gender bending casting, it becomes clear that these are actors' roles, and these are skilled actors playing them. They are not cross-dressing, they are metamorphosing."[26] With these women, Wolpe has achieved her aim.

In her own rehearsal room, Wolpe walks the line between a traditional male authoritative approach and a more feminist model of collaboration. She maintains a clear vision of what she wants from the production while seeking input from the other artists working with her. In fact, once her company was established, she began to hire outside directors on occasion. Being the producer and acting a male protagonist is enough. She can allow someone she trusts, such as Maureen Shea, former director of the now defunct Company of Women, or Tina Packer, to direct.

Part of what prompted her creation of her own company was her frustration in working with a male director who was guiding an all-woman company in a production of *King Lear* in which she was playing the title role. Although Wolpe has nothing against male directors, she saw that the male leadership in this case prevented the production from evolving into all it could have been.[27] "I think there's a different dynamic in the room when there are only women. There's more freedom. I'm hoping that builds a level of trust that develops deeper emotional freedom." Emotional freedom in the rehearsal room exhilarates Wolpe, and it is part of the journey on which she wants to take other women as well:

> If you're playing Richard III, you have to be able to wheel on somebody and go right up in their face and almost bite them, and then say, "Fuck off!" and turn away and not apologize and say, "Was that OK?" You have to be free to be fucking evil and powerful. And people just have to take care of themselves a little bit around that. Which is great. It's great when you have the trust to do that with each other and say, "Yeah. We're going to that dark place." . . . You're taking a leap and you're playing all that you can muster that's like that. And it's like a free fall because the text is taking you on this journey, and you're not afraid to go because someone is asking you for everything and more. . . . [In order to justify the responses the text apparently requires,] they need you to be everything you are.

She has also created a safe space for both homosexuals and heterosexuals to work:

> We have gay women and straight women working happily together—some bring their kids to the production, and some bring their girlfriends. In the rehearsal room, there is respect, humor, and an excitement at the permission to play with other women without having guys around to define a traditional hierarchy and sexuality. As a result, a tremendous power arises in the exploration of who these women really are.[28]

In dealing with gender issues as a person and as a director of an all-female company, her goal is less to portray gender as purely a social construction and more to question how society has constrained women so that they do not speak or act on what they feel, do not fulfill their whole potential. One of her goals is also to provide positive role models for women and girls.

And yet perhaps what is most important to Wolpe's work and what she is most proud of, which the organization of her mission statement implies, is the truly multicultural ensemble she supports: forty percent black, ten percent Hispanic, ten percent Asian, and forty percent white—what she believes approaches a microcosm of the larger world. This emphasis has led her away from the trap of constructing "woman" as white and middle class. She is sad, in fact, when women say that she is presenting "the woman's point of view," because in her mind, every woman has her own point of view, although this idea exists in tension with her earlier assertion concerning ways that men and women typically behave.

Wolpe tries to be fair in her casting, and she believes that race usually does not become an issue in the rehearsal room because of her commitment to multiculturalism. However, she does not cast the roles racially blind. She enjoys inverting traditional casting. Extending her ethic of casting women in the roles of princes and warriors, she finds an added richness in casting minorities in the most powerful and heroic roles of canonical Western literature. But that does not become a given, because allowing women to fulfill a range of roles refutes generalizations and stereotypes about their abilities. She wants audience members to think, "Playing the clown is that elegant black lady, who was the king in the last play, who was the lady in the play before. I'll never generalize about what a black actress can or cannot do." Such casting destabilizes normative assumptions about race and gender. Casting against type also encourages the audience to view the actors as actors instead of "some sort of titillating piece of meat" and to consider the body's nonsexual markers.

But at the same time, she does not resist the audience's tendency to sexualize the actors, because she realizes it is inevitable. She believes that both men and women actors are viewed as sexual objects at some point by audience members, but she hopes that if her actors embody the text well, they will give the audience something to think about other than appearance. In theory, Wolpe said she would use nudity onstage if it were integral to the production, but never gratuitously. In her twenty-five years of work, however, she has never found it necessary.[29]

As Artistic Director of LAWSC, Wolpe is also conscious of wanting to leave a legacy behind her. Aside from wanting "mastery over a body of work that I'm proud of," she would like history to recognize her achievement as something different, something no one else was doing in quite the way she was. The institution of LAWSC offers tremendous opportunities for Wolpe and virtually no constraints other than economic, which every American theatrical institution faces to one degree or another. Even in this area, she has developed substantial support from corporate, civic, and individual donations.

Tina Packer

Born in Wolverhampton, England,[30] Packer trained at the Royal Academy of Dramatic Arts (RADA) where she won the Ronson Award for Most Outstanding Performer, and won a three-year contract as an associate artist with the RSC. In addition to acting with repertory companies in Glasgow, Edinburgh, Leicester, and Coventry, she also worked for the BBC and ITV television companies and in film. She has acted with John Barton, Peter Hall, John Schlessinger, Ian McKellan, Paul Scofield, Janet Suzman, and Ian Richardson, among others.[31] She never went to university. Particularly at RADA, however, she was dissatisfied with the overly "outside-in" approach to acting, conflicts within the company, and limitations placed on her because she was not "right" for leading roles. She was also unhappy with being forced to abandon her native accent for the forerunner of Received Pronunciation.[32] She felt "limited and powerless as an actress in England."[33] Packer came to America to form her own company partially because she believed America's acting community, generally trained more deeply in psychological realism than England's, would provide her with a stronger pool for creating the committed, passionate, and emotionally truthful work that has become her hallmark. Even ten years ago, John Gielgud remarked that discussions of motivation were more American than English, and in England "one simply had to trust the verse."[34]

Although Packer's first Shakespeare and Company dissolved in 1973, the second is alive and well, and she has directed forty-four productions with this ensemble. She has recently begun plans for reconstructing the Rose Playhouse in Lenox, Massachusetts, which has become an international project. Packer has written a trilogy of plays exploring Shakespeare's women characters, called *Women of Will,* which was supported by Guggenheim and Bunting Fellowships in 1994–95. She holds honorary doctorates of letters from Emerson College, Trinity College, the Massachusetts College of Liberal Arts, and the Berkshire Business and Professional Women's Organization named her 1998 Woman of Achievement. Packer teaches both workshops and semester-long classes at numerous colleges and universities, including MIT and the Columbia Business School, but she has lectured or been the keynote speaker at over thirty institutions of higher learning. In conjunction with John O. Whitney, professor of management at Columbia's Business School, she has just published a new book, *Power Plays: Shakespeare's Lessons in Leadership and Management.* In 1999 she won the Massachusetts Commonwealth Award, the state's highest honor for cultural and arts achievement. Helen Hayes has called her company "a national treasure."[35] She is currently working on a book about adapting Shakespeare's stories for children.[36]

Working closely with Kristin Linklater in the early years, Packer developed an approach that focused on the importance of the voice, which she believed had been largely ignored in American actor training. Instead, actors had been encouraged to develop an internal focus of soul-searching. She currently trains her company extensively in bodily relaxation and release. While her work with actors is deeply psychological and often realistic, she claims to have a different focus than Method acting:

> What I am saying is that as actors, words should shape us, not the other way around. The classics are a vessel for human emotion. They may be stories, but they are "true." Otherwise they would not have lasted. In the Method, you may think of your own mother if you're playing Hamlet, and if you're lucky, the words come out of your mouth. But you're also lucky if anybody else can hear it. With us, it is not only your own personal experience that is the trigger but also, always, the larger psychological truth which rests in the poetry of text.[37]

While she somewhat unfairly suggests Method actors cannot project fully enough to be heard in performance, she does work hard at integrating all areas of actor training. Because American actors tend to use language, especially offstage, for reporting rather than expressing, she focuses on creating and releasing, as her (life and art) partner Dennis Krausnick has said, "a history of the words in their bodies." The object is less about breathing life into Shakespeare than about allowing "Shakespeare" to breathe life into the actors, which they share openly with the audience.[38]

In other words, it's less about actors and directors adapting Shakespeare to themselves and making him their contemporary than about adapting themselves to Shakespeare, or at least "find[ing] a way of doing Shakespeare that [is] both true to him and true to us."[39]

Institutional Opportunities and Limitations

Like Wolpe, Packer has enjoyed the freedom to develop her own approach to Shakespeare. Shakespeare and Company is one of the few theatrical institutions in this country that not only produces Shakespeare, but also offers actor training to those not in company productions, and an extensive educational outreach program for grade school and high school students. It has sponsored workshops for high school teachers as well, and has won a number of grants from the NEA. The company itself is run collectively by the actors. Although this organizational structure was initially adopted as a survival technique when funding for the arts dried up several years ago, most members of the company have found a real benefit from participating in both the artistic and the administrative work of the company. The structure is also responsive to Packer's goal, first formulated in 1978, to develop a democratic theatrical institution in this country. Each actor gets a vote, and they all live on the grounds, cooking and cleaning as well as rehearsing.[40] At the same time Packer has placed herself solidly in the center as artistic director and president of the board: "I'm the only person in the whole organization who can't be sacked," she laughs. Shakespeare and Company has been accused of being incestuous, and indeed, a number of members have fallen in and out of love, married, divorced, and remarried, though apparently shifts in such liaisons were even more loose and numerous before the advent of AIDS.[41] When people live and work together so intensely, however—especially since her approach encourages vulnerability, passion, and acting on impulse—shifts in combinations of lives seem almost inevitable.

Packer always wants to be directing any Shakespeare play because it provides her "an adventure in growth." She begins to have perceptions about whatever he was working on in the play. She speaks of the Bard from a generally universalist, essentialist viewpoint, as if he is both a sage and a comfortable old house: "I absolutely trust his insights about humanity. I feel very relaxed inside Shakespeare. I always know that he knows more than I do."[42] In many ways, her abiding trust in Shakespeare's texts reflects her early training under John Barton, a student of F. R. Leavis.[43] Scholars trained under the school of New Criticism believed the author's intended meanings could be discovered by mining the text, a naïve notion. Her focus in production is always verbal rather than visual. From her perspective, "All Shakespeare's plays reflect every age anyway." Although she expects actors to understand and invest in the given circumstances of their roles, historicizing the plays has never been her focus, which eliminates a potentially powerful form of critique from her productions.

Packer also aligns herself with acting theories that came of age in the sixties concerning the truth contained in the body. Commenting on the differences between Dustin Hoffman's Method approach, which demands that the actor experience the character's life, and Olivier's more classical approach, which depends more on sheer imagination prompted by externals such as costume and physicalization of the character, she said, "I agree that an act of imagination can take an artist anywhere. But our bodies hold all the good and bad things that have ever happened to us. The good things tend to pass through the body—we let them out with a laugh, for example—while the bad things stay."[44] Opposed to Olivier's view that acting is just convincing lying, Packer believes it is ultimately telling the truth, and Shakespeare is dead unless the actor finds the truth of the character within him or herself.[45]

In order to facilitate the actor's discovery of the text's meaning and to forge a psychic connection between the actor and the character, Packer has developed a training tool she calls "dropping in," which is the first step in the process of any production Shakespeare and Company mounts. During that process, a coach says a word or phrase from the text to the actor, who is generally sitting directly in front of and maintaining eye contact with her scene partner. The coach then asks the actor a question that draws randomly from either the actor's imaginative creation of the character or the actor's own personal history. The unexpected intertwining of questions is part of what encourages an imaginative fusion between character and actor. The actor then says the word to her scene partner with her emotional response to the question "on the text." In other words, *the way* she says the word expresses her response. During this process, the actor is encouraged to allow the breath to drop deeply into the body and to keep her mouth slightly open. This not only assists in fully oxygenating the body but also creates a physical experience of openness for the actor. Both encourage the release of the actor's responses.

As a participant in the intensive program, I watched a demonstration of this technique before engaging in the process myself. The workshop leader chose two other participants and cast them as Macbeth and Lady Macbeth in the scene right after he has killed Duncan. When the coach working with the actor playing Macbeth got to the word "sleep," he asked some of the following questions, always following the question by repeating the word "sleep" and pausing for the actor to vocalize this word in response. The coach always signaled the shift to a new word by simply saying it once and having the actor repeat it after him before free associating a list of questions:

Sleep.
(The actor says, "Sleep," etc.)
When was the last time you were asleep? Sleep.

>How did you sleep last night? Sleep.
>What is it like to go for a long time without sleeping? Sleep.
>What has your sleep been like in Scotland these last few weeks? Sleep.
>When will you sleep again? Sleep.
>What is it like to sleep with Lady Macbeth? Sleep.
>Do you sleep in the same bed with her every night? Sleep.
>Who usually initiates sex when you sleep together? Sleep.
>What is your sexual relationship like? Sleep.
>Would you rather be sleeping with the person across from you right now rather than doing this exercise? Sleep.

Most words do not get such a lengthy list of questions, but because this word is so crucial and resonant in the play, the coach spent more time with it. At a good pace, one can drop in about eighty lines in an hour.

This process has proven effective but controversial. Some critics claim it is too much like therapy, too emotionally wrenching, saying the same connection can be reached by less "violent" ways. Some have also speculated that it could create a kind of codependency between actor and coach, or at least actor and process. But Packer believes no other process creates as deep a connection between the actor and the text. She recognizes the potential pitfalls and tries to avoid them: "As a feminist it's really important that there isn't a power relationship going on here. I always acknowledge the other person as my equal as we work. I don't think you'd find any dependency around me. In fact I'd never allow it to happen."[46]

I found my first experiences with "dropping in" somewhat disturbing, partially because the process seemed invasive, and I felt I was judged unfairly by my coach.[47] Emotions rocketed out of me, and although the faculty gave tacit approval for me to "take care of myself" and step out of the process if necessary, it was almost hypnotic, like entering another state of consciousness where I felt I did not have enough control to make such a decision. However, after working with the process more, I have come to feel comfortable with it if my coach is someone I know and trust. Under those conditions, I find it an enormously useful technique when preparing a role for performance.

Packer's use of this process means that she typically comes to rehearsal with nothing more than a general idea of the play. She works very collaboratively and understands the play through the actors. Although her casting choices are sometimes partially limited by the current composition of the company, she generally has a strong pool from which to choose. Her casting of Allyn Burrows as Angelo, for instance, was based not just on his abilities but on his physical likeness to Jack Kennedy. She wanted an all-American golden boy who appeared to be a real gentleman because evil often looks attractive. She also wanted the potential for sexual chemistry between the actors playing Isabella and Angelo, as well as between Isabella and the duke. Most of the time, however, she makes intuitive guesses based on her sense of the congruence between the essence of the actor and the character. Of course, by the time an actor has been through one of her training programs, where all the faculty discuss all the students' work, she has a rather strong sense of who they are. Since this production of *Measure for Measure* (1996) was part of the Bare Bard series, which mimics Shakespeare's playing conditions for a traveling company—only six or seven actors and a minimal set—and the production concept doubled "opposing" characters, the actors in this production also needed to be extremely versatile.

Packer sees Shakespeare's attitude toward women changing throughout the course of his career, which she has embodied theatrically in a series of monologues called *Women of Will*. Apparently looking for a unified and progressive development, Packer developed a concept that, unfortunately, oversimplifies the representation of women throughout Shakespeare's career. From her somewhat simplistic viewpoint, early on, he largely accepted the virgin/whore split. In the middle of his career, women were literally dying to speak the truth, only protected if they went underground by cross-dressing. Women's voices were crucial; they existed outside the power structure, so they had the insight to criticize it. Toward the end of his life, he most identified with the "feminine element" and allowed it to come into power, showing how the daughter redeems the father. But because women in his society were not in power, he could not tell the story realistically and had to move into the form of the myth or the storyteller. Even in *The Taming of the Shrew,* however, Packer sees his ambiguity about his culture's view of sex relations. Her challenge when she directed this was to make something coherent out of the harsh story of Kate and Petruchio and the strongly comedic elements in the rest of the play.

When she has to cut the text, she cuts what bores her, never to eliminate contradictory elements or unsavory material. So despite some postmodern elements in her production style, she is at heart a modernist searching for a unified interpretation of the text. Perhaps it is her very focus on the text that creates and delineates her perspective. "I think the essence is: What's the text saying and how honestly can I play this? And until you really know the text, until you're right inside the words and your imagination is really understanding the depth of that, the other stuff [primarily design elements] is background noise."

Packer attributes her position in the world as a feminist partially to the result of tapping into "the deeply feminine part of Will Shakespeare." In her mind, even though "the plays are embedded in the patriarchal structure . . . all great art is actually not invented in the structure. . . . What I see great artists do is align themselves to their feminine sides, which is why women are represented [as important in the plays]." By feminine side, she means, "an interest in relationships, being in touch with one's feeling, interested in what the collaboration and celebration is, as opposed to only achieving 'The Goal.'"[48] Audiences fail to perceive this, Packer believes, because they frequently see productions directed by men in which the women "don't have their voices" or do not truly understand their roles. Packer's feminism is in many ways outdated by current academic standards, but is genuine nevertheless. Beyond her feminism lies a broader agenda: to structure society so people can live creative lives. And yet, the two are connected in her mind, because breaking out of patriarchal structures requires creativity. Not everyone, of course, wants to live a creative life. And Siegel has appropriately taken Packer to task for interpreting Hamlet's tragedy as his failure to listen to his feminine side, which would have prompted a discussion with Claudius rather than his murder.[49] But he has also said that her productions always have a "feminist and often a pacifist overlay," and the "remarkable aspect of her work is that she rarely strays from the text, or from history, to pull it off."[50] Her goal to change the society so that people can achieve a better quality of life is admirable. Despite my reservations about some of her beliefs, interpretations, and working methods, I find Packer a warm and generous woman, a talented artist, and a powerful producer of Shakespeare.

Ellen O'Brien

Ellen O'Brien, as her bio says, "leads a double life as theatre practitioner and Shakespeare scholar." She began her career with a PhD in English from Yale University, but she also holds advanced and postgraduate degrees in voice studies from Central School of Speech and Drama in London. She has published in *Shakespeare Quarterly, Shakespeare Survey,* and *Selected Proceedings of the World Shakespeare Congress, 1996.* She taught and directed at Guilford College, North Carolina, from 1978 to 2000, initially in the English department but moving to the department of Theatre Studies in the mid-eighties. She is now a voice and text consultant for the Shakespeare Theatre of Washington, D.C., and voice and speech teacher for the Academy for Classical Acting, an MFA program affiliated with the Shakespeare Theatre and George Washington University. During her tenure at Guilford, she coached numerous Shakespeare productions for theaters such as People's Light and Theatre Company, Shakespeare Santa Cruz, Charlotte Repertory Theatre, and the North Carolina Shakespeare Festival. She has also led workshops on Shakespeare's verse and language for a wide variety of institutions—theater companies, colleges, universities, Shakespeare Association of America, Association for Theatre in Higher Education, and the National Council of Teachers of English. O'Brien is perhaps the best-equipped director in this study to bridge the gap between theory and practice.

Like most good directors, O'Brien believes that Shakespeare's plays "are not history lessons or museum pieces but explorations of issues vitally important to our own time."[51] At the time of our interview, six years after the statement above was made, O'Brien laughed a little about this dogmatic phase, but still believes in using Shakespeare to interrogate our current situation. She is particularly drawn to the exploration of power in the plays and how a political approach to production might bring class and gender to the forefront.[52] Like Packer, she recognizes that Shakespeare is language-centered, and she does not want the set, or even stage business, to detract from the spoken word.

O'Brien very much enjoyed the collaboration in directing with Jack Zerbe, the head of the Guilford theatre studies department, and misses the opportunity to codirect with him. After directing *Measure for Measure,* she started doing more freelance work. Although she recognizes that collaboration can be very difficult with the wrong person, and that, in fact, truly successful collaboration is rare, she and Zerbe helped each other think more deeply about the play than either one could have alone. Their initial discussions showed them that they had very similar viewpoints. They also brought complementary strengths to the production and frequently ran simultaneous rehearsals with O'Brien working primarily on the text and Zerbe working primarily on staging. Not all of the choices in the production were explicitly made by O'Brien. However, for simplicity's sake, I will focus on O'Brien's choices, as revealed in the interview. Usually Zerbe shared and contributed to her vision. Where relevant, I will discuss their differences.

Institutional Opportunities and Limitations

A small liberal arts institution, Guilford College attracts primarily upper-middle-class white students, many of whom major in the arts and humanities. The college offers a BA in Theatre Studies. Two professors and a technical director make up the department. Not having a costume shop, they have to buy most of their costumes, so are somewhat limited in that regard. Occasionally they hire freelance professionals as designers. Not feeling the need to record their work for posterity, they have no formal archive, so much of the department's work exists primarily in the memories of the directors, and O'Brien freely admits hers is faulty.

Although North Carolina is a generally conservative state, the faculty and administration are more liberal. The institution in no way censored O'Brien's work. If it did, she would not have worked there. When she has needed to use nudity onstage, she has gone to the administration to inform them of her choice and her rationale to prevent later backlash, and the administration has always approved her decision. It has also never criticized her choice of plays.

She had been "blessed" by not being governed by the box office, which gave her more freedom than her colleagues in the professional theater. Individual audience members have sometimes complained about certain elements of her productions, but never the college. The audience for theatrical productions at Guilford is largely students, which guided the way she told the play's story, but she tends to challenge as well as cater to her audience. Part of why she chose to do *Measure for Measure* was not only because she believed the theater majors needed to do some Shakespeare, but also because the largely homogenous, protected population of the bucolic campus needed to consider problems concerning class and race. Limited to casting largely untrained actors meant she could not work as collaboratively as she would have liked, but she worked hard at training and preparing them for this production. In addition to running double rehearsals, she designed a course for the actors that met weekly and included readings and exercises specific to the challenge of acting Shakespeare. Many of the actors had also taken classes with her or Zerbe prior to this production, so she had not only participated in their previous actor training but also developed a relationship with a number of them. She had a stronger pool of talent than Koszyn and enjoyed a shared history with some of the actors on which to build.

As opposed to Packer's rather neat and oversimplified chronological ordering of Shakespeare's depiction of women, O'Brien does not subscribe to any theories about how Shakespeare's plays depict women or how she portrays them in production:

> I think for me it would probably be a different take with every play, which will have to do with the play, the particular moment of my life, the particular historical moment, quite possibly also with the company. What is the company capable of? . . . Almost any question you give me, I don't think there's one answer to, and I think that's particularly true with this stuff. I think what matters is thinking about it, and deciding which way is going to work best in the given situation.

Unlike Packer, she does not look for a way to make the play coherent. "I'm less and less interested in a solution which obliterates the problem moment, and more and more interested in framing the moment."

Similarly, she has changed in her attitude toward the text. Categorizing herself formerly as "a real hard-nosed purist," she now believes that consciously cutting and reshaping is also a legitimate enterprise. In this production, O'Brien and Zerbe cut obscure jokes and not much else. Taking a similar approach to her direction of *Henry V*, she realized in the middle of rehearsals that if she were going to deconstruct the myth of heroism in the way in which she wanted, it really required some reconstruction of the text. Aesthetically, she is very leery about adding lines to try to imitate Shakespeare, but comfortable with a production that draws clear boundaries between his work and hers. At this point she feels it is most important to understand what she cuts, guided by her realization that she does not need it or that it is in her way. Precisely because the plays are cultural icons, she feels such intervention is important, even though it then becomes an adaptation rather than Shakespeare. Some plays require reconstruction to permit a feminist interpretation. She says of *The Taming of the Shrew*, "I can't imagine doing that text straight and saying anything I want to say to anybody."

O'Brien agrees that classical and Renaissance plays can reinforce patriarchal values if the plays are reproduced to accept the structures as given rather than examining them and finding ways to undercut them. But she believes putting women in the roles of women characters changes everything, and it is dangerous to disown the past. "It's partly acknowledging the suffering that happened under [Elizabethan governance and American slavery]. It's partly remembering where we don't want to go back to, and it's partly just acknowledging that change is slow and imperfect, and that people cannot transform themselves overnight, much less cultures transform themselves overnight." It seems then that transformation exists as a value by its absence in most of O'Brien's productions. She also believes not everything "touched by patriarchy is worthless" and recognizes patriarchal attitudes in ninety percent of the films currently made, whose impact is probably more damaging because their distribution and consumption is so much more substantial. But she validates both those who want to start from scratch, and her own approach, which is to rework the inheritance of past theatrical tradition.

Since her approach was so clearly political, I asked O'Brien what she wanted audience members to do when they left the theater. She admitted that the production did not suggest any clear directive, but she hoped people would begin viewing the world differently, seeing the way power is used inappropriately and to be more actively involved in the political system at least at the level of voting. She also hoped for more subversive activity, aware that the battlefront keeps changing. While no "magic cure" exists, she wants people "to make justice a priority."

Abigail Adams

Although Abby Adams works occasionally as a freelance director, as she did for the production I'm studying, her primary work in the theater is as the artistic director of The People's Light and Theatre Company in Malvern, Pennsylvania, a suburb of Philadelphia. In some ways, her journey is similar to Packer's. She was not part of the original four founding members in 1974, but joined the company soon after in 1975 and has been active with it ever since. To date she has directed over forty main stage productions. The company began with the structure Packer's has recently adopted: the actors did all the work of administrative, production, technical, and janitorial staffs. The company was run collectively, with each member getting a vote. As they sought to expand, they reluctantly gave up that power to a board whose financial clout could garner more substantial grants, but the board has always supported rather than dictated the company's artistic vision.[53] At the time of the interview, the theater's mission statement was: "We believe that excellent well-produced drama provides a powerful way to affirm, question and explore contemporary life. Thus, our mission is to bring together artists of the highest caliber with large and diverse audiences in a welcoming environment in order to celebrate the joys and fears of living in an increasingly complex world."[54] In its Basic Operating Tenets the theater affirms the values of collaboration, challenge, and risk-taking to produce a compelling story relevant to its audience.[55] Adams believes that theater serves a civic as well as artistic purpose, and she has worked hard to provide outreach to the community, whether through taking productions to prisons and schools or offering some performances for free. Not surprisingly, she describes her work as a director as "very, very collaborative."[56]

Adams has been described as a "Renaissance artist" because she has worked not only as an actor and director but also a writer of children's plays.[57] People's Light's arts education program, Project Discovery, is the largest outreach program in the state, serving over forty thousand students and allowing seven thousand to see productions for free. Through their Theatre School, resident artists teach a wide variety of courses for both children and adults.[58] She also directs New Voices Ensemble, created through a partnership between People's Light and Swarthmore College for predominantly students from the city of Chester, Pennsylvania's most depressed city. New Voices Ensemble was awarded the 2000 Coming Up Taller Award by the National Endowment for the Arts and the President's Committee on the Arts and the Humanities, an award granted to outstanding arts programs for youth at risk. She is also a board member of the International Association of Theatre for Children and Young People (ASSITEJ/USA). In 1986 and 1987 she received a TCG Observership grant. Although she has taught at the University of Pennsylvania, New York University, Bryn Mawr College, and Carnegie Mellon University, in addition to serving on the faculty of Swarthmore College, she describes herself as "so not academic."[59]

Although Adams is the artistic director and hires most of the staff and artists year-round, People's Light also engages guest artists each season from all over the country. The theater has two black box theaters, which seat 375 and 180, and hosts over

100,000 patrons annually. The company has produced over three hundred plays, including more than one hundred world and/or regional premieres. While a number of People's Light productions have moved downtown into Philadelphia, others have gone on to Washington, D.C., Chicago, Mexico, Budapest, and Cyprus. Many national and local organizations have given grants to the theater, including the Connelly Foundation, the Lenfest Foundation, the National Endowment for the Arts, the Open Society Institute, the William Penn Foundation, the Pew Charitable Trusts, the Shubert Foundation, the Surdna Foundation, TCG New Generations, the Lila Wallace–Reader's Digest Fund, and the Fund for New American Plays.[60]

Institutional Opportunities and Limitations

The North Carolina Shakespeare Festival (NCSF) was founded in 1977 by Mark Woods and Stuart Brooks, "two actors tired of the jaded audiences, dingy showcase theaters and high production costs of New York plays."[61] Because it was located in the relatively small town of High Point, many doubted the success of the company, especially since the summer months, when locals vacationed, was the only time they could rent the High Point Theatre. The company had grown not out of a grassroots desire for Shakespeare but rather out of the founders' own goals. But they marketed the festival "as a statewide cultural asset," and drew eleven thousand people to their first season's twenty-four performances.[62] Like many theater companies trying to survive year-round, they developed an educational component to their program. Eventually, the repertory also expanded to include non-Shakespeare classical and modern plays. The company tours not only to schools but other cities in the state. The festival's statement of purpose is:

> The Festival is dedicated to producing great plays of social and political relevance in a variety of theatrical forms and styles. We want to present theatre that is entertaining, exciting, passionate and culturally and educationally stimulating. The Festival is committed to non-traditional casting, to developing the strongest ensemble acting company possible, and to complementing the work of our actors with a creative technical and administrative staff working on the highest professional level. We hope that the Festival can grow, along with our audiences and the greater North Carolina community, toward realizing the possibilities of regional theatre as an integral part of our culture.

The festival will serve the audiences and citizens of tomorrow by touring its productions to schools throughout the state and nation, reaching youth in their formative years and broadening their vision and understanding of themselves, the world and the theatre.[63]

In a region where people still sport Confederate flags in the back windows of their pickups, an explicit commitment to nontraditional casting probably helps NCSF deal with questions that could arise from potentially provincial and prejudiced audience members concerning their casting choices. In rural areas or small towns in North Carolina, the cultural centrality of regional theater also needs argument. Unlike more metropolitan areas, not everyone acknowledges it as an important contributor to cultural life. Ideologically within the Bible Belt, North Carolina is home to residents who may regard the theater as spiritually dangerous, particularly those who are older and highly religious. I have heard it described in this region as predominantly "the devil's playground." Adams knew that she would not be able to stage nudity at NCSF, but then that did not become an issue because the production did not require it. She usually feels little restraint concerning potential audience members' objections when directing.

Shakespeare, however, is considered a priori by many, especially conservative and less educated, Americans to be a proper and morally correct writer. Many have not read any or much of his work. Similar characterizations, conversations, or plots in plays by other playwrights might be condemned. But the name of Shakespeare covers a multitude of sins.[64] The cross-dressing and perceived same-sex attraction in *Twelfth Night,* for instance, might have been problematic were it not for the legitimacy that Shakespeare's name affords. In fact, at one point when NCSF produced only one Shakespeare play in its season, their subscribers complained, which resulted in three productions the following season. Partly because his plays consistently draw larger audiences, NCSF now plans for at least half the program to be Shakespeare.[65] One of the ways in which it does resist conventional expectations of the Bard is producing the plays primarily in non-Elizabethan periods.[66]

The summer of 1996, when Adams directed for the NCSF, was something of an exception. Rarely can she get that much time away from People's Light, but she does enjoy a break occasionally, relishing the freedom she gains from just directing and not having any other concerns. Working at this particular juncture with NCSF, however, was sometimes trying. The incompetence and/or obstinacy of the technical staff limited her. In fact, the technical director was fired at the end of the season. Her ideas about creating a sense of the sea were largely abandoned and became "a casualty" of the "technical disasters." She also had to give up her plan for having upholstered screens for Orsino's household. Instead, they changed the furniture, and two different gobos projected different designs on the backdrop. The gobo for Orsino's household projected undulating white lines reminiscent of a heart; for Olivia's, sets of straight long and broken rays emanating from a vortex at the bottom and spreading out to create an arc of about 100 degrees. Both structured and sunlike, the design suggested Malvolio's strictness but breaks in his control of the household, which contained a powerful life force. Although she was not specific, Adams also had a difficult time with the costume designer, saying at another point that there were "disasters in the sewing." She felt frustrated by her inability to have more control over color and set decisions. Because Adams began her work in the theater as a designer, her need to be involved in the design process and her criticism of design failures are probably stronger than most directors.

At People's Light, Adams has solved part of the problem of design work preceding and therefore limiting what can happen in rehearsal through a process she calls "phased development."[67] Typically, she workshops a play for a couple of weeks to see what emerges, then leaves it for several months, during which time the design is developed. Then she begins formal rehearsal, which culminates in the production. She had to work in a shorter rehearsal period than usual for NCSF, which proved sufficient only because she had directed the play twice before. She would not have directed any other play under such conditions.

But a long-term benefit for directing this production was making professional associations. Four of the NCSF company members have moved to Pennsylvania and joined People's Light. She also met Ellen O'Brien, who was the text coach for this production, and who recommended that I interview Adams because O'Brien admired her work as a director. In terms of their viewpoints concerning politicizing theater, however, they represent opposite ends of the spectrum.

Adams would not generalize about how Shakespeare's women are depicted in the other plays because she did not know them. She also believes that genre has little to do with the depiction of women. Adams reports that she generally only cuts obscure jokes that she thinks will go over the audience's head, unless she is doing a production for young audiences and needs to cut for time. Although I did not study her cuts in the promptbook closely, I noticed that she cut a section at the end of 2.5 after Malvolio's exit. The text she cut was perfectly intelligible, but my guess in this instance is that she found a very strong ending for the first "act" of the production—Malvolio looking at the reflection of his mouth in the back of a silver spoon and attempting to smile. The hideous expression he ended up with was hysterical and provided a much stronger theatrical closure than the subsequent discussion by the on-stage audience.

She is something of a pragmatist at this point in her life: "A great story is a great story. . . . Maybe [Shakespeare's stories] do reinforce the culture, but it's certainly a culture that I'm never going to escape. It's part of who I am, and I do not renounce it. I think a lot of it can be changed." Adams's viewpoint straddles the fence between resignation and reformation. She believes that significant aspects of feminist theory are indirectly making it into practice. Although she does not view herself as a feminist, she recognizes that some of the choices she has made in her life and profession may be viewed by others as feminist.

Melia Bensussen

Until the birth of her son about seven years ago, Bensussen worked primarily as a freelance director and is still a member of the Society of Stage Directors and Choreographers. A Caucasian Jewish native of Mexico City, she is also a translator. After graduating from Brown University, she worked as an associate artist for several years with the New York Shakespeare Festival. She has received fellowships from the Drama League of New York and the Theatre Communications Group, which published her adaptation of Langston Hughes's translation of Federico García Lorca's *Blood Wedding*. She also received a Dorot Research Fellowship to study in Israel. In 1993 she received the Princess Grace Statuette Award for Sustained Excellence, and in 1999 she won an Obie Award for her direction of Jeff Hatcher's *Turn of the Screw* at Primary Stages. In New York she has directed for the Manhattan Class Company, Playwrights Horizons, WPA, the Women's Project, Ensemble Studio Theatre, Home for Contemporary Theatre, Theatre for the New City, the Village Gate, and the Puerto Rican Traveling Theatre. Regional theater directing credits include productions at the San Jose Rep, Repertory Theatre of St. Louis, Actors Theatre of Louisville, Cincinnati Playhouse, Denver Centre Theater, Cleveland Playhouse, Berkshire

Theatre Festival, North Carolina Shakespeare Festival, Portland Stage Company, Philadelphia Drama Guild, New Mexico Repertory, University of Missouri–Kansas City, and Fordham University. Bensussen has served as an on-site evaluator for the National Endowment for the Arts; as the American representative to the First International Theatre Workshop for Latin America in Havana, Cuba; as the ITI delegate to the former Czechoslovakia; and as the Hispanic Literary Consultant for the Arena Stage. From 1996–2000 she served as the head of directing at Southern Methodist University and is now an assistant professor as well as the producing director of the Emerson Stage in the Department of Performing Arts at Emerson College.[68]

Bensussen likes to work very collaboratively. Before coming to rehearsal, she has a general sense of what the play is about and what the dominant mood of the production will be. She tries to elicit suggestions from the actors especially in the beginning. She's most comfortable editing and giving feedback to ideas the actors try on their own initiative. Although she does do a fair amount of dictating late in the process, in the beginning she enjoys experimenting.

Bensussen used to have a relationship to the text similar to Packer's: it was her job to make the lines work and cutting them was a "cop out." But her views are now more in line with O'Brien's, that editing, changing words, and reshuffling scenes is valid. Her view is partially based on her knowledge of how the plays were originally constructed—"cobbled together . . . [and] the writer didn't even write them down, and we don't know about the scene order being right, and inserts and speeches and lines and jokes . . . which are so obviously, 'We don't know how to end the scene.'" She doesn't believe the plays are "brilliant" or "sacred." She admires Akalaitis's "brave" work with the texts.

Similar to the other directors I have interviewed, Bensussen admits a sexism in the plays but also thinks that a contemporary context and thoughtful interventions by directors and actors can significantly shape or comment on the meaning of the text. She doesn't see "overt misogyny" but rather "class expectations that hurt everybody." She also has some new arguments to add:

> As a woman and as a Jew, if I don't do literature that doesn't respect me, I am limiting my field of artistry significantly. . . . I think the job is to wrestle with the play. . . . I think we do ourselves a great disservice by ignoring the text, because someone else is not going to ignore it. So if people who are politically intelligent choose to ignore it, then

it will absolutely stay in a very rigid reactionary place, but those of us who disagree with the plays are exactly the people who should do them and we should wrestle them to the ground and try to wrestle some truth out of them because they are too good to be ignored.[69]

Even though she knew *The Merchant of Venice* was a melodrama that depended on Shylock's defeat to succeed, she felt the need to wrestle with the play, and the play won.

Bensussen does consider herself a feminist, "partly because I resent everybody saying they're not anymore. I think women are not yet viewed as powerful, as positive as men are." However, in a somewhat odd contradiction with her work, which reveals the constructedness of gender and performance, in the interview she collapsed differences among women: "I don't have to work at finding the woman's point of view because that's always the point of view I'm living in." She believes her work in the theater is not as productive as it could be in terms of social change because there's so much "preaching to the choir." But she does believe she can contribute to creating a better society for women in small ways:

> You hope you're bringing some surprising image or idea, and I think the empowering of the female is definitely one of them. The notion of female sexuality being a strong, positive thing and wit and power in a woman being not intimidating things are important messages. By somebody in an audience loving a Rosalind or loving a Viola, they are appreciating an aspect of the female experience, especially if you do it with dignity and give these women their due. They're really young women with power, and I think that is rare still to see onstage.

Bensussen enjoys casting young women to show them coming into strength. She also enjoys casting against type. She cast a black actor as Portia in *Merchant of Venice* despite repeated references to her blue eyes, fair skin, and blonde hair. In this way, she called attention to and destabilized conventional normative standards of beauty for heroines. She thinks that in some ways it is "truest to the play" to highlight the tension between text and performance since originally the women characters were played by boys.

Institutional Opportunities and Limitations

The Oregon Shakespeare Festival holds the title of the oldest Shakespearean festival in the United States. A drama professor at what is now Southern Oregon State College in Ashland, Angus L. Bowmer (1905–1979), founded the festival in 1935. Bowmer followed what he knew of Elizabethan staging, producing plays virtually uncut, with fluid scene changes and minimalist design. He also encouraged the actors to work in a relatively quick tempo while maintaining a realistic aesthetic that highlighted character and conflict. In the 1970s, two additional theaters were added, a large indoor theater, named after the founder, and a small black box named the Black Swan. In 1983 OSF won a Tony Award for its history of achievements and the National Governors' Association award for distinguished service to the arts, the only theater in the country to earn this honor. It began touring some of its productions. When it added a satellite operation in Portland, OSF became the largest not-for-profit theater in the United States, although later deficits in this operation caused them to transform the Portland company into an independent organization.[70]

OSF has been referred to as "Bardway," a "Shakespearean Disneyland," and "Disneyland for people with Masters degrees."[71] A 1994 survey revealed that 48 percent of the playgoing respondents had taken graduate courses, and the median household income was $75,022.[72] It's the American equivalent to Stratford-upon-Avon with the oldest full-scale, half-timber Elizabethan theater in the country.[73] Virtually only the mountains remind RSC actor Christopher Luscombe that he is not in Shakespeare's birthplace in England.[74] But its long tradition and generally mainstream appeal have sustained a norm of white actors in period costume following, in the opinion of *San Francisco Chronicle* critic Steven Winn, "a sort of safe, centrist aesthetic party line." Even productions of non-Shakespearean plays, introduced in the 1960s, "have tended toward straight-ahead realism." The management has been hesitant to tamper with the festival's overwhelming popularity and success,[75] despite longtime company member Shirley Patton's claim that its leaders have been risk takers.[76] Leadership has been extremely stable. Not surprisingly, for many years the festival had a very "deliberate and calculated style."[77]

In 1991, popular actor and director Henry Woronicz, who had been with the company since 1984, became the festival's third artistic director. Wanting to build on past successes, he nevertheless had a vision for change. Intent on a more inclusive, diverse company, four of the 1992 season's first five plays were directed by women, and he also encouraged the hiring of minority actors.[78] He began to choose more daring, controversial plays typical of urban theaters. But overtones of AIDS and graphic language in Terence McNally's *Lips Together, Teeth Apart* and Paula Vogel's *The Baltimore Waltz* prompted walkouts midshow and a number of angry letters. In addition to choosing a more eclectic season, Woronicz did not renew contracts for a number of longtime actors, which allowed an infusion of new talent and a more streamlined, creative approach to productions. Anonymous sources in an *Ashland Daily Tidings* article labeled the move a "bloodbath."[79] In a more popular move, he established a training program for the acting company including text work, voice, and movement.[80] Woronicz wanted to make OSF the premier American theater company.[81] Unfortunately, he resigned for personal reasons in 1995. Former OSF director Libby Appel took over in 1996, continuing Woronicz's more inventive approach to production but choosing plays less likely to offend the audience.[82] In 1997 *New York Times* writer Ben Brantley praised the OSF productions as better than most Manhattan productions. They were better at suiting the action to the word and the word to the action because the actor spoke not as if Shakespeare were a foreign tongue but in ways that made the plays intelligent, accessible, and dramatic.[83]

OSF has now produced the Shakespearean canon three times, a feat unparalleled in American theater history.[84] It also maintains one of the largest programs for theater education in the country. It performs for over 150,000 students a year. In addition, it sponsors workshops at OSF for teachers and students. The general public may attend concerts, lectures, and discussions, in which actors, directors, scholars, and other theater artists from OSF and around the world participate. With a budget of $15.1 million, OSF produced eleven plays in the 1999–2000 year, four of which were Shakespeare, for a total of 762 performances for approximately 150,000 patrons.[85] Daniel Watermeier and Felicia Londré end their entry in *Shakespeare Companies and Festivals* by calling OSF "one of the 'treasures' of the contemporary American theatre."[86]

While OSF's financial stability and strong company offer significant opportunities to guest directors, the institution is not without its limitations. By Bensussen's report, the OSF artistic staff "had definite ideas of who needed to be in what roles," so her choices were limited not just by the company's composition but also by administrative pressure. The OSF artistic staff wanted a racially mixed cast without trying to make a statement about the association of race with role. She ended up with an African-American Orsino and an Asian Olivia. While Bensussen is not opposed to racially blind casting, the staff's choice of LeWan Alexander for the role of Orsino, as discussed below, proved problematic.

Another aspect of OSF's system that interfered with her normal way of working was that tech was scheduled only one-third of the way through rehearsals. Bensussen often does significant finishing work during tech because she finds actors particularly receptive at this stage when a similar suggestion earlier in the process might have prompted more resistance or at least a longer discussion. She habitually saves some of her refining notes until that phase of rehearsal, which for this production she completely lost since it came so early. Despite recent changes, Ashland also remains a rather bucolic place. Bensussen thinks that its cheerfulness, in part, kept her from making the production darker. She also admits that she is too restricted by the expectations of the audience and the artistic staff, especially the first time she directs for an institution. She calls her desire to please in this context "destructive." These elements made her feel she got "eaten up by the Ashland machine, and it turned out to be a much cheerier production than I'd intended, oddly enough. I think that happens." Now that she's more familiar with the way things work, she would like to direct there again. She could not accept an offer to direct her second show because her son had just been born.

Some of the actors also resisted Bensussen's open and collaborative process. They wanted her to tell them exactly what she wanted and didn't seem to trust her because she would not do that early on. The previous year, Woronicz had just tried to introduce a more process-oriented method of rehearsal.[87] Apparently, some equated explicit and detailed direction from the director starting day one with competence and more open-ended work with a lack thereof. Interestingly enough, the characterizations that resulted from actors unwilling to work in the way she requested were, in her mind, not "hers"; yet that had to have involved more structured input on her part. The two actors most open to her way of working—Robin Goodrin Nordli, who played Viola, and Bonnie Akimoto, who played Olivia—created characters that she thinks were more reflective of her ideas, even though the actors contributed more to the characterizations. Bensussen envies Adams's situation for both the phased development structure of rehearsal and the opportunity to work consistently with people who know and trust her. Bensussen says:

Abby has got it absolutely right. You've got your company, you've got your place. You build from there. If they don't like your work, they stop coming, but you've got enough people who do to build community. I don't have that, and I wish I did. I do not have a community that sees my work all the time, that has faith in me, that I can trust. So I feel like I'm always being judged for the first time. And there's some theatres now that I've gone back to, and that's lovely. Then I start to relax, and then you can start doing good work. I don't know what one does about that problem.

Freelance directors generally experience more difficulties or at least complexities with the institutions that hire them than those who work consistently with their own company or school.

Barbara Gaines

Gaines's experience with the theater began early in life. Raised in Port Chester, New York, she frequently went to Manhattan with her grandparents to see theater. Her father, a television director who believed in treating everyone on the set exactly the same way, also taught his daughter that there was a creative solution to every problem. She went to Northwestern University for its theater program. Wallace Bacon, a Shakespeare professor there, taught Gaines that Shakespeare was a humanist, a view she came to embrace herself.[88] She also studied at the American Academy of Dramatic Art and with Patrick Tucker, former director of training for the RSC.[89] After graduating, she worked in Manhattan for four years, primarily as an actor. But she missed Chicago. She moved back in 1980, and while recovering from a knee injury,[90] she offered to teach a Shakespeare workshop to a dozen actor friends. Within two months, the core of twelve had grown to forty. In 1985, the workshop produced a showcase of selected scenes entitled, "To Shakespeare, with Love," which played at the Second City theater for three weeks. The following year, she founded the Shakespeare Repertory Theater, which performed *Henry V* on the roof terrace of the Red Lion Pub. In 1987, her theater embarked on its first season at the Ruth Page Theater with *Troilus and Cressida*. Gaines was the artistic director of what became, reputedly, the only theater in the country performing only Shakespeare year-round.[91] Although at a couple of points in the interview she said her instinct was responsible for the decision to produce lesser known plays at the outset, at another point she admitted that she gravitated toward those plays because she had not seen them, and therefore, she knew her own imagination would be freer to work.[92]

By 1993, Shakespeare Repertory was considered "a cherished staple of Chicago theater."[93] Gaines's work became known for its accessibility, clarity, and elegant staging.[94] She has now directed twenty-five of Shakespeare's plays for her theater, recently renamed as the Chicago Shakespeare Theater. She has won a number of Jeff Awards (awards for Chicago theater): Best Production (*Hamlet, The Tale of Cymbeline,* and *King Lear*) and Best Director (*The Tale of Cymbeline* and *King Lear*). She is a member of the artistic directorate for the Globe Theatre in London and also serves on the Board of Trustees for Northwestern University. She has been honored by Loyola University's Humanitarian Award, YWCA's Outstanding Achievement Award for Art,[95] and Shakespeare Repertory Theater Day instituted on April 23, 1997, by Chicago Mayor Richard M. Daley and the Chicago City Council. Her theater was praised by the mayor as "a rich and important addition to the cultural and educational life of all Chicagoans and a source of great civic pride." Gaines and her company have been credited with attracting "many of the finest directors and actors in the world," and her educational Team Shakespeare program has been recognized for "enriching the cultural and educational life of our city."[96] She was named one of the seven 1999 Chicagoans of the Year by *Chicago* magazine, a title conferred on her by *Chicago Tribune* arts and entertainment writers as well. She has worked on panels for the National Endowment for the Arts and currently serves as a board member for the *Chicago Reporter.* With the International Theatre Institute of United States, she participated in the first Delegation of American Theatre Artists, which traveled to Czechoslovakia.[97]

Gaines takes a universalist, populist approach to Shakespeare that is sometimes explicitly antiliterary and antiacademic, which, paradoxically, she developed largely as a result of taking Wallace Bacon's course. "Shakespeare was not meant to be read. His plays were to be seen,"[98] she says, and she's proud of the number of converts she's made by dragging people to the theater. She explains her version of Bacon's humanist view:

> What that really means is that Shakespeare just didn't write beautiful words. He wrote about human behavior under those words that is absolutely universal. I think people are tired of all the schlock in the world. They want to get back to who we are as human beings because a lot of us feel so isolated in our lives, and Shakespeare—when he's

done well—expands the human heart. Look what's happening in the schools, with all the art and music being cut. We could easily become a nation of monsters.[99]

She puts perhaps too much stock in the power of art and Shakespeare. But the payoff for her is in the audience response of high school kids hooting and howling because they are emotionally involved,[100] or homeless people shouting "Bravo!" after every scene of Shakespeare Repertory's first outdoor production in 1994, *Shakespeare's Greatest Hits*. She interprets their enthusiasm as a sign that "there's not a person who can't relate to these lines." It was a revelation to her about "the power Shakespeare has over people."[101] Although Shakespeare well performed is certainly capable of inspiring enthusiasm in many different segments of American society, her interpretation of why these audiences responded the way they did is dubious.

Gaines's views are typically characterized by certainty and confidence yet not always seasoned by critical reflection. Frequent Shakespeare Repertory reviewer Hedy Weiss writes of an interview with Gaines concerning her production of *The Taming of the Shrew*: "[A]s in all her encounters with Shakespeare, she clearly and passionately talks about the text of the play, illuminating the psychological and emotional lives of the characters with information she insists Shakespeare himself provides."[102] Qualifying her interpretation with the admission that she "may just be a hopeless romantic . . . [who depends on her] deep personal connections to a script," Gaines nevertheless sees Petruchio as instinctively understanding Kate, loving her at first sight, and knowing how to free her to become happy.[103] Petruchio gives her "a chance to re-create herself, liberate herself, by modifying her behavior with civilization and with people. It's a very romantic play, and not at all political."[104] She explains that her interpretations are all based on common sense, that every clue she gets is from the text, but then never questions why her interpretations are different from those of the past four hundred years, or other contemporary directors also working from a primarily psychological viewpoint. Perhaps she would say other directors are carrying baggage, her term for any ideological viewpoint that guides one's interpretation of the text—a hindrance from which she believes she is free. In a rare moment, she admitted to me that she knew that with every decision she made regarding a play, she was narrowing and therefore hurting Shakespeare's text, a knowledge that made her very sad. But this comment came in the context of saying Shakespeare, because he was a humanist, was incapable of writing a sexist or racist play: "He was the least judgmental writer of any writer ever. He had the greatest range of human sympathy. He was way beyond any 'ism.' He was so of all of us, of all people, and never judged. He just let us see it. He put real life on the stage without judging, and then we could make our sense of this."

Despite these claims, which deify Shakespeare in a seventies, liberal sort of way, she also says he is "just a man," and the plays should not be treated with reverence as if they were holy. She ascribes the reverent approach to scholars and critics, whom she routinely defines herself against. Treating Shakespeare reverently would lead to bad theater. In Gaines's view, Shakespeare, after all, was not "academic" but rather "a theater person, which means a man of action." She uses the First Folio for all her productions because the punctuation provides definitive clues to the subtext.[105] Gaines does not seem to notice some of the ideological problems raised by her generalizations. She is an excellent director, but not one informed by or particularly responsive to feminist theory—which does not mean that feminist spectators cannot read her work from their own framework.

Writing about an interview in early 1992, Weiss began her article, "When Barbara Gaines talks about William Shakespeare, she sounds like one of those women who have devoted themselves unreservedly to a long and intensely passionate marriage with a complicated genius."[106] The love affair has not waned. Despite the fact that she "detests labels," she accepts the humanist one willingly, as if it weren't one, as if it were the ideologically neutral position because Shakespeare was, in her mind, a humanist. Humanism for Gaines is taking each character personally, a feat she is confident she accomplishes: "The men are inside of me as strongly as the women." But her antifeminism seems to be based on a popular misunderstanding of feminism, as if all feminists are antimale. She thought I would consider it "heresy" that she feels for the men as well as the women. Although feminism has often regarded humanism as an enemy because of its blatant blindness to plurality and diversity, they share an interest in affirming the individuality of each person.[107] Director Zelda Fichandler, for instance, calls herself a feminist but sees her feminism as an extension of her humanism.[108] Like many feminists, however, Gaines sees an intractable divide between the two. Her antifeminism also seems to have some familial roots. She quoted her nephew, "Men are people too," and then said, "Boy that tells you something, doesn't it?" Apparently there is some strong cultural feminism within her family.

But others who work with her detect at least a woman-oriented perspective. Scott Wentworth, a member of the Stratford Festival company in Ontario, played Petruchio in her *Shrew*. He told Terry, "I guess the major difference for me, working with her the first time, is that few women direct a Shakespeare play—or, for that matter, a Shakespeare company. It's a very male-dominated industry. There's a sense of feminine energy here, whereas doing Shakespeare usually is like being in a locker room with the guys. So it's interesting to see a filtering through of a female consciousness."[109] Although puzzled that anyone would consider her work feminist, Gaines admits that "perception is everything," and that people will see different things in her work.

Institutional Opportunities and Limitations

Like the other artistic directors in this study, Gaines has tremendous freedom to pursue her work, especially since she espouses a populist approach. Her dream of creating a permanent home for her Shakespeare theater came true in October of 1999 when the brand-new Chicago Shakespeare Theater (CST) opened on Navy Pier, a tourist area with shops and restaurants. The theater is a 525-seat courtyard-style auditorium wrapping around a 30-foot deep thrust stage modeled loosely on the RSC's Swan Theatre. No seat is more than 30 feet from the stage. Three tiers of wooden balconies are made from lightly stained ash, and the seats are plush green velvet. Also in the seven-story, seventy-five thousand-square-foot, $24 million building is a two-hundred-seat studio theater, a rehearsal hall, costume and wig shops, a cafeteria for the actors, a parking garage, a skyline terrace, an English Garden, a pub-style bar, a book shop, and a teacher resource center.

Gaines has developed relationships with a number of famous English male directors: Peter Brook (who stopped at the Chicago Shakespeare Theater with his world tour of *Hamlet* in May of 2001), Michael Pennington (who directed a production of *Twelfth Night* for Shakespeare Repertory in 1996), Michael Bogdanov (who directed a production of *Timon of Athens* for Shakespeare Repertory in 1997), Peter Hall, Trevor Nunn, and Mark Rylance (of the Globe), who brought his highly acclaimed *Twelfth Night* to CST in the fall of 2003. When invited to visit, Brook reportedly said, "I want to meet the woman who got her city to build her a Shakespeare theater." Through a new International Actor Exchange Program, an English actor from London's Globe Theatre performed in the Chicago Shakespeare Theater's opening season's *All's Well That Ends Well*.[110] British Consul General Robert Culshaw, who watched the construction from his home on East Chicago Avenue, has said, "This is a real link between Chicago and the U.K." He believes it will increase tourism in both localities. Peter Hall told Gaines, "You have one of the best, if not the best, Shakespeare spaces in the world."[111] In her publicity materials for the 1996–97 and 1997–98 seasons, she quotes the *London Independent* as writing "Shakespeare Repertory is one of the best Shakespeare companies on a continent that's dotted with them." The backing of the Brits is probably partially responsible for her success, although she separates herself from the RSC in praising her actors for tapping into their passion, something she hasn't seen much at Stratford.[112]

But Gaines has also appealed to Chicagoans' sense of pride and she has solicited their support, asking them to support a high standard of quality of the arts in Chicago. The theater's executive director, Criss Henderson, told reporter Judith Newmark: "From the start, Barbara has followed two threads: Shakespeare and Chicago. She loves Shakespeare, who was the greatest humanist and the greatest storyteller who ever lived, and she loves Chicago. She wanted to give Shakespeare to Chicago as a shining light—a shining light in a dark world."[113]

Her genuine passion shrewdly marketed has paid off. As one of more than two hundred professional theaters in Chicago, the Chicago Shakespeare Theater is the third largest not-for-profit theater company in the city, following the Goodman and Steppenwolf. The 1998–99 to 1999–2000 subscription base went from seventy-five hundred to over sixteen thousand, and the theater played to over one hundred twenty thousand people in the 2000–2001 season. Their 2003–2004 season budget was $12.4 million supported by a subscription base of twenty-two thousand. The Team Shakespeare education program now reaches fifty thousand students and teachers annually. The theater offers student matinees as well as the typical pre- and postshow discussions about the plays with artists and scholars.[114] Gaines is grateful for the support she has received from friends and artists, which has contributed to her success and protected her from the battles that many women directors face. The theater has also become the family she never had.[115]

Although Gaines sometimes casts the same actors over and over, for instance, Lisa Dodson, whom critic Stu Feller calls "one of the most gifted (and consistently interesting) performers in Chicago,"[116] and Greg Vinkler, she has resisted forming a solid company because she feels that would force her to make compromises. For every production she holds an open audition, excited by the "fabulous, fertile, and extraordinarily talented group of people in Chicago." For Imogen, she wanted "a leading lady" who "was very strong yet incredibly vulnerable, and could speak the language really really well." Lisa Dodson exemplified those qualities. She wanted a Posthumus who would form with her a visually attractive couple, but someone also capable of finding the "great sadness" in this "tormented character." Ultimately, she wanted the audience to like both the characters and desire their union. Otherwise, "Why would anyone want to sit for three hours of Shakespeare?" For Gaines, the hero and the heroine need to be appealing so that the audience can identify with them. Yet at another point in the interview she claimed that she does not know what her audiences expect so their expectations do not influence her work. Perhaps she was referring to interpretations of specific plays, but clearly she assumes that her audiences need to be entertained by productions that ascribe to fairly conventional interpretations of various dramatic roles. To her credit, she sees the characters in *The Merchant of Venice* (which she had just directed at the time of the interview) as predominantly shallow, including the selfish hero and heroine, whom she does not see as happy in their marriage. However, the shallowness of all the characters became her focus and her way of evading questions about anti-Semitism. She consistently avoids political issues in the plays.

JoAnne Akalaitis

Growing up in a working-class Lithuanian Catholic family in Cicero, Illinois, a suburb of Chicago, Akalaitis would seem an unlikely candidate to become "one of the great provocateurs of the late 20th [century]."[117] After attending parochial school, she was the first in her family to go to college. Although now an atheist, she is grateful for the sense of ritual and spectacle that her Catholic background brings to her work. She enrolled at the University of Chicago as a premed student, but then became a philosophy major. After graduating with a BA, she entered graduate school at Stanford University to continue her study of philosophy. At this point she began to direct theater, and it led her to quit school, move to San Francisco, and study acting. She met composer Philip Glass, and later they married and had two children together. Although they divorced, they still maintain both a personal and professional relationship. He has composed the music for a number of her productions, including *Cymbeline.* In the sixties, they moved to Paris, meeting Ruth Maleczech, David Warrilow, and Lee Breuer there. She also worked briefly with Jerzy Grotowski before returning to the States in 1970, when she became cofounder of the experimental theater group Mabou Mines, comprising herself, Glass, Maleczech, Warrilow, and Breuer. The group created cutting-edge original work using mixed media and working very collaboratively. Its acting style was emotionally truthful but nonrealistic. During its twenty-two years, Mabou Mines won numerous Obie Awards, including one in 1976 for Akalaitis's direction of a work adapted from Beckett's radio play *Cascando.* She resigned in 1990.

Akalaitis has worked primarily as a freelance director, staging productions for numerous theaters, including American Repertory Theatre, Lincoln Center Theater, New York City Opera, Goodman Theatre, Mark Taper Forum, Court Theatre, and Guthrie Theater. She has worked as the artistic director of the New York Shakespeare Festival, Andrew Mellon Co-Chair of the directing program at Juilliard, and she is now a professor in the Theater Department at Bard College. She has won an Edwin Booth Award, four Obie Awards for Distinguished Direction and Production, earning a fifth for Sustained Achievement, a Guggenheim Fellowship for experimental theater, a Rosamund Gilder Award for Outstanding Achievement in Theatre, as well as National Endowment for the Arts grants for writing. Akalaitis has taught at a number of institutions, including Yale University, Harvard University, the University of Illinois, Mount Holyoke College, New York University, and the University of Chicago. Since 1998 she has been a fellow of the New York Institute of the Humanities.[118]

Akalaitis has been one of the most controversial directors of the late twentieth century, acclaimed by some as an innovative, inspired genius who opened brave new worlds in theater, but descried by others as gimmicky, narcissistic, and overly intellectual. When Joseph Papp named Akalaitis his successor at the

New York Shakespeare Festival in 1991, he said that she "has the most original mind in theater today."[119] Likewise, Peter Zeisler, the former executive director of Theatre Communications Group (TCG), whose board Akalaitis served on, has praised her "extraordinarily brilliant mind."[120] But she is also known for her visual imagination and her meticulous attention to detail, considering what every movement onstage communicates to an audience. In fact, an anonymous friend reported that "the wonderful thing about her is that she operates from a gut level. The bad thing about her is the same."[121] Akalaitis is particularly well known for her revising of "the classics," which has provoked vitriolic responses from traditionalist New York critics. Interviewed recently, however, she said with alarm, "I hope I'm not being written about as a controversial person. . . . I'm the most ordinary director in the world." Arena Stage Artistic Director Molly Smith said that was a "classic comment" from Akalaitis, whom she has known for nearly a decade. "But," Smith added, "she really is extraordinary."[122]

Akalaitis's work has never been mainstream, yet when she took over as artistic director for the Public, she insisted, "We are about making art accessible and important."[123] At the same time, she said of the festival's subscribers, "they didn't understand the work . . . were essentially dull people [and] did not appreciate especially what we might call more adventurous theater."[124] A supporter of racially blind casting since the early years of her work with Mabou Mines, she wanted the demographics outside the theater to be present inside it, both on the stage and in the audience. But the audiences at the Public during her brief tenure were the "richest, youngest, best-educated audiences in New York."[125] One wonders if a more diverse audience would actually appreciate her work more than established, white, middle-class audiences, and in a recent interview, she conceded, "It's not as if large numbers of diverse people want to go see *Hamlet*. That's not what's happening. The show has to be very culturally specific, like *Freak*."[126]

Akalaitis insists that her work is not guided by an aesthetic, that theater for her is an open field, "an emotional and intellectual playground for spiritual development."[127] But she has never been interested in psychological naturalism, looking instead for the right gestalt,[128] although she rejects the deconstructivist label often applied to her: "I have never deconstructed a line of text in my life. There is this dopey, old-fashioned concept that if you have a cigarette or a piece of pizza onstage, you are deconstructing the text."[129]

She admits that some of her trademark gestures have been influenced by the work of neurologist Oliver Sacks, who has described in *Awakenings* the "otherworldly movements" of encephalitis patients.[130] Not surprisingly, Akalaitis finds the speech of English actors "to be uniform and boring."[131] She also admits to liking "a lot of music in a play, almost like a movie.... I like emotional underscoring."[132] Fluorescent lighting and very physical acting tend to be part of her signature.[133] Dramatic characters in her productions are generally not strongly individualized; rather, they tend to represent their race, religion, gender, or class. The actor serves as "image as well as agent."[134]

Although Akalaitis is known for interpretive and editorial liberties with the text, she rejects that criticism because she does not interpolate other words into the author's play: "I don't have a free hand with texts. I basically do the play. I don't adapt them or change them. I sometimes cut scenes or rearrange scenes, but basically the words that are spoken are the words the playwright wrote."[135] In my review of various promptbooks for the production, it was clear that the editing process was evolutionary. Sometimes lines would be cut and later restored, but as far as I could tell, only one line was changed. Cloten's line in 4.1, "This is the very description of their meeting-place, and the fellow dares not deceive me" (ll. 24–25) became "Where is this damn Milford Haven?" a change probably motivated by its comic effect. Perhaps it is because her vision is so unusual that what seems like adaptation to most audiences is merely how the play speaks to Akalaitis. Deborah Saivetz, who has worked as an actor and dramaturg with Akalaitis and interviewed her extensively, describes her "often irreverent stagings of classic plays" as "radically reinterpreted, though textually faithful."[136]

With the exceptions of *The Taming of the Shrew* and *Othello*, Akalaitis tends to see the women in Shakespeare's plays as strong: "Shakespeare wrote wonderfully for women. The language expresses such passion about relationships, about sex, about power. It seems equal to me. It doesn't seem like a man's world." Yet then she made another exception of *Henry IV*. When she was lying in bed after having given birth to her daughter, she went through all the female characters of Shakespeare, deciding to name her daughter Juliet. Clearly she has felt a deep affinity for Shakespeare.

Akalaitis does consider herself a feminist, but believes that feminist performance theory is limiting. She finds its categorizations literal and unimaginative. She describes her feminism as "very, very practical, but in everything I do I am a feminist." She brings food to rehearsal, for example: "That could be kind of a reverse sexism, filling in the blanks by doing too much, by being too nurturing. It happens to be my nature, but in every aspect of my life, it's there. But it's not a theory; it's just a way of life." She believes that directing and theater in general is fundamentally about human relationships: "[It's about] being a decent person, somehow to involve a community of people in a vision, or project, and not be mean to them, not manipulate them."[137]

Akalaitis is also interested in sexuality onstage: "I always try to have it onstage because I think the theater is very sexy, so I have sexual scenes onstage that are more explicit perhaps than the text calls for, because I think it's fun for the audience, actually." She does not worry about the objectification of women because her experience has been that men in the audience "are very uncomfortable with sexuality onstage. It's not like a movie." When I told O'Brien this, she replied that while she would like to think it was true, it was probably more dependent on whether or not the men were with their wives.

Institutional Opportunities and Limitations

Beginning as a Shakespeare Workshop led by a blue-collar, high school-educated Brooklynite in the basement of Emmanuel Presbyterian Church, the New York Shakespeare Festival became the premier nonprofit theater in the United States.[138] In 1954, Joseph Papp (1921–1991) got a provisional charter from the New York Educational Department that allowed him to establish his nonprofit theater. Its goal was to "encourage and cultivate interest in poetic drama with emphasis on the works of William Shakespeare and his Elizabethan contemporaries, and to establish an annual summer Shakespeare Festival."[139] By 1957, Papp was touring his productions in all five boroughs of New York City on the back of a truck that opened out into a forty-five-foot platform stage. One day, the truck broke down in Central Park, and Papp decided to perform on the spot, which started the tradition of Shakespeare in Central Park. As a result of some savvy fund-raising, in 1961, he built a permanent outdoor theater there, the Delacorte Theater, which opened on 18 June 1962, with George

C. Scott starring as Shylock in *The Merchant of Venice*. With a thrust stage, the Delacorte became capable of seating nearly two thousand spectators. By 1964, NYSF was once again performing in parks in all five boroughs.[140]

But Papp had an even greater vision for the festival. He wanted to produce contemporary works as well, and in 1965 arranged with the city to purchase the old Astor Library in the East Village. Dubbed the Public Theater, its first production was the musical *Hair,* staged in 1967. By 1977, the NYSF was producing theater on eight stages. Papp staged the works of new American playwrights, foreign premieres, and new translations. As a leader of a theater in one of the most international cities of the world, Papp also supported artists from ethnic and cultural minorities. Several times he developed companies of black and Hispanic actors. In addition, NYSF has served as a host to other theater artists such as Richard Foreman, Andrei Serban, and Joseph Chaiken. It developed an educational outreach program for both performance and playwriting, as well as a Latino Festival, and a Film Festival.[141] As *Shakespeare Companies and Festivals* editor Ron Engle writes, "Perhaps no other company in American theatre has launched as many acting careers and new American playwrights, designers, and technicians as the NYSF."[142] An English reporter remarked that the NYSF was "an institution as close as anything in America to a National Theatre—six houses playing agitprop, Shakespeare, avant-garde, amiable musicals."[143] It is still dwarfed, however, by the RSC, which has a budget of approximately $50 million, seven hundred employees, and twenty-one hundred annual performances.[144]

After directing on and off at NYSF for fifteen years, Akalaitis was appointed as an artistic associate in 1990. Papp developed cancer and, in June of 1991, his son died of AIDS at twenty-eight. Two months later, Papp appointed Akalaitis artistic director, and on October 31, he died. Along with drastic cuts in funding and the closing of the extremely profitable *A Chorus Line,* which Papp had produced, his leave during his illness had resulted in a financial crisis for NYSF. The number of new productions were cut by half, the staff was cut from 120 to 60, and the budget went from $13.5 million to $10.5 million.[145] *Los Angeles Times* theater critic Sylvie Drake remarked that Papp's death came as a hard blow "to an increasingly dysfunctional New York theatre scene."[146] After a troubled twenty months, Akalaitis was fired and replaced by a playwright director on the artistic staff, George C. Wolfe, who remains the artistic director today. For the

1999–2000 season, the Public ran seven performance spaces: five theaters in their headquarters on Lafayette Avenue in addition to a cabaret/bar and the Delacorte Theater in Central Park. They produced eight shows, three of which were by Shakespeare, for a total of 378 performances. Attendance was almost two hundred sixteen thousand and the budget was $12 million. Although they do not have an official educational outreach program, their Community Affairs department works with schools to get students into the audience and hosts postshow discussions with the actors for the students.[147]

Akalaitis was able to cast from the available acting pool in New York City, probably one of the most substantial in the country. She was primarily looking for "a good actor." But for Imogen, she wanted someone "spunky and alert, bright, funny." She wanted the brothers in the woods to be "sexy and exciting," and the stepmother to be also "sexy and exciting in a complicated way." She also says that she never thinks about the expectations of her audience "because that kind of dooms you." Concerning the controversies over her work, she has said, "It does not inform or define my life or my work. I go from project to project, from job to job. And I mean it. I wake up in the morning and think, What am I going to do in rehearsal? When am I going to eat tonight? Two months from now, what show am I going to direct? What class am I going to teach? It's not, What is the arc of my career?"[148] Her refusal to cater to mainstream audience expectation has allowed her to produce some extraordinary work, and also perhaps some gimmicky work. But clearly, she feels more freedom than Bensussen does.

Shortly after Akalaitis's dismissal, *New York Times* critic Frank Rich, who had both praised and slaughtered her productions, wrote a telling article about the state of American theater in the early nineties. He remarked that Akalaitis's "failures at the festival have little to do with her gifts as an artist. She has been and will continue to be a talented director," citing her lack of substantial, more mainstream productions as one of the causes of her demise.[149] But he also noted, "Both the nonprofit and commercial American theater are at a crucial juncture in their history, beset by a leadership that is aging and frequently out of touch, severe economic cutbacks, racial divisions and a shortage of new producers." But what disturbed him most was "how little the theater community stirred itself either to help the fading theater or to call attention to its plight. Do the art or dance communities stand idly by when comparable institutions like the

Whitney Museum or American Ballet Theater are in crisis? . . . [T]he Akalaitis fiasco dramatizes the timid everyone-for-himself mentality that now seems to drive the theater community."[150] While Akalaitis had substantial finances and a well-established venue for her production, the cutthroat New York theater scene, of which Rich is a part, doomed her *Cymbeline* to critical failure. Fortunately, the critics did not keep audiences away, and *Cymbeline* played to full houses for most of its run.

The Productions

1
Destruction Wrought by Domestic Violence: Jayme Koszyn and Lisa Wolpe Direct *Romeo and Juliet*

*R*OMEO AND JULIET IS A ROMANTIC TRAGEDY, THE FIRST TO APPEAR on the stage.[1] Both chance and irrational hatreds destroy two extraordinary youths whose unbounded, passionate love blossoms with heartbreaking strength and beauty, youths whose union might have healed the enmity infecting the playworld like a deadly disease. Part of the tragedy lies not just in their deaths but in the misfortune that, as Ronald Knowles has written, "only death came from their love, not the renewal and thus reaffirmation of life."[2] In fact, the sense of tragedy is intensified because the potential for a happy ending is so near.[3]

The protagonists have no real space of their own, and their attempts at withdrawal into forbidden and only temporarily protected spaces is finally not enough to ensure their survival. Despite Romeo and Juliet's partial transcendence of their culture's ideologies, particularly the one that demands their separation, they are also inescapably products of their society.[4] Lloyd Davis has written, "The oneness felt by the lovers appears to signify mutual presence, but such intersubjective moments are overlaid with social and historical pressures."[5] At least their love ruptures Veronian ideologies and thereby denaturalizes them.[6]

Romeo and Juliet also explores the connection between sex and violence and how it is culturally and politically constructed. While the play presents a particular girl/woman in a relationship with a boy/man, it also presents violence as a fundamental part of male sexuality and the corresponding attitude that mutuality in a love relationship results in weakness and is, therefore, dangerously feminizing.[7] So the major hurdles facing women directing this play include how to represent the patriarchal familial and cultural structures, Juliet's sexual subjectivity, her intersubjective relationship with Romeo, and the ways in which particularly masculine violence nearly ubiquitously yet not inevitably informs the ideology and action of the playworld. In contrast with most 1990s American, British, and Continental productions, both performances I researched for this project explored in different ways the connection between sex and violence and, in particular, the cultural ideology that connects male sexuality with violent dominance. They also created a vital and balanced relationship between the protagonists. But their primary focus was the way Capulet sought to control his daughter's sexual choices through violence.

Staging violence is in itself potentially problematic. Studies on the effects of violence in the media or theatrical representation are inconclusive. The majority of feminists writing on the arts, however, assume that representation impacts not only individuals but, if the distribution is extensive enough, more widely held cultural conceptions. The logical extension of this belief is that art must therefore be held to certain ethical standards. Claiming that media violence significantly contributes to real violence and denying the possibility for critical reflection after the theatrical event, fight choreographer J. D. Martinez claims that the dramatic context for violence is irrelevant since its impact is largely visceral and therefore precludes a rational cognitive assessment.[8] Martinez perhaps gives too much power to represented violence, but like most writers on the subject, he treats violence as a monolithic entity.

Violence can, however, have a range of values, especially for women. John Marshall Townsend's sociological study on male and female psychology and sexual behavior cites numerous examples of women claiming that, despite their own feminism and attempts to develop long-term relationships with men who were gentle and considerate, they frequently grew bored and found themselves gravitating toward men who were more aggressive and dominant, even though they claimed not to want someone who was domineering or likely to interfere with their career choices. One interviewee was particularly explicit: "I need a lover who can say, 'Shut up, Bitch!' once in a while and then rip my clothes off. I think most women need that too but they can't admit it.... I want a man who loves me and is considerate, but if he can't stand up to me, I can't respect him and it won't work."[9] Townsend inserts a footnote after this quote distinguishing between ravishment and rape, explaining that "Pat" is referring to the former because all women hate rape.[10] True enough, but some women may be reluctant to articulate their desires precisely because of the danger of being misunderstood. Even Janice Radway, who interviewed approximately forty readers of romance novels in a small town in the southern Midwest, considers her readers' distinction between "forceful persuasion" and "true rape" both "curious and artificial," attributing it to women's need to understand how to deal with male power and their desire to reject responsibility for their own sexual feelings and actions.[11] Radway apparently needs to condemn violence regardless of the context.

The context exists, to some degree, within the definition of violence itself. Webster's first definition is our common understanding of the word: "exertion of physical force so as to injure or abuse." But parts of the third definition are probably what Radway's interviewees had in mind when they referred to "forceful persuasion": "intense, turbulent, or furious ... vehement feeling or expression: fervor." Joan Ozark Holmer points out, "Romeo is violent in the nature of his love, as the friar would not have him be, but Romeo is not violent in his physical relationship to Juliet, as the sexual stance of men like Sampson and Mercutio would have him be, that is thrusting women to the wall (1.1.14–16) or being rough with love (1.4.27)."[12] This provides a useful distinction, though even this boundary is not completely stable for by its very nature, physical violence is in some ways sexual because it is tactile.

Scholarly research concerning men using physically harmful, nonconsensual violence against women are numerous. Citing Nancy Chodorow, Radway argues that, in our society, men's need to differentiate themselves from women is a fundamental source of their violence against them.[13] *Gender Violence: Interdisciplinary Perspectives* (1997) offers a wide array of readings, many authored by men. One of the editors, Laura L. O'Toole, cites various scientific studies and writes about the ways in which children come to understand the construction of masculinity, which includes, for men, acceptance of violence as a means to maintain their hegemony. She then explores the way various subcultures further indoctrinate members into beliefs that permit not only an acceptance but also an encouragement of rape.[14] Edwin Schur discusses the influences of American life that contribute to sexual coercion, again discussing the linkage between American masculine sexuality and conquest.[15] And so on.

While such studies are needed in order to address certain variables that may allow for intervention and change, I would like to argue that our society capitalizes on and distorts deeper structures in the psyche.[16] While I was sorting through these ideas, a colleague e-mailed me a succinct and perceptive articulation of the complex connection between sex and violence: "Life is intrinsically violent, and sex is intrinsically violent as well, which is one of its loveliest qualities. My nonviolence is social/political/ethical, having to do with things like war and the death penalty and disciplining children. Physical relationships between lovers are another matter. Our society's moral confusion all too frequently is based on a conflation of public and private values. As long as no one gets hurt, violent sex is a thrill. Violence as sex is a crime." Although some women may eschew any kind of violence connected with sex, which is often the result of past abuse, this formulation resolves a number of apparent contradictions. Sexual violence, depending on its form, offers dangers or pleasures, and nonabusive sexual violence need not be ranked as a less evolved impulse of life.

The distinction between violent but nonabusive, consensual sex and violence as sex is clear for most women but perhaps not so clear for many men.[17] Depicting (and writing about) the connection between sex and violence onstage in a way that acknowledges its allure while condemning its abuse is particularly challenging. However, *Romeo and Juliet* seems in many ways an ideal play for experimenting with this area. Directors can easily depict two individuals in a mutual, loving relationship, despite the pressure on Romeo, in particular, to adopt a ruthless, nonconsensual physically violent relationship with women. Violence can be given a range of values.

Nevertheless, the recent stage history of *Romeo and Juliet* suggests that many directors, at least American ones, bypass this opportunity.[18] A notable exception is former Cornell University Theatre Department Chairman, Bruce Levitt, who directed the play in 1996 for the Heart of America Shakespeare Festival in Kansas City. However, his conception of the play is much clearer from the interview than the review of the production itself, perhaps partially because the reviewer saw a sharp divide between Romeo and Juliet's passion and the violent society that destroys it.[19] Irene Lewis may have had a similar concept for her 1997 production at Center Stage in Baltimore, but the reviewer merely noted that the same raised platform "eerily" served for both Romeo and Juliet's marriage bed and bier.[20] Other than including the required sword fights, American productions rarely focus on the violence of the play.[21] This may be partially related to

America's relationship with Shakespeare. In his book *Shakespeare's America: America's Shakespeare* (1990), Michael Bristol argues that American institutional attitudes toward "the Bard" reveal the belief that Shakespeare is a reconciler of social contradictions. His writings "are often celebrated as remedial and therapeutic, reconciling or transcending conflict within the social landscape depicted in the plays."[22] *Romeo and Juliet* is often considered "family entertainment" and is many students' first exposure to Shakespeare. Producers are probably reluctant to present a dark view of this play for fear of alienating audiences, particularly in nonacademic settings. It is not surprising, then, that American productions of this love story usually do not problemtize the society's construction of gender and sexuality and how violence enters the equation.

In her survey of post-World War II to mid-1980s productions, Felicia Hardison Londré argues for the greater popularity and success of *Romeo and Juliet* productions in continental Europe as opposed to England or America. She attributes this to two early landmark productions in England: the 1935 New Theatre production starring Laurence Olivier, John Gielgud (alternating between Romeo and Mercutio), and the "never to be equaled Juliet," Peggy Ashcroft; and Zeffirelli's triple incarnations of the play. She also argues that English critics have often been dissatisfied with actors' abilities to deliver the verse both poetically and passionately.[23] And perhaps America is just overcoming its inferiority complex.

The two "productions" of *Romeo and Juliet* most familiar to American audiences are Zeffirelli's film and *West Side Story*, though Baz Luhrmann's *Romeo + Juliet* has also made a substantial cultural mark on today's youth.[24] Zeffirelli's film did evoke a culture of masculine violence, which for the astute observer was also connected to sexuality. The visual sequence at the beginning, where Sampson's codpiece is literally underlined with the bottom of the frame as he bites his thumb, establishes him as "a young man in love with his own sexual prowess which he expresses through his violence."[25] But the emphasis of the play was on the youth of the lovers, the generation gap with their elders, and how the hot summer days, hence climate rather than culture or politics, played a large role in the escalating violence. Many of Zeffirelli's cuts simplified Shakespeare's more complex exploration of the Veronian masculine culture of violence.[26]

West Side Story is perhaps even better known. I'm currently teaching in a small liberal arts college in central Illinois where the students have not been educated particularly well in the arts, but most in my Introduction to Theater class have seen *West Side Story*. And in the Movement for Theater class I recently taught, I used an exercise for exploring Greek choral work that revealed how ingrained in teenagers' consciousness this film's group dynamics have become. There were two groups, and each had a leader. The group followed whatever their leader did and the two leaders were instructed to have a movement conversation. Immediately, although both the leaders were women, the "dialogue" became playful citations of gang interactions—which continued until I asked them to become more abstract. In a skit which they were asked to develop based on the theme of "surprise attack," one group chose to be a gang who snapped as they encircled their "prey," a young couple whom they—quite seriously, for I specified the tenor of the action as dramatic rather than comic—robbed and beat up. While the film capitalizes on American urban racial tensions, it tends to romanticize violence without genuinely questioning our attraction to it.

Countries that have suffered under a politically repressive regime often produce Shakespeare in more politically progressive ways than their democratically ruled counterparts in the West. His plays have been a vehicle for expressing their criticism of the government and their intense discontent without crossing the border into revolutionary propaganda. Despite the productions' political edge, feminist concerns are generally subordinated to those of class, economics, political agency, civil rights, government corruption, and racial or intracultural hostility. The productions studied for this project took a more feminist approach than most.

JAYME KOSZYN'S *ROMEO AND JULIET*

The Director's Vision

Koszyn was struck in reading the play over and over that, with the exception of Romeo's mother, who dies offstage from grief, all the people who die in the play are children:

> It was this *tremendously* tragic inversion of the children dying before the parents did. The play is filled with children killing children—a kind of infanticide—and I wondered, what is this world like? And what I concluded was, this is a world that is a completely violent

world, a world driven by hate. Hate starts at home, and the relationship between the children and their parents—their basic home life—was totally lacking in love and affection.[27]

Koszyn admitted that her viewpoint was influenced by both her past and present. She grew up in the Bronx, and while preparing for rehearsal, an MIT student was murdered when he resisted a robbery by three Cambridge Rindge and Latin High School students. The youngest, sixteen-year-old Shon McHugh, allegedly stabbed the victim once through the heart, and then threw his knife into the Charles River. All three students had previously been charged with murder and armed robbery.[28] During a protest march by about two hundred Cambridge Rindge and Latin students, Rosalie Barnes told *Boston Globe* reporters, "We have to change a society that views violence as normal, acceptable and commercially profitable."[29] Koszyn saw a real connection between the world of the play and the world in which the students lived. But she also believes that the violence of our culture grows out of an older framework: since the medieval era in England and the Colonial era in America, people have developed traditions for using weapons ritualistically, traditions that continue to this day. However, rather than simply portraying a universal narrative of human experience, she recognized the ways in which both her own personal history and the local, historical present contributed to her reading, a recognition that shaped her production choices. She was thereby able to contribute to a localized production meaning.

Koszyn did not want to embody her ideas in what Robert Brustein calls "simile directing," where the play is set, for instance, in Northern Ireland, yet she did want to communicate the play's current relevance. Elements of her set design brought both ideas together. She created an unlocalized world with no backdrop and very few set pieces (relatively nondescript chairs, benches, and bed), but costumed the characters in modern dress, so the playworld would be clearly analogous to the world the audience inhabited. The only more expressionistic element of the set was a scrim sometimes positioned lengthwise across the stage and usually used to signify forces separating Romeo and Juliet or imprisoning them.

In contrast to the opposition between public and private, political and personal that society has often constructed along gender lines, Koszyn viewed the civic feud as a *result* of domestic violence:

The bloodlines were violent bloodlines, and the energy in Verona was the energy of hate between those two families. But it was between those two families because it was in the households themselves. The relationship between Capulet and his wife is not unlike the relationship between wives of men who are abusing their children, where the wives are completely devoid of emotion because they are steeped in denial and passivity. The husband is violent, masculine, opposing, and everyone is silent around him. The city was so tremendously violent because people were being beat up at home.

The fighting *between* the households arose because the fathers were perpetrating abuse *within* their own households. The domestic sphere, then, was not marginalized or considered inferior to the public sphere. Rather, it held a primary place as the origin for the dynamics of civic life. Although social and domestic spheres exist in a dialectical rather than unilateral relationship—both influencing each other rather than one dictating the dynamics of the other—at least she reversed the typical traditional formula.

The domestic sphere was also not defined as the woman's domain. Even here, the father dominated. This was especially evident in the relationship between Juliet's parents. Because Lady Capulet knew her husband was abusive and did not want to face either his rage or their daughter's and her own victimization, she essentially cut herself off from her emotions. She was a shadow of who she could have been.

Capulet's abuse of his daughter when he threatens to disown her aided by his wife's ultimate complicity (3.5) was a central scene in the production. Although the women rarely participate in public life in this play, Koszyn's view emphasized that in the Veronian society no place is safe for women. She therefore deconstructed the patriarchal polarization along gender lines of public and private, active and passive, visible and invisible. The production also showed connections among gender, family, state, and other cultural codes.

It is somewhat surprising, then, that within this harsh environment, Romeo and Juliet love. The production revealed that each became the other's only haven, and the society would ultimately destroy even that sanctuary. Koszyn observes:

> The movement of the play has to do with two people who believe against this world energized by hate, Romeo and Juliet. The only reason that Romeo and Juliet in their souls even know what love is (because certainly their parents were not giving that to them) is because they each have a surrogate parent who loves them: Romeo has the

friar, and Juliet has the nurse—what Alice Miller calls the only compassionate "witness" a child needs to survive.

In her view, the disenfranchised in the society became the true source of love and nurturing. In the concrete world of a violent Veronian society, seeds of love were planted by these surrogate parents in the receptive hearts of Romeo and Juliet, where the seeds took root and grew. The design used to advertise the production was a cityscape of buildings with a balcony in the center expanded out like a distended belly. Through this image, Juliet's balcony symbolized the place where healthy love could gestate and thrive, but also break familial bonds. Because it was abnormal in this society, their love was represented as distorting architectural lines. At the entrance to the doors opening out onto the balcony stood a frail but tall, potted tree, an image suggesting that their love was alive but vulnerable because the environment would not support it. For Koszyn, the love between Romeo and Juliet was not "sweet but fanatic, obsessive, almost pathological" because their souls were entwined, and they knew that the other was the only one in the world with whom they could feel this way. Every time Romeo and Juliet were onstage, it was "like a shot of adrenaline, or if you're a drug addict, a shot of dope in your arm," while the relationships with and between the parents were very cold.

Although Koszyn would normally read literary criticism and reviews of other productions while preparing to direct, because her vision was so strong, she avoided the criticism, wanting to stay within the world of the play as she saw it. However, she was aware of more subtle influences. She had been reading John Barton, who believes, like many Shakespeareans, in trusting the imagery of the text, and this led her to follow Romeo's celestial imagery by making Juliet an angel in the balcony scene. She had also seen Peter Brook's film of *King Lear,* which contributed to how she staged Romeo's murder of Tybalt.[30] Not surprisingly, the models Koszyn drew from were those of highly acclaimed British RSC men.[31] Koszyn was grateful for the interview because it gave her an opportunity to reflect on the production and see what she was trying to achieve in a way that she was not fully conscious of at the time. Who knows how much mediation happened between her work as it was happening and her view of it several years later, but it does seem—at least from our post-Freudian vantage point—that sometimes an artist's work is partially unconscious. And the sense artists make of their work after the fact is in some ways just as important as the sense or lack thereof that they make of it while in the press of creation.

The Play in Performance

> "Allwayz gotta fuck at a wedlock
> I like it when the pussy goes snack crack and pop"[32]

When spectators entered the MIT Kresge Little Theater to see Koszyn's *Romeo and Juliet* in November of 1992, they entered into a space charged with sex and violence both visually and musically.[33] While listening to NWA and Gangsta rap, they watched a dumb show of a Veronian rite of passage. Sampson, about fifteen, was ritualistically teaching the approximately ten-year-old Gregory how to use weapons. On the lip of the forestage the weapons were spread out over a red cloth. Koszyn notes:

> The ritual has to do with the history of the society, from the medieval maces all the way up to Uzis. There's a sense that instead of learning to love or learning to get married and procreate, these children grow up in a society where they learn to use weapons ritualistically.

The movements were very stylized and sexual, taking their rhythmic cues from the music. Their rehearsal was interrupted by the entrance of the Montague servants coming down the aisle. They shifted from practice to performance once encountering their enemies, and the acting flowed into action.

The apparently male-generated union between violence and sexuality was undercut by the cross-gender casting of Sampson and Gregory. The audience first saw two young women dressed as boys who used weapons in a sexual way. Koszyn was not trying to question the culture's construction of gender, however. The cross-gender casting occurred only in minor roles and fulfilled a need to cast a company that had more women than men. Despite its practical rather than theoretical aim, such casting, if only at an unconscious level, would not allow an audience to associate the connection between sexuality and violence exclusively with men. With this combination of production concept and cross-gender casting, Koszyn accomplished two things at once: she portrayed the culture's patriarchal construction of sexuality and violence, while showing women as capable of complying with, resisting, being victimized by, or actively generating such cultural codes. Women were both passive and active, and while their passivity was often the result of male domination, as

1: DESTRUCTION WROUGHT BY DOMESTIC VIOLENCE   97

Gregory teaching Sampson how to use weapons in the preshow to Jayme Koszyn's *Romeo and Juliet*. Photo: Eric Levenson.

in the case of Lady Capulet, their agency, as is true of any human being, could be used positively or negatively. In this way she revealed the society's oppression of women while deconstructing the paradigm that posits sex-based differences in people's responses to violence. Her casting and directing choices challenged the common belief that men are innately more brave and aggressive than women.

Since the production did not call attention to the cross-dressing, it is difficult to determine how much the audience questioned cultural gender construction as a result. A comparison to Lisa Wolpe's work discussed in the second part of this chapter proves informative here. Los Angeles Women Shakespeare Company's productions do not particularly highlight the cross-dressing, and in fact, reviewers say they forget about it after the first few minutes.[34] But Wolpe claims that reviewers are especially critical of her fight scenes, as if anticipating that the women will not be convincing warriors, even though they ignore weaknesses in fight scenes of other productions cast with men.[35] This shows a heightened awareness of at least some audience members concerning men's and women's potentially differing relationships to violence. Especially since the first thing the audience saw in Koszyn's production was the cross-dressing, and it occurred in the context of a violent dumb show, I would suspect it at least raised these issues for many.

ACTOR AND AUDIENCE

Koszyn used a realistic acting style for this production because she wanted the audience to connect her vision of the play with contemporary issues, but she did not follow all the theatrical conventions of realism. She broke the fourth wall by having the actors enter and exit through the aisles. Still, the actors rarely made eye contact with the audience. Koszyn used the space this way primarily to make it more interesting, but she actually believes that was a mistake because her intent at the time was to create a sense of the characters being imprisoned, which she partially achieved through the use of a scrim. If she had thought more clearly about the implications of her staging, she would have maintained the fourth wall to engender the sense that there was no escape from this world. Koszyn has, thus, moved from a very basic concern of making a forestage proscenium space "interesting" to a more theoretical consideration of how the actor/audience relationship communicates something more specific about the play to the audience. Although Koszyn had not read feminist criticism at the time of our interview, her instinct to use the fourth wall as a sign of imprisonment is precisely Patricia Schroeder's suggestion in "Locked behind the Proscenium: Feminist Strategies in *Getting Out* and *My Sister in This House*."[36]

THE VIOLENCE CONTINUUM

Koszyn sees the issue of violence and its relationship to political authority differently than many feminists. She does not maintain a blanket distrust of hierarchy and unilateral authority. The Prince, she believes, is enlightened. At the top of the hierarchy, he could have benefited the city if it had listened to him. The rest of the characters felt and sometimes acted on their violent impulses, and the production charted their decisions along a continuum. When the Prince called a halt to the civic brawl, some people knelt and listened respectfully, others knelt grudgingly, but Tybalt (Orin Percus) refused to kneel. He merely threw down his weapon angrily. Koszyn explained of Tybalt, "He can't even observe courtesies toward an enlightened man that even the most violent individuals observe, because Tybalt is too far gone." Characters on the violent side of the continuum, such as Tybalt, Paris, and Capulet, were dressed in a more regimented fashion, in dark suits and ties.

The Prince and Tybalt represented opposite ends of the violence continuum. Dressed in a white suit and separated from everyone else by the scrim while admonishing the fighters with stern dignity, the Prince seemed a humanist substitute for God. Koszyn's desire to criticize the violence of the society was so strong that she presented the corrective voice of reason as nearly divine. The Prince literally seemed to be from another world, an embodiment of an idea, which contrasted with an otherwise realistic performance style. She derived her connection of the Prince with the forces of good and peace primarily through her analysis of his speech, the superior viewpoint he espoused, rather than viewing the larger picture of the play's dramatic action and considering the civic violence he allowed.

Romeo and Juliet lived, as did Benvolio, the only youth in the play who survives, on the Prince's peaceful side of the continuum. The protagonists' love contrasted sharply with the hatred and violence of the feud, yet at least Romeo could not completely escape from internalizing the violence of his culture. In the fight with Tybalt, Koszyn wanted to show the cost to Romeo of living in this world: "Romeo has suppressed all of this rage, living in a world like this and being who he was, but when he finally crossed the threshold into violence—again, he did grow up in this world—he just can't stop it. It just keeps falling out of him."

VIOLENCE-INF(L)ECTED SEXUALITY

The end of the fight also revealed Verona's destructive connection between violence and sexuality. When Romeo (Eugene Chiang) killed Tybalt, he straddled him and stabbed him rhythmically several times, the intensity and rhythm of Tybalt's screams resonant of a female climax. Koszyn felt the fusion of sex and violence in this moment grew partially out of Romeo's jealousy over the closeness between Juliet and Tybalt. Although Koszyn was not specifically trying to evoke a homoerotic moment, certainly this staging potentially suggested such a dynamic, a dynamic supported by the strongly homosocial world of the play. But all sexualities in this world were in some way inf(l)ected by violence. According to Koszyn, "In the world of the play, sex and violence are carried on the same genome—except in the case of Romeo and Juliet."

The Capulets' party also embodied this liaison between sexuality and violence. The dance centered around swords. Sometimes the women held the swords horizontally over their heads while swaying their hips back and forth. Sometimes the sword passed between the partners seductively. Some of the dance steps imitated the stylized fight moves in the opening. Romeo and Juliet did not participate together in this dance, but Juliet did dance with Paris and Tybalt.

I asked Koszyn if Juliet had escaped this conditioning. Her answer suggested that Juliet had been subjected to the conditioning but she had not internalized it. She mentioned a ballet of *Romeo and Juliet* she had recently seen performed by a French company where Juliet had clearly been stamped by the violence of her culture. Koszyn admitted that she herself had not really addressed this question. By instinctively exempting Juliet and the other female protagonists as well from initiating violent acts, her production portrayed a connection between sex and violence that was predominantly male. The women in the sword dance accepted this construction of sexuality, but they were not portrayed as perpetrators of violence.

Koszyn also believes that without love, the whirlpool of violence becomes too strong to resist. Although not consciously seeking death, Mercutio pursues his duel with Tybalt partly because he has lost Romeo, the love in his life. Without that love, he is drawn to the brink of death. But Koszyn also used this fight as a way to denaturalize the Veronian codes surrounding violence and "honor." Consistent with his character's affinity with the fool, Mercutio (Ryun Yu) mocked the conventions of sword fighting by playfully overacting in Koszyn's production. Once when he had his sword at Tybalt's throat, he pretended it was a bow and Tybalt his violin, a staging that suggested not only the power but also the ridiculousness of violence. Whereas the Veronian society had highly developed rituals meant to elevate the status of violence and support its centrality, Koszyn devalued it as a lofty ideal. But, appropriately, the comic tenor of the scene became tragic when Mercutio realized he would die. This shift reminded the audience of the consequences of violence, and potentially, of Veronian codes for masculine behavior.

Koszyn portrayed the society's violence as disturbing, yet despite her critical attitude, the power of the playworld's vision apparently infected her. She identifies Romeo's rite of passage from boyhood into manhood at the moment of Mercutio's death, the moment when he becomes willing to fight. She also believes, somewhat inconsistently, that the love between Romeo and Juliet brings him to this point, that it, in Koszyn's word, "politicizes" him. She notes that his language becomes less metaphorical after Mercutio's death. Thus she relied on the authority of the text to direct her, as she often did. This shift was not strongly marked in the production and so was probably not communicated to the audience. But when she accepted the logic that, in this particular world, true manhood is defined by the willingness to kill, her critical feminist viewpoint succumbed to a textual analysis dominated by the cultural power of violence.

TAKING UP "ARMS" WITH A DIFFERENCE

In her first appearance, Juliet (Monica Gomi) presented the antithesis of ruthlessness and violence. The audience saw her behind the scrim—which ran the full length of the stage, dividing it in half from front to back—dressed in white, barefoot, wearing a headband, and jumping rope. She appeared to be an obedient child who was somewhat uneasy around her mother (Stephanie Gellar), but very affectionate with and close to the nurse (Rosa Ren). The party that evening began with Juliet's "coming out," still in white, but with her hair pulled back in a ponytail, as it would be for the rest of the production. The nurse began the ritual. Juliet had been wrapped in a long white cloth that resembled a shroud, foreshadowing the tomb that awaited her. The nurse held the end of the cloth while Juliet spun out of it in a dance. Koszyn sees the Veronian society as very ritualistic. She is a Jew who has attended Orthodox weddings, which led her to imagine this ritual as part of a premarriage ceremony. It was also significant that the mother did not take part, because she was not truly a mother anymore, having been "replaced" by Juliet's surrogate mother, the nurse. The cast had sympathy for the mother, thinking she may have started out as having the strength and will to support her daughter, but Koszyn and the cast saw Lady Capulet as needing to protect herself from the abuse of her husband. The only way she knew how to achieve this was to stop feeling anything. In fact, during Capulet's (Orin Tempkin) first interview with Paris (Sean Ningen), she sat silently off to the side. At one point, she turned and stared numbly at the audience. As a viewer I was startled and disturbed by her vacancy and brokenness.

Koszyn wanted the audience to read Lady Capulet's gesture as a plea for help.

The party was set behind the scrim as well. Romeo and his cohorts entered from the aisle and went behind the scrim, but Romeo came back out to the forestage down left to deliver his monologue in praise of Juliet before returning to the party. Throughout the scene, the couple was often separated by the scrim, but their meeting happened on the forestage. Their encounter was seen by Tybalt, the nurse, and Lady Capulet, who all stared at them from the other side of the scrim, but the couple was oblivious to them. The second kiss was more passionate than the first as they both discovered the desire they ignited in each other. When Romeo left, Juliet ran to the edge of the stage to see him, as if scarcely able to let him leave her sight. Koszyn said, "I wanted it to be beyond the kind of love we typically imagine—almost like a twins-separating-from-each-other-in-the-womb-and-now-reconnecting kind of love." Koszyn wanted each time the couple parted to be enormously painful, as if they could barely live without each other. She wanted no pretension that the audience was unfamiliar with the story, or that the story would end happily, and the love scenes were "infinitely tender" within that scope. When Juliet found out who Romeo was, a male guest was standing immediately behind her, holding a sword horizontally in his hands. Everyone in the audience knew the tragic ending, and the anguish of their fate ran underneath all their scenes.

Even in these first two scenes, the audience could see a progression in Juliet from a girl who followed direction and did not think much for herself to a young woman who has begun to make choices on her own. Juliet was alone in front of the scrim for the first time when she chose to stay outside the party and sit on the bench downstage left. She did not go back inside with Paris. When Tybalt left, she was curious about his anger and moved toward him as if to find out more while keeping her distance and not returning to his space. With the awakening of her love for Romeo, she suddenly knew what she wanted and began to assess the cost of achieving it. The difficulty of negotiating the barrier of the scrim in conjunction with the violence of Capulet suggested that the cost would be high.

Like most directors and scholars, Koszyn sees Romeo as much more immature than Juliet in the beginning. She noted that his only language for love is rhetorical, primarily in the form of overly romanticized, gushing metaphors. He is much less direct

1: DESTRUCTION WROUGHT BY DOMESTIC VIOLENCE 103

than Juliet in the way he communicates. Koszyn played up Romeo's apparent intoxication with rhetorical flourishes. Although the actor playing Romeo seemed to genuinely feel his emotions, his language was clearly a performance. His speech in the garden is full of celestial imagery, so with the use of the scrim and lighting, Koszyn created an image of Juliet floating in midair like an angel, a *Romeo and Juliet* "without a balcony." During this scene, Juliet moved between the excitement and inexperience of a girl and the passion and determination of a woman. The love was maturing her, and she tried to encourage Romeo's growth as well. This meant taking herself off the pedestal he had put her on and reminding him they were children of warring families. The last time she returned to speak to him, she descended from her perch and came to his side of the scrim, meeting him on the forestage once again. They did not touch this time, and yet it seemed as if they could hardly breathe when they had to leave each other.

Koszyn's inventive approach to this scene staged a masculine construction of female subjectivity that was undercut by femi-

Romeo (Eugene Chiang) wooing Juliet (Monica Gomi) in the balcony scene in Jayme Koszyn's *Romeo and Juliet*. Photo: Eric Levenson.

nine resistance to that construction. Romeo knew very little about Juliet or about love, and he had created an image of his lover that separated them and prohibited the possibility of a genuine intersubjective relationship. Juliet realized this and took the initiative gently to replace his fantasy with the reality of who they were and the world they lived in, a world not inhabited by angels and underlings, but by flesh and blood people, some of whom were full of hatred and violence and who would seek to destroy them. The production suggested that Romeo tried to objectify her, not because he wanted to control her, but because he did not yet have any other models for loving a woman. As Juliet's subjectivity emerged, she instinctively rejected this imbalance and offered another model. Rather than be worshiped from afar, Juliet suggested that they enter into the social, legal, and spiritual union of marriage, a marriage in which their lives and bodies and souls would be united. She was willing to take this risk, and Romeo met her. At their wedding Juliet chided Romeo one last time for his dependence on rhetoric. After they were united in marriage, he dropped his performance of love and just loved her, his speech and gestures beginning to follow more realistic conventions. The staging and the acting style for each of the protagonists reinforced Juliet as an agent who actively sought to create an intersubjective relationship with her lover and a Romeo who followed her lead, an interesting reversal of traditional gender roles in which the man is always the leader and initiator.

A CONSUMMATION MOST DEVOUTLY WISHED

After her marriage with Romeo, Juliet's peach-colored, spaghetti strap, low-cut, satin nightgown was always visible underneath her white dress or gray cloak, as if her secret passion and marriage constantly inspired her life. Her love was maturing her and giving her the courage to stand alone. The change her love for Romeo was effecting was also evident when the lights came up on the couple after their wedding night. Their heads were at the foot of the bed, the top of it untouched. Their position was symbolic of the inversion love had brought to their lives. Everything had been turned upside down. Koszyn was careful, however, not to have the sexual consummation of their love as a rite of passage for either character. In many productions, Juliet's transition from girlhood into womanhood is marked by having sex, her growth dependent on her physical relationship with Romeo, while Romeo's maturation is connected only obliquely to his relationship with Juliet and not specifically with having sex. In Koszyn's production, sex was just one more step on their journey.

This scene was frustrating for Koszyn, however, because she wanted both actors nude, a naturalized representation of a couple's state of undress after making love, particularly if it's for the first time. But they were not willing to be so. Nudity is rarely used in productions of *Romeo and Juliet* in the United States. None of the reviews of American productions I read indicated the use of nudity, despite its occasional use abroad.[37] Apparently not considering the stylized rituals in the production as unrealistic, she felt it was the one moment when reality was "thrown out the window." She did not worry about the audience ogling Juliet because Romeo would also be nude.

To hide the lack of nudity in this scene, Koszyn devised a creative alternative. The red satin sheet they had been sleeping under became a symbol both of their love and the womb, a symbol of their "twinness." During their waking moments while still in bed, except for one moment when Romeo closed in over Juliet's prone form, they shared the initiation of touch and usually responded in reciprocal movements. Hearing the nurse's call threatening their nest, Juliet leaped out of bed and wrapped the sheet tightly around her. When Romeo started to leave, Juliet wrapped him in both the sheet and her embrace, as if their love could hold him to her, oblivious in that moment to the danger. This time it was Romeo's turn gently to remind Juliet of the world in which they lived. He slowly unwrapped himself from her embrace and crossed her arms across her chest, a gesture that signified simultaneously his bidding her to hold on to their love and a foreshadowing that their love would bring her to her death. The tomb and the womb were the same thing. When she asked if they would meet again, he grabbed the sheet in his fist as he responded, "Doubt it not." Each time he moved away from her, he backed away to arm's length and struggled painfully to pull his hand away from her body. He descended into the orchestra pit stage right and headed toward the center aisle. She ran to the edge of the stage, as if looking out the window closest to his departing path. Only the sound of her mother approaching tore her away from her tormented fury against their fate, which demanded their separation. She ran back to the bed, sat up near the top, quickly hid the sheet underneath the covers, and pulled them around her protectively. She wrapped them around her chest, as if wanting to hide her vulnerability. She had good reason.

VIOLENCE BEGINS AT HOME

In sharp contrast to the dynamic of the previous scene, Lady Capulet was aggressive and menacing, chasing her daughter out of the haven of her bed. Her behavior in this scene was inconsistent with Koszyn's view of her as having given herself "an emotional lobotomy." Koszyn probably made this choice to strengthen the sense of Capulet's abuse against the women in the household and Juliet's complete isolation. But perhaps also this glimpse showed us a Lady Capulet driven to violent behavior because of the violence inflicted on her, a behavior pattern that surfaces occasionally from her otherwise numbed condition. After her brief awakening into protectiveness, Lady Capulet sank back into sullenness and abandoned her daughter. She felt helpless and could not deal with her daughter's pleas. Tybalt's death had been particularly hard on her because there was a repressed, incestuous desire between them. On her knees, she cleaned his blood from the ground, and during Paris's second interview with Capulet, she sat behind the scrim, huddled over an urn of Tybalt's blood. This dynamic created yet another contrast of cold, warped sexuality against the pure and healthily erotic love of the protagonists.

The tension between mother and daughter set the stage for the tumultuous confrontation between father and daughter. It began very tenderly, almost too tenderly. Koszyn said, "The father's terrible, violent reaction is simply the reaction of seeing the daughter growing up and—when it's pathological—not allowing the daughter to cross the threshold because of the sexual possessiveness of the father. Capulet's behavior in this scene is very disturbing." Capulet held Juliet and stroked her hair on his opening lines.[38] Her staging suggested the source for his extreme anger when he discovered her resistance to his control of her marital and sexual fate. He seemed surprised initially at her rejection, though quickly moved into fight mode. He started circling her. This was not a man who questioned why his daughter was changing, but a man determined to annihilate any resistance to his command. The audience's first real taste of Capulet's violence had come in his wrathful and physical rebuke of Tybalt at the party, which attracted attention from the guests. All throughout the production, the servants in the Capulet household moved nervously and often knelt on the edge of the space. Koszyn had a sense that they knew they could be killed for something as trivial as setting the table wrong. Capulet's anger is often staged physically in this scene with blocking that borders on abuse, but the intensity of his assault in this production was unusual and startling.

In an effort to connect the domestic and civic violence, Koszyn used some of the same choreography from the public brawls in this confrontation. At the close of Capulet's first series of questions (3.5.141–45), they ended up facing one another on either side of Juliet's bed, further emphasizing that Juliet's power of sexual choice lay at the heart of this argument.[39] In his "chopped logic" speech (3.5.149–57), his growing aggression changed first into an ugly mocking scorn, his verbal taunts soon becoming physical jabs. In a series of slaps and shoves he drove her to the other side of the stage where he threw her down for a second time and barely prevented himself from backhanding her (3.5.163). Juliet then ran toward her mother and the nurse, huddling at their feet. They knelt down and protectively covered her with their arms, but Capulet divided them, first pulling the nurse up and driving her across the stage much as he did Juliet. He told Juliet she could die in the street with cold indifference but still with an authority that would not suffer to be crossed. His line, "Look to it," was delivered as a warning to all of the women.

Capulet (Orin Tempkin) struggling to force his daughter (Monica Gomi) into submission in Jayme Koszyn's *Romeo and Juliet*. Photo: Eric Levenson.

Koszyn believed that his assault would have been even more sexualized—as Romeo's was on Tybalt—if the other women had not been present.

STRUGGLING TO ESCAPE

Following a generally common approach to the end of this scene, Juliet reached for the nurse as her last hope, but the nurse disappointed her. Convinced that the nurse would no longer help her, Juliet turned from her on, "Amen" (3.5.228), and walked swiftly toward her bed. She planted herself there to finish her conversation and deliver her monologue after the nurse had left. At this point the production introduced a less typical interpretation. From this place, where Juliet and her husband had slept, she drew her strength when everyone in her family turned against her. She also delivered her resolution that rather than betray Romeo she would take her own life as a discovery both disturbing and comforting. She was not traditionally heroic (automatically and uncomplicatedly ready to die for love), which made her seem a particular young woman contemporary with her audience. Underneath her words ran a current of defiance.

This defiance was still smoldering when she met Paris outside Friar Lawrence's cell, but she also felt threatened. Her attitude wavered throughout their encounter, but after a particularly saucy reply, she checked herself, seeming to realize that such behavior might arouse suspicion. The obedient daughter had become merely a role she played, a role that two days of remarkable experience had made her unfit to play. She chafed at its constraints. Sean Ningen's Paris, made up and costumed as a large, middle-aged man, closed in on her, using his powerful physical presence to dominate her. She spoke her replies like lightning, wanting the dialogue and his nearness to end as quickly as possible. He revealed his Capuletlike angry, controlling, possessive nature on, "Thy face is mine" (4.1.35). She had escaped to Friar Lawrence's (Vinu Ipe) side, but Paris took her by the arm and pulled her away, back to himself. She accepted his kiss on the forehead, but when he hungrily tried to kiss her mouth, she turned her head sharply away.[40] A marriage to Paris would not only have been a betrayal of Romeo. She would have been committing herself to live the rest of her life with someone like her father, and Juliet was desperate to avoid that at any cost. She lived every day with the price her mother had paid. The language and staging of these scenes encouraged the audience to see how Paris and Capulet viewed Juliet's body as a site for their own inscriptions. For Capulet, the marriage of Juliet to Paris would reinscribe his parental honor and authority. For Paris, the smiling face of his wife would increase his own cultural capital by signaling not just his possession of her beauty but his competence at "husbandry." Juliet was terrified at the prospect of being put into the family vault, but her resolve returned when Friar Lawrence told her Romeo would be there when she awakened. Her individual subjectivity and relations with her husband were developing as a result of her experiences of oppression and pleasure, a development happening through a telling mix of socially constrained and self-directed choices.

The false reconciliation with her father was clearly difficult. They were again facing each other across the foot of the bed. When he read her repentance as genuine, he raised her from her knees, stroked her, and held her again, but she was wooden. The kind words seemed awkward in his mouth. When he said, "My heart is wondrous light" (4.2.46), he took a step toward his wife and the nurse, and they both took a step back, as if perceiving the possibility of sexual abuse and resisting it. The staging here simply and deftly suggested the hidden histories in this household. He returned to the more "pliant" Juliet. She flinched when he cupped her head in his hands before leaving. Lady Capulet imitated her husband's gesture, a stiff and awkward moment for both mother and daughter. This was not their usual way of relating. The touch was hollow and therefore frightening because it signaled an alliance with the brutality and false tenderness of the father.

Juliet returned to sit on the foot of her bed to take the sleeping potion. She slipped to the floor when imagining waking too early in the vault. Having symbolically left the space of love, she was nearly overwhelmed by fear. When she felt threatened by Tybalt's ghost, she crawled underneath the covers of her bed, pulling them around her protectively once more. But then she discovered the satin sheet she and Romeo had slept in. Juliet returned to her love. Her present tactile experience of the cloth and the memory it evoked restored her from madness to sanity and renewed her resolve. She was tense after drinking the potion, waiting to see what effect it would have. But then she lay herself down and gave herself over to her only chance to be reunited with her lover.

THE SILVERED LINING

The tragic conclusion was softened by a ray of hope. When Romeo found Juliet in the vault, he kissed her lingeringly. Then suddenly, he backed away and pulled out the poison, as if his soul had divined her life but his mind harshly reiterated her death and the necessity of his own. When Juliet discovered his form covering her, she moved from beneath him and came around behind the bier. Their positions were exactly reversed, a visual image confirming the reciprocity of their relationship. She did not even look at the friar, her attention riveted to her husband. Rather than stabbing herself, she slit her wrists, providing a more contemporary method of suicide that would probably resonate more deeply with a modern audience. Then Juliet crawled onto the bier to lie beside him in death.

The cost of their deaths to the families was heavy but not without redemptive power. Juliet's death was the final blow to Lady Capulet. During the final scene, Lady Capulet stood against the back wall in her white satin robe, her arms folded across her body and her head hung to her chest. But the children's deaths did finally break the enmity between the warring households. In the final moment of the play, the two patriarchs knelt by the bier. Capulet took Romeo's hand and Montague took Juliet's. They joined the hands of their children, then looked at each other, realizing that this reconciliation had come far too late and at far too high a price. Once again, Koszyn seems to have drifted into the realm of the ideal in order to make her point. Certainly the patriarchal choice to end the feud is a step in the right direction, but it cannot erase the violence within the Capulet family or within the broader culture.

LISA WOLPE'S (AND ERICA BILDER'S) *ROMEO AND JULIET*

The Director's Vision

Wolpe had directed *Romeo and Juliet* prior to this production and felt she knew the play well. Although she codirected with Bilder, I did not realize this at the time of the interview and Wolpe never mentioned it. Apparently, Bilder served more as an assistant than a codirector. In the *Romeo and Juliet* production archive section of the LAWSC Web site (www.lawsc.net), Wolpe is given the title "Director," while Bilder is given the title "Co-Director." Bilder was on loan from Company of Women so was familiar with Wolpe's way of working. Wolpe describes Bilder as the "perfect foil" for her in the process and a tremendous help in sharing the burden of creating a complex show with four weeks of rehearsal. Their views diverge, however, particularly at the ending, which Wolpe saw as rather bleak. In contrast, Bilder writes that "love can conquer all" and the deaths of Romeo and Juliet "forged a peace" not previously possible. Wolpe may have worked collaboratively with Bilder, but she retained ultimate artistic control of production choices.

Wolpe originally wanted to do the production with the title characters represented as clowns, because she is interested in the theme of innocent fools who stumble into a hostile and dangerous world. Because fools do not know how to cope, they meet violent deaths. But the clown character does not speak very much, and she found that trying to cut the text to fit the trope meant that she was cutting poetry she could not bear to lose.[41] So she returned to the idea of a more traditional production.

When she cast Juliet, Wolpe was looking for a "really alive girl" who had to be "great with text and very passionate and interesting, nothing stereotypical." In an effort to create the illusion that she was male, she wanted a Juliet who was shorter than she, which is a stereotype, but Donya Giannota, the actor she chose to play Juliet, is not in any way a stereotypical beauty. Wolpe also knew she wanted a powerful Capulet. Wolpe thought that Capulet's rage against Juliet critically shaped the story of the play.

She was excited by the prospect of playing Romeo. Wolpe's goal was an integration of thought, feeling, and physicality: "It isn't simply a question of behaving like a man, but incorporating how a man moves with how he thinks and talks. This is key to me, since I play Romeo, and teenage guys don't talk a lot about their feelings, but rather, run away from them. Romeo, though, can confront his emotions almost as a poet would."[42] What some others have seen as a rhetorical and insincere expression of emotion, Wolpe sees as a poetic expression of feeling, and when she spoke the lines in the balcony scene, she filled them with a moving and romantic passion. Wolpe also believes that her lightness, openness, and vulnerability are probably closer to those of a fourteen-year-old boy than a man in his thirties playing the role with a long history of conquest. Both of Wolpe's parents committed suicide, and she felt she truly embodied Romeo's anguish in a way that someone with less tragedy in his or her life could not have.[43]

Although she is certainly not the only female actor who has played Romeo, her performance of this role is far from common. Charlotte Cushman, one of Wolpe's earliest and most notable American predecessors, accomplished a similar feat, which was much more risky in her era than in ours. She was masculine by contemporary standards, erotic in her wooing, and powerfully passionate. *Romeo and Juliet* has always enjoyed immense popularity, and she succeeded for much the same reason Wolpe believed she would: Romeo is more youth than man, and especially 150 years ago, men felt either incapable of expressing Romeo's passion or unwilling to in public.[44] When I first viewed the video of the balcony scene, I was stunned at how convincingly Wolpe portrayed a male youth.[45] Giannota commented that when she looked at Wolpe playing Romeo, she saw an adolescent boy.[46] Wolpe makes "very few claims to feminist agendas," but by having women convincingly portray men in major roles, even more forcefully than Koszyn, she is situating women between bipolar categories of analysis as well as interrogating the construction of gender and the female body. Although critics report forgetting that women are playing men, lesbian audience members attest to the powerful erotic arousal of seeing two women actors portraying a love scene between a male and female character.[47] Representation inevitably becomes a subject of the performance.

Wolpe is also aware of the connection between sex and violence in the play, though this was not as central in her production as it was in Koszyn's:

> Everyone who is impatient for one thing is impatient for the other. Capulet's fingers itch, which means either he's having a heart attack over all of this angst, or he wants to hit somebody, but he also wants to get somebody married off immediately at the age of thirteen. And he's flirting with women all over the masquerade ball scene. And Romeo wants to have Rosalind one second and have Juliet the next second, and in between is a meeting on a hot August afternoon and blowing up and killing people on the street, or at least he kills Tybalt. So it's a very excitable Italian temperament on a very hot summer day with a lot of hatred and a lot of sex. They talk about it during the whole play, so it's on everybody's mind. . . . There's definitely pervasive violence in the society. It's what they come in talking about at the top of the play, "We will fight." And then they immediately go to, "We will rape their women."

Similar to Koszyn, Wolpe sees the sex and violence connection as perpetrated by the men rather than the women. Although

1: DESTRUCTION WROUGHT BY DOMESTIC VIOLENCE 113

Lisa Wolpe as Romeo in the balcony scene in her production of *Romeo and Juliet*. Photo: LAWSC Archives.

Juliet's rejection of the nurse is emotionally violent, none of the women think about doing physical harm to the other characters of the play. On the Web site, Bilder also writes of the strong presence of violence in this "quintessential love play," though doesn't articulate a connection between them. She seems to have a more oppositional sense of the two forces because she writes that violence usually overpowers love, and she encourages the audience to act on the message of the play, to transform the "war-cry into a love song . . . before it's too late."

Viewing him as slightly more aggressive than Koszyn, Wolpe portrayed Romeo as acting from a place between the poles of violence and nonviolence. Wolpe thinks that despite Romeo's losing his head, he is more loving and less given to violence than his juvenile friends. When Tybalt (Erin Erlich) was speaking with Mercutio (Diane Robinson) before the fight scenes, they were on the stage floor, and Romeo appeared from above, descending to them on the grand staircase. In the beginning of Romeo's encounter with Tybalt, he approached his new relation, who had his sword drawn, with open arms. Tybalt was taken aback, but the strategy worked. He put up his sword and started to walk away, but Mercutio insisted on a fight. Wolpe sees a death wish in Mercutio. His monologue suggests that he has been troubled

Benvolio (Karole Foreman) urges Romeo (Lisa Wolpe) to leave after killing Tybalt (Erin Ehrlich) in Lisa Wolpe's *Romeo and Juliet*. Photo: LAWSC Archives.

by the war and by women as well because he talks about whores in one breath and about soldiers in the next. Following the typical Method tactic of writing a biography for characters' histories prior to the play's beginning, the actors conjectured a past for Mercutio, agreeing that he had contracted syphilis. Although Wolpe did not mention any way this was specifically staged, the actor based her portrayal of the character on the knowledge that the violence he suffered in the war then spilled out into his social relations in Verona.

Wolpe loves violence and is very interested in exploring it. She feels "there's something appealing about incredible force because we're all members of the animal kingdom." But she does not find that all women are as interested in this subject as she. Even the women who are have usually had little or no training, a lack compounded by a four-week rehearsal period. Wolpe is quite good at sword fighting and clearly committed to both the physical and emotional action this requires to be convincing. However, the other actors cannot quite match her, a fact Wolpe herself admits. The fights were a little slow and too evidently choreographed. Some reviewers have been impressed by LAWSC's fight choreography, but others have commented that this is one of the few flaws of its productions. Company of Women, the Massachusetts-based all-women Shakespeare troupe that also grew out of Shakespeare and Company, staged the battle scene in *King Lear* as a dance, but they were seeking to highlight the female in nearly every institution and interaction, and Wolpe does not share that aim. She would rather encounter the violence full-faced and straightforwardly.

Violence has a range of values in this production. Wolpe allows it to be exciting in the lovers' interaction and in the fight scenes. But she condemns it in the tyrannical Capulet.[48] In this way, her production concept is more complicated and potentially confrontive than Koszyn's, where violence had no positive value. This difference in overall concept may also explain the differences in the way the two directors view Tybalt. In contrast with Koszyn, Wolpe sees Tybalt as, "beautiful in his strength. . . . So a woman who plays him is seen as incredibly strong, incredibly beautiful, and absolutely female at the same time. You don't lose your femininity in playing a man but you gain in power." Casting women in men's roles, particularly when those characters are violent, participates in Western avant-garde projects that, in the words of Laurence Senelick, "reclaim the anti-social and disruptive elements of performance that confront and overthrow norms, gender norms among them."[49] It also helps to call attention to how not only gender but also the female body itself has been marked. In *The Explicit Body in Performance* (1997), Rebecca Schneider outlines the goal of many contemporary feminist performance artists using the nude female body as the center of their work: "Making any body explicit *as socially marked*, and foregrounding historical, political, cultural, and economic issues involved in its marking, is a strategy at the base of many contemporary feminist explicit body works. Manipulating the body itself as mise en scene, such artists make *their own bodies* explicit as the stage, canvas, or screen across which social agendas of privilege and disprivilege have been manipulated."[50] I would argue that cross-gender casting, particularly in roles where the character defines himself according to traditionally masculine traits, performs an analogous function to women performance artists' use of their own nudity onstage.

Clearly for Wolpe, femininity and masculinity are flexible constructs that can be adapted or abandoned, but it seems important to her that the women actors are not subsumed completely into masculinity by playing male roles. She seems to desire a specific supplemental experience of power for the actors and audience members identifying with them rather than a more fluid or substitutionary experience, which might result in replacing femininity with masculinity. But this goal is based on the apparently unexamined and more patriarchal than feminist assumption that power is male. Her characterization of Tybalt as powerful also reveals Wolpe's instinctive understanding of the connection between the willingness to use violence and power, a partially accurate but uncritical viewpoint. If she has resolved the tension between an attraction to violence and power and a condemnation of its abuse, she did not clearly articulate that in the interview.[51] Since the video shows only selected scenes, it is difficult to tell how clearly the distinction between use and abuse of violence and power came across in performance.

Wolpe was not conscious of influences of literary critics or previous productions, though in some ways her conception of the playworld is indebted to Franco Zeffirelli and Peter Brook.[52] In a striking similarity with Koszyn, her central concerns were the passion between the lovers, the creation of an intersubjective relationship between them, and the violence of Capulet against Juliet. She wanted everyone to recognize the cost of tyrannical parenting and domestic abuse. Her fundamental practice of producing all-women Shakespeare innately stimulates the audience to consider the cultural construction of gender and women's bodies.

The Play in Performance

THE ARTISTS' EDEN DISRUPTED BY THE PLAYWORLD'S VIOLENCE

The power of patriarchy in the society was reflected in the set, which appeared to be either the impressive interior or exterior of a nobleman's house. It was used as both. The massive stone structures were cream-colored. A staircase with two landings descended stage left. As in Koszyn's production, characters entered from backstage as well as from the house through the aisles. The costumes were historical, from the early Italian Renaissance.

Although both Wolpe and Koszyn created preshows, they were dramatically different. While Koszyn presented information about the culture's rituals, Wolpe presented her ideal of women artists in collaboration. At the beginning of Wolpe's *Romeo and Juliet,* the audience was greeted the way it usually is at the beginning of a LAWSC production, by the sound of women's voices raised in song. The actors establish their identities as women before beginning to portray men. The concept of transformation, key to Wolpe's entire project, was therefore highlighted:

> Women's voices in song are really powerful and magical. . . . You get a number of women blending their voices together, and it's distinctly female. . . . I think there is something transformative about song and the reverberations or the resonance of the singing voice . . . so I use it whenever I can. . . . It's very human and specific to theater for me also. It does things that film and video can't do. It really makes the hair on the back of your neck stand up, and it changes the way your heart feels and your stomach feels. It's very visceral I think. And I love collaborating with composers. And it just creates a kind of otherness that is very theatrical in the space.

Her love of collaboration extends to her desire to bring other art forms into the theater. The play proper began with a puppet show. Sometimes she also uses video and projection. The layers of art forms create a more impressive production. But for Wolpe, it is also a way of "manifesting," testifying to the power of these women artists. The puppet show was integral to the play and Wolpe's vision. Harsh words in the puppet drama erupted into a sword fight. Yet despite the violent nature of the content, the participants in this onstage theater connected to one another, in both giving of themselves and appreciating the other, an analogue to the work ethic of LAWSC and the value they hope their productions have for their audiences. Wolpe says that the community supports their work and believes it is important or they would not continue. The audience for the puppets were the singers, blurring the distinction between entertainer and audience. Wolpe always breaks the fourth wall as a way of including the audience. But such an easy crossing of boundaries and harmonious collaboration between artists could not survive in the Veronian society. Entertainers on both sides of the puppet booth were scattered by the brawl between the Capulet and Montague servants. Acting flowed into action. The one element of harmony surviving in Verona was the relationship between the protagonists.

AND SHE SAID, "LET US MAKE MAN IN OUR IMAGE"

Wolpe believes the potential romance onstage can actually be increased when both lovers are played by women. In an essentialized overgeneralization, she stated that women can create male characters who are even more romantic and satisfying than real men because women know what they want—men who are sensitive and actually listen and do not take women for granted. In some ways, this is reverse sexism since women are constructing "man" according to their own desires. It is also difficult to achieve, given Shakespeare's construction of male characters, but this becomes a site of her intervention through performance. Although Wolpe did not discuss women's attraction to dominance at this point in the interview, her comments elsewhere suggest her awareness of women's desire to inflame men into a passion that is violent but never physically harmful to them. For example, when discussing her portrayal of Henry V for the Company of Women's production, which ridiculed the character and resisted his violence and military competence, she said, "The fact is, if you're a world conqueror, people do lie down for you. For one thing, they are your conquests and have to. And for another thing, there's something appealing about incredible force." These two models for attractive men present a contradiction that, again, may be integrated in Wolpe's mind but which she did not articulate.

As to physical intimacy, the text does not often call for it and sometimes even creates distance between the lovers, as in the balcony scene. Wolpe believes such architectural structures for expressing love exist in the plays because Shakespeare originally produced them with all-male companies. When she creates romantic scenes between male and female characters, she wants to get beyond the same-sex titillation of two women actors. But the company does not shy away from physical expressions of love if the situation calls for it. She departed, for instance, from the usual tenderness and playfulness depicted in the lovers' first meeting. When Romeo said, "Give me my sin again" (1.5.109), he pushed Juliet up against the wall and kissed her hard. Wolpe did not want the interaction to be governed completely by courtliness and believed that the violence and passion in Romeo would prompt him into such an action. Romeo was able to channel these twin impulses into a healthy erotic energy that excited Juliet because it was never abusive. However, within the range of interactions in the playworld, this was the exception rather than the rule.

In the lovers' next meeting, the balcony scene, Juliet took the lead. For Wolpe, she is the more mature of the two, and she agrees with Koszyn that Juliet is constantly trying to bring Romeo down to earth. She sees Juliet as very practical and intelligent, much

1: DESTRUCTION WROUGHT BY DOMESTIC VIOLENCE 119

more so than Romeo. Juliet makes the contract for the marriage, not Romeo. Wolpe believes playing Juliet is much more difficult than playing Romeo because her thought process is so quicksilver. On the contrary, a mediocre actor can play Romeo because he is not particularly clever.

Romeo spoke much of his praise of Juliet to the audience and asked them, "Shall I hear more, or shall I speak at this?" (2.2.37). During his speech, he had been hiding in the shadows of the enormous staircase stage left. On his first line, "I take thee at thy word," he leapt up three or four stairs onto the first platform to make his proclamation, which sent Juliet crouching behind the balcony wall, but only for a moment. Each time he wished to make a proclamation, as when he offered to swear by the moon, he instinctively mounted the platform, trying to use this higher-level stage as a place of strength, resolution, and performance. But Juliet kept bringing him back to the space under her balcony, where he sometimes tried to scramble up the pillar, though its smooth surface prevented him from reaching her. Romeo's vacillating activity contrasted with Juliet's fixedness at the corner of her balcony closest to him, a kind of urgent constancy. Both his false and real exits were taken through the aisle.

Romeo (Lisa Wolpe) trying to scramble up the pillars to Juliet's (Donya Giannotta) balcony in Lisa Wolpe's *Romeo and Juliet*. Photo: LAWSC Archives.

Wolpe sees the couple's romance as maturing both of them, and particularly making Juliet a woman with a strong and active subjectivity. Wolpe focused on their falling in love and "finding something greater than themselves, because before they were not heart whole." She noted Juliet's earlier passivity and willingness to be compliant with whatever her parents wanted for her. But when she fell in love, everything changed. According to Wolpe, "She says, 'No, I need this, or I will die.'" And from this point on, she begins engaging in more sophisticated strategies to get what she wants.

Wolpe also worked to create reciprocity in the couple's relationship. They were both initiators: "She wasn't just taken in by him. She was also seducing him. I think they fell in love equally and completely." For Wolpe, the morning scene after their wedding night was very intimate. She felt they were more connected, more centered, partly because the language is no longer so hyperbolic. They were relating more as husband and wife and they had "a deeper grip on being together." Wolpe too, however, fell into the trap of seeing Juliet's progression to womanhood as largely dependent on her losing her virginity, whereas Romeo becomes a man as a result of his banishment. Don Shirley, reviewing for the *Los Angeles Times,* complained that their wedding night was too chaste because Romeo "hardly removes a stitch of his clothes." For him, it was the one scene that defeated the "gender bending."[53] The reviewer, like many, is overly dependent on the exposure of flesh to signify the consummation of passion. With an all-woman cast seeking to maintain the illusion of representing different sexes, nudity for both characters was not an option. Having Juliet nude and Romeo clothed in this context would have signified imbalance in their relationship, which was clearly at odds with the director's concept.

THE SERPENT OF PATRIARCHAL VIOLENCE

The scene where Capulet fights for his dominance of the household was also central to Wolpe's production. At the beginning of 3.5, Lady Capulet (Caroline Ducrocq) was withdrawn. Wolpe created a history for her that included domestic violence. Having been beaten by her husband, she was unable to speak up for her daughter. She did not look at her husband when she spoke to him. The detachment of Lady Capulet in both productions extended a common interpretation of her as generally passive or unhappy, a vision that prefigured the intense emptiness and drug addiction of her character in Baz Luhrmann's film.

1: DESTRUCTION WROUGHT BY DOMESTIC VIOLENCE

Capulet (Leigh Curran) carried a walking stick, and by "Proud me no prouds," he was scraping it agitatedly across the floor. As someone who had been beaten before, Juliet recognized the sign of his gathering rage. She quickly ran down the stairs to the stage floor, and her mother briefly came out of her world with concern, following her husband and the nurse. The three women formed a unit together center stage, while Capulet paced up and down, dominating the space. He then barged through their group to separate them, the same strategy Koszyn had Capulet employ. When Juliet tried to rise to her feet, he raised the stick with the command, "Do not answer me." Likewise, he silenced the nurse (Fran Bennett). When the nurse spoke up for Juliet, Capulet drove her across the stage and she shrank to sit on a bench where she stayed until the end of the scene. By dividing the women, he crushed their resistance and maintained control. Wolpe read the nurse's argument, "I speak no treason" (3.5.172) as a sign that Capulet ran his household like a little kingdom. As in Koszyn's production, his line "Look to it" was a warning to all the women.

Lady Capulet followed the same exit path as her husband, signaling her renewed submission. The nurse ended up following that path as well. She was uncomfortable with the advice she gave but felt it was the only solution in that context. Fran Ben-

Capulet (Leigh Curran) threatens Juliet (Donya Giannotta) with his stick while Lady Capulet (Caroline DuCroq) watches passively in the background in Lisa Wolpe's *Romeo and Juliet*. Photo: LAWSC Archives.

nett commented that she did not feel the nurse betrayed Juliet but tried "to get her to live in the real world. After all, this is what she's going to have to do."[54] Clearly, Juliet was not ready to abandon her love and return to the society from which she had momentarily escaped. In her final monologue, she worked her way up the staircase, and made her final resolution from her bed, as in Koszyn's production, a place of strength. Both productions presented Juliet's love, sexuality, and desire as empowering her. When the audience next saw her, Juliet was defiant as she met Paris (Diane Mountford), a rich man who viewed her as an ornament and was marrying her for money. She twice rebuffed his sexual advances. Both Wolpe and Koszyn shared a similar interpretation of Paris since the patriarchal oppression of Juliet was central to their production concepts.

THE UNIDEALIZED WORLD

Unlike Koszyn's somewhat idealistic conclusion, Wolpe's portrayed the apparent reconciliation between the households as superficial. Also at odds with Koszyn concerning the Prince, Wolpe perceives him as having tremendous power but not using it particularly well. He was not strict enough to control the violence of Verona. She also believes he is a very political person not particularly interested in truth. He wants to ameliorate the rich people rather than prevent youth from being killed in the street. The final tableau was of the children in the center dividing the Capulets and the Montagues. The patriarchs' speeches about raising statues in gold suggested a return to the values of image and money.[55] They shook hands, but Wolpe said she did not see that "as a sign of incredible deep wisdom having been learned. I don't think that's what happens in the world, so it was no Hollywood ending."

AUDIENCE IMPACT

One of the core members of the company, Bennett said that in talking to people after the show, they commented that for the first time, they really heard the words in the balcony scene. Rather than seeing the scene through the general haze of a generic romance, they saw two people trying to get together. She and the audience members she spoke with felt they perceived the scene in this way because both actors were women, that somehow that difference did not allow them to generalize about the scene without really hearing it.

Dolan rejects identification between audience members and dramatic characters as a positive strategy for feminist performance. She writes that the Women's Ensemble, for instance, "operated within a system that worked to de-emphasize difference and distance [between performers and audience] and to emphasize identification and proximity."[56] Dolan expresses a surprising contempt for identification: "Rather than succumbing to the seduction of the illusionist text—which fulfills a need as base and transient as consuming a meal (hence, Brecht's term 'culinary theatre' to represent such illusionism)—the spectator in epic theatre is given an 'exercise in complex seeing' and asked to 'think above the stream' rather than to 'think in the stream.'" She believes this critical, reflective position disrupts the process of identification that normally pulls the spectator through the text, subjects him or her to the authority of narrative closure, and offers the relief of catharsis.[57]

For Dolan, identification continues to reify sexual difference, the foundation of traditional theater, and Dolan's goal is the erasure of this difference. Like Laura Mulvey, Dolan argues that theater must disrupt visual pleasure because visual pleasure promotes reification of traditional gender relations and social hierarchies.[58] But Dolan believes that perhaps the most successful way of preventing the objectification of women onstage is to represent the lesbian as an actively desiring subject, especially when she quotes gender roles. She can deconstruct gender and the sign of "woman" because her performance demonstrates that gender is merely a role and signifies that women are not objects for male desire and/or consumption.[59] Dolan's desire to disrupt hegemonic meanings is so powerful that she advocates performances of gay and lesbian pornography (a pornography that is explicit in its difference from heterosexual sex and from romanticized sex, which stresses a relationship between the couple) because it is a transgressive act, "the most constructive choice for practicing cultural disruptions."[60]

This prompts the question, is disruption worth any price? And what does it, after all, actually achieve? Certainly the audience response to Wolpe's production suggests that cross-gender casting can disrupt the assumption of sexual difference and the typical trajectory of heterosexual narratives without resorting to staging homosexual pornography.

Drama-Logue critic Larry Jonas praised the production as being "staged with imagination, taste and passion." Jonas's evaluation suggests that the actors' characterizations did indeed avoid stereotypes. Especially the leading actors achieved an appropriate tragic stature while still creating protagonists particular and realistic enough for the audience to identify with. Jonas noted the "individual characterization" that the actors created: "If Romeo and a glowing Juliet (Donya Giannotta) are depicted as larger-than-life characters, they are never less than real lovers facing real situations. And, yes, their vaunted balcony scene is staged with grace and empathetic ardor."[61] *LA Weekly* reviewer Judith Lewis made a similar remark concerning the gender bending: "What's amazing about it all is how convincingly women can play men without lowering their voices or relying on macho posturing, but instead with a subtle physicality and conviction that comes from the inside out."[62]

Shirley compared Wolpe's production to another playing in town at the same time (produced by A Noise Within), citing Wolpe's "all-women's multicultural version" as the more interesting of the two. He particularly praised Wolpe's performance of Romeo: "Though her frame is hardly big, even by women's sizes, Wolpe has recast herself as a young man to an uncanny degree. Her voice is the key—low, mellow, authoritative, but her posture and even her haircut play their parts as well. And it isn't just the gender switch that she has down so well; she also has Romeo himself well in hand, moving fluidly from melancholy to ardor to tragedy."[63] While he differs from Lewis in his opinion of how Wolpe uses her voice, my own viewing of the video suggests the truth lies between the two—she uses her lower registers without straining her voice. His remarks reinforce the performativity of gender that Wolpe's productions inevitably enact if the women perform the male gender convincingly, which in his estimation, by and large they did. Shirley criticized the other production for a Juliet who was "far too sophisticated," and Romeo who was "too boyishly hyped-up from the beginning," characterizations that clashed and also did not develop, whereas in Wolpe's production, "we can see Donya Giannotta's Juliet growing up before our eyes."[64]

Only Lewis suggested that LAWSC's production criticized the protagonists' rebellious love. She noted that they treated their "courtship with defiance": "There's a spiteful rebellion behind their words that makes you consider their passion (and love itself) from a less sympathetic angle."[65] Although Wolpe never mentioned this viewpoint in our interview, she had this section of Lewis's review reprinted on a page with other *Romeo and Juliet* reviews to be used as publicity material, so it must not significantly misrepresent the production. But this remark also came within the context of Lewis's opinion that the cross-gender casting opened up unusual interpretations of the play, particularly concerning characters' motives, and certainly this achieves one of Wolpe's goals.

Two other recent productions directed by women serve as a valuable context for Koszyn's and Wolpe's. Bonnie J. Monte, artistic director of The Shakespeare Theater of New Jersey (formerly New Jersey Shakespeare Festival), directed a production of *Romeo and Juliet* in 1999. Juliet's sexuality was nearly obsessive and newly discovered—but before she ever met Romeo, thereby establishing her sexual subjectivity as developing independent of Romeo. But in this rather realistic version of the play, both youths mistake sexual attraction for love and are clearly flawed, distancing the audience somewhat from identifying with them. Neither of them understands what death is, as evidenced by the surprised look on their faces when it begins to overtake them—another refusal to romanticize them and their violence.

Similarly to Koszyn, Monte saw the public and private spheres tightly intertwined, an idea partly conveyed by the unit set that alternately represented interior and exterior locales. Even during supposedly private scenes, other people kept intruding, and the couple's oblivious belief in their ability to sustain private lives in this world was part of their downfall. Also similar to both Koszyn and Wolpe, Capulet was overbearing, though the reviewer (John Timpane) does not note specifically his violence. Capulet is also occasionally neglectful. In general, characters in the Capulet household were self-absorbed while trying to keep everyone else in order, an effort that only succeeded in pushing people apart because of each's devotion to his or her own interests. Monte's tactics encouraged an audience's critical reflection, and she revealed a sick, corrupt playworld producing children rushing headlong into tragic error.[66]

Karin Beier's *Romeo and Juliet* (1993) premiered in Düsseldorf Germany, although later it toured in England and across Europe. Somewhat unusual for German directors, Beier was unafraid to present the protagonists' genuine love credibly. While not seeking to return to a purely romantic idealism, she senses that audiences are "longing again for great emotions. . . . And of this longing and how impossible it is to satisfy, theatre can tell in vital seriousness and through the full deployment of its comic and ironic means. We cannot go back on the once won freedoms . . . but we can tell of the surviving atavisms with verve and spirit."[67] Wilhelm Hortmann described Caroline Ebner's Juliet as "childlike, passionate and absolute . . . the magnet which drew the production together."[68] Like a number of other European directors, Beier had the couple nude for their wedding night and morning-after scene. But she framed their interaction with Lady Capulet and Paris dancing a tango sensually while Mercutio's followers marched across the stage in vaguely militaristic fashion. The audience's point of view was therefore complicated and destabilized, making it difficult to objectify the lovers sexually.

Impinging on their love was the society's latent violence, which she, like Koszyn, choreographed and stylized. At various points between scenes, soldiers would march over the stage, stamping rhythmically. At Capulet's ball, the choreography for the dancers exhibited a growing wildness barely restrained by order as the movement developed toward an orgiastic climax. This scene helped to cement the connection between sex and violence in which both men and women participated, and yet by framing the action of the play as a whole with military movements carried out by male soldiers, Beier suggested that the patriarchal structures of the society largely defined and perpetuated this connection. Closer to Wolpe than Koszyn in her view of violence, Beier allowed it to be both disturbing and thrilling.[69] What began as playful sparring, however, became increasingly menacing and dangerous.[70] As did Wolpe, Beier saw the Prince as ineffectual and so characterized him as "an infantile fairy-tale Prince."[71] The ending was even more bleak than Wolpe's. Not only did the parents continue the cycle of rhetoric and commercialization without realizing the need for change, but also the legend they created rewrote the actual terror of the "original" ending. Romeo tried to vomit up the poison once he swallowed it, although it still took his life, and Juliet realized with horror that she did not have the resolve to slit her wrists.[72] Her final position was reminiscent of the victim felled by the firing squad in Goya's famous *The Third of May 1803. The Execution of the Defenders of Madrid of 1814.* While English reviewers were not favorably impressed with the production,[73] such an ending graphically juxtaposed different historical and cultural frameworks, smashing the illusion of idyllic heroism and "love conquers all" with the frailty of youths trapped in a virtually loveless society.

Bristol argues that Shakespearean critics', editors', and scholars' work within America's "patriarchal dispensation" has traditionally articulated "specifically masculine subject positions."[74] Women taking a position of authority in the cultural production of Shakespeare, even when working in the trenches with amateurs in low-profile situations, is in itself an act that challenges the largely male-dominated institutional control of Shakespeare and potentially more conventional interpretations driven largely by traditionally masculine ways of seeing. But Koszyn also had the opportunity to influence a group of college students, some of whom may have either directly or indirectly suffered from domestic violence, many of whom were still in a process of defining their subjectivities and the way they wanted to relate to significant others. Raising feminist issues for a thoughtful audience in its formative years is not as high-profile as an all-woman professional production in Los Angeles, but both productions were potential vehicles for positively contributing to social change.

2
"How do poor people live?":
Tina Packer and Ellen O'Brien Direct
Measure for Measure

IN *MEASURE FOR MEASURE,* FEMALE SUBJECTIVITY AND SEX RELAtions are far more complicated than in *Romeo and Juliet* because sex and violence are more intricately intertwined. Angelo's abuse of his power as the highest civic authority also complicates the equation. His outrageous coercion forces Isabella either to consent to be raped or leave her brother to be tortured and killed. Apparent virtue in Angelo and the duke, the other prominent male character, masks currents of cruelty and deceit in both, and it can be argued that they have designs on an unwilling partner. In some ways, the various characters and plot strands in *Measure for Measure* force the audience to consider the ways sexuality and violence manifest their relationship when implicated in different material and metaphysical realms of existence—the social, the political, and the spiritual.

Categorized as a "problem play," *Measure for Measure* is not often produced, but it has garnered extensive literary criticism. Perhaps no other Shakespearean play focuses on sexuality so relentlessly, and perhaps no character other than Isabella has attracted such starkly opposing viewpoints. Earlier twentieth-century criticisms of her as "rancid in her chastity, " a "Vixen in her Virtue," "hard as an icicle," or on the other hand, an "angel of light," have been superseded by more sophisticated analysis.[1] But even within the last twenty years, she has been referred to as a "cold virgin" whose "self-protective chastity" does not allow her to be an "integrated woman,"[2] "a rather brittle [and cruel] character who has never loved life, or ... never found anything lovable in life,"[3] and as someone unaware of her own self-absorption and lack of charity.[4] Defenders of Isabella, however, note she is an "articulate and compassionate woman,"[5] exercising her "sexual freedom" with "a self which has the potential to be faithful to its own idea of truth."[6] Kathleen McLuskie goes so far as to argue that the play allows no point of entrance for a feminist critique, but Marcia Riefer takes this difficulty as a basis for her approach, which focuses less on judging Isabella's character or behavior and more on analyzing the effects of a strongly patriarchal society on the women characters and the play's conclusion.[7]

At the heart of these opposing views is Isabella's "unmanageable" sexuality. Her chosen vocation as a nun resists the way the men in her culture want to position her. In different ways, both Angelo and the duke attempt to put her back into a male-dominated sexual economy, to erase her disturbing independence. Her life in the nunnery gives her a kind of freedom and autonomy that she would otherwise be forced to forfeit. Consequently, chastity in *Measure for Measure,* as in much of Western civilization's history, is valued by the men only as a prelude to marriage, as a temporary state. Traditionally, for a woman to refuse sexually every man but one has been considered one of her greatest virtues, because it assures the "legitimacy" of her husband's heirs. But to refuse sexually all men for life, substituting relationships with other women and a marriage to Christ for marriage to a man makes Isabella abnormal, her position attacked by other characters in the play and some contemporary critics alike. Jonathan Dollimore notes that critics who prescribe a more "normal" development for Isabella affirm the playworld's unjust refusal to accept her choice.[8]

But Isabella's choices also need to be seen in the larger context of the play. The Viennese society offers little support for affirming, intersubjective sexual relations. Most sexual activity in this world is punished or belittled by those in power, often resulting in subjugation and degradation, especially for women. Presumably, sexuality expressed within a fully sanctioned marriage is acceptable, but the play does not include any characters in this kind of relationship. Barbara Baines argues: "Isabella's power, place, and value in society are so determined by her chastity that its forfeiture would constitute for her a form of social and psychological suicide."[9] However, my recent direction of this play and my review of its production history suggest that such views are not common among particularly American and English theater practitioners and their audiences. Sonia Massai claims that theatrical embodiment of Baines's view preceded its appearance in literary materialist criticism, citing Charles

Marowitz's adaptation of *Measure for Measure* in 1975, but this is an isolated example.[10]

Isabella provides a particular challenge to a woman director, especially in the nineties where chastity is valued as a choice in some circles—an attitude prompted from the right by religious conservatives and from the left by cultural feminism's insistence on women's ability to control their own bodies. But even cultural feminists do not usually value this control above a sibling's life. Isabella is not so uncomplicatedly sympathetic as Juliet. Her problematic character and silence at the play's conclusion allow for wide-ranging interpretation. Feminist productions of this play are likely to diverge significantly from productions not informed by feminist theory or at least a female consciousness—the consciousness informed by the experience (or understanding) of living in an inequitable society where sexual harassment is common and often viewed quite differently by the sexes, where lifelong celibacy is often judged as abnormal.

Isabella appears to be, not surprisingly, more sexualized on stage than in literary criticism. Linda Macfarlane writes that many productions suggest Isabella encourages Angelo,[11] enacting the idea that when women say no they mean yes. Jan Kott claims that, in order for the audience to view her sympathetically, "there has to be some kind of natural attraction between Angelo and Isabella," and that the play seems to demand that Isabella lose her virginity.[12] Similarly, David McCandless argues that even though the text does not "overtly substantiate Isabella's attraction to Angelo," staging at least an unconscious attraction is "the strongest, most emotionally generative choice, the choice that sets up maximum conflict for Isabella."[13] Clearly, such critics value the audience's identification with Isabella and assume that heterosexual attraction and internal conflict are the paths to spectators' involvement. Although these assumptions may be generally correct for mainstream audiences, they suggest an attempt to cater to rather than question or challenge the audience's ways of seeing.

The portrayal of Isabella has also been tied to changing views of the duke. Through the 1950s and 1960s, the duke was generally staged as a benevolently divine figure, and it was assumed that Isabella would happily marry him. The women's movement and criticism of the Establishment in the late 1960s challenged that view. The movement of women into the workforce also meant that they had options other than marriage for surviving in the world and could achieve financial and personal independence.¹⁴ But while Jon Barton's RSC production in 1970 stripped the duke of his religious aura and Isabella was at least unresponsive to his proposal, she was still portrayed as having a "hysterical fear of sex which scarcely allows her to speak of her brother's fault, and leads directly to her unlovely attack upon him in prison."¹⁵ Similarly, Jonathan Miller's 1975 production staged Isabella as rejecting the duke but turned her into a psychotically nonsexual woman escaping from an incestuous relationship with her brother, thrown almost into madness by the duke's proposal. Feminist literary and cultural criticism have gradually influenced the theatrical culture regarding this play.

RSC Artistic Director Adrian Noble encouraged Juliet Stevenson to create an Isabella not sexually repressed. But given the Viennese society, she chose monastic life so as not to become a slave of worldly passions. Stevenson believed the attraction to Angelo was overt but to give herself over to him would be to forsake order and to capitulate to chaos.¹⁶ This somewhat humanistic interpretation at least allows Isabella an active sexuality, as well as a deep self-knowledge, a critical appraisal of the world around her, and an active mind and will capable of choosing her own path—a valid choice from a feminist perspective, but certainly not the only one and distinct from at least Kott's view. Perhaps the (male?) need for Isabella to accept the rite of sexual initiation as opposed to a spiritual initiation that renounces intimacy with men has led many directors to create a benevolent duke and build a relationship between him and Isabella that supports Isabella's decision to marry him, a decision the text explicitly leaves indeterminable, given her silence.

Our current notions of marriage based on erotic love that, to be credible and lasting, must mature over time encourages directors to build the development of romantic feelings between Isabella and the duke into stage business throughout the play if Isabella accepts the duke's proposal at the conclusion. A historical reading of the play suggests that the duke may have offered marriage simply as a way of erasing the public blot on Isabella's reputation, which she suffered as a result of following the plot he devised.¹⁷ However, for contemporary theater practitioners and audiences unfamiliar with and unattuned to Elizabethan cultural conditions—or not particularly concerned with the original historical conditions that framed the play—the attraction of an apparently mutual dynamic in sex relations is more compelling. Historicizing a play's cultural values is a primary tenant of feminist materialist performance criticism, but it is sometimes difficult, as in this case, to enact effectively.

Recent American productions have been in some ways responsive to feminist criticism that supports Isabella—her right to choose how she will use her body is at least partially respected rather than viewed with contempt, and the duke is sometimes portrayed as manipulative. As early as 1971, Herbert Coursen reported on a Shakespeare festival in Monmouth, Maine, that portrayed the duke as manipulative and Isabella as naïve but with a clearly latent sexuality, a "real woman and novice nun."[18] Some productions, however, still represent Isabella as a cold, unyielding prude or at least as "frumpy."[19] One reviewer of a 1987 London production rather shockingly complained: "Saskia Reeves [Isabella] has so hammered away at the small-voiced, shrill and shrewish young girl—a promising point—that one begins to wish Angelo had threatened her with a fate worse than bedding. So that the knot which the duke steps in to untie concerns us rather less urgently than it should."[20] Wish her a fate worse than rape, which for some women results in a living death they wish had been ended by murder? This male reviewer is criticizing the director and the actor for not making Isabella more sympathetic. But his view of Isabella as unsympathetic because of her sharp insistence and the quality of her voice, and his lack of sympathy that leads him, even in jest, to suggest the audience wants Angelo not only to rape Isabella but also to violate her physically in some other way represents a deeply sexist and dangerous response. A more subtly condescending review of a 1996 Washington, D.C., production described the actor playing Isabella as giving "an emotional performance, sobbing and sniffing as Mr. Goodwin's increasingly enraged Angelo puts the screws to her."[21] This male reviewer of a male-directed production suggests Isabella's overly emotional response to the threat of rape, making the scene almost comical with his choice of the word "sniffing." But at least he's not rooting for Angelo. Isabella's choice tends to be viewed more negatively abroad, perhaps the result both of a stronger cultural feminist movement and a greater moral and sexual conservatism in this country.

At the other end of the spectrum, directors must choose how to represent the "lowlife," a choice that can impact how the audience views other instances of oppression in the play, particularly Isabella's. Michael Friedman has helpfully categorized typical portrayals of these characters in *Measure for Measure* as "conventional," "lascivious," and "adverse."[22] The first approach is theatrically the most traditional and emphasizes the comic appeal of the tattered but feisty and humorous band, which minimizes the upper class's role in sustaining class divisions and the potential evil they perpetrate. The second approach emphasizes the sexual appeal of the prostitutes, encouraging the audience's own voyeurism or at least sexual arousal and perhaps also encouraging them to view Isabella as repressing her sexuality, which makes Angelo's proposal seem less nonconsensual and violent. The third approach portrays more realistically the suffering of women and sometimes children who are exploited by the sex trade. Friedman notes the inherent tension between the potential comedy of the low-life characters, substantiated by their warmth, life, and vigor, and a feminist materialist approach that reveals their living conditions more realistically, thereby making their depiction almost exclusively tragic. Portraying "the full spectrum" of the low-life characters' "virtues and shortcomings" presents a difficult challenge.[23]

Both productions researched for this project portrayed Isabella sympathetically and highlighted the sexual politics of rape, which were intensified by Angelo's abuse of power. One of the directors took a specifically feminist materialist approach, which is rare for productions of this play.

Tina Packer's *Measure for Measure*

The Director's Vision

Measure for Measure was the first play Packer directed (1971 at the London Academy of Music and Dramatic Arts) and she very much enjoyed returning to it—so much so, that she directed Lisa Wolpe's company in a production the following spring. Packer was conscious of only one production that influenced her approach to the play. When she was fourteen or fifteen, she saw a production at Stratford with Marius Goring, who flagellated himself as Angelo. She wanted to incorporate that bit of stage business into her own production.[24] She reports that most of the time she sees other productions to discover what she does *not* want to do.

Packer sees the play working on political and deeply psychological levels, raising the complementary issues of how those in power should rule and how the underclass lives. The quote in the title for this chapter comes from my interview with Packer (a question she adapted from Pompey's "I'm a poor fellow that would live" [2.1.220]) where she expressed something of a Brechtian/Marxist attitude: "How do poor people live? And the answer is, they live the best they can."[25] Although Packer's English upbringing attuned her to class issues, she still espouses a generally essentialist viewpoint. She sees those at the bottom of the social system as not having the luxury to think about their relationships with God, the possibility of a monastic or political career, and even more specifically, what order of the church to enter, or what laws and approach to their enforcement to institute. The humor, tenacity, and vivacity of the lower-class characters are the opposite side of the high poetry and philosophy expressed by the upper-class characters in *Measure for Measure.* She believes that a state based on utopian visions always turns out badly and destroys some of its members, and an absolute enforcement of overly strict rules usually leads to some kind of explosion. Packer states her ideal philosophical basis for moral and political systems, however, in more liberal humanist terms: "There is only the acceptance of human nature and muddling through. That's all there is. Let's muddle through as best as we possibly can, and as honorably as we can, and doing as little harm to people as we can." Such a mix of philosophies is actually quite common for the British left wing, which is more anti-authoritarian than genuinely materialist.

For Packer, *Measure for Measure* explores complex relationships among violence, sex, and spirituality. She believes Shakespeare wrestled with these forces, writing about them over and over. In her view, the violence in this play exists on two levels, political and personal. The first is the violence that the state commits against its prisoners in the form of capital punishment. Packer astutely observes that, in the nexus of the personal and political, Angelo confuses power and sexuality, substituting one for the other. When Isabella's mind and spirit awaken his sexuality and she refuses his offer of "love," threatening to expose him, shame then also awakens his latent potential for violence, and his sexual and dominant urges merge. Packer believes the play explores sources of violence and sees Isabella as quite vengeful. Opposed to this violence, Mariana was central to her production as an agent of redemption and mercy. Packer defines real holiness as "ask[ing] forgiveness for the person who has sinned against you." She sees the two women kneeling together and using their power to influence the decision of the state as one of the most important moments of the play. Their spirituality forestalls greater violence.

In Packer's production Isabella was mature spiritually but more like a child psychologically and sexually. She was strong, warm, intelligent, disciplined, and vibrantly spiritual, struggling to reconcile her commitment to and belief in the law with her more compassionate impulses. Her naïveté, resistance to sex, and volatile emotional responses revealed the childlike side of her disposition. Packer saw Isabella's reaction to her brother's desire to live at the expense of her chastity as extreme, and the sign of an unbalanced woman who does not know herself. Angelo's proposal was almost a rape that Isabella in no way encouraged, though Packer believes there was an undercurrent of attraction between them. In this playworld, the desire to rape was encouraged by repression. Packer believes that great spirituality is sexual and great sexuality is spiritual, a marriage that leads to pure ecstasy in the first half of *Romeo and Juliet* but pure misery in this play, partly because Angelo and Isabella divide sexuality from spirituality so starkly.

Although the duke was rather inept at personal relationships and even occasionally cruel, a part of his character Packer did not understand, she portrayed him as largely benevolent, a well-meaning "idiot . . . at his wit's end to know what to do." Admittedly somewhat skirting and mystifying the ending, she referenced Michelangelo's *The Creation,* and moved the production to a more archetypal level, with the duke reaching out to Isabella as God does to Adam. But apparently, she initially directed a different ending. According to one critic, Isabella slowly gave her hand to the duke in silent assent, qualified by a friendly but guarded look.[26] This ending must not have ultimately satisfied Packer, and she retreated from the human level into an allusion to the divine to make the ending more ambiguous.

Also central to her concept was the thin line separating virtue and corruption. In many ways, her concept merely extends her belief that no experience is completely foreign to the actor, that within each person is the obedience of Ariel and the rebellion of Caliban,[27] or, in the case of *Measure for Measure,* the spiritual strivings of Angelo or Isabella and the sexual licentiousness of Mistress Overdone or Pompey. She embodied this theatrically by double casting each actor to play a spiritually struggling and a low-life character (e.g., Isabella and a whore, Angelo and Abhorson, Mistress Overdone and Escalus) and says she likes this con-

Angelo (Allyn Burrows) tries to force Isabella (Kristin Wold) to accept his proposition in Tina Packer's *Measure for Measure*. Photo: Richard Bambery.

The actor playing Isabella (Kristin Wold, right) in her role as prostitute with another bawd (Robin Hynek) and Lucio (Walter Wilson) in Tina Packer's *Measure for Measure*. Photo: Richard Bambery.

cept so much that she would not want to direct the play any other way. In addition, at certain points actors appeared on stage with clerical outer garments but then stripped to reveal gaudy outfits or sexy lingerie underneath. She thereby deconstructed the virgin/whore as well as the minister/profligate polarities. Her combination of neo-Brechtian and -Stanislavskian techniques was ideally suited to this purpose. *Boston Globe* critic Ed Siegel especially praised Packer's production concept as embodied by the double casting: "The conceit works beautifully as if puritanism inevitably leads to biological backlash."[28] Packer's concept shows the dangers of intrapsychic sex relations and makes present and powerful the marginalized prostitutes.

Michael Hattaway describes a similar casting in a 1992 production at the Opera House in Buxton, England, performed by the Compass Theatre Company and directed by Neil Sissons. Remarking on the way the double casting forced the audience to consider the misogyny in the plays and resulting likeness between Claudio and Angelo, Isabella and Mistress Overdone, he described the production as "undoubtedly brilliant and, equally undoubtedly, a post-feminist production."[29] This judgment is puzzling, however. Perhaps Hattaway is referring to the way the double casting leveled distinctions among men and women who made very different choices and lived under very different conditions, but because he attributed this leveling to the misogyny in the play and praised the production for its insight, it is difficult to understand why he considered such a production postfeminist, a term which I'm assuming he uses to designate attitudes resistant to feminism.

The Play in Performance

OPENINGS

The set for this production was simple yet stylized and suggested many of the tensions and contrasts the performance would reveal.[30] Two slides of carpet, one blue and one black, hung from ceiling to floor on either side of the stage, intended to symbolize roads to heaven and hell. A solid white primitive throne-like chair was placed centerstage. Draped across it was a priestly-looking robe. Other cloaks hung on hangers in midair. Packer wanted to suggest the conflict between being and seeming. Behind the chair was a ladder, and a white down light suggested a path to heaven. A couple of other ladders were behind the proscenium arch. Scattered somewhat randomly over the large forestage where most of the action was played, predominantly stage left and stage right, were simple black wooden chairs. A dummy sat in one, a representation of the ever-present spectator.

Like both Koszyn and Wolpe, Packer chose to begin the production with, somewhat literally in this case, a preshow foreplay, which was reprised at the end of the first half (the end of Shakespeare's third act). The actors emerged in long black clerical robes, their measured and stately movement culminating in a V-formation. They looked straight out into the audience. Then they ripped open the clerical gowns, the sound of the quick succession of metal snaps opening an appropriate aural corollary to the visual scene of bodily restraint moving through tension into release. Bright flame-colored silks and rosy flesh was revealed underneath the austere black poly/cotton robes. The actors moved their hands over their bodies. Against the slow organ music, composed for this production and intermingling both medieval and modern tonalities, sounded the hissing and heavy breathing of sexual arousal from the actors. Although this "lascivious" approach may have encouraged the audience's sexual objectification of the actors, the destabilization of what can be definitively known as "being" and "seeming" probably also promoted a self-consciousness about the outward appearance and inward desires of the spectator. During the play proper, the lowlife was generally presented more conventionally, so despite Packer's apparent class consciousness, the production utilized these characters for their entertainment value rather than for their potential social commentary. Such a choice is both easier to stage and probably more popular with mainstream audiences.

"ALL THE WORLD'S A STAGE"

Central to Packer's approach to theater is the connection between the actor and the audience: "The relationship with the audience for me is the key relationship in any Shakespeare play." During the intensive actor training program I participated in, she made an exaggerated and oversimplified claim, maintaining that the theater was declining primarily because actors were not willing truly to share themselves with the audience. Declaring fourth-wall realism the "stupidest" theatrical convention ever constructed, she encouraged actors to speak their lines directly to the audience whenever possible without breaking character. In fact, for the presentation of our final scenes, we stood before the audience for a moment, acknowledging each other's presence both before and after the performance. But Packer's focus on this relationship also springs from an endorsement of Jaques's comment that "All the world's a stage, / And all the men and women merely players" (*As You Like It,* 2.7.139–40), a sentiment echoed elsewhere in Shakespeare as well. Making a somewhat illogical connection between performance and personal responsibility, she believes Shakespeare's frequent metatheatrical references in his plays signal his belief that "the very act of acting is what our lives are like, and so there is a philosophy that he is espousing that we generate our own lives, and that implies responsibility for your own life." But then she extends this philosophy into a belief that apparently designates each person as the author of even tragedy in his or her life: "Just to think that whether you're the rapist or the rapee, you're both actors in this and what's your responsibility in that?" At other points in the interview, she made it very clear that Isabella never incited Angelo to rape her or provided him any justification. Perhaps her remarks concerning responsibility refer only to dealing with the consequences of whatever happens. But her attitude seems to verge on blaming the victim, which is clearly problematic from a feminist perspective.

However, her staging of this imperative for actor and audience interaction is often effective. When Mistress Overdone first appeared onstage, she invited the audience to visit her establishment. Later in the production, Pompey clapped his hands with a look toward the back of the auditorium, and the light board operator responded by bringing up the house lights. Able to see individual audience members, he picked out a few to tease about having been patrons at the brothel. But this moment also called attention to the theatrical apparatus and thereby made representation a subject of the production. Such an anachronistic moment juxtaposed two different histories, creating a temporal anomaly and bringing the present into sharp relief. Similarly, at one point Lucio was onstage alone, cutting lines of cocaine on a mirror. Suddenly he became aware that the audience was watching him. Embarrassed but determined to make a quick cover, he cited the contemporary slogan, "Just say 'No.'" The unexpectedly modern text and the character's obvious hypocrisy created a comic response in the audience.

Having the actors sit onstage and watch the action further highlighted Packer's concept that the distinction between actor and audience is somewhat artificial. The one time I found this disturbing was when the actor playing Isabella came on stage to watch the play shortly after her character had nearly been raped by Angelo. Her head covering was off, and she clearly enjoyed the comic scene, smiling at the actors'/characters' antics. I found it difficult to disassociate her from her character at that moment, feeling it outrageously inappropriate for her to be so carelessly mirthful after such a traumatic experience. But certainly it prevented me from fusing the actor and the character and thereby splintered my coherent viewpoint, upsetting typically stable positions for theatrical exchange. As audience members we witnessed the actor's pleasurable experience outside the representational frame, which clearly contrasted with the character's experience of oppressive gender and sex relation codes within the playworld. The actor was also performing what may have been common practice backstage, a practice usually concealed from the audience in realistic theater because it would break the illusion. And yet Packer's own theory about this element of her productions stems from a desire to communicate that what happens onstage happens in the world and vice versa. Rather than shattering the mirror realistic theater supposedly holds up to life, Packer seeks to reinforce it through different means. The impact of this production style on the audience is probably not uniform, but at least audience members recognized that they were witnesses to an artistic event in which the director wanted to implicate them: "If you don't get what [the actors] are saying or you don't feel this is part of you, then there's something wrong somewhere." And yet her goal is not merely identification. In her production of *Henry IV,* Falstaff actually instigated a discussion with the audience on the meaning of honor. This was the actor's (Johnny Epstein) idea, and Packer thought it was brilliant because it forced the audience to think about the central theme of the play.

THE IRON FIST IN A VELVET GLOVE

At the end of the preshow, an actor climbed an upstage ladder. When he came down and forward, the others began buttoning up. A couple of actors held one hand to their throats while others raised a hand as if in praise, perhaps suggesting different characters' responses to the law. As the play proper began, the duke (Philip Bryce), Escalus (cross-gender cast with Karen Beaumont), and Angelo (Allyn Burrows) continued to look out toward the audience without making eye contact. Once the duke was safely robed in his cream-colored outer garment, he began to make eye contact with the other characters in the scene, who were similarly dressed. The actors not in the scene sat in the onstage chairs and watched.

The duke wore a grape-vine crown, an allusion to Christ. Packer made this choice because she wanted to remind people that the crown originally symbolized the halo: the ruler was meant to be God's anointed, appointed by God because he (in most cases) was the most holy and spiritual person. His spirituality was originally what gave him the right to rule. The duke certainly fell short of this ideal, but the tension between the ideal and the real was thereby highlighted for some audience members—certainly for me it was. It may have influenced others to consider his actions in a more positive light than they deserved. He took off the crown when he put on the friar's robe and began the journey toward discovering how, from his perspective, to keep his state from "going to hell in a hand basket," as Packer said.

The alternative of strict enforcement, however, had nearly disastrous effects. To underscore Angelo's harshness, Packer had him bring in Claudio (Jason Asprey) and Juliet (Robin Hynek) with their hands tied to a bar that passed behind their necks. He forced them to kneel. I still remember the startling and unsavory pleasure and vehemence with which he later pronounced Juliet a "fornicatress" (2.2.23). When the Provost (played alternately by Burrows, Beaumont, Hyneck, and Walton Watson), a more sympathetic person in power, spoke of Claudio's "offense," he quoted the word, clearly conveying his sense that Claudio had not, in fact, offended any reasonable standard of law and morality. In Packer's words, he had done only the "natural" thing. This staging underscored the way Angelo abused his power. He delighted not in justice but in dominance. Juliet and Claudio's loving and committed sexual relationship was also supported since they were subjected to Angelo's cruelty and gained the audience's sympathy.

SEX AND THE CITY

Critics have complained that a play so decidedly focused on brothels and sexual license oddly excludes the prostitutes from the text. Packer not only put them on stage, but put them in their sexual dalliance "on top" of the men, specifically Lucio, who, portrayed as a bisexual, enjoys "having things done to him," as Packer says. But for her, it is also a small measure of power that women can get men to pay for access to their bodies. The brothel is perhaps the only place where whores, at the bottom of the social strata, *can* reverse the typical hierarchy. The production never suggested the cost the women paid for this themselves, however, and the price for their financial and moral independence could not have been cheap.

Lucio's intrusion into the nunnery revealed yet another response to the complexities of living in the world—withdrawal. Act 1, scene 4 began with women on the ladders singing a Kyrie. One of the postulates had her head covered. When Lucio mistook one of the nuns for Isabella and pinched her cheek, she threw her veil over her head. When the woman with her head covered heard Lucio say "with child," she gasped, crossed herself, and withdrew. Isabella herself had apparently cut off all contact with her brother and her best friend Juliet, going into the nunnery just about the time Juliet became pregnant. Packer was curious about how and why this separation occurred. Although some scholars and practitioners believe there is no subtext to Shakespeare, that the text reveals everything there is to know, Packer believes that what is not said is just as important as what is. For Packer, this is a sign that Shakespeare intuited the subconscious forces at work in "human nature." Her essentializing of humanity and reading of Freud back into Shakespeare are problematic, but Shakespeare was probably aware of the ways in which language was not always sufficient to express what people thought and felt at any given moment, which for a contemporary mainstream American audience probably translates into something like Packer's assessment.

STAGING THE GAZE

The eruption of subconscious forces fired the first meeting between Angelo and Isabella (2.2). The staging of this scene established the acting style and two important symbolic uses of space. Stage left became identified with an absolute adherence to the law, with judgment; stage right became identified with the plea for mercy. Isabella was stage right, and Angelo remained stage left with the ever-present white throne between them. Isabella felt discomfort early in this scene partly because she had entered unfamiliar territory. During the prison scene with Claudio, her position was reversed and she was stage left while Claudio was stage right. Packer also used trends in the history of visual art as an intertext for the staging. In a broad approximation of different historical viewpoints, strict enforcement of an unreasonable morality was staged through the characters facing front, Packer's translation of the two-dimensional style of medieval painting. When characters were relating more to the desires to live in this life as fully as possible, they faced each other to suggest the three-dimensionality of Renaissance painting. Packer cites the Renaissance as the birth of our individualism and the desire to live in one's body, of recognizing sex is for pleasure, of wanting to be with the person one loves because he or she offers pleasure. Claudio, in her mind, honorably symbolizes this viewpoint. Although certainly this division is oversimplified, and I did not make an intellectual connection between the staging and historically different perspectives, I did register a more generalized sense of engagement versus disengagement.

The blocking in 2.2 promoted a very interesting way of staging the gaze. Throughout the scene, Isabella and Angelo rarely made eye contact. Torn between two modes of belief, one for herself and one for her brother, Isabella divided her look between Angelo and facing front. Angelo faced front for most of the scene, but as Isabella began to move him, his eyes would snap toward her, almost against his will. The moment she turned to meet his gaze, he guiltily withdrew it, moved by her spirituality, her mind, and her touch. At her entreaty, he consented to consider her case, subconsciously if not consciously anxious both for her to leave and return again. Gratefully, reverently, but with no sense of her sexual power, Isabella knelt, took Angelo's hand, and kissed it. Angelo's face showed a mixture of anguish and ecstasy. Physically he both gave into and resisted her. Her affection inflamed him, and he hated himself for being inflamed—terrified, excited, and disgusted by his response to her—the first time any woman had moved him this way.

THE ROSE AND THE FLAME

Angelo referenced "What's this?" (1.163) in the following soliloquy by putting his hand to his heart. Throughout the speech he clearly fell into fantasizing about her, pulling himself back to reality abruptly, and slipping back into his fantasy. Packer believes that "conversations are the sexiest things that are," and that Angelo has never met someone this clever who can challenge his mind in spiritual conversation. She thinks that he really did love Isabella in his own immature way, an interpretation difficult to square with his later behavior. Part of the tension arose because he was divided against himself: his professed allegiance to the

Rose of Sharon was, in his mind, threatened by his attraction to Isabella's "rose," and it was no longer just the Holy Spirit's tongues of fire that moved him—although it could be argued that his former commitment to Christian law was born of duty and will and never truly moved his heart in the first place.

Before their second meeting (2.4), Angelo entered from his side of the stage making a sound of disgust. But once he crossed into Isabella's space, he softened. In one sense, her influence was humanizing him. However, he returned to his own space prior to their meeting. Before Isabella entered his presence, she climbed the ladder at the back of the stage, as actors often did, particularly when they were pleading for help or mercy. When she said that she would kneel to ask forgiveness for the sin of begging her brother's pardon, he took the initiative to touch her in this scene, but it was to raise her from her knees, for he needed her to be not quite so spiritual. Then they separated and Isabella looked forward while he looked at her, now indulging his gaze a little more freely. When he insultingly brought her womanhood into question (ll. 133–37), "predicat[ing] female identity on insemination," they were finally facing each other.[31] Isabella looked away on his proclamation of love (l. 140). When he touched her, she gasped and jumped. A more "advanced character," in Packer's words, would have respected Isabella's rejection, but when Isabella metaphorically "slams the door on him and says, 'I'm going to shame you,'" it triggers his own inherent violence. Isabella tried to run away but he grabbed her, picked her up, and carried her downstage. He lay her down parallel with the front edge of the stage but stage right—his territory—and her head covering came off. He ripped open her gown and thrust his body between her legs. She remained stiff and terrified. When he rose, he shoved one of her legs further open, a disgusted gesture. She came to sitting as she protested, but when he said, "Who will believe thee, Isabel?" (l. 153), he knelt behind her, grabbed her around the waist, yanked her to her knees, and hissed his words into her ear.

SEX AND VIOLENCE: TAKE 2

Packer wanted to represent an "all-but-penetration rape," prompted by her own experience and experiences of women friends encountering the difficulty of being outside the power structure. Angelo was not just talking about violation; he meant it, and Packer wanted the audience to recognize unmistakably his brutal abuse of power. At the same time, she found it interesting that he did not become violent until he was threatened with public shame by Isabella (ll. 150–53). Packer identifies shame as one of the primary causes of violence. Angelo's sexual violence is distinguished clearly from the sexual licentiousness of the brothels, which are not violent spaces. His violence also comes out of the absence of love, so is "not natural," Packer said, citing that 99.9 percent of all murderers grow up in violent households, though she does not suggest specifically what kind of household Angelo grew up in. Indeed, the play does not suggest any kind of history for him. But clearly it's an important issue for her: "Unless we understand the link between sex and violence, we're not going to get anywhere."

For Packer, the moment after the near rape allowed Isabella to see her "insides outside," and she did not recognize that part of herself. Once Angelo had left, Isabella slowly got to her feet. She looked down at the black negligee underneath her habit before she looked out at the audience. Packer's favorite way of costuming this moment is to have nothing underneath the clerical robe so that Isabella sees her own bare breasts: "And why I prefer that is because the whole vulnerability is so exposed at that point, the softness of the skin, the real vulnerability." Vulnerability is central to Packer's acting ethic. And yet to use nudity at this moment to express her vulnerability would potentially sexualize Isabella in an unhealthy way by linking a violating act with sexual stimulation. A woman's bare body onstage functions as more than a material and symbolic exposure of the character. Such a staging would not necessarily highlight the way the body is socially marked and mediated. It would be more likely to prompt an uncontextualized arousal that subconsciously might even strengthen the link between sex and nonconsensual violence. The black negligee is actually a better choice in this context since it suggests vulnerability but also protects the actor.

Packer believes there is an undercurrent of attraction between Angelo and Isabella, which in many ways weakens Isabella's credibility. To suggest this she double cast Angelo with Froth and Isabella with Elbow's pregnant wife, who appeared onstage when Elbow was trying to get Froth arrested. During this scene, Froth managed to get Elbow's ill-kept, simple, and flirtatious wife on his lap, which Elbow never really registered. In a stunning moment, Froth picked up Elbow's wife like a man carrying his bride over the threshold, and handed her over to Elbow himself, who was double cast with the actor playing the duke. This choice perfectly exemplified the concept of women used as an object of exchange between men.

(A)STIGMATIC VISION

Packer thinks that precisely because of the nun/friar relationship, Isabella and the duke could come to know each other because the possibility for a sexual relationship was put aside. She admitted that if she had discovered the duke could have stopped all her suffering and did not, "I might have been really pissed." She also recognizes as problematic the duke's use of his power in saying he is going to marry Isabella and change her vocation of being a nun. But unable to understand his moments of cruelty in the context of the rest of his character, she more or less covered them under the shield of his well-meaning ignorance. At least he was trying to discover how to rule the state more pragmatically, and Packer thinks that perhaps the duke rightfully takes Isabella out of her order because she does not really belong there. Isabella does not, after all, retreat back into the nunnery after Angelo's assault, but tries to remedy the difficult and painful situation by staying in the world. But such a value judgment seems predicated on assumptions antithetical to Isabella's choices. Packer sees Shakespeare as clearly portraying a woman "obsessed with rejecting sexuality," which means she is "neurotically sexual." Packer supports this interpretation by citing Isabella's decision to go into the nunnery. Quoting Isabella's thoughts she said, "I'll have nothing to do with anybody," which is hardly true of life in the community of a convent. Her misconception of the nunnery is predicated on a perceived lack of communication between the nuns and others in their world.[32] Jessica Slights and Michael Morgan Holmes have recently argued that Shakespeare supported Isabella's pursuit of convent life, a place of "personal security and tenderness" where she could be creative, self-defining, and loving in a woman-centered social environment, as opposed to the patriarchal society in which she lived.[33] Although Packer said Isabella's choice could be justified if she defined her chastity "as her relationship with God and the most spiritual thing about her," rather than radically attacking her brother, I doubt that she could ever truly support such a choice.

The representation of the duke and Isabella's growing relationship onstage was compelling. One of the most convincing moments was when he told Isabella he would not be present for the final judgment, and as a child who feels she will miss someone she is very fond of, she embraced him. Surprised and moved by her gesture, he slowly and gently returned her embrace. At his first proposal of marriage, he had taken her hand. She withdrew her hand and went to Claudio, disturbed. Soon afterward, Claudio brought out his and Juliet's child in a blanket, which delighted Isabella. She moved a little toward the duke, but at the play's end, everyone started to exit, and she was left alone onstage. Pensive, she seemed suddenly to notice her isolation. She turned to look for the duke, and he had climbed the ladder, reaching out toward her, a white down light bathing him. Seeing the duke reach to her from the path to heaven, she seemed almost ready to accept his proposal, but the white spotlight on their hands, which were moving in a dance around each other, faded to black before they touched. The image was powerful and moving, and for this very reason, any sense of the duke's insensitivity and potential abuse of his power dissolved.

REDEMPTION AND TRANSFORMATION (NOT)

The duke's proposal to Isabella in this production seemed partly predicated on his close observance of Isabella's response to the chain of events he set in motion in the final scene. For Packer, the turning point in the play is Isabella's decision to kneel and pray for Angelo's life. Mariana is the person who brings her to this point. Earlier in the play, Isabella's righteous anger always builds into threats, sometimes of physical violence.[34] The duke had been the one to restrain her through his spiritual authority, his calls to reason, and in one instance, an embrace. As Isabella was crumpled and crying on the floor after the duke lied to her about Angelo having killed Claudio (4.3), he came up behind her and wrapped his arms around her—a gesture of comfort that restored her to calmness. When Mariana asked Isabella to kneel with her, her first response was to run away as if appalled by the proposition. The duke in no way interfered this time, but keenly watched. The dramatic situation led Isabella to question her views of right and wrong, to consider acting mercifully. Although kneeling can be a submissive posture, Isabella did it so frequently, so naturally and easily even when not pleading, that it had come to represent a genuine expression of her spiritual self. Kneeling for her was almost like breathing. Her decision to join Mariana in petitioning the duke for Angelo's life, a decision she continued to struggle with as she spoke, seemed in some ways a form of reconciliation with herself, a healing that was hopeful and appropriate for a comedy. *Measure for Measure* is a problem play partly because Angelo deserves a more severe judgment. But here, too, Packer chose not to fight or undercut the ending. Her concepts of holiness and forgiveness seem in many ways divorced from the context in which they appear. I would argue that personal forgiveness should not necessarily release a rapist and murderer from his crime's social consequences—imprisonment. Only the comic genre disallows the full damage of his intended actions. The women's "power" is to excuse a corrupt and abusive officer of the state, thereby belittling their own suffering and the atrocious acts he very nearly perpetrated against others. The play itself demonstrates the annihilation of boundaries between personal desire and political responsibility, boundaries that in this case are better upheld than removed. To pin the legal system's responsibility to execute justice on Isabella's personal spiritual journey is troubling. As is typical of her work, Packer followed her sense of what the text suggests without seeing the problems it raises. She may, at times, trust Shakespeare a little too much.

Another problematic aspect of the play that Packer's production elided is Mariana's continued desire for Angelo even though he cruelly broke off their engagement upon discovering that she had lost at sea her fortune and her brother, "pretending in her discoveries of dishonor" (3.1.227). But Packer sees her as a redemptive force, key to the spiritual meaning of the play. At one point when she was speaking with the duke, the backdrop was lit by a gold cross. Packer's interpretation was also reinforced by the actors' views of their characters, which provided a sympathetic interpretation of Angelo. Her initial analysis led her to believe that the bed trick was a brief and essentially loveless interaction:

> My thought about it was that it had been a quick, you know, three thrusts, he came, and she was out of there kind of thing. But they thought that was not true, that it was a somewhat tremulous meeting, and that there was great tenderness between him and Mariana, and that what happens to him in the last scene when Mariana starts pleading for him, is that actually he begins to perceive who Mariana is.

Packer already believed that Angelo changed, that when he asks for death, which she staged as him lying on the floor in a crucifix position, he is truly sorry for what he has done. He finds humility in Christ's true teachings rather than the institutions set up to enforce them. In her view, at this point of genuine repentance, the duke is right to release Angelo from his earlier sentence. Although certainly there is not much love in his initial encounters with Isabella, his profession to love Mariana and his commitment to be faithful to her signals to Packer that something has changed him. Following the actors' intuition, she came to believe this change was rooted not just in his public exposure but also in his encounter with Mariana. In a sense, when what he fears most has come to pass, and when he is forced to confess publicly his sin and yet is forgiven and loved, he is inspired to become a new man. Packer observed, "He's obviously going to be a very different person from the one before. I like plays in which people are deeply changed in the course of the events. It's a very satisfying play in that respect." This is an idealistic view of the play's ending, but certainly the text does suggest a change in Angelo (5.1.364–72, 472–75), which allowed her to fulfill her desire to stage his transformation.

The power of a repentant sinner and the power of the people to plead for mercy and sway the duke's decision were demonstrated in a somewhat comic reprise. When Lucio was exposed as a slanderer of the duke, he adopted Angelo's crucifix position on the floor. His insincere performance of confession was thereby contrasted with Angelo's genuine confession, which gave the latter more strength partly through the recognition that repentance is not always genuine and can be used merely as a ploy to escape punishment. When the duke began to deliver his sentence for Lucio with, "Thy slanders," the rest of the company onstage dropped to its knees smiling. In apparent response to their request for leniency, he continued, "I forgive" (5.1.517). Here the duke showed mercy to the one who had sinned against him personally. He did not ask from others what he was not willing to give himself. His personal response in this political situation, his attention to the corruption within the state, and his attempts to reform those who had broken the law suggested that he had learned much about ruling during his sabbatical. The personal transformations he instigated were depicted as a step toward a humane reformation of the social order.

Ellen O'Brien's (and Jack Zerbe's) *Measure for Measure*

The Directors' Vision

O'Brien's take on *Measure for Measure* is the most consciously political of the directors in this study. Before going into production, O'Brien and Zerbe developed their ideas into several pages of "Director's Notes." Both their names appear on the first page, but having worked with both of them, I hear Zerbe's voice more strongly, and the use of the singular for "Director's" also suggests that although the notes reflect both their input, he primarily composed this document. Still, their visions were largely shared, and because it was composed just before they went into rehearsal, it represents one of the most accurate primary sources available. This was the concept as it appeared in the director's notes (1991):

> Power is a weapon wielded by rulers for their own glorification, the maintenance of upper-class male privilege, and the perpetuation of the socio-political structure that ensures the continued repression of the disenfranchised members of society. The nature of power is both self-serving and oppressive. *Measure for Measure* is an image of what our society will become if existing socio-political systems continue to develop on their present course.

The world of the play was seen to operate under the power of fear. Performed at the end of the Reagan-Bush years when many social programs were cut and the country's rich and poor had grown further apart, this production also sought to suggest the failure of Republican capitalism and the need to find an alternative vision. As opposed to Packer's approach, which examined the qualities of ruling in terms of absolutism and strictness versus leniency, O'Brien's far more sophisticated reading of the play was more specific in its criticism of the current American political and economic systems.

In the directors' view, the corruption in the Viennese state literally determined every other area of life. The polarization of the society between rich and poor and the disappearance of the middle class meant particularly women had very few options for survival. If they were not married to a self-serving political official, they were almost forced to be either virgins or whores. An ethic of governance that served to promote the privilege of its leaders and the upper classes rather than serve the needs of the people legitimized the victimization of the disenfranchised. Shutting down the brothels did not clean up the city or result in a net gain in public morality. It merely denied a significant segment of the population its only means of survival. Economic hardship rather than immorality spawned the thriving prostitution ring in Vienna. Assuming that the brothels in the city served the upper classes and that those in the suburbs were lower-class establishments, O'Brien saw the split in Angelo's edict, which allowed the city brothels to stand while demolishing those in the suburbs, as motivated by an ethic of protecting upper-class privilege. The individuals in this system and the choices they made were less important than the system itself, which significantly limited their choices. This concept also allowed the directors to interrogate the construction of gender and the female body, and show connections among gender, family, state, and other cultural institutions.

O'Brien and Zerbe disagreed most in their interpretations of Isabella. While Zerbe wondered if she were "just a prude," seeing the nunnery as an unhealthy escape from the world, O'Brien and the actor playing Isabella, Anna Ribble, believed Isabella was not a prude but someone who "had some very strongly held beliefs that were genuine, and she was put in a tremendously difficult place."[35] Her desire for a strict order was consonant with the seriousness with which she approached her vocation and her desire to embrace completely this chosen path. The nunnery was one of the few safe places in this world for women and one of the only positive choices she had. But life in the convent was not just a last resort. It was something she wanted, even if in another world she might have made a different choice. The extreme reaction to her brother in prison came as a result of him pinning her to the floor as Angelo had, and her sense of oppression. According to O'Brien:

> She was boxed in, pushed around, used by all the males. . . . I mean, clearly it's a world in which sexuality is demonized, and so if you're going to be good in that world, it's very hard to have sexuality be a part of your life at all, and I think that's part of Isabella's struggle.

The duke in this production was a manipulator of his public image. He set up Angelo in his place because his popularity was waning, and he knew Angelo would be a worse ruler than he. His return would, therefore, be welcomed by the people. O'Brien and Zerbe's "Minimum Casting Requirements" for the duke called for the actor to be "credible as an intelligent leader between early Reagan and Bush, able to play the role of the leader, some charisma and personal charm." O'Brien believes it was important that the iron fist was hidden by a velvet glove, for then it was both more credible and more dangerous.

From the directors' viewpoint, Angelo began as someone who genuinely believed in an absolute law, but his newly appointed position of power corrupted him, allowing him to put himself above morality and the law. Power had this effect on him partly because his beliefs were more intellectual than personal. The casting requirements for this character included "passion with power, powerful lust, icy person with animal lurking inside, dangerous. Healthy ego. Verse [which I am assuming is shorthand for "handles the verse well"] and visceral." O'Brien thinks he is incapable of love, which she defines as "concerned for mutual well-being." As opposed to Packer's more humanistic and existential approach to the thin line separating virtue and corruption, O'Brien examined what kinds of social and political structures encouraged people to take benevolent or malevolent action. She defines an action as benevolent or malevolent not so much in sexual or spiritual terms but in terms of personal and political service and disservice, that is, whether one makes self-serving versus other-serving choices.

Like Packer, O'Brien's reactions to previous productions, both those she had seen and those she had read reviews for, going as far back as the nineteenth century, informed her about what she did *not* want to do. Most had Isabella happily accepting the duke's marriage proposal. Literary and cultural criticism of the play, however, had a profound effect on her approach. Works such as *Shakespeare Reproduced, Political Shakespeare,* and *Alternative Shakespeares* featuring new historicist and cultural materialist criticism excited both her and Zerbe. They knew they wanted to produce the play in such a way that gender and class politics featured prominently.

The Play in Production

HALLS OF POWER

Set designer Nephelie Andonyadis created an upper level of the set, constructed as a silver- and gold-lined corridor of power. Just beneath it was the squalor of the prisons and the brothels. The visual contrast and spatial relationship between these acting areas portrayed a sharply divided and hierarchical world. The director's notes remark that Vienna is

> a world of enclosures.... Although the places of power and the places of the powerless are pressed up against one another, they are carefully walled apart.... A dark, decaying world: everything but the Halls of Power has been allowed to fall into disrepair because the wealthy use the resources to serve their own ends rather than the public good.

Large sections of scaffolding covered parts of the set, conveying the sense of a "wrecked city."[36] Aside from a city in decay, O'Brien also wanted to depict a state trying to hold back those elements it feared, especially the lower classes that might "pose a threat to the upper-class patriarchy if they ever mobilized.... In this claustrophobic world, doors, gates and the prison become powerful symbols of repression, enclosure, restraint and denial."[37] At the beginning of 2.3 when the duke entered the prison, prisoners poured out from underneath the scaffold into the space to the accompaniment of sirens and whistles. As in Packer's production, the provost was the most humane man in the correctional system, trying to soften the impact of the state on its victims but ultimately having little power. O'Brien wanted to create an echo of the Berlin Wall in the set:

> Like that wall, the walls here may serve in theory to keep intruders out, but in fact their function is as much to keep the inhabitants in as to keep others out. Imprisoned by the structures of power and the psychologies of subjugation which those structures instill, the people of this play can only escape their worlds by walling off private sanctuaries (however perverse) within the city walls.[38]

For O'Brien, people's identities and behaviors are predominantly the result of the sociopolitical system they inhabit.

The sociopolitical distinctions among rich and poor, powerful and powerless were strongly reinforced in the costumes, also designed by Andonyadis, to convey upper or lower class with nothing in between. But hierarchical distinctions were also developed within the upper class in terms of power, wealth, and conservatism. The lower classes were "not scum or jolly poor folks. These people are struggling to survive economically." The costumes provided a narrow definition of the self that was less complex than reality.[39] Bodies were marked according to social class, and as far as the upper classes were concerned, little else about the person mattered.

ACTOR AND AUDIENCE

Unlike Packer, O'Brien did not articulate a philosophical creed concerning Shakespeare's attitudes on acting or the actor's responsibility to open herself to the audience. But for this production in particular, she did want the audience to feel the pressure of the playworld, to consider the possibility that they might be living in such a place in the not-too-distant future. She set the play in the twenty-first century. The gray stone wall of the set surrounded the seating area, and actors entered and exited through the aisles. The city gate was a chain-link fence with barbed wire through which the audience entered the auditorium. There was literally, then, no action that happened outside the representational frame, and because the frame was shifted from its usual site, representation became a subject of the performance.

Never much given to realism or a fourth-wall production style, O'Brien wanted direct contact between the actors and the audience. She believed this would be most effective in encouraging not just an intellectual but also a visceral response in spectators. Although she used some Method terminology and techniques, such as asking the actors to play objectives and actions, she also wanted to create some Brechtian alienation effects: "The dynamic of the play in performance should follow the Brechtian principle of alienation: emotional involvement followed by shock, surprise, or sudden turn of events that forces the spectator to step back and recognize the injustice of the action."[40]

Like the other directors studied so far, O'Brien developed preshow activity. The prostitutes solicited audience members for business. She thereby established an intersubjective mode of relation between actor and audience that initially upset stable positions for theatircal exchange. Although she cannot remember this certainly, she may also have had various groups of the cast move through the acting area to establish the distinct and separate social segments of the society.

POSITIONING THE PROSTITUTES

Since *Measure for Measure* is ostensibly largely concerned with sexual and ethical choices, I found the following idea in the director's notes initially startling, but in many ways a natural outgrowth of the core concept: "The real question of morality in this play has nothing to do with sexual license. The hypocritical use of power to perpetuate privilege is the only real immoral act in the play." Wanting to criticize this action and show its effects, O'Brien took the "adverse" approach to the lowlife, putting the prostitutes onstage not just at key moments but quite often. This decision was prompted partially by the desire to include more women in the production, but the prostitutes provided a useful commentary on the playworld. O'Brien wanted the audience to see the disenfranchised, and although the play includes lower-class men, the lower class women are largely excluded from the text. Lucio "kicked the prostitutes into action" when Mistress Overdone entered. The gentlemen enjoyed the prostitutes' advances during relatively idle conversation but shoved them aside when a topic of genuine interest arose. The gentlemen were also in league in taunting the women, in one case stealing a hat and tossing it among them. Revealing the gentlemen's callousness may have worked to alienate male audience members' propensity to identify with them and to question ways of viewing and representing women in the culture. It was certainly likely to stimulate a "gender-aware gaze," which Goodman identifies as one of the goals of feminist performance.[41]

But O'Brien also worked with the women to keep them from having too much fun. At one point in the rehearsal process, their actions conveyed the sense that a life of prostitution was a happy one, which was the opposite of her intent. She moved the actors toward professionally performing their "happiness" for their clients, while revealing that ultimately their lot was unhappy. I asked O'Brien if she worried about repeating the sexual objectification of the women in the playworld by subjecting them to the gaze of the audience since they were necessarily somewhat scantily clad. She admitted that it was an insoluble problem in putting a prostitute onstage. She felt it was an important question, and she might solve it differently for another production. But despite her "adverse" approach to representing lower classes, the production was not without humor. In fact, she saw the humor as a way of drawing the audience into emotional identification with unscrupulous characters, which then could be alienated through disgust at the recognition of abuse and injustice.

THE HUNTERS AND THE PREY

Isabella and Angelo's (Tim Hanna's) encounters were also strongly politicized: "The interactions between Angelo and Isabella carry a great deal of weight as a symbolic exchange between the powerful and the voice of the disenfranchised."[42] To this end, the scenes began with Angelo appearing on the upper stage level and Isabella approaching from the ground level. The upper stage was connected to the lower stage by a set of stairs with a landing midway up. As Isabella began her suit, she climbed the stairs to the landing. Little of the actual staging is recorded in O'Brien's promptbook, but she followed the action cues inherent in Lucio's (Aaron Bohn's) lines. One element in

Isabella (Anna Ribble) approaches Angelo (Tim Hanna) to ask for her brother's life in Ellen O'Brien's *Measure for Measure*. Photo: Nephelie Andonyadis.

staging the scene came from their initial rehearsals. O'Brien usually begins by trying to embody physically the psychological space of a scene. Angelo circled Isabella like a predator closing in on its prey. Because this action seemed right to her and the actors, they built on it in the production.

The actors' clear development and delivery of Isabella's and Angelo's rhetorical arguments were equally as important to O'Brien as having them play the characters' intentions. Her promptbook also reveals in many places a close attention to scansion, especially the irregular and short lines, which she feels suggest some kind of action. The action can be physical, or the character can be experiencing some revelation or intense emotion that propels him or her toward getting something she or he needs. Isabella often used Angelo's word choice as a way of engaging with his current mode of thought but with the aim of moving the argument onto a different level, to a more personal and religious level. Isabella was trying to suggest, for example, that "there's a more important way of thinking about a forfeit of the law, and it's that we are all sinners, and you are too." O'Brien recognizes the unfortunate consequences of Isabella's powerful rhetoric: "And, of course, what that ultimately does is work against her, and it seems to bring him closer and closer to the idea of trying to have sex with her." Angelo had previously considered the appearance of moral superiority as the basis of manhood, but once Isabella's personalized beliefs reached him on a more human level and the power structures allowed him to abuse his position, violence entered the equation.

Angelo was a man who swung between extremes and who was incapable of love. O'Brien's understanding of the distinction between lust and love is clear. Even though Angelo is attracted to Isabella's intelligence and passion, which is ultimately more sexy to him than a shapely body, what he feels is still lust because it is focused on his own desire. O'Brien noted, "That's not, 'I love you, I want you to be happy, I want to share life with you.' It's, 'I have to be in bed with you.' And I can't read that as love."

Apparently Angelo did not come down to Isabella's level (the landing) until well into the second encounter when he asked her to prove her "womanhood" (2.4.130). Zerbe's memory of the staging is that his descent suggested Isabella might have a chance; however, at this point, it seems the audience would have a sense that Angelo is plotting something against Isabella. What he remembers most clearly is that Angelo pinned Isabella violently, and the violence was difficult to stage because they had so little space on the landing. After that, she wanted to get as far away from him as possible, never having felt any attraction for him. After threatening and degrading her, Angelo climbed back up to his Hall of Power before exiting through the upstage center door, his typical space of entrance and exit.[43]

Most important to O'Brien was Angelo's intended violation of Isabella's very being, and although Claudio did not intend to violate Isabella, he pressured her to accept Angelo's violation. Consistent with a production concept that displaces personal choices, especially those related to sexuality, into more political frameworks, virginity was not the central question for Isabella, according to O'Brien:

[It was a symbol for] maintaining your purity, whatever that is, maintaining who you are, and not being forced into something that is not who you are. For me, the importance of maintaining Isabella's virginity wasn't virginity itself, but the sense of a violation of all her values and norms and desires, and the violation of thinking that a

Isabella (Anna Ribble) pleading more urgently with Angelo (Tim Hanna) in Ellen O'Brien's *Measure for Measure*. Photo: Nephelie Andonyadis.

woman should just give herself to some man who wants her for any reason.

The threat of Angelo's violation to Isabella was not about one woman losing her virginity through coercive sex but the sexual politics of women becoming subject to men's desires to violate them. O'Brien and Zerbe staged the larger implications of Angelo's threat by having Claudio (John Bray) physically imitate Angelo's blocking. Up until this point, Isabella had been very close to Claudio, but then someone she loved and whom she thought understood her begged her to submit herself to what was inconceivable. She reacted so violently precisely because she loved him and he betrayed her to the point of physically pinning her as Angelo had. The similarities between Angelo's and Claudio's behavior staged the female body as a site of inscription whose other social markers were often ignored by men.

Spiritually, Isabella and Claudio were also in very different places. His vision of death was annihilation and hers was union with God in a life far superior to this one. Isabella felt that what her brother was asking of her was worse than what she was asking of him, which was to accept the consequences for what he had done. For once, the production allowed for differing beliefs and actions not tied to sociopolitical background. This production may have overemphasized material conditions as a determiner of behavior, but at least it provided a corrective to many productions ignoring this crucial element.

The duke's (Chris Reid's) involvement with Isabella was depicted as manipulative, an extension of his function throughout the work as a playwright, and generally consistent with the way the other men treated her. He was smitten with her from the very

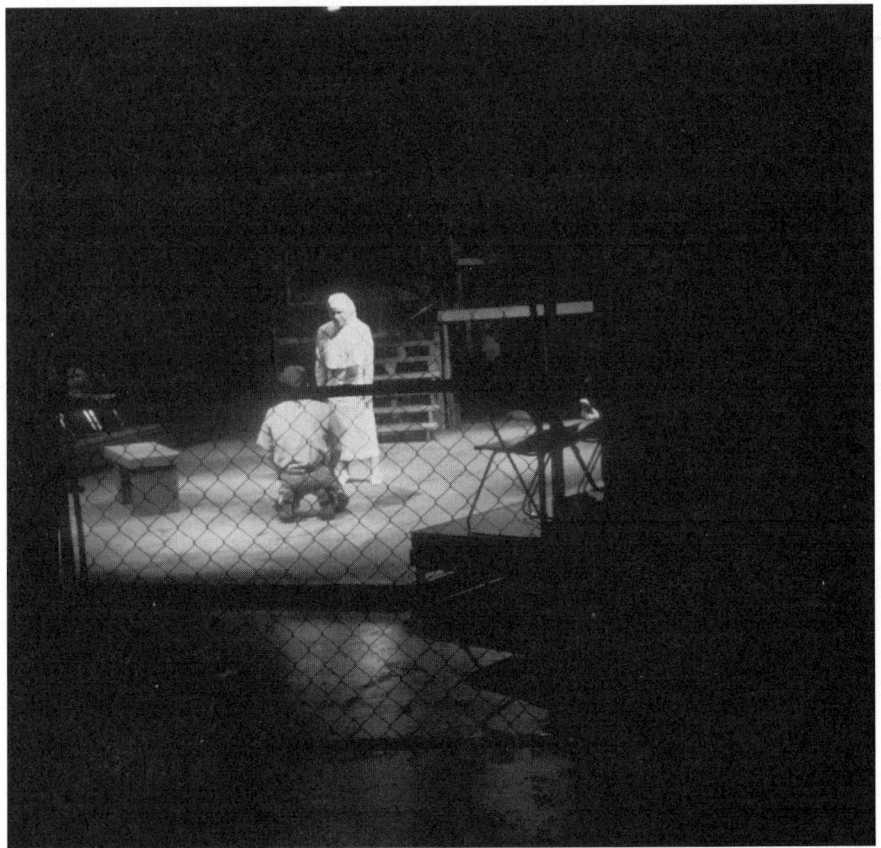

Claudio (John Bray) pleads with his sister (Anna Ribble) as seen from the outside of the fence surrounding the audience in Ellen O'Brien's *Measure for Measure*. Photo: Nephelie Andonyadis.

beginning and tried to develop a more romantic relationship with her, partly because he knew it would improve his image to marry a nun. His feelings were more developed than the purely intellectual lust Angelo felt for her, but O'Brien was unwilling to call it love because it still lacked mutuality. Zerbe titled the scene where he lies about Claudio's death as "The Betrayal," a concept he probably shared with the actors in rehearsal. Because Isabella's focus was elsewhere, she did not notice the duke's interest. O'Brien's reading of nineteenth-century stage history of the play revealed that many of those productions portrayed the duke as a saint. She understood that choice as consistent with a more solidly patriarchal society, but she also felt that the text allowed a deconstruction of the duke as benevolent ruler without turning the play "on its head." In their production, the duke merely played the *role* of the benevolent ruler, lying to the public in order to set himself up as God.

CONTINUING THE CYCLE OF ABUSE

In a drastically different interpretation from Packer, O'Brien sees Mariana as an abused woman who has bought into her victimization. She was portrayed as a very unhappy woman, trapped by her desire to embrace Angelo and "everything that's wrong with him." Even more so than Packer, she recognizes that women without power do not have many choices, but she does not support Mariana's capitulation to male dominance. In O'Brien's production, Mariana's thinking was, "What else is a woman going to do? How do you gain power but by submitting to the power and pleading for mercy when you have no power yourself?" Her kneeling was a logical extension of her psychology. The significant act of kneeling was Isabella's, but O'Brien believes that it was not primarily about learning compassion or forgiveness. Isabella's rationale was, "This is my sister. I have a bond with her. I think she's stupid to want this man, but if she wants him, she has suffered enough to deserve him. I will do this." They had become close in the scene just prior to the fifth act. Throughout the play, the production had shown Isabella forging strong relationships with the other nuns in her community. Her sense of solidarity with other women was her base of support and ultimately more important than any of the relationships she had with men. In this way, she destabilized her culture's normative construction of her gender. The opposition between her choice and male expectations of her also clearly revealed that her self-directed construction of her subjectivity, her gender, and sex relations was clearly opposed to the culture's oppressive codes.

O'Brien does not believe that Angelo fundamentally changed. Mariana was clinging to Angelo, and he clearly did not want to be there. She thinks that if Mariana is lucky, he might learn to love, "but I'm not holding my breath." Under these conditions, the duke's sentence of marrying them merely perpetuated a cycle of abuse. The importance of the duke's own ego rather than the well-being of those he was sentencing also surfaced in his vicious attack against Lucio. Slandering a prince was the worst crime of all, and his sentencing was a warning to the rest of the crowd, who were, nevertheless, taken in by him and fully supportive.

But the duke's self-centeredness loomed largest in his proposal to Isabella. In complete disregard for her chosen vocation, he believed that the greatest reward he could give her was himself. This production allowed for no truly intersubjective relationships between men and women and in fact starkly marked this absence. The staging of the play's ending evolved to intensify this lack of intersubjectivity and extend its resonance into social and political spheres. Initially, Isabella had gone off with the nuns and rejected his offer. In an odd echo of the play's dynamics, during tech weekend, Zerbe thought that choice was not working and was having the duke drag Isabella up the stairs with him. O'Brien was away at a conference, and the transition was difficult for Ribble. She almost called O'Brien because she was very uncomfortable with the change, knowing she could depend on O'Brien for support. What finally happened was that the duke took Isabella's hand and took her part way up the stairs, but then released her to wave to the crowds. As usual, he was completely oblivious of the negative impact he was having on others. The nuns were also deeply distressed by this move, for they were the only ones who saw through the duke's sham: "The nuns have just turned into themselves because there's no place else to go." The crowd was cheering. The production ended with Isabella in shock, theatrically framing the choice being thrust upon her at the last moment without showing a clear decision. Although Ribble found the first ending more personally satisfying, she was ultimately happy with this staging.

Only one review of the production was in Guilford's files. The reviewer, Abe Jones for the *Greensboro News and Record,* the city's major newspaper, was impressed with the production and understood the overtones of political repression. However, he

The duke (Chris Reid) greeting the welcoming crowd as he attempts to bolster his image by securing Isabella (Anna Ribble) as his wife in Ellen O'Brien's *Measure for Measure*. Photo: Nephelie Andonyadis.

missed the implications of the final scene: "[A]ided by his religious disguise, [the duke] manipulates events so right triumphs in a final act emphasizing the virtue of forgiveness."[44] The text certainly validates this reading, but clearly the production tried to create a different interpretation.

Packer and O'Brien are both self-proclaimed feminists, and they both take a text-based approach to Shakespeare. But their differences are much greater than their similarities. Packer did not go to college partly because while studying for her entrance exams, she "could not bear the time she spent sitting in classrooms," interested only in boys and theater.[45] Throughout her career, O'Brien has willingly engaged in extensive study. O'Brien is much more of a materialist and a postmodernist in her thinking and practice. She frames Shakespeare in a highly politicized way rather than merely encouraging the individual actor to find the truth of the character within herself while seeking to understand the larger truth of the play. Not dependent on the box office, O'Brien is much freer to create such unconventional productions. Constantly searching for money, Packer needs high production values but cannot afford truly risky interpretations. In fact, when she took over The Boston Shakespeare Company briefly, it had gone into debt largely because the previous director had alienated the company's subscribers with critically acclaimed avant-garde productions.[46] Such is the fate of more radical Shakespeare companies in America.

In a sense, they have both found lives that allow them to work out of their strengths, and in different ways, they are models for this book. When I was developing my theories concerning feminist acting, I became aware that my fundamental premise of engaging with the audience in character through a fusion of Stanislavskian and Brechtian approaches was the core of what I had learned with Shakespeare and Company.[47]

Packer has quite a high profile in the American Shakespeare community. Her productions have now reached thousands. Her celebratory approach focuses on individuals, as actors and characters, grappling with the human condition. But O'Brien has found ways to put truthful acting into more fully developed theoretical approaches to the plays. O'Brien's production fulfilled more elements from the above-outlined array of feminist strategies than any other in this study. Her work also exposes developing actors to a more theoretically informed way of viewing and enacting the text. Women actors trained as "resistant readers" can use the strategies they learn in their future work, especially when supported by directors like O'Brien. The popular audience is not as prepared for O'Brien's interpretations, but perhaps she and others like her can encourage spectators to take the next step, to adopt a more critical awareness of problems Shakespeare's work raises concerning power, gender, and class.

3
Whose Gender Is It Anyway?: Abigail Adams and Melia Bensussen Direct *Twelfth Night*

THE PLAYWORLD OF *TWELFTH NIGHT* CONTRASTS SHARPLY WITH those of *Romeo and Juliet* and *Measure for Measure.* Most significantly, the consequences of the characters' actions are much less severe. A magical land where law is never an issue, Illyria is filled with characters who long for something beyond their reach; the obstacles, however, lie within themselves or within the objects of their desire rather than in the state, family feuds, or even moral codes. The threat of serious violence emerges only briefly in the last scene, and sexual compulsion is absent. Although the world is still divided by class, no one struggles to survive. Removing the characters from conflicts with institutions, family, or material conditions, the play delves into issues of gender construction and its relationship to sexual attraction. Even though the play ends with the marriages typical of comedy, the majority of the play's action disrupts heterosexual norms of relation. Through its depiction of role playing, *Twelfth Night* also explores the art of theater itself.

Viola's assumption of a male disguise differentiates her from Juliet and Isabella because she does not represent herself as a woman to others, and Viola's clear expression of desire further separates her from Isabella. But she shares with Juliet an obstacle to consummating her love, which the genre allows her to overcome, and she shares with Isabella a hierarchical relationship with a man who is attracted to her. Since Isabella rejects Angelo's advances, she also shares with Viola resistance to unwanted sexual attention, but the power dynamics in their situations exert markedly different pressures. Despite some similarities, then, these individuated female characters in distinct environments act quite differently. Seen together, they offer a number of different constructions of "woman." In addition to Viola, two other women in *Twelfth Night,* Olivia and Maria, are also active in the story and engaged in romantic liaisons. Olivia's sexuality awakens under Viola's unintentional coaxing, which leads her to pursue actively the object of her affection, and Maria marries a man who is potentially charming but also probably an alcoholic.

Unlike the heroines in many Shakespeare plays, Viola clearly plays the central role. Providing the catalyst to change Illyria's stasis, her actions drive the plot to its conclusion. But her impersonation of a young male servant complicates her status and creates the primary conflicts. As a woman impersonating a boy, an action that both protects her from detection and excites erotic energies that are sometimes misdirected, she can deconstruct the concept that either gender is fixed or innate while also exposing the personal and social difficulties of moving between the poles of male and female genders.[1] But her marriage with Orsino, a vain, self-centered man more in love with love than loving, is potentially problematic[2] and may end up subduing her.[3] Because Viola's love also develops while she is posing as a servant to the duke, a subordinate rather than mutual paradigm can be explored.[4] Paradoxically, despite the subordination of her performed class, Viola gains a kind of equality with Orsino through her performed gender. However, Viola has been viewed by both literary critics and directors as the least active of the comic heroines, largely because she lets Time unravel her destiny and is constrained by her position as a servant.[5] In *RSC Directors' Shakespeare: Approaches to Twelfth Night,* Terry Hands (RSC artistic director, 1980–90) in particular remarked that the role she chooses to play "makes her a wonderfully still centre [of the play] and wonderfully passive," although later he remarked that in using the word "passive," he meant that things happen *to* her. Neither he nor RSC director Bill Alexander sees her as an active heroine.[6]

In contrast to some critics' and directors' perceptions of Viola's passivity, the majority of the productions I have seen or read reviews of portray Viola as an alive and energetic subject, which suggests that this choice may be motivated by more generally theatrical than specifically feminist concerns.[7] This points to the divide between literary and theatrical cultures, and even something of the divide within theatrical culture—between a director's ideas and the practice of performance. Although Olivia has been portrayed in the past as rather cold and stern, in the nineties, she is often a much more vibrant character, or at least warms considerably once she falls for Cesario. In general, the women characters in this play have recently been portrayed as sexual subjects, though sometimes they are also oversexualized,[8] which tends to place them within the virgin or whore dichotomy, their subjectivities defined primarily through their attitudes toward sex.

Eva Bergman directed an ideologically sophisticated production in Sweden in 1993. She set the play in "a scruffy modern [English] town populated by raffish characters and afflicted by homelessness, crime, alcoholism, alienation, and other typical urban problems." Viola was threatened by "some night-crawling local characters." Discovering that she had taken her brother's backpack in the confusion of the shipwreck, she discarded her own women's clothes "that [made] her vulnerable prey," and took the very real protection of a boy's clothes.[9] More clearly than in most American or British productions, this production created both a material, sociological environment to motivate Viola's disguise, *and* it exploited the humor of sexual excess beyond the bounds of realism. The director allowed the actors to add improvised dialogue, implicitly challenging the authority of the text. In this way, the production surprised the audience and resisted their expectations, thereby upsetting stable positions for theatrical exchange, especially for those who knew the play well.

Another challenge that directors must negotiate is the mismatch of Orsino and Viola. Occasionally critics remark that the duke is not a suitable husband for Viola. Still, they are clearly in the minority.[10] *Boston Globe* critic Bill Marx noted that in Penny Metropulos's production, Michael Wiggins's Orsino "is so dashing you can see, for once, why Viola falls for such a self-indulgent, albeit poetic, prig." His self-knowledge made him attractive: "Wiggins gives a terrific performance that exudes danger and irony—this Orsino knows his hot fits of jealousy and love are ridiculous, but the guy can't help overdramatizing."[11] Although British codirector of Cheek by Jowl, Declan Donnellan, has remarked that the three couples are "extraordinarily mismatched" at the end of the play, he goes on to say that "they show many signs of surviving and they are just like the marriages of all our friends."[12] Likewise, RSC director John Caird noted that the play is "not exactly a classic happy-ending story," but attributed it to the characters ending up with people other than those they originally wanted.[13] Only slightly more pessimistic, Terry Hands believes that Olivia and Sebastian, and Viola and Orsino will probably have successful marriages, whereas Toby and Maria's will probably fail.[14] In general, performance seems to increase the drive toward consummation. RSC director John Barton has discussed the need for Orsino's "danger and weight" in the production. Otherwise, "he just becomes wet, and that trivialises Viola's feelings and the whole chemistry of the evening is affected."[15] As an audience member at Adams's production, I was aware of my identification with the characters and my resulting frustration at their failure to get the love they wanted. By the end of the play, I *really wanted* at least someone to succeed and be happy, which overcame my initial feeling that Orsino was not the right match for Viola. I did not have these feelings while reading the play. So while the text certainly raises various problems, the embodiment of performance and experience of viewing actors in the roles inflects them with a difference. In some ways, this lets a director "off the hook," while still offering the possibility of thoughtful intervention.

Most productions that suggested discord at the play's conclusion resisted a happy ending not specifically because of the problematic marriages but more in response to a general sense of decadence, bleakness, or disillusionment that pervaded the production as a whole.[16] Miranda Johnson-Haddad has noted that melancholy productions of this play have become almost standard.[17] Former RSC Artistic Director Peter Hall (1960–68) created autumnal 1958 and 1978 productions that have been viewed by some as definitive.[18] By contrast, some women directors have moved against the grain or found an interesting combination of melancholy and festive humor. Lisa Wolpe's production was surprisingly cheerful. In an interview with Johnson-Haddad about the production, Wolpe reported that for her "Shakespeare is usually a message of healing," which is why she highlighted the comedic elements.[19] Apparently, her view has shifted somewhat since she resisted the reconciliation at the end of *Romeo and Juliet*. Using a different approach from either a melancholy or cheerful playworld, Cindy Gold directed a production for the Southern Festival Theatre at the University of Mississippi. The actors came on stage in neutral-toned cotton outfits and began to create their costumes while the audience heard the sound of crashing waves. Once dressed, the cast began to create the sound of the storm, which built into a flamenco-style dance celebration of the Epiphany. Although a fanciful, Spanish, almost cartoon look predominated a festive production, at the end of the play, the actors tore the costumes off one another and departed alone. Feste was left to sweep up the confetti.[20] While ultimately highlighting the theatrical apparatus and the theatricality of the play, seeing the actors almost violently disrobe one another and then scatter in isolation certainly cast a chilling pall over the prospect of living happily ever after either in Illyria or in life.

This play can be performed, as it is often read, as dramatizing bisexual or homosexual energies. Although some directors of productions for which I read reviews chose to highlight this aspect, most portrayed the characters as heterosexual.[21] But in the spirit of extending the gender-bending, a number of directors chose to cross-dress or change the sex of other characters. The characters most often changed were Feste, Antonio, and Malvolio, although one changed the sex of Sebastian. Excluding one all-woman (LAWSC) and one all-male production, four out of the eight productions changing the sex of the character or casting across gender were directed by women.[22] Although still a small minority of artists directing Shakespeare in the nineties, women seem to choose or be asked to direct this play somewhat more frequently than *Romeo and Juliet* or *Measure for Measure*. This may be attributable to the centrality of the Viola/Olivia relationship. Perhaps also because of the higher number of gays or bisexuals on the West Coast, this play is apparently produced in California more than any other area of the country.

Abigail Adams's *Twelfth Night*

The Director's Vision

This production provided Adams with her third opportunity to direct *Twelfth Night,* although she freely admits that she is "not a huge Shakespeare fan" and he is not the writer she most wants to direct. *Twelfth Night* is her favorite Shakespeare play and the one she knows best. She has acted the role of Viola twice: her first large role at eighteen in drama school and her last role, which she played in her midtwenties. Although her view of the play has changed over the years, she has always loved the story, the balance in the two plots, and the idea that Viola always tells the truth, even though she is not often believed.[23] This assertion can only be true, however, if limited to Viola's words, and seems blatantly to overlook her adoption of a disguise. Her silent deception essentially makes the play happen. Perhaps Adams would concur and has merely focused on the interesting opposition between text and action.

Adams explored class issues in the first production she directed in her late twenties. She was interested in how the status of being a servant would account for the characters' impulses and intentions, and she "was determined to . . . give the servants as much attention as the lovers."[24] In her program notes, she describes this as her "political" phase, although when I asked her about this in the interview, she admitted that her use of the word "political" was somewhat "flip." She was not trying to make a political statement about the injustice of class inequities; rather, she sought to explore how the experience of class differentiations affected characters' thoughts, feelings, and behaviors. Indeed, the very title of her program notes, "Director's Notes: Power, Sex, Class, and Shipwrecks," sets up an expectation of a political approach, which she then overturns with "shipwrecks." The second time she directed the play, when she "didn't much worry about what I thought any of it was about," she remarks, "You see, I was growing up."[25] At the same time, she believes that "when you have characters who can express an inner life, you have characters with real ownership and power over their journeys."[26] She is more humanist than materialist in her worldview. When I asked her about whether she tended to depict the strength and power of women characters or their oppression in a patriarchal world, she responded, "I am so not interested in politicizing meaning that I really don't make decisions about that. . . . I'm interested in audiences creating meaning, in using the available resources well to make a compelling theatrical event."

Certainly she is right to give the audience an important role in the creation of meaning. However, her apparent abdication of the potential to politicize the plays inherently limits the kinds of meanings she will make available to her audience. She does not seek to historicize the plays either, largely because she is "not very interested in [Shakespeare's] time." Rather, she seeks to create identification with a modern audience. However, she acknowledges that whatever issues she is personally engaged in at the time affect her view of the play. This time around, the play was about change, its causes and effects.

Adams tends to work very improvisationally, having clear ideas about space and the world of the play when she enters rehearsal but allowing the rehearsal process to determine the specifics. Even her initial ideas are open to change. In this production, she wanted the scene changes to be "entirely fluid," which she achieved partly by having the actors do the changes, her practice in all the productions she directs and a pragmatic rather than political choice. The physical landscape informed her view of the play and set choices more than a sociological analysis: "I wanted the garden, I wanted air. I wanted a sense of the sea."

The costume designs were in the art nouveau style. She used flowers quite a bit in the production, partly for practical reasons, because they gave the actors plenty of activities, but also because they conveyed the sense of wealth, particularly since they were cut flowers. She also wanted "to have as many dressings and undressings" as possible. Aside from the interesting resonances in terms of masks and identity, she used them as methods for creating intimacy between the characters or revealing a character's desire for intimacy.

Adams views the women as initiating all the action and Viola in particular as "incredibly active. I think that's one of the neat things about playing her." But she also admits that she always sees every character as active because drama is about doing; that is what differentiates it from narrative: "To have a character that's passive would be completely unproductive for me as a director. . . . Even though the audience might find that character passive, that's never how we would work on it or think about it. So I don't have any ideas about passive; everybody's active or you don't have the drama. All are doing." Adams's essentialism concerning the necessarily active quality of every dramatic character is accurate to some degree, but the tendency to stage every character as active (both intentionally and physically) is certainly reinforced by contemporary American notions about theater, which generally favor a Stanislavkian approach and a stage picture in nearly constant movement—especially true of verse drama and part of contemporary theater's competition with film. In considering a character's passivity or activity, the different ways literary critics and directors see and work are often at cross purposes.

Aside from a general sense of the characters as active, however, Adams sees the women as sexual subjects, openly expressing their desires. She remarked that she would have gone even further in that direction if she had had more time. Viola is not androgynous in her view, but the disguise allows her to discover another side of herself. Near the end of rehearsals, they started exploring Viola's *in*competence at performing the male gender, even though initially she worked at a convincing portrayal of a boy. Such a choice suggests that Viola is more essentially feminine than chameleon. The company was interested in exploring what would happen if Viola and Olivia became close, although they never brought sexuality into that choice: "It's just that they really like each other, and that's a whole different world from this partnering up with the right man." This is an area Adams will explore more fully if she directs the play again, which could present the audience with an alternative to the typical drive of comic narrative.

Although she views Orsino as "incredibly vain," Adams does not think about the potential mismatch between him and Viola: "I never think that way because the text is the text, and that's the story that you're going to make happen, so I never have any opinions about that. That's who she ends up with, and then I think you figure out a way to make that be an interesting choice." Her work as a director is consciously focused on fulfilling rather than critiquing the text. And yet her awareness that Viola and Olivia would make "a great combo" and her desire to work toward revealing their connectedness while recognizing its resistance to the comedy's trajectory shows a mind receptive to many different possibilities the text may be shaped to support.

A similar tension arose in her conception of Maria and Toby's relationship. Toby drank a lot in this production, and Adams never thought about what it meant for Maria to continue her involvement with an alcoholic, except for seeing that she covered for him because she loved him. What interested her more was Maria's desire for revenge and her response to Toby when he more or less backed out of the plot. Her need for revenge was fueled in part by class consciousness. In this production, Maria was from a higher class than Malvolio but poor. She resented his assumption that he could ever marry Olivia, but there were many "stored histories" of past indignities she had suffered from Malvolio. Once again, Adams's sense of the character's psychological response is in some ways at odds with the text, and the text became the final arbiter.

> We talked a lot about that in rehearsal, whether she should go off and take care of [the drunken Toby] or whether she should be pissed at him [for withdrawing his support]. I'm not sure we ever really resolved that, but it was too harsh for her to be pissed at him; the text didn't give her quite enough to do that with, so she went off, but we tried to give that moment a kind of bafflement for her, a kind of betrayal, although she was going to make sure that she got him to bed.

Shakespeare's open silences are not particularly open for Adams.

Adams reports that she researches the world of the play but never literary criticism or past productions. Her own productions are supposedly the only theatrical influence, although later in the interview she admitted that her ideas of dressing and undressing in connection with this play arose from not only productions she had directed but also those in which she had acted.

The Play in Production

AN ORGANIC, DREAMLIKE ILLYRIA

The High Point Theatre houses a traditional proscenium stage with a small forestage.[27] The stage was raked slightly for this production, the curtains open when the audience entered the auditorium. The backdrop was lit in blue as if it were evening. The set used natural, organic, and more highly stylized elements. A large, freestanding gate flanked by candles in tall, vinelike metal candleholders was upstage center. It was quite airy, however, because aside from the frame of the two doors topped with two golden, gently arced lines, like an improvisation on an eyebrow window, the doors themselves were nonexistent, save for a few wires again suggesting vines. The audience could clearly see the backdrop through the gate. Upstage left was another slightly smaller gate of similar composition. Upstage right was a fence of sorts, whose posts were topped with shapes suggestive of half a teardrop or cattail and bound together by a serpentine wire. There were also a couple of trees with green trunks and golden branches drooping almost like willows. Illyria appeared to be a fanciful and inviting place.

ACTOR AND AUDIENCE

The pianist, wearing a beret and contemporary clothes, entered doing a dance step before taking his place at the far downstage right corner. He remained onstage for much of the action. When Adams uses music, she usually uses a live musician and tries to integrate him or her into the playworld. Without this integration, the production lacks cohesion, an important value for her.[28] Soon after Feste (Michael Kamtman) entered, he suddenly "discovered" the audience. Most of the soliloquies were delivered in direct address. For Adams, breaking the fourth wall is a method of including the audience as much as possible, not of challenging the male gaze or drawing attention to the theatrical apparatus.

The night I saw this production, a particularly funny interaction developed between the actor playing Malvolio, Graham Smith, and the audience. As he came forward to the lip of the forestage to confide in us at one point, a woman a couple of rows behind me cackled loudly, apparently quite amused at the self-important and conspiratorial look on his face before he even began to speak. Completely in character, he looked at her, horrified, and backed away, deciding it was safer to begin his speech to the other side of the house, which raised a huge gale of laughter from the audience. He had just enjoyably upset stable positions for theatrical exchange. At another point as he was crossing the stage, he threw a look over his shoulder to sneer at the woman, raising more laughs. She became the object of his gaze. Although these interactions were governed by his character, the audience became aware of the actor's pleasures of performing and viewing and experienced an increased pleasure in its own viewing.

A LITTLE OUT OF STEP

An expanse of silk represented the sail and the sea. Viola (Elizabeth Slaby) appeared in a long blue velvet gown and wearing a headband. She had long curly blond hair, a picture of femininity. But as Cesario, she had short hair, a striped shirt and light jacket, ankle boots, and at times, a straw hat. Her movements were quick, light, and energetic, sometimes even bold and vigorous. However, her sexual identity was not entirely eclipsed by her boyish physicality. One of the lighting changes was cued to when Viola used her hips in 3.1, at the beginning of the scene when she is talking to Feste (Michael Kamtman), who seemed to know she was a woman. Drawing attention to the pelvis, the bodily site wherein sexual difference is most pronounced, inevitably called attention to Viola's and the actor's female body beneath the masquerade of male identity.

Viola's subjectivity was also a blend of typically feminine and masculine traits. While at some moments she revealed a touching vulnerability, she also exhibited strength, determination, and conviction. In the most surprising and delightful gender reversal, at the beginning of the sword fight with Andrew (Lucius Houghton) in 3.4, she adopted a classic fencing pose. Andrew's comical yells of intimidation that he had been practicing sporadically around the set while pretending to fight became a yell of dismay and fear as he ran away. *Charlotte Observer* critic Tony Brown aptly wrote of this moment: "Sir Andrew Aguecheek's war whoop collapses into a whiny wimp's yodel."[29] The traditional interpretation of Viola as afraid to fight, lacking the supposedly masculine attributes of courage and prowess, was reinscribed as merely a reluctance to fight, although she was perfectly capable of defending herself if necessary.[30] The vision of a woman taller and clearly more fit than Andrew raising her weapon in a manner that suggested years of training shifted the balance of power generally assumed in physical fights between men and women. The production departed from the normative response of a woman in a culture a century earlier than ours. In some ways reminding us of both contemporary women who have taken self-defense courses or martial arts and characters who have become action heroines—for example, the enormously popular Buffy the Vampire Slayer—this moment also juxtaposed colliding histories. Elin Diamond argues that when an actor suggests the "historicity of the character in contrast to the actor's own present-time self-awareness onstage," it fosters a critical awareness in the audience. "The body's emphatic ('live') presence is offered as a momentary habitus of what is not present—the forgotten objects and cultural detritus that constitute a piece of the 'historical experience of women.'" This coupling of discontinuous historical images allows for spectators to experience a kind of recognition that can lead to transformation.[31]

Adams chose this staging partly based on the actor's particular anatomy. Since Slaby was a "six-foot Amazon who could really clobber him, it would be pretty silly to think that she couldn't actually fight him. She just didn't wish to because of the trouble that would ensue." By adopting this interpretation, Adams also clearly highlighted a particular attribute—unusual for her sex—of this actor. Such a choice can also suggest that bodies are marked not just by sex but by a multitude of differences, including, for instance, race, class, sexuality, age, and mobility status. The normative becomes increasingly broadened until it almost disappears, presenting "multiple and fluid possibilities of differential embodiment."[32]

In his introduction to *Gender in Performance: The Presentation of Difference in the Performing Arts,* Laurence Senelick writes persuasively about the performative nature of gender:

> Gender *is* performance. As a cultural construct, made up of learned values and beliefs, gender identity (if one can posit such an absolute) has no ontological status. Whatever biological imperatives may order sexual differentiation, whatever linguistic patterns undergird it, it is outward behavior that calibrates the long scale of masculinity and femininity in social relations. Like a Berkeleian universe, gender exists only insofar as it is perceived; and the very components of per-

ceived gender—gate, stance, gesture, comportment, vocal pitch and intonation, costume, accessories, coiffure—indicate the performative nature of the construct. Even when the projection of gender becomes second nature, it can, like any performance, vary in plausibility, verisimilitude and persuasive power. . . . Consequently, gender roles performed by "performers" never merely replicate those in everyday life; they are more sharply defined and more emphatically presented, the inherent iconicity offering both an ideal and a critique.[33]

Certainly *Twelfth Night* offers an ideal opportunity for exposing gender as a cultural construct, especially since Viola must learn how to perform plausibly the gender expected of the opposite sex. Despite their criticism of classical drama, both Dolan and Case praise Simone Benmussa's *The Singular Life of Albert Nobbs,* which presents a storyline almost identical to *Twelfth Night* (a young woman falls in love with her employer, who is in love with another woman, and she decides to disguise herself as a man) precisely for its ability to interrogate gender and, as Case writes, to reveal "how social constructs are inscribed on the body."[34] In the instance of the sword fight, Adams's direction encouraged the audience to see how individuals may break from social constructions of the gender typically attached to their sex.

Gender reproduced without such exposure can work to reinforce a repressive gender polarization. Diamond writes: "When spectators 'see' gender they are seeing (and reproducing) the cultural signs of gender, and by implication, the gender ideology of a culture. . . . To paraphrase Gayle Rubin, women and men are certainly different, but gender forcibly translates the nuanced differences in sexuality into a structure of opposition."[35] The sword fight, or perhaps more accurately, the pre-sword fight, not only resisted the gender-based typical structure of opposition for this scenario but also completely reversed it. These are the kinds of interventions that allow classical texts to be theatrically reappropriated to create new meanings.[36]

DEVELOPING DESIRE

Orsino (Mark Kincaid) was acted broadly, stressing his high opinion of himself and melodramatic tendencies. Probably in his forties, a bit overweight, and only moderately good-looking, he was certainly not an obvious match for the young and beautiful Viola. Yet despite his pompousness, he was friendly, expansive, and affectionate in ways that salvaged his potential appeal.

The first time the audience saw Orsino, he appeared in a towel, having just worked out with "the boys," a bit of stage business inspired partly by Adams's sense of his vanity. He went behind a screen to get dressed and had Cesario bring him his clothes. She ran quickly in behind the screen and just as quickly out, comically abashed. But when she reached the other side of the stage, she went up on tiptoe and tried to see over the screen when he was presumably naked. I asked Adams if she were intentionally trying to stage a reversal of the male gaze. "No," she said with a smile, "I never thought of it in those terms. I just thought that's kind of what a girl would do." She also said it was a way to reveal quickly how intimate Viola wanted to be with Orsino. But I found it interesting that she generally assumes most women will act on their sexual desires in this way, although perhaps her use of the word "girl" conveys her sense that this behavior is primarily characteristic of young women. Still, only Orsino's vanity and Viola's nonthreatening romantic attachment removed the taint of violation potentially present in a woman trying to see a man nude without his knowledge or consent.

While Adams's view in some ways constructs women as "woman," at least it's a radical reconstruction of the typical formula. Eli Simon directed a production at the University of California at Irvine that also contained a bath scene, but when Orsino was in the tub, Viola was "studiously trying to keep her eyes averted."[37] While Simon acknowledged Viola's desire, it was represented in its repression rather than expression. Removing Viola further from sexual subjectivity, Adrian Noble's RSC production placed Viola in a locker room with several naked male bodies "for Viola to wince from."[38] From this description, she seems an uncomfortable adolescent rather than a woman in love. In these instances, the female director portrayed Viola as a young woman whose sexuality was blossoming whereas the male directors portrayed Viola as uncomfortable with sexuality. Trevor Nunn straddled the fence with a similar scene in his film of the play. Orsino called Viola into a shed where he was bathing alone, and although initially reticent, she was eventually sweeping the sponge across his back with pleasure and stopped herself. Adams thought Viola was a virgin, but her lack of sexual experience was not portrayed as an absence of sexuality.

In Orsino and Cesario/Viola's second scene together (2.4), their relationship was staged to show clearly their developing intimacy, which occasionally disturbed Orsino. The hierarchy inherent in their master/servant relationship figured almost imperceptibly in the way they actually related to one another since the duke so clearly favored Cesario, holding "him" in his heart more like an equal than subordinate. When Orsino asked, "But died thy sister of her love, my boy?" (l. 120), he seemed on the verge of returning her affection, the intensity broken this time by Viola with her offer of returning to Olivia. Her position in the household provided her with opportunities for intimacy she would not otherwise have had, her male disguise prompting a close friendship while simultaneously prohibiting openly sexual interaction. She also passionately argued for the strength and constancy of women's love, unlike the image she painted of herself as a woman sitting "like Patience on a monument" (2.4.115). She thereby highlighted, as Casey Charles argues, "the constructedness of both Orsino's and her own depictions of gender paradigms."[39] In her relationship with Orsino, Viola destabilized master/servant and heterosexual norms of relation as well as cultural constructions of gender.

SLIPSLIDING AWAY

Far from the stern woman sometimes depicted, Olivia (Tess Malis Kincaid) was warm, funny, and active right from the start. A surprising element of her characterization was that she smoked, a behavior of which Malvolio clearly disapproved, and she wanted to avoid his censure. She hid her cigarette when he entered unexpectedly. While not wanting to endure Malvolio's criticism, she occasionally engaged in comic self-deprecation. When Cesario left for the first time, she repeated her question to him, "What is your parentage?" (1.5.293), embarrassed and disbelieving that she could have said something so stupid, and wryly self-aware of her ability to become tongue-tied when falling in love. It got an enormous laugh from the audience. Olivia was also compassionate and protective of her household, genuinely upset at Cesario when it was reported that "he" had wounded Andrew and Toby. More than any other character, Olivia adopted different behaviors for different situations and audiences, revealing not just her individuality but her shifting positions in various social formations.

Viola's scenes with Olivia showed in some ways a greater sensitivity and a deeper connectedness between the women than between Viola and Orsino. In their first meeting (1.5), Viola had at one point taken Olivia's hands unconsciously as she spoke intensely. Suddenly she realized what she was doing and grew un-

Olivia (Tess Malis Kincaid) sizing up Cesario (Elizabeth Slaby) in their first encounter in Abby Adams's *Twelfth Night*. Photo: Richard Haggerty.

comfortable, dropping Olivia's hands as if conscious that she could be misrepresenting herself and leading Olivia in the "wrong" direction. Her heterosexuality and compassion were clear when realizing Olivia's attraction after Malvolio brought the ring to her (2.2). During their second meeting (3.1), Viola once put her hand on Olivia's shoulder to comfort her, but when she said she pitied Olivia (l. 124), she also gave the ring back.

After Olivia started to fall for Cesario in their first meeting, she fluctuated between feeling happy and disturbed. At one point, she even watched Cesario's hips. But once she decided to pursue "him," she revealed her passion in various ways. The intermission separated their first two meetings, and the backdrop was lit in light blue and gray, suggesting dawn and awakening. Initially, she was dressed in a rich purple velvet gown with a high-collared light-colored shirt underneath, decorated with a small floral design. She wore her hair in a bun from which a few curly tendrils escaped. At the beginning of their second meeting (3.1), she had opened her heavy velvet gown to reveal a thinner, lavender gown underneath. At one point Olivia chased Viola across the stage and took her shoulders from behind, which Viola gently resisted, clearly sympathetic but ill at ease, again reasserting both her compassion, even affection for Olivia but also the limits her sexual orientation necessarily set.

My responses as an audience member to the characters' genders and sexual orientations shifted in interesting ways that destabilized my own gendered spectatorial position. Michael Shapiro writes that in same-sex wooing scenes, the audience becomes more keenly aware of emotional and sexual intimacy suggested by the lines, and more conscious of bodily action as well.[40] This certainly resonated with my experience. In most of the notes I took during the show for Viola as Cesario, I used the pronoun "he," which was an instinctive rather than critically examined choice based on my perception as an audience member at that moment. I accepted Viola's intended impersonation—her successful performance of the male gender—just as the other characters did. But when the stage business explicitly reasserted Viola's sexual difference and subjectivity, as in this moment, I unconsciously switched the pronoun to "she." My record of this moment in the performance reads: "Olivia takes him by the shoulders from behind—she stiffens." This moment of intimacy and the various tensions it produced created a double awareness of Viola's sex and adopted gender.

But another dynamic may have also been at work. Both of these characters are sympathetic to the audience; they are likable and the experience of unrequited love is common to virtually every audience member. When Olivia actively pursued Cesario, I identified with her and her perception. However, when Viola actively though carefully resisted while Olivia remained still for a moment, hence, in some ways, became passive, I identified with Viola. The active subject drew my identification. The corresponding quicksilver shifting sense of Viola's gender more radically destabilized gender as a marker even more than Viola's cross-dressing and adoption of a male persona for most of the play. Yet at the same time, it reaffirmed the apparently essential quality of Viola's true sex and sexual orientation, at least in terms of how she identified her orientation. Orsino's and Olivia's heterosexual orientation fluctuated into bisexuality while Viola's remained stable. This mix of fluid and firm boundaries and markers in both personal and social realms is most resonant with the collective life experiences of spectators. It offered nearly everyone some point of identification and some challenge to that identification—a serendipitous and in many ways ideal relationship to engender between production and audience.

The subtle threat or discomfort this may have produced for certain audience members who otherwise tend to hold Shakespeare in high regard is suggested by Tony Brown's review for the *Charlotte Observer*—a delicate balancing act. He equated homosexual love with a "disquieting subject," not surprising considering that a production of Tony Kushner's *Angels in America* created an enormous upheaval in this city. He writes, "Adams also roots out the troubling side of Shakespeare's view of mortals in love. Almost all the characters have ulterior motives. Orsino and Olivia's mutual attraction to Viola, disguised as a boy named Cesario, has homoerotic nuances. Madness is referred to repeatedly."[41] Aside from the shaky assumption concerning Shakespeare's view, Brown's disturbance over the play's homosexual overtones that was, nevertheless, overcome by his praise for the production reveals the general conservatism of this region ameliorated by a Shakespeare play well performed. He began his review by describing the production as "hysterical yet introspective," noting that the play offered "a highly complex examination of romantic love." He thereby reaffirmed the artistic mastery, sophistication, and depth of the Bard. Intent on the director's supposedly dark interpretation of a troubling play, he saw Feste as reminiscent of the emcee in *Cabaret,* the "knowing sadness" of his final song signaling that "no happiness is ever pure."[42] By contrast, *Triad Style* reviewer Leslie Mizell viewed Feste as "a constant reminder of the playfulness of the action."[43] Brown refrained from casting judgment on the characters, however, by appealing to the play's subtitle as "more fitting. . . . You are to make of these confused human beings *what you will.*" While registering his discomfort, he ultimately abdicated his cultural authority to Shakespeare.

THE COSTUME OF DESIRE

By the time of Cesario/Viola and Olivia's third meeting (3.4), Olivia was demonstrating the height of her passion through her costume. In anticipation of Cesario's arrival, she removed her outer gown, revealing her shoulders under gold pearl spaghetti straps. She was also wearing sandals, and let down her long, thick, dark brown hair.[44] Reading Olivia's appearance rightly as a further attempt at seduction, Viola was completely stiff, sending an unmistakable message. After this scene Olivia put her outer robe back on but left it open and left her hair down. Her initial defeat was not enough to make her shut down her sexuality again. Her costume suggested a slightly protective openness. In this guise, she met Sebastian (4.1), imagining, of course, that it was Cesario. His greater openness renewed her hope, and she touched his cheek. Responding in precise opposition to Viola, he melted. When he agreed to be ruled by her, her "O" (l. 64) became

Olivia (Tess Malis Kincaid) in a more seductive dress as she attempts to woo Cesario (Elizabeth Slaby) in their third encounter in Abby Adams's *Twelfth Night*. Photo: Jim Koch.

Feste (Michael Kamtman) addresses Olivia (Tess Malis Kincaid) after her marriage to Sebastian in Abby Adams's *Twelfth Night*. Photo: Jim Koch.

an exclamation of pleased surprise. Sebastian (Ted deChatelet) was handsome, earnest, good-humored—critics referred to him as "lively and lusty,"[45] "chivalrous and hot-blooded"[46]—a worthy substitute for his sister. When they met to elope, Olivia initiated the first kiss, going up on her toes to meet his lips. They kissed twice more during this scene, despite the priest clearing his throat. The disapproval of a conservative man with authority no longer inhibited her. Once married, she put her hair up again, but left her outer gown open, signaling a sexuality simultaneously monogamous and active.

BEHIND DOOR NUMBER THREE

The third couple demonstrated a greater ease and intimacy from the very beginning. Maria (Alison Shank) and Toby (Allan Hickle-Edwards), long past the initial courting dance, appeared quite comfortable with each other in their opening scene (1.3). Toby kissed her early on and at another point in the play hugged her around the waist from his knees. In this scene, he was changing clothes, and Maria occasionally helped him. This created an immediate contrast with Viola's mingled eagerness and shyness inspired by the duke's lack of clothes. But this couple was also occasionally prone to conflict. He was drinking from a silver flask, and Maria was reproaching him for his nightly drunken revels because they were likely to get him in trouble. But more pointedly, Maria did not appreciate Toby encouraging Andrew to court her. When she said to Andrew, "I pray you bring your hand to the buttery bar and let it drink" (l. 69), she took his hand and put it on her breast with the air of a saucy barmaid and a reproving look at Toby. The comfort with which she used her sexuality in various ways contrasted sharply to Andrew's discombobulated stuttering. Adams views Andrew as a lonely character utterly baffled when confronted with real sexuality, clueless about how to respond when offered any kind of connection with a woman.

Maria was more comfortable with her sexuality than any other character in the play, but she was never oversexualized. Although Maria came initially to quiet the revels in 2.3, she soon joined in, dropping her shawl to dance with Toby. She was wearing a long, white cotton nightgown. At one point she kissed him, looked at him seductively, and began to undress him. Although usually comfortable with her advances, in this instance, he looked at her quizzically and pulled away. Adams was trying to show that she "got him," began to arouse him when he was not in control. Despite his resistance toward social constraints on his own conduct, as a lord of misrule he paradoxically needed to be in control of his relationship with Maria. Adams and the actors went back and forth concerning how physical their intimacy had become. They ended up thinking that Maria was a virgin, but very close to Toby at the play's beginning, but had probably made love with him by the play's end. As in Koszyn's production, sex was not a rite of passage that changed Maria from girl to woman but merely one more step in the couple's journey toward increased intimacy and marriage. The play presents a number of people of different class and sex pursuing various objects of desire. Adams staged these individual sexual subjectivities and attempted couplings with a multiplicity of valences.

WHOSE HAPPY ENDING? EVERYONE'S

The final scene presents in many ways the most intense passions of the play before resolving them. When Olivia entered (around line 95) and approached Viola, Viola used the duke as protection, crossing behind him with "my lord would speak, my duty hushes me" (l. 105). Nervous that Olivia might express her love and further remove Viola's chances with Orsino, she used her subordinate position as a servant to avoid potentially dire consequences. But when he began to upbraid Olivia a few lines later, she put a hand on his back as if to calm him and end his attack, an action more like an equal than a servant. Her compassion overcame her fear, however. When Olivia moaned, "Ay me detested! How am I beguil'd!" (l. 136), she collapsed to her knees. Viola knelt in front of her on the next line, trying to discern what grieved her. But she withdrew once Olivia called her "husband." Not only was this potentially dangerous in light of Orsino's feelings and position of power, but such an exclamation must have seemed the ravings of an unstable mind beyond Viola's help. If she had any hope of convincing Orsino that she had not betrayed his trust, she necessarily had to perform her true intentions, past and present, by backing away.

But the damage had been done. Orsino had already decided to kill Cesario because he intuited Olivia's love for "him," and wanted both to remove that obstacle and spite Olivia. Such a decision, although made with difficulty—he touched Viola's hair on, "And whom, by Heaven, I swear I tender dearly" (l. 125)—overthrows one's confidence in his ability genuinely to love anyone.[47] He advanced threateningly on Viola, and she retreated. He grabbed her and slung her toward Olivia, changing his resolution from death to banishment. When he moved to exit, Viola ran after him, not smart or perceptive, but constant. Despite this tension, the light on the backdrop was pink near the bottom, reassuring the audience that the potential violence would not be executed and all would end well.

When Sebastian entered and asked Olivia's forgiveness for hurting her kinsman, he knelt, took her hand, and kissed it. Puzzled, Olivia leaned to look at his face. Discovering both Viola and Sebastian, her exclamation, "Most wonderful!" (l. 223), became an expression of delight that two such desirable beings existed. Yet when Sebastian told her that she had been betrothed to a man and maid (l. 261), she laughed uncomfortably, trying to feign politeness but clearly horrified to have been so deceived and not ready to accept consciously and publicly her potential bisexuality—a reaction fitting for this cultural venue. Both responses got huge laughs from the audience.

When the duke apologized to Olivia, they held hands and she kissed his cheek in acceptance of his apology. Orsino initiated the first kiss with Viola, but she leaned up to meet him. The men generally shook hands with one another. At the end of the play, everyone was "family," and everyone was happy. All the gates were open. Adams's unequivocally happy ending resolved tensions perhaps better left in flux.

Melia Bensussen's *Twelfth Night*

The Director's Vision

Bensussen had directed three Shakespeare plays before directing *Twelfth Night,* and she had been enjoying the work.[48] She had just recently finished directing a production of *As You Like It* before accepting OSF's offer to direct *Twelfth Night.* What Bensussen most liked about the play when she first started preparing to direct it was its melancholy. She was also surprised by the sense of urgency in the play, the ambitions and insatiability of its characters: "I felt it was all about people chasing something and then not wanting it when they had it, and I liked that quality about it, that never-satisfied longing."[49] Her sense of the melancholy, then, directly resulted from her view of the love relationships in the play. The characters seem young to her, more infatuated than committed to love, and partly for this reason, the marriages at the end are "dicey."

Bensussen sees the play as thwarting ambitions of social mobility, although this was not a particular focus of this production. She believes most Americans are shocked by a philosophical resistance to upward mobility, but she sees the prohibition against desiring something beyond one's class as "essential in Shakespearean work." For this director, concerns about class are clearly not part of a political phase to be outgrown.

Bensussen also worked out of a more historical sense of gender and sex relations than Adams: "The notions of what a relationship between a man and a woman can be in [the playworld] are not very interesting, whereas the ramifications of a relationship between men is very interesting: it's conversation, it's companionship, it's all these things that you don't hear about men getting from women. What's exciting about men and women is the chase." She sees the greatest satisfaction happening in the perceived same-sex relationships. The play was set in no particular era, but an eclectic range of styles all suggested a time at least one hundred years removed from our own.

Bensussen's ideas about the play are, however, in some significant ways similar to Adams's. She also sees the theme of change. Her program notes quote Claude Lévi-Strauss's argument that people like to arrest moments of delight. The shipwreck changes the static rhythm of the island and sets everything in motion. People chasing what they believe will complete them "becomes the catalyst for change, and forces them to journey from their own selves to a connection with others." Contrary to Adams, she sees "a surprising, unresolved quality to the play." Closely connected to her ideas of change is each character's different sense of time, which is out of sync with that of every other character: "Time seems magical in Illyria only because it expands or contracts to suit one's emotional life." And yet she questions whether our sense of time is any more "real," commenting on the way memory rewrites the past.[50] Bensussen worked with both similarities and disjunctures between the historical conditions of the playworld and our own.

In her view, the women characters are all active and sexual subjects. She shares exactly Adams's sense about the active/passive split: "I don't see what you gain by choosing to see her as passive. In theatrical terms, it doesn't give you anything. . . . So choosing to make any character passive I think would go against what you're trying to do in any production. You're always trying to find what's active, so even though in critical terms it might be absolutely true, it would never cross my mind to want to go that way. You're going to find the active choice in letting time unravel things." For her, Viola's decision to let fate straighten things out is a sign of maturity on her part. She is not delivering her whole life over to fate, but "this insanity of, 'She loves me, I love him, he loves her, this is absurd.'"

Bensussen tries to create particular, idiosyncratic representations of the characters, often taking clues from the actors, which was particularly true for Viola. Although Bensussen is aware of how the historical playing and social conditions in Elizabethan England contributed to homosexual and bisexual energies in performance, she did not pursue those in this production, partly because they were not her focus, and also because Bensussen thought that Robin Nordli, who played Viola, was "very 'golly gee whiskers. . . . I'm a straight girl from the country, gosh darnit.'" They explored Viola's desire to play the boy's part well

Viola (Robin Goodrin Nordli) working on her role as Cesario, the duke's manly servant come to woo Olivia in Melia Bensussen's *Twelfth Night*. Photo: David Cooper.

along with her difficulty in achieving a competent performance. She began with a feeling of, "'I'm just trying to *do* this, and I don't know how to do this part.'" She was not androgynous, and although she was able to express traditionally male traits well by the end of the play, "the nature of the actress was to always feel more female than not. I think that's a very specific actor state."

Bensussen realizes the different levels of comfort different individuals have with performing the gender assigned to their sex or the opposite sex and worked with Nordli's own proclivities in this area. But Nordli's "actor state" regarding gender performance did not significantly deviate from Bensussen's view of the play. While the loss of Viola's brother frees her to explore being male, which empowers her, she also feels bereft. But "tough and spunky," she is able to make her way in the world and, with experience, gain competency if not complete comfort in performing a different gender.

Bensussen sees the difficulty of the match between Viola and Orsino, but the mismatch is not based on their particular traits or Orsino's inferiority as a mate. It is based on the historical limitations that gender and sex relation codes put on male/female relationships. She conceived of Orsino as almost homophobic, so his discovery of his attraction for a young boy was necessarily upsetting. Yet because the relationship was so intense when he believed Cesario was male, his discovery that the boy was a woman was actually disappointing in the end.

Bensussen also recognizes the darkness of Toby.[51] She thinks Maria genuinely loves Toby while knowing his faults, but Bensussen does not see this as problematic. While she does not see this as a virtue, she sees it as particularly "human": "You know, we do love awful people sometimes, right? We all do that." Maria was also significantly older, closer to Toby's age, than Adams's youthful Maria. She was not upper class, so marrying him would be marrying up, although that was not her primary motivation.

Bensussen wished she could have been more prepared for directing this production. Although unfamiliar with feminist performance criticism at the time of the interview, Bensussen had recently been reading art criticism concerning objectification and believed it was a lack on her part not to be more conversant with feminist theory. She had also reviewed some literary criticism and stage history for the play, "terrified," she said somewhat hyperbolically, by the weight of creating an original production when it had been done so many times before. She had read interviews with RSC directors who had directed the play, and she had seen two productions, although the most recent one at the Delacorte Theater in Central Park with Michelle Pfeiffer and Jeff Goldblum was so "hideous" she left at intermission. She thinks that in directing Shakespeare plays, the first attempt is not going to be particularly good. It has to be gotten out of the way before a director can start to do her best work, and despite many lovely things she achieved, her own dissatisfaction with the outcome is foremost for her. She would love to direct *Twelfth Night* again. Early in the interview she said, "I feel like I was another person doing that show, and I would do it so differently now." One of the things she would change is to make the restoration of order in the last act disastrous for everyone. She believes that the fifth act of the comedies can be trite and not particularly meaningful to a modern audience. She worked on deconstructing gender in the production as a way of making the play more relevant, although wishes she had pursued this further as well. Clearly, her goal is to comment on, and not just embody, the play.

The Play in Production

ILLYRIA AS A TROPICAL CARNIVAL

When the production in the large Bowmer Theatre started, which housed a proscenium stage with a large forestage, the lighting reproduced a night storm: a blackout punctuated by flashes of lightning. Projections pictured a ship on a stormy sea. The set was covered with a large blue expanse of fabric. As the storm subsided, it was flown out. Gradually, a warm light came up on Orsino's court.[52] The set design was inspired by contemporary Cuban painter Lydia Rubio, who uses an eclectic mixture of visual elements. The result was a colorful, partially abstract design suggesting life on a tropical island.[53] Orsino's court was built with a small pavilion stage right, a kind of stage onstage bordered by tall columns and raised by two steps that curved around its front. Two ropes stretched from inside the roof of the pavilion to the tall pillar stage left, and off one of them hung a series of pennantlike fabric ornaments, which suggested a carnival. The height and space indicated Orsino's wealth. A live trio of oboe, viola, and bass played. The sky began to lighten as if it were dawn, revealing ferns and palm trees in the background.

The set was on a revolve, and when the scene changed, doors at the back of the stage would open so the revolve could be reversed. Sometimes people would look at one another as they were being moved on or off stage, which heightened the sense of time moving people forward as well as people pursuing others usually beyond their grasp. During these changes, the backdrop revealed not only sky and trees. People could also be seen walking behind the revolve—other inhabitants of Illyria—so there was always a sense of the world beyond the more prominently staged action, a silent but surprising supplement to the playwright's work. It challenged realistic staging conventions, which tend to hide everything beyond the story of the play.

Two sets of curved stairs, one stage right and one stage left, led down to another central platform and also allowed the actors to enter and exit through the audience. Olivia's house indicated wealth as well. A large structure with three or four openings and a hallway behind it suggested a cloister. Two tall, thin, highly manicured evergreens were stage right. Both sets had a bench close to center stage, although Orsino's was completely rectangular and Olivia's had legs shaped like swans. A couple of cut off columns also served as seating areas.

ACTOR AND AUDIENCE

Bensussen used direct address to break the fourth wall and also used the live musicians as a way of revealing the constructedness of the theatrical apparatus. The musicians interacted with the audience, and the actors visibly cued them at various points. They had been playing, for instance, during the scene when Malvolio (Paul Vincent O'Connor) returned the ring to Cesario. The music underscored Malvolio's pursuit of Cesario and stopped in the middle of the scene. As Malvolio started to exit, the musicians started up again, and both Malvolio and Cesario turned to look at them as if to say, "What are you playing for?" The musicians stopped. Bensussen frequently uses musicians in this way and believes Shakespeare in particular is written constantly to acknowledge spectators in the theater. Bensussen likes the nakedness of theater, which prompts spectators to use their imaginations. She's most interested in creating theater that encourages a dialogue with the audience. But with Shakespeare especially, it's part of how she deals with the politics of the play. A play that suggests only royalty can marry royalty is not as harmful if she constantly reminds the spectators that it's only a play. In a further twist, for this particular production two of the musicians were women dressed as boys. Somewhere between technical staff and actor, the musicians were thereby characterized in ways that connected them to the play's action. It disrupted the audience's typical positions of exchange with accompanists.

REVEALING CONVENTIONS

Bensussen also used the first wooing scene between Viola and Olivia to accentuate the theatrical apparatus. Viola came with flowers and musicians, and the musicians played to underscore the text she had practiced. Clearly they had rehearsed their performance with Viola. But when she stopped to find out if she were really delivering it to the right audience, the musicians stopped also. When she saw that her set speech would not be successful, she sent the musicians away. Such interactions denaturalized the emotional support to staged action that music conventionally covertly gives. The process of rehearsal was clearly evident in the product of performance.

The sword fight provided some of the best humor because the characters played with sword fighting conventions in order to avoid fighting. Neither of them really knew what they were doing, but Viola imitated whatever Andrew did. It began quite slowly but gradually picked up speed and became almost a dance. At one point Andrew (Mark Murphy) came out of the fighting area and locked arms with Feste (Clayton Corzatte), taking him into a square dance-type turn before moving back into position with Viola. Andrew and Viola enjoyed exaggerating the moves,

Viola as Cesario (Robin Goodrin Nordli) and Sir Andrew (Mark Murphy) try to figure out how to perform a sword fight without getting hurt in Melia Bensussen's *Twelfth Night*. Photo: David Cooper.

knowing they were not really hurting each other. At another point, Andrew made a swipe at the ground and Viola stood still, looking blank. He pointed at her feet as if to say, "You're supposed to jump." Her expression changed, indicating, "Oh, okay, I get it." He made a swipe again, and this time she jumped appropriately. When Andrew fell, she bent down to give him his sword because she was upset, and he thanked her before they remembered they were supposed to be fighting. Eager to prove their earnestness to their companions, Andrew held his sword over his head, and Viola took the bait, locked her own against his. They circled one another, screaming in mock fury while periodically looking over their shoulders at Toby (Dennis Robertson) and Feste as if to say, "See, I'm really doing it." For Bensussen, playing with convention was a way for them to have fun and create a completely safe space to protect them from doing what neither of them wanted to do. By revealing the harmlessness of fight choreography, Bensussen disrupted the typical equation between manliness, strength, prowess, and sword fighting. Such revelations prompt questions concerning other supposedly exclusive male rituals and values. The staging also reminded the audience they were in the theater seeing a play produced with a nonillusory aesthetic.

Reviewers differed in their ability to read the ideology of this work. Unlike most productions around the country, OSF typically draws Shakespeare scholars who write reviews for academic audiences. Robert Hurwitt of the *San Francisco Examiner* criticized the sword fight as going "well beyond the logic of her comic premise." In an attempt to get a cheap laugh, the "mock duel" turned into "a pointless dance."[54] By contrast, veteran OSF reviewer Alan Armstrong discussed the sword fight in the context of the secondary characters' "comic vitality": "[Andrew's] well choreographed comic duel with Cesario is predicated this time on their simultaneous discovery of the stylized art of stage combat, in which they engage at first with desperate relief, then with growing theatrical enthusiasm."[55] In this instance, the more highly educated critic knew how to appreciate Bensussen's playful and theatrical approach to the production. Judging from the laughter I heard on the video, many other members of the audience also enjoyed the sword fight but may not have recognized its citation and disruption of theatrical convention.

Another instance of questioning both social and theatrical conventions occurred in the night revel scene. Malvolio's pink curlers under his night cap revealed once again the rehearsal inherent in performance—hair does not shape itself like a curler without various products applied in private. But it could also remind the audience of the odd cultural conditioning that prompts us to admire beauty yet ridicule those who work at it, who try to mold their natural form into culturally and historically specific models for beauty. Having Malvolio enter with curlers also deconstructed the female gender as the only one that works at its appearance, partially by juxtaposing our current history with an earlier one in which men worked almost as hard. Malvolio's hair probably took more labor to achieve its performance than that of any other character.

"WHY CAN'T A WOMAN BE MORE LIKE A MAN?"

As in Adams's production, Viola first appeared in a beautiful dress that made her look like a princess. Her long skirt even had sparkles on it, and her ways of speaking and gesturing were very feminine and upper class. As Cesario, her long-sleeved white shirt still billowed around her arms. She wore a finely plaid vest with gold buttons, a silk cravat, and knee-high boots to match her tan suit. Her wavy blond hair was pulled back into a ponytail. She was quite awkward at first, and when someone else in Orsino's court reached for his sword, she jumped and let out a faint, startled cry. Her initial attempt at imitating masculine movement was a swaggering caricature. Later, the audience saw that some of her gestures and ways of speaking were actually imitations of Sebastian's. During Sebastian's monologue, he imitated some of Viola's more feminine gestures and intonations.[56] Gender became a field of experiences allowing for similarities and differences between male and female genders but devoid of rigid oppositions. Such staging also destabilized the supposedly natural and absolute connection between sex and gender, revealing gender's mobility and performativity.

Although Viola gradually became more confident and convincing in playing a boy, under stress she always collapsed her body inward, unable to maintain a polished façade. These moments occurred primarily when other characters responded to her as a man rather than a person. The audience was reminded in these moments of her female sex and her particular personality that had difficulty adapting to playing a man. Discarding or adopting gender markers comes more easily to some than to others. In some ways, the no-man's-land (or perhaps here, more accurately "no-gender's-land") between genders erupted when a threat broke her performance of Cesario but did not allow her to return to her accustomed feminine performance of Viola. The production suggested that gender may be unstable, but it is virtually impossible to live without. In those moments she was unable to commit to a performance of either gender. Her ventures into foreign territory proved freeing and exciting but also potentially dangerous, largely because she was not who she pretended to be and could not fulfill the expectations of others. Her female gender had restricted as well as protected her from certain kinds of threats.

B(E)ARING HER BODY

Bensussen has the sense that Viola is always trying to protect the huge secret that is her body. She cannot let anyone touch her, and yet other characters feel comfortable with her, and so they keep initiating touch, which she then has to deflect. Although unable to find the right place in the performance, Bensussen had an idea of a moment where all the men would take off their shirts and Viola had to find a way to get out of it, like an undercover agent. She sees Viola as the outsider passing in a male community. Sebastian (Raymond L. Chapman) and Viola did look alike, but Feste was aware of their difference. He had initially discovered the secret of her body when he playfully grabbed the outside of her upper thigh in 3.1. She shrank from him.[57] The moment reasserted Viola's female body and the differences in various sex relation codes. Feste's discovery saddened Viola, because she had been close with him before and now felt she had to avoid his questions and knowledge. When Feste ran into Sebastian in 4.1, he adopted an aggressive stance. Sebastian matched it, which suggested to Feste that perhaps this was not Cesario. Bensussen's actual and imagined staging highlighted (or would highlight) both the essential nature of male and female bodies and cultural constructions concerning how they are performed.[58]

IDEALIZATION AND LIMITATION

Orsino was infatuated with an idealized love. In the opening scene, he had his back to the audience because he was painting a portrait of Olivia in the pavilion. Concurring with a common interpretation, Bensussen believes his feelings had nothing to do with Olivia. He was in love with a portrait, and he needed to have an idealized other because he was lonely and incomplete. His unreasonable testiness about women not loving as deeply as he (2.4) drew a laugh from the audience because of his comical arrogance. Bensussen thinks that in some ways, Viola may be drawn to him because she has lost her twin and feels incomplete herself, looking for her other half. And yet she also thinks Viola feels conflicted about being in love because "it's such a dopey state to be in and she's an eminently practical person." In her production, Viola could not deny her growing desire.

However, as opposed to the active, passionate nature of the "patient as a monument" speech in Adams's production, in Bensussen's it was very melancholy—more in tune with her production concept. Similar to Adams's production, 2.4 was the scene of greatest intimacy between Orsino and Cesario/Viola, and the moment where Orsino was closest to acknowledging his affection was at the line, "But died thy sister of her love, my boy?" Almost unable to bear hiding her love, aroused by his nearness and concern, Viola stepped back with her question, "Sir, shall I to this lady?" But when he handed her the jewel, she had to "tell" him. She took his hand and made love to it, kissed it with all the passion her words concealed. This could have eroticized her subordinate position but did not because of Orsino's response. Disturbed, he withdrew his hand, resisting his homoerotic feelings, however, rather than a hierarchical love relationship. Unfortunately, the violence with which he executed this move in performance suggested disgust and rejection when Bensussen wanted to convey discomfort. The actor playing Orsino was quite ill. Bensussen tried to accommodate his needs, but he died before the end of the run. Partially as a result of his critical condition, he developed an antagonistic relationship with both Bensussen and Nordli. Bensussen knows the weakest part of the production was Orsino and Viola's relationship because in the end, she had little control over it.[59]

THE VIRGIN QUEEN

Olivia was portrayed as a young woman coming of age. She was clearly in mourning at the beginning of the play, melancholy and dressed in black silks and satins with her hair up. Aware that Olivia has often been played by an older actor, Bensussen nevertheless sees her as very girlish. Like a number of other critics, she thinks the mourning is a little self-indulgent. She was also influenced by some reading she was doing that suggested Olivia was an analogue for Queen Elizabeth, or an earlier version of Queen

Elizabeth, a young virgin queen not taken seriously as a ruler at first because she is a young woman. Bensussen sees Olivia as a young woman with power and not quite sure how to handle it. Although probably doing a better job than people give her credit for, she is not investing herself in running the house the way she should, and her kingdom is not truly under her control. The trick against Malvolio occurs partially because of this. Bensussen also sees that Olivia and Orsino are very much alike, their class dictating their identities as "indignant autocrats" much more than their gender.[60]

COMING INTO HER OWN

The relationship between Viola and Olivia is Bensussen's favorite. In her mind, Olivia's attraction to Viola is not the result of bisexuality but of a young heterosexual virgin initially attracted to a safe sexual interest. Bensussen thinks that some virgins conceive of sexual experience as dark and potentially frightening, so creating intimacy without the genuine possibility of sex is an appealing way to begin the journey. For Viola the relationship is always sisterly. When Malvolio returned the ring to her and she realized Olivia's attraction because she had convincingly emulated a young man, she laughed, pleased with herself at her successful role-playing. But it is precisely the various kinds of role-playing in which Viola and Olivia engage that allows for an unusual release of emotion. The prompt book reminds the actors in 1.5, "Watch anything that shuts down scene. Everything needs to open scene—wide range of emotions."[61] Although initially reticent, sparring with Cesario, Olivia started to open up and flirt with him. Similarly to Adams's production, Viola found herself holding Olivia's hands, unconsciously impelled by her earnestness during the "willow cabin" speech as they were sitting together on the bench. But the prompt book notes that Viola releases Olivia's hands and moves away as she remembers that Cesario's class is beneath Olivia's, making their intimacy inappropriate.[62]

The social consciousness motivating Viola's movement may not have been evident to the audience. However, such a motivation also opens up an interesting dynamic between self and role. Viola had in one sense so fully invested in her mission that she adopted a lover's words and actions. She was no longer displacing Viola for a representation of Cesario. She was displacing Cesario for a representation of Orsino. But she was representing

Orsino not through merely conveying the substance of his sentiments, as his servant and messenger might, but through almost becoming Orsino, or at least performing Orsino's feelings as only Viola knew how. It is partially the passionate embodiment of the message rather than merely its delivery that makes Viola a rival to her master rather than a retainer in her master's service. For

Olivia (Bonnie Akimoto) woos an understanding but reluctant Cesario (Robin Goodrin Nordli) in Melia Bensussen's *Twelfth Night*. Photo: David Cooper.

the purpose of moving Olivia's affections, she is a better Orsino than Orsino. Whereas Orsino uses conventional expressions of courtly love devoid of any individuality because he loves the image of Olivia rather than the woman, Viola is unintentionally successful because her own love, knowledge of women, and present experience with Olivia lead her to create a far more effective text and performance than Orsino ever could. The change it effected in Olivia was stunning. At "You might do much" (1.5.280), she paused between each word and brushed a tear from her cheek, almost trembling. For Viola, the role of lover allowed her to release some of her own romantic feelings. In a sense she became herself by being someone else. But both her own passion freely expressed and her assumption and transformation of Orsino's passion removed her too far from her role as Cesario, which she needed to protect herself. Olivia, too, backed away from her earlier vulnerability, feeling the need to protect herself as well, but by the end of her monologue (ll. 294–304), she had opened up again, and a flash of lightning signaled the tumultuous changes ahead. The emotions that each released in her performance were broader in scope than an actual encounter between Viola and Olivia would inspire. The play in general and this scene in particular invites considerations of the relationship between self and role in both personal and social spheres. Bensussen's staging of having Viola move away when Olivia asks "What is your parentage?" (1.5.281), a question reminding Viola of her actual and adopted histories as well as her present social status and passion, served to highlight some of these issues for the spectators. Viola's own awareness at that moment of the ways in which her hidden personal aims and the various roles she played could produce results in her onstage audience that were at cross purposes may have prompted a similar awareness in the offstage audience.

POWER AND DESIRE

By their second meeting, Olivia had become increasingly seductive and open. Her desire for Cesario led her to be much more aggressive. At the conclusion of the scene, they were facing each other across the bench, and Olivia had Cesario's hands in hers. During "his" last speech, Olivia grabbed Cesario's shoulders, and at its conclusion, she kissed "his" mouth for a long moment.[63] Viola had been trying to stop Olivia's pursuit of her and to escape this moment of entrapment but did not succeed. She backed away, stunned. She collapsed, her physicality reflecting her earlier more awkward bearing. Rather oblivious to Viola's reaction, Olivia was thrilled because, in Bensussen's words, she had "take[n] charge. And Olivia can't believe she's *done* this. So she's delighted that she *did* this. She made a pass. It was delicious to her."

The two academic critics differed in their view of the relationship between Viola and Olivia. While Armstrong recognized that Viola's feelings for Olivia were sisterly, Felicia Hardison Londré, whose article focuses on various constructions of gender in the production, saw Viola discovering her bisexuality in her encounters with Olivia: "Viola-Cesario was terribly conflicted throughout [3.1], but mustered her resolve to leave and clasped Olivia's shoulders mannishly on 'Adieu, good madame.' Olivia in turn grasped Viola and kissed her on the lips, an arresting image to end the act."[64] She also viewed Viola's response to Feste's prod as an instinctive reaction to sexual harassment, but according to Bensussen, that was not the issue. It seems that once Londré correctly perceived a feminist viewpoint in the director, she saw it in places, as I initially did, that Bensussen did not consciously stage it. But such is the ability of a well-executed and thoughtful production to prod its audience in unexpected ways.

The next time Olivia appeared, she had shed her mourning dress for something long, flowing, and sexy and let down her long, dark, curly hair. In preparation for their third meeting, she exchanged the bench with a chaise lounge. At this point in the production, the back doors remained open after the set change, suggesting her greater openness to the world. For their final meeting, the prompt book reads, "Regardless of Cesario's response, Olivia will not give up. Has response for any way Cesario responds."[65] She was less sensitive and more determined than Adams's Olivia, but still never oversexualized.

Falling in love and taking charge empowered Olivia. When she came in to stop the fighting between Sebastian and Toby in 4.1, her strength and commanding authority were startling and impressive. Her growth was instrumental in transforming an infatuation into a love capable of sustaining a marriage. Sebastian's strength, confidence, and good looks made him an exciting match for Olivia. Bensussen worked hard on building to the excitement of Sebastian's acceptance of Olivia and her delight at her success after long experience with rejection. The prompt book notes that for Olivia, her response to his willingness to be ruled by her ("O, say so, and so be!" [l. 70]) is a leap of faith.[66] Love was building her maturity and courage.

TWO OLD DOGS

Maria (Eileen DeSandre) and Toby had a relationship different from all the others. They were, in Bensussen's words, like two old dogs, having spent considerable time together and become quite comfortable with one another. Interestingly enough, Toby was getting dressed in this scene, as he was in Adams's, although only missing coat and boots. In Bensussen's view, Maria is the only real adult in the play. She is not looking for an ideal love. Practical and ready to marry, she wants to settle down with Toby. However, she knows she doesn't have him yet and is always trying to win him over.

The triad scene with Andrew was quite different from Adams's. The buttery bar line was seductive, and Maria put her hands on her hips, presenting her breasts to him. It was Toby who took Andrew's hand and put it on Maria's breast, proceeding to jiggle it. The original staging had her put her hand over Toby's. In the video of the performance I saw, Toby dropped his hand, and Maria stroked Andrew's before moving it away and releasing it. Bensussen saw Toby's use of "his woman's breast" in this way as dark and coarse. According to Bensussen, Maria enjoyed humiliating Andrew a little, but she was primarily doing it for Toby.

As in Adams's production, the night revel scene (2.3) included dancing between Toby and Maria, although Toby's affection more clearly softened Maria's initial sternness. She did, however, try to quiet them again before Malvolio came in. Malvolio inspired more open ridicule than fear. The seriousness of his threat was in some degree neutralized by the pink curlers under his night cap.

WHOSE HAPPY ENDING? TOO TENTATIVE TO TELL

For the final scene, all the back doors in the set were open, and the revolve was stopped between set changes, a spiral staircase centerstage. The "Whom I swear I tendered dearly" line was warm here as in Adams's production, but Orsino merely started to move toward Cesario and then caught himself rather than actually touching "him." Viola was intent on following Orsino, and Bensussen recognizes that as very specific to Nordli, that her Viola just kept trying. Orsino got more violent after hearing the priest's confirmation that Cesario was Olivia's husband, circling "him." But when he started to exit, she physically restrained him.

Viola as Cesario (Robin Goodrin Nordli) chases after the enraged duke (LeWan Alexander) as a troubled Olivia (Bonnie Akimoto) looks on in the final scene of Melia Bensussen's *Twelfth Night*. Photo: David Cooper.

Sebastian bounded onto the stage at his entrance and knelt at Olivia's feet. Olivia's recognition on "Most wonderful!" that two such lovely beings existed followed exactly the same impulse as Adams's production. In contrast to Kincaid's Olivia, she did not seem disturbed by her apparent bisexual attraction. But she was somewhat disturbed by Malvolio's suffering. She recognized her responsibility in the trick. And Toby was quite cruel to Andrew when he abandoned him with his own exit. Sebastian's entrance temporarily rescued a tense, uncomfortable group of characters.

When the confusion was resolved, Viola knelt behind Orsino, and he turned to raise her. When he proposed, he knelt to her, but Bensussen did not create this staging to signal mutuality but merely his performance of a courtly ritual as a gentleman. She does not see any real warmth on his part toward Viola at the end, so his final lines were spoken facing not her but the audience. She thought he loved her, but their relationship was tied to gender, and without it, in a traditional marriage, they would not be able to have the kind of relationship they had when Viola was dressed as a man. They would lose their equality and intimacy. Although not able to achieve it in this production, she believes the last scene could be genuinely heartbreaking.

At the conclusion, Olivia cued the musicians, and they began a dance. Bensussen had the couples come through the arches side by side without holding hands because she wanted to communicate that they were strangers. The second time, Orsino ended up holding hands with Sebastian, which upset the men more than the women. The third and final time they came through the arches, the couples were matched according to marriage and holding hands, but a thunderclap suggested a storm. No one could be sure what the future would bring.

Differing expectations among the audience probably accounted for different perceptions of Viola and Orsino's final union. While Armstrong noted a tentativeness between them, *Ashland Daily Tidings* reviewer Robert Miller was completely oblivious to this tension, seeing Orsino as "only too happy" to accept Viola for his wife. Miller probably assumes that all comedies should end happily in marriage.[67] But what Armstrong had no way of knowing was that the tension between *the actors* was more responsible for the tentativeness than Bensussen's direction, offstage difficulties coloring onstage interaction.

Armstrong was, in fact, most critical of the production for Bensussen's treatment of the play as "an essentially unproblematic romance." He derived his opinion partly from the set design, which he characterized as "reminiscent of a child's pop-up book," but also in the casting and directing of Malvolio as someone without credible authority or threat.[68] A number of other critics also noted the generally cheerful tone, but no one else faulted it on this ground.[69] Typically, elements largely outside Bensussen's control were attributed to her purpose. Only Londré sensed an undercurrent of melancholy throughout the production.[70]

Audience reaction to the couple's mismatch in the final dance reveals another tension between audience expectations based on past experiences and the director's attempt to communicate something against the grain. When Sebastian and Orsino ended up holding hands, upset by this mistake, the audience viewed their reactions as comic and laughed. Bensussen directed them to be disturbed by what had happened. However, the long tradition of comic homosexual intonations in theatrical representation, particularly in comedy, encourages the audience to laugh at such blunders rather than to consider their potentially disturbing resonances for the characters. Their previous readings of similar situations led them to interpret this interaction as they had in the past, glossing over a potentially different innuendo.

Resistance to a happy ending was also prominently featured in Karin Coonrod's production for the Court Theatre of Chicago. Rearranging the text, she staged the characters freezing in the middle of their exit during Feste's closing song, "smiles faltering from their faces." The actor playing Feste started to remove his makeup while sitting on the edge of the stage and throwing his paper money into the air. At this point, a crash of thunder signaled Malvolio's return to threaten vengeance, and his tirade closed the performance with an "ominous and unhappy note."[71]

In addition to drawing attention to the theatrical apparatus by having an actor reveal his typical postshow behavior, Coonrod furthered the theatricality of her production in a number of ways. Characters directly addressed the audience and used the auditorium aisles for entrances and exits. A shadow-puppet pantomime portrayed the opening shipwreck. She quoted earlier historical eras with Orsino's imitation of Elvis Presley and London 1960s costumes for his courtiers. She drained the appearance of life out of her modern-day Illyrians by having them made up in white face. By contrast Viola looked "full-blooded" (though sported a pencil mustache as Cesario), and Feste, rather critical of his culture, was made up half white-faced and half normal. Chatting with the audience before the show and hustling them back into their seats after a brief interlude in the first half of the show, he also knocked elements of the set askew. The rather artificial environment included rows of three-dimensional paintings of bushes, which encircled the seating area, thereby including the audience within the world of the play. Feste made sure all of them were cockeyed.[72] By positioning Feste between character, actor, disruptive audience member, and overly forward house manager, Coonrod, too, upset stable positions for theatrical exchange. A metatheatrical, postmodernist approach is characteristic of her work.[73]

Either the reviewer, Justin Shaltz, was not particularly attuned to problems in the couple's liaisons, or they were not highlighted in the production. Toby was portrayed as a heavy drinker and Maria was "sassy and sexy." Orsino is described as having an "extravagant angst" that has grown tiresome within his court. Viola was a "refreshing presence" who was, nevertheless, clearly uncomfortable in her role: "Slouching and shuffling, frequently stuffing her hands into her hip pockets, she passes for an Illyrian until she breaks into desperate asides." Role playing, or at least taking on the opposite gender, was apparently alien to her. Sebastian and Olivia's union became a source of humor because the pair "not only kiss but grope and grapple with each other like salacious teenagers, clumsily moaning and cooing their way offstage, through the audience, and out of the theatre."[74] Olivia and Maria seem to have been given a sexual subjectivity, and if Olivia's was somewhat comical and oversexualized, at least so was Sebastian's. The disturbance at the end, however, comes more from Malvolio's threat than from potential problems in the marriages, though clearly seeds were sown to suggest less than perfectly happy alliances.

More than any other director in this study, during the interview Bensussen became the characters she described. She acted out their responses, and at one moment cast me as Orsino to her Viola when Viola kisses Orsino's hand. Developing intellectually in her ideas about performance, she nevertheless instinctively embodied the answers to my questions. When I questioned her about Londré's interpretation of Viola as bisexual, she registered the difference between directorial intention and critical interpretation in a humorous and self-deprecating response acknowledging the typical divide particularly between academic reviewers and directors: "And the way we set up the kiss was that she gets trapped. It was very clear I thought, but what do I know. I mean, there's critics, and they know things, and us poor schmoes, we just keep putting up plays, and then other people can tell us how we suck. But we worked very consciously at the entrapment of it." A relatively young director (just past forty) Bensussen will continue to develop as a feminist director through both study and practice. And now that she's teaching, she can pass on her insights to a new generation of women directors.

Adams's growth is not likely to follow a consciously feminist path. But as artistic director of a thriving company, whose programs reach thousands every year, her awareness of women's issues will find its way into her choices in more subtle ways. She has recently directed Beth Henley's *Abundance* and Charlotte Keatley's episodic *My Mother Said I Never Should,* played by four women actors who tell the story of four generations of English women spanning from World War II until 1985. Although the latter is not a well-known play, Adams said, "I know it had a remarkable effect on our audience. And the kind of resonance it had with women in particular was huge." She will continue to cocreate with her actors individual, active women characters who are sexual subjects. She will continue to support the work of women playwrights and find as much space for women actors as possible. She will continue to explore same-sex and opposite-sex relationships in ways that do not always follow the assumed trajectory toward heterosexual marriages. Despite her disinterest in politicizing meaning, such choices have political resonances. Such choices offer alternatives to male-centered power structures and traditionally masculine ways of seeing.

4
Once Upon a Time: Barbara Gaines and JoAnne Akalaitis Direct *Cymbeline*

W<small>RITTEN LATE IN HIS CAREER,</small> *C<small>YMBELINE</small>* <small>IS ONE OF</small> S<small>HAKESPEARE'S</small> most heterogeneous plays. Roger Warren describes the play as a "combination of myth and pseudo-history."[1] No fewer than twenty-four threads of action are explained or resolved in the final scene. Containing a number of improbable events, including the appearance of Jupiter, this drama reaches beyond the bounds of anything remotely resembling realism. Although the play has received scant literary analysis and has not been produced often, it has recently garnered more attention. Adrian Noble believes that the play is "consonant with the mood of the last years of the century because [it is] about change and the journey of the spirit."[2]

Because *Cymbeline* is a romance, a genre that focuses on familial rather than erotic relationships, the play allows the heroine Imogen an even less active role than Viola, despite its cross-dressing episode. She shares with Juliet a secret marriage against her father's wishes, but the courtship and marriage happen before the play's action begins, and the couple spends most of the play apart, so we have little chance to see them interact. Her sexuality is presented ambiguously, for although she clearly loves her husband, Posthumus reports that she often resisted his sexual advances, even though they were his "lawful pleasure" (2.4.161). Like Angelo, he is enticed by her "pudency so rosy" (2.4.163), but while the plot hinges to some degree on her fidelity, her excessive modesty has no other consequence. The broad sweep of the romance also focuses less attention on individual characters, which tend to become more stereotypical. Because contemporary audiences usually expect characters to represent people, a director must either disrupt this equation with a clearly unrealistic approach to production, which could include playing up the stereotype *as* stereotype, or create a strongly individualized heroine if she wants to resist a conventional and oversimplified construction of "woman."

Noting the difficulty erotic relationships face in *Cymbeline,* David Bergeron argues that sexuality in the entire play is misdirected and thwarted until the very end.[3] Female subjectivity and how it functions erotically with men in this play is particularly problematic for a feminist director. Although Imogen begins spiritedly, she gradually wanes throughout the play,[4] and she becomes a victim of violence and abuse by Iachimo's psychic rape and Posthumus's striking her so hard Pisanio thinks he's killed her.[5] Upon discovering Posthumus's false accusation and order to assassinate her, she becomes a martyr who pleads for death.[6] The feminist director is faced with a choice of accentuating her passivity and criticizing the forces constricting her as well as revealing her own personal collapse, or creating visual imagery through energetic movement and delivery to counteract her weakness. She may choose the latter simply as a way to make the production more dramatic and appealing for the audience, but Imogen's slip from active subjectivity toward a more stereotypically passive existence presents a challenge unlike the other women characters studied in this project. While a feminist performance need not always present strong women, to present the heroine as weak and passive tends to reinforce essentialist notions that good women are passive and weak if none of the men are presented that way and if her choices are not seen within the context of cultural conditions—especially when the one other female character falls into the evil witch/stepmother stereotype.

Posthumus, too, is a seriously tarnished hero, initially, whose flaws may be glossed over. In some ways he resembles both Iachimo, by succumbing to the villain's mercantile objectification of women, and Cloten, by his threat to murder and dismember his wife.[7] As a number of scholars have pointed out, to his credit, he is the only Shakespearean hero who forgives his wife *before* learning of his error and her actual fidelity. Even in the final scene, however, his enormous self-absorption, resulting in an attack on the "page" for interrupting his theatricals,[8] and his passive adoration of Imogen[9] suggests that their marriage may not be perfectly happy. His character complicates his relationship with Imogen and the audience's perception of Imogen for remaining loyal to him. In fact, George Bernard Shaw wrote a play entitled *Cymbeline Refinished* in which Imogen does not stay with Posthumus at the end.

When *Cymbeline* is produced, these issues are frequently suppressed. Neither Posthumus nor Imogen is often depicted as problematic.[10] Particularly mainstream theater has a tendency to further idealize protagonists into characters the audience can identify with, a phenomenon supported by actors who, typically, want to be liked onstage. Although one review by a woman in an academic journal describes Imogen as occasionally passive, most describe her as strong and passionate, one even calling her a "modern woman."[11] In terms of her sexuality, once again when the text describes a woman who unequivocally repels a lustful suitor, on stage Imogen is sometimes tempted by Iachimo.[12] The sexualizing tendency of live performance operates here as in *Measure for Measure*. Imogen and Isabella are different characters who have made different sexual choices, but their choices have removed them from the sexual economy of exchange between men.[13] Is it simply more exciting to double the site of conflict so that it builds not just between characters but also within a character? Kott certainly thinks so: "And if we think of Isabella as someone trying to deal with a ferocious repression—a woman who goes to the cloister because she cannot deal with her overwhelming sexual desires—that too makes the character, for us, more exciting."[14] A psychoanalytic interpretation uninformed by feminism might see this as merely Freudian baggage, a projection of the spectators' fundamental sexual drives onto the character as a means of identification. Such projection is especially intense if a character confronts a forbidden object of desire. But although the text suggests that only the man is divided in his attitude toward the forbidden woman, the stage productions sometimes open a rift in the woman's resistance, as if these directors needed to project their anxiety onto the other, and to suggest that women will necessarily succumb to "unlawful" male desire. A woman's capitulation to another man is precisely what her partner fears. However, when a man pursues a woman already "spoken for," her capitulation to him is precisely what he desires. Staging this potential certainly raises the excitement level in the audience (even if in the form of anxiety), and most audiences want to be excited, which any good director knows.

Lawrence Danson argues that Shakespeare's male characters are frequently tormented because they fear they lack control, both of themselves and their wives, particularly regarding their partners' sexual appetites. He suggests that Shakespeare portrays "the tragic failure of male possessive desire" and opens the possibility of recognizing "a realm of female self-possession; and that recognition (again, on the optimistic reading) is the pre-condition for a conceivable state where a man knows a woman's sexuality neither as threat to be expelled or possession to be controlled."[15] In production, however, Posthumus is generally represented as a sympathetic character, particularly in the speech where he fears his wife's infidelity.[16] Only one review suggested that the staging mocked his excessive ranting.[17] The productions for which I have reviews other than Akalaitis's and Gaines's were directed by men. In a play where the possibility of adultery figures prominently, the preponderance of male-directed productions seems to implicate Imogen and excuse Posthumus too readily. Male critics also contribute to this perception. Warren discusses Robin Phillips's (1986) highly sexual staging of the scene where Iachimo comes out of the trunk and ends up "riding" Imogen as she writhes underneath him in troubled sleep. He notes that Imogen "seemed much more soiled than usual."[18] Many reviewers remark in some way about this "rape" scene, but the perception that the victim retains the "soil" of the crime misrepresents even a psychic rape.

Barbara Gaines's *Cymbeline*

The Director's Vision

Gaines views the play as a fairy tale, which she conveyed partially by billing the production as *The Tale of Cymbeline*. She also thinks it is "a fabulous adventure story." But the element that moves her most is the sense that the characters are "guided by an invisible thread." She draws this interpretation largely from Pisanio's lines, although in the interview she remembered them as coming from Jupiter. She transferred these lines to the storyteller who framed the production: "All other doubts, by time let them be cleared, / Fortune brings in some boats that are not steered" (4.3.45–46). She is drawn to the beauty and spirituality of this idea, that despite all the things that befall Posthumus and Imogen, a providential hand moves them together. This pronouncement is the heart of the play for Gaines, "Otherwise, it's just an adventure story. There's no meaning to it." Gaines doesn't seem to consider the possibility that even adventure stories can convey meaning.[19]

Making meaning is clearly important to Gaines, and she obviously believes it's important to her audiences. She wants the audience to be able to take something away with them, to believe that "when things are just crashing down in your life, maybe there *is* hope. You don't know, do you? So you can't give up." The particular kind of meaning she gravitates toward, however, is liberal humanist aphorisms. But they are drawn, in part, from her experience of life and her needs for sustenance from spiritual values. In an interview with Weiss just before *Cymbeline* opened, Gaines said:

> I think what appeals to me about *Cymbeline* at this point in my life is that it's about the struggle of just getting through the day. And more than that, the characters not only persevere, but they come to the enormous revelation that if they let go of their pain and their animosity, they are able to forgive. And with forgiveness comes light.[20]

Her approach focuses on individual rather than social concerns, though her ideal of redemption does potentially have social implications.

Imogen is a very active, brave woman, in Gaines's view. She bases her view primarily on the fact that Imogen survives in the woods, a feat she herself could not perform. But this seems a view held in odd contradiction with her fundamental view of the story as fairy tale rather than realistic documentary. Within the genre of fairy tale, going into the woods does suggest confronting evil or at least the unknown, but the test is psychological or spiritual, not physical—or at least physical tests generally stand for other kinds of trials or threats. She thinks the criticism of Imogen as passive is "horseshit," and told me I could quote her on that. She added, "It's why you shouldn't read critics and scholars." Her staunchly antiacademic bias may have softened somewhat in the last few years because she included "A Scholar's View" of *The Taming of the Shrew* (written by University of Chicago professor Wendy Doniger) in her autumn 2003 playbill. As further proof of Imogen's admirable character, Gaines points to Imogen's faith in her husband. Imogen resists Iachimo because she knows her husband would not betray her: "How many women would trust their men quite like that?" Of course, she also trusts him not to order Pisanio to kill her, and only Pisanio's love and wisdom save her life. At least Gaines believes Imogen is right to be angry at Posthumus for doubting her own fidelity.

While pointing to the characters' exceptional qualities to commend them, she cites their common humanity when defending their flaws, saying that we are all flawed human beings. Of Posthumus's extremely misogynist speech in 2.4, she says:

He thinks he's been betrayed. We're *all* that way. That speech is merely a reactive, knee-jerk response to thinking that Iachimo had made love to his wife. And there isn't one person in this world, if you're passionately in love and find out, or think you've found out, that your lover has betrayed you, that isn't going to respond with that anger and hatred and horror when you're alone in your bedroom. It hurts. Again, it's common sense human behavior.

I'll grant that to be hurt and angry at betrayal may be a nearly universal response, but to paint one's own sex as completely innocent and the other as completely corrupt and hell-bound, feelings that later lead to commanding someone to murder one's spouse for suspected infidelity—this is more common than it should be, but thankfully, it is not universal. Gaines forgives this in Posthumus because he later shows remorse, and his grace in letting Iachimo live proves he is not a murderer. Had his intention to kill Imogen been fulfilled, the murder would have been, she admits, very difficult to forgive. "But that's not what the story is about. The story *is* about forgiveness and grace, as are all dramatic romances." Here, the play's genre and conclusion drive Gaines's interpretation concerning what occurs earlier in the story a bit too charitably. Ultimately, she believes the couple lives happily ever after because they have grown up together, know each other well, have "been through hell and back," and realize at the end "just how lucky they are." Again, Gaines moves unconsciously between romance genre and life in her interpretations of the characters and the play.

Gaines typically goes into rehearsal with some general ideas about the play and some specific visuals she wants to create, which usually end up in the final production. She does not do any research: "I love starting without having any information about any other production or any take." Although at most points when she mentioned critics in the interview, she did so with an implicit sense of superiority, once she admitted that she was confused by them, not understanding their views. She attributes the source of the confusion, however, to the scholars' lack. "Most scholars," she began, then a little more diplomatically said, "not most, many scholars don't know anything about theater."[21] Her repudiation of scholarly criticism sometimes leads to a naïve sense of discovery. In an interview with Sid Smith about her production of *Othello,* she reported watching another production and thinking that other productions always made the story about Iago, which was wrong—though in the theater, Iago is frequently the central character. In Gaines's mind, the story was about Othello, and he falls into Iago's trap because he comes from a different culture that is not valued in Venice. "He remains an outsider . . . in a strange land, where he will never be accepted as an equal."[22] Hardly uncommon, this view was proposed by Jim Siemon to his undergraduate Readings in Shakespeare class in 1990 at Boston University, certainly partially the result of other research. Although speaking of the much more frequently produced *Twelfth Night,* Bensussen is more realistic. A friend once said something to her that she keeps in mind whenever she approaches Shakespeare: "'When you think you're being original, you just haven't done your homework.' Because it's all been done, and so you have these moments where you get this great inspiration, and you think you're so brilliant. Then you look at the variorum that night, and of course it was done in 1634 by—and in the late 1800s so-and-so tried that bit but didn't find it as successful." Certainly not everything has been done before, but awareness of one's choices within the context of at least theater history and pertinent criticism provides for a more informed approach. Working from a supposedly blank slate—while certainly freeing—also allows one to maintain the illusion of originality.

When Gaines began directing *Cymbeline,* she knew that it would be a fairy tale, that there would be snow at various points, that the time frame would go from winter to spring, that the battle at the end would be stylized with flags. In an interview article just before *Cymbeline* opened, Weiss reports that Gaines's recent trip to Czechoslovakia had changed her approach to directing. Quoting Gaines, she writes: "Watching some of the Czech productions helped me to cut some of my own strong ties to realism."[23] This led to a more stylized production, but she still believes that, fundamentally, acting is response—one human being responding to another in the moment.

Gaines has also become more collaborative over the years. Now she leaves most of the moment-to-moment work to what is created in rehearsing with the actors. She admitted that when she directed *Cymbeline* in 1989 and 1993, she was much more controlling and had more definite ideas about how things should be played. According to Gaines, the productions were virtually the same despite cast changes. She has become more convinced that the actors need to make most of the decisions:

> The actor is the one ultimately who is playing this part every night, so every actor has got to be absolutely committed and comfortable

with what he or she is doing. It can't be the director's play. It has to be the actors' play. Mostly I think a director right now for me is just guiding a lot of talented people around so they can do their best work.

She notes that, at this point in her career, some ideas "never see the light of day" because the actors either disagree with them or are not capable of performing them. She does whatever is necessary to make the scene "work." What works tends to be shorthand for theatrical viability, what will be compelling for the audience. But of course nothing works for everyone. Still, this concept tends to be a bottom line for directors and often takes precedence over other concerns.

Gaines claims that her decisions about textual editing are guided by "pure instinct." While starting to make a claim that every director works intuitively in this area, she revised her statement to say that her friends in England and she work with what they perceive as the rhythm of the play. "You get into the rhythm, and somehow inside of your blood and your marrow, that pencil works in an intuitive way for me. So I can't tell you how I do it." She cut about seven hundred lines out of *Cymbeline,* predominantly for time.

The Play in Production

ENTER THE STORYTELLER

As the audience took their seats in the fall of 1989 around a thrust stage awaiting the beginning of *The Tale of Cymbeline,* they saw a large circular piece of fabric on the wooden stage floor while pleasant music played in the background.[24] Then the music and the lights faded. The music came back up, but was much more magical than the preshow music, a Philip Glass composition. The stage became smoky. A figure walked down the center aisle and up a ramp to the stage. Barely lit, he dramatically leaned down to the ground and picked up the circle, which became his cape. Then the lights came up, and he began to tell the story to the audience, which took the place of the first scene in the text. The other characters came on to the stage and stood around the perimeter looking at him. The lights rose on each one as he spoke of him or her.[25] Gaines was trying to create a picture of the characters identified and illuminated as if in a cloud before they were set down to do their work. Gradually, they all left the stage, leaving Posthumus sitting alone on the down left edge of the stage, looking out over the audience but clearly waiting for something or someone.

At the close of the production, the storyteller appeared on the stage and turned to look at the scene with his back to the spectators, his arms outstretched. His gesture suggested that this was the final tableau of the story he had painted for the audience. It also suggested that the future of the characters, particularly the lovers, would grow seamlessly and perfectly out of this moment. As if wanting to maintain the image of fairy tale characters and not drop completely to actors receiving applause, during the curtain call, Lisa Dodson, who played Imogen, and Peter Aylward, who played Posthumus, kissed. Although playful and engendering a laugh in the audience, it fed the illusion of continuity between offstage and onstage actor dynamics that American audiences particularly cherish.

ACTOR AND AUDIENCE

Gaines always uses direct address for soliloquies, following what she believes to be Elizabethan stage practice.

"'I want *you* to know how *I* feel.' That's what I tell the actors. I want everyone in that house to be pulled in by your eyes. You need their help as the actor. 'I need your advice. What would you do?'" For her, the dynamic she creates between the actor and the audience with this technique is "very active . . . so startling and powerful. It's great. I don't know why more theaters don't do it." She so wanted me to experience this supposedly rare hallmark of her theater that she gave me a ticket to her sold-out *Merchant of Venice* that was playing soon after our interview concluded. She believes the technique is especially potent if handsome actors talk to individual audience members who are attracted to them. By her report, the women in the audience loved it when Posthumus accused them individually of various vices in his long monologue in 2.4 because Aylward is so handsome.[26] So she uses direct address primarily to achieve the audience's emotional involvement with the production, one of her primary goals: "Everything you do onstage should be done to create some emotion, some feeling."

Scenically, Gaines used grates in the floor and smoke, relatively common scenic elements for her productions, because of the environment and ambience she can create with them. She likes the sharp and dramatic quality of up lighting in particular: "It's a very kind of ghoulish, severe, fun thing, just the lights coming from underneath." She particularly wanted to create a sense of the cold of the palace in winter, which smoke suggested. At some points she also had people warming their hands over the grates. In general, however, scenic elements were minimal. But the wood paneling of the stage walls wrapped completely around the audience. The set designer made that choice because he wanted the audience to feel safe and secure. Perhaps he thought this simulated the sense of a child in bed or in the arms of a loving parent while being told a story. This choice also physically included the audience in the clearly fantastical world of the play, encouraging them to leave behind the world they inhabited everyday. Remarking on the 1993 "faithfully revived" staging of the original 1989 show, Lawrence Bommer (*Chicago Tribune*) wrote that the conviction of the production effected "a suspension of disbelief strong enough to overcome all contrivances."[27] It seems that the overall design and execution of the play encouraged an escapist rather than critical mode of spectatorship. The audience was encouraged to enter into the fairy tale rather than to judge it.

THE FAIRY-TALE PRINCESS COSTUME

Despite the modern psychology, the production was set in the Renaissance. The costumes for the production were borrowed from the Stratford Festival in Ontario. Dodson, a beautiful full-figured brunette, was wearing a very low-cut gown and corset, showing plentiful cleavage. When I asked Gaines about this costume choice, she cited the Renaissance period as the primary reason. When I began to pursue the choice further, asking, "Do you ever worry that the costume—" she cut me off and responded a little testily, "Why wouldn't I show cleavage? I don't understand. I don't understand the question. You're the first person that's asked that question." When I started to explain about feminist performance critics' concerns about objectification of women onstage, she cut me off again with her "horseshit" line. But then she resorted to a number of somewhat peculiar defenses, including Queen Elizabeth as a model and legitimator of such a practice:

> I think if it's period, and it was, and it's beautiful, and it was, and she's a young princess in a romantic setting for two scenes before she becomes this boy, you want her to look as beautiful as you can, because she's going to look horrible for the rest the play. I wanted everyone to remember that, indeed, she is a princess. And princesses wore dresses

with cleavage, as Queen Elizabeth did and so many other people did in nobility; well, then we'll do it too. Besides that, it's a gorgeous costume, and every princess would want one.

Interestingly, staging the construction of the play as a fairy tale rather than realistic drama—which extended to a broad acting style—did not lead her to question the conventions generating the fairy tale genre itself.

A critical change in costume and bit of stage business did potentially highlight the way conventions for particularly the heroine's dress encourage women to display their bodies for the visual consumption of men. When Iachimo first meets Imogen and says, "Hath nature given them eyes / To see this vaulted arch" (1.7.32–33), she suddenly feared he was referring to her breasts and self-consciously covered with her hands the flesh her gown exposed. Although the moment was comical, at least it revealed the potential dangers of wearing sexually suggestive costumes for every audience.

A later scene marked a slight costume departure from the fairy-tale genre. When she appeared the next morning, frantically searching for her bracelet as Cloten tried to have a conversation with her, her appearance was quite different, the theft of the bracelet effecting an erasure of her public image. She cared little about how she appeared to any audience. Her hair was down and disheveled. She was wearing a headband, and her clothes were, while still rich, much more casual—not the typical dress of a princess. Her breast was also covered, almost as if she sensed the violation that had happened. For Gaines, the shift was probably intended to signal how important the bracelet, and hence Posthumus, was to her. But it also served to frame the conventions governing her earlier costume. The public/private distinction became clear as well as the imperative of male desire driving the design of the princess costume.

THE CRUEL MISFORTUNE OF HERO AND HEROINE

The audience's first view of Imogen in the play proper occurred at the opening of 1.2 as she was running across the length of the stage to meet Posthumus in an embrace. But as soon as they touched, the Queen's voice intruded from upstage. Despite the Queen's assurances, Imogen moved away from Posthumus when the Queen promised to "deliver you the keys / That lock up your restraint" (ll. 4–5). Clearly, Imogen intuited the wicked stepmother's genuine design. Only when she left did they rush back together again. The scene was punctuated by a number of kisses, conveying an intense passion between them. Just before the king entered, they were kneeling on the floor, holding and kissing each other.

In an interesting and modern twist illuminating a subtext directly opposed to the literal import of the lines, when Imogen gave Posthumus the diamond, saying, "But keep it till you woo another wife, / When Imogen is dead" (ll. 43–44), she gave him a warning look, as if to say, "You better not." Aylward's Posthumus, handsome, blond, the image of a golden boy, genuinely reassured her.

Dodson portrayed Imogen as a spirited daughter. After the king separated the couple, commanding the guards to lead Posthumus away, she performed a ritual of respect by curtseying lightly to her father. But this relic of Renaissance behavior soon vanished as she rose like a powerhouse to fight the man who had separated her from her love, her anger and determination no longer cloaked beneath obligations of parental deference and honor. Cymbeline physically restrained her at one point from walking out on him, and after "Thou foolish thing!" (l. 81), he raised his hand as if to strike her. She dropped to the ground to shield herself, but her move was still characterized by grace and dignity. She never cowered before him. The queen's entrance stayed his blow. Imogen moved away with her back to the royal couple, turning with concern only at Pisanio's report that Cloten had drawn his sword on Posthumus. This Imogen displayed a strong and passionately sexual subjectivity.

Gaines succeeded in getting the audience to sympathize with the couple and long for their reunion. Reporting for the *Reader*, Albert Williams noted that Dodson and Aylward created "a robust and passionate couple whose strong temperaments nearly drive them apart."[28] Perceiving exactly what Gaines hoped to convey in Imogen, *Skyline* critic Paul Faberson believed Dodson was "perfectly cast.... She is lovely, regal, vulnerable yet strong, and she communicates Shakespeare's poetry with intelligence and clarity." Aylward's Posthumus earned only the comment that he was "fine-looking" from Faberson, although elsewhere the character was described as a "heroic lover," certainly a product of both the director's and the actor's interpretation.[29]

THE VILLAIN'S VENTURE

With dark hair and eyes, a shaggy coif and beard, Henry Godinez as Iachimo looked the villain. Philario's house in Rome, the setting for 1.5, appeared to be a brothel. Prostitutes were hanging around the perimeter. The lighting was dark for the scene, primarily blue center stage and red around the edges. Iachimo and Posthumus casually circled each other, alternately taking stage and retreating. Iachimo confidently dallied with the women on the edge of the stage while talking about how he would seduce Imogen, and Posthumus remained upstage in the shadows, barely visible, before he finally came forward and took up Iachimo's challenge. The proposal unnerved him. Clearly he did not completely trust Imogen's commitment to him, but the audience's experience of her suggested the problem lay in Posthumus's own insecurity rather than in any well-grounded suspicion. The scene ended with each slapping his hand against the other's—clearly a contemporary gesture—and a blackout, after which the men in the onstage audience laughed derisively.

The scene where Iachimo tests Imogen (1.7) revealed a usually generous, modest, and chaste woman momentarily captured by Iachimo's spell. She initially received Iachimo, dressed in black with a black cape and purple sash, with buoyancy and warmth. When Iachimo kissed her hand in greeting and looked up at her, he was smitten by her beauty. Perceiving how she had moved him, Imogen became uncomfortable and withdrew. Her compassionate nature reasserted itself, nevertheless, when she suspected Iachimo was ill (l. 51). She put a hand to his forehead, as if checking for a fever, and he melted. She became melancholy and pensive when Iachimo told her her husband frequented prostitutes, almost as if she were in a dream. Iachimo continued to weave his hypnotic spell, gradually increasing their physical intimacy—taking her hand, whispering into the nape of her neck or her ear, and finally, on his knees, kissing and caressing her hand. He pulled her hand to his face and stroked his beard with it.

Gaines cut the first "What ho, Pisanio!" (l. 139), apparently to continue the spell a little longer. In the following line, Iachimo says, "Let me my service tender on your lips." She was kneeling with him at this point, an echo of her earlier scene with Posthumus. He took her in his arms and kissed her. In an interesting inversion of the typical fairy-tale plot, the villain's kiss broke his own evil spell. She came back to herself and sharply rebuked him. Iachimo had one final trick up his sleeve. He kissed her cleavage, but this only prompted Imogen to leap up, run upstage, and call for Pisanio. It gave her very clear motivation for threatening to make her father "acquainted of thy assault" (ll. 149–50). The similar staging and different conclusions emphasized the contrast between her relationships with the two men and asserted her fidelity to her husband. True to the fairy-tale frame, she waivered only when influenced by Iachimo's hypnotic powers, but she uncovered his deception and triumphed over him. Once Iachimo said he was only testing her, she became calmer, but was still wary, and she started to leave before he called her back with his request for her to guard his trunk.

WAYS OF SEEING

The trunk scene was sexual but limited the audience's voyeurism. The lighting in her bedroom chamber was very blue with some reds. Emphasizing her innocence, part of the bedroom decor was long, white, silken ceiling-to-floor swaths of fabric. Once she was asleep, Iachimo slithered out of the trunk barechested and sweaty. He kissed her, and she remained motionless. During his long monologue, he spoke to the audience frequently, which would have encouraged their complicity, an invitation that may have made some uncomfortable. In order to get off her

A publicity studio shot emblematic of Henry Godinez's Iago, a seductive villain who invites the audience's complicity in his betrayal of Imogen (Lisa Dodson) in Barbara Gaines's *Cymbeline*. Photo: Jennifer Girard.

Iachimo (Henry Godinez) having just climbed out of the trunk once Imogen (Lisa Dodson) is asleep in Barbara Gaines's *Cymbeline*. Photo: Lisa Ebright.

arm the bracelet Posthumus had given her at their parting, he took off his sash, slipped it between the bracelet and her arm, and slowly lured it from her. The movement and image it created was somehow resonant of his undressing Imogen by removing her belt. Even more carefully, he pulled back the sheet, lifted up the neckline of her gown, and looked at her breasts. Once discovering the secret bodily mark he needed to clinch his "proof," he leaned over and kissed her breasts, but then suddenly pulled away saying, "No more." In its original context, the words begin an explanation of why he will not write down anything else; it is "screw'd to [his] memory" (2.2.44). But the staging here suggested that he felt he had violated her, and he needed to leave before he violated her further. The self-awareness of the character at this point allowed the audience to criticize his actions with him and perhaps become aware of their own voyeurism rather than merely participating vicariously in Imogen's violation.[30]
The nudity in this staging was for Iachimo's eyes only, and in fact, a similar staging in Olympia, Washington, where Iachimo untied her gown and looked inside drew gasps from the audience.[31] By contrast Bill Alexander's 1987 RSC production had Iachimo unbutton her gown all the way to her navel, where he had "difficulty restraining himself." Yet the reviewer, Stanley Wells, comments that in the scene the actor was "suave and understated."[32] As early as 1962, William Gaskill's production had Imogen nude under the sheets, and when she turned, one of her breasts was exposed. Similarly, Peter Hall's 1988 production at the National also had Imogen nude under the sheets.[33] Once again, the American productions and presumably the audience response were more conservative regarding the degree of nudity staged.[34]

PROTECTING THE HERO

The scene where Iachimo convinces Posthumus of Imogen's infidelity was played relatively realistically. As opposed to his earlier uncertainty, Posthumus was casual and confident when Iachimo returned. He barely listened to Iachimo, until Iachimo called Imogen "so easy" (2.4.47). At first he was angry, but then the doubts invaded again. Throughout most of the scene he was tossed back and forth between confidence and anxiety. In his moments of security, he could walk away from Iachimo, but Iachimo always found a way to lure him back. And finally, Iachimo's knowledge of the mole on her breast completely broke him. Evidently in excruciating pain, he sat down, dropping his head into his hands, but he roused to shake Iachimo's hand from his shoulder, rejecting the villain's feigned comfort. Then he started running over the stage like a man whose sanity and control were slipping, finally collapsing at the end of the scene.

The lights dimmed and everyone else exited. He crawled back to the bench that was upstage right and pulled himself onto it to deliver his monologue to the audience. The speech's potential venom was restrained, and the monologue became slightly comic at points, making it easier for the audience not to take his anger here seriously, to see it as an aberration in Posthumus, a momentary reaction. Of course, this "moment" extends to him writing a letter to Pisanio, ordering Imogen's assassination. But the audience's admiration of and sympathy for him were reestablished when he bravely fought in the war, vanquishing and disarming Iachimo without killing him, and when he suffered in prison, sitting on a grate lit with blue up light, the rest of the stage dark, a huge metal collar around his neck. His redemption was sealed by the ghostly support of his family and the spectacular proclamations of Jupiter.

AND THEY LIVED HAPPILY EVER AFTER

The transition to the final scene was scored by hopeful, Yanni-like New Age music. The back of the stage opened to reveal a pale blue cyclorama, foliage gobos making it appear as if sunlight were shining through trees. People began slowly assembling. Posthumus emerged, framed in light for a moment before taking his place. In fact, to give him this somewhat regal entrance, Gaines moved it from where the text marks it later in the scene. Then the King walked out and came downstage to his throne. The scene proper began. Like the rest of the production, it moved between dramatic, serious moments and more playful, comic moments. The scene's many revelations often caused a broadly acted response of, "Ahhh . . ." from the onstage audience, again highlighting the play's nonillusionistic dramaturgy. Iachimo was genuinely repentant, and his speeches were appropriately serious. By the time Imogen asked Posthumus why he threw her from him, she was quite confident, knowing he behaved the way he did because he did not recognize her. But his momentary unprovoked violence against someone clearly not his equal either socially or physically was largely glossed over. His line when she has embraced him, "Hang there like fruit, my soul, / Till the tree die" (5.5.263–64), was motivated by his own inability to embrace her since his hands were cuffed behind his back. When she pulled back to look at his face, they kissed. At another point in the scene, they were separated, kneeling on the floor on either side of the king, their eyes locked on each other. But in the final moment, they were kneeling together and kissing, back lit.

Faberson wrote that the final scene left "everyone living happily ever after, audience included."[35] Tom Simpson of the *Chicago Maroon* wrote that in the final scene, "Gaines brings us to a kind of romantic leap of faith, where everything works out perfectly at the end just because we want it to so very badly."[36] Only Bommer complained that in the 1993 version the last act was even more broadly performed than in 1989: "Not all is as fine as in '89. The broadly acted final scenes seem self-consciously hip, as if, deferring to our supposed sophistication about fairy tales, the characters mean to mock the miracles they've undergone. Careful—it's not nice to fool around with Father Shakespeare."[37] I doubt mockery was the intent, but Gaines does think Shakespeare should be "fun." At least one critic for Chicago's major newspaper, and perhaps more, is too conservative to accept happily an intervention by the director calling attention to contemporary "problems" with Shakespeare's dramaturgy. But Simpson ended his article by noting Shakespeare Repertory's challenge to the bigger, more well-established Goodman: "Barbara Gaines has done a brilliant job on a modest budget. As such, this late romance comes at a perfect moment, throwing down a kind of local, low-tech gauntlet to this season's Big Shakespeare Event, *The Winter's Tale* to be directed by Frank Galati at the Goodman. Will Galati, with Goodman's cash-flow and resources, be able to do as much?"[38] With only its second production, Shakespeare Repertory led by Gaines was clearly making an impact on the theater scene in Chicago.

The fairy-tale frame became a convenient aid in telling the story but was not consistently followed throughout. In some ways, the production shows Gaines's blend of stylization and psychological realism at this point in her career, a blend that was probably almost unconsciously chosen. Noting the self-conscious yet committed handling of the fairy tale, Weiss particularly praised the "exuberant stagecraft and extremely physical, extroverted approach to acting" as well as the "playfulness and directness of [Gaines's] methods . . . at once sophisticated and childlike."[39] Clearly, Gaines managed to make the production both accessible and emotionally compelling for her audience.

JoAnne Akalaitis's *Cymbeline*

The Director's Vision

Akalaitis did not write program notes for this production, but one sentence on the cast list page of the program announced that this *Cymbeline* took place "[i]n the Midst of Celtic Ruins—a romantic fantasy in Victorian England." The production was not set so much in the Victorian era, as in the Victorian imagination. Imogen was enormously popular with nineteenth-century audiences.[40] When I asked Akalaitis if she wanted to highlight the historically constructed nature of fantasy, she answered affirmatively.[41] And yet when I asked more specifically about why she chose the Victorian era, she admitted that the choice was relatively superficial, not having anything to do with the content of the play but rather with how it looked. She had read that it was Tennyson's favorite play and that he was buried with a copy of it. She likes the Victorians' clothes, she admitted, laughing, although elsewhere she has said that costume design is important because "the audience is able to locate themselves in relation to clothes."[42] Rather than making choices based on any intellectual or political idea, more often, she just "[sees] it that way." Visual imagination is essential to her: "My thing about a play is if I don't have a visual picture of something, then I shouldn't do the play. . . . It doesn't mean that the play is good or bad; it means that I should not be doing it."[43]

Although Akalaitis often likes juxtaposing the historical and the contemporary, such choices seem to be more about layering meaning and perspective to create an artistically and intellectually rich experience for the spectators than about fulfilling some agenda. She never thinks, for instance, about gender relations in Shakespeare's time. She did admit at the beginning of the interview, "I can't remember a lot of things. Usually when I do work, I forget everything about it."

She had never read *Cymbeline* until Papp suggested that she direct it as part of the Public's Shakespeare Marathon series, which ultimately included every play in the canon. In fact, this was the first Shakespeare play she directed.[44] But when she read it, she was delighted, especially by Imogen, whom she sees as "so spunky, and so loyal, and so intelligent in her choices." She is also attracted by the extravagance, fantasy, and richness of the play—"unending delights." She likes all the characters, even "the wicked stepmother." But unlike Gaines, she never spoke of the play being about anything in particular. In fact, at one point she said, "There's no plan about how the performance turns out."

Like Gaines, she sees Imogen as an active heroine, and somewhat surprisingly, considering her more intellectual and sophisticated approach, uses a similar logic: "She goes on this voyage alone, she ends up in this forest, she's drugged, and then she joins up with the Romans. She's not passive at all. She does things that most of us could never do. It's like hitchhiking across Texas alone, or something. She is an amazing girl." Both directors seem to ignore the fantasy context for Imogen's choice in this situation. Akalaitis also sees the play, in general, as "very sexy." While she characterized Imogen's passion for Posthumus as adoration, she remarked on the bestial sexuality in both Posthumus and Cloten, noting in particular that Iachimo "is unbelievably sexy."

Unlike Gaines, Akalaitis thinks Posthumus is a "jerk," despite her concession that his real torment concerning the imagined infidelity should not be dismissed. Similarly to Gaines, she maintains a fairly democratic viewpoint: "We've all been victims of that kind of torment." But implicitly, her statement suggests that her recognition of the common *experience* the audience shares with Posthumus does not extend to a belief in a common *response* or a consequent evaluation of his extreme misogyny in this moment as only "natural." His later acts of mercy do not completely erase his faults. Posthumus, however, was largely sympathetic in this production. Akalaitis attributed that to the work of the actor rather than her choice:

> What you have to understand is that a director doesn't say, "This character is sympathetic. This character is unsympathetic." I mean, you do, but I never use the word "sympathetic "or "unsympathetic" for any actor. There's no such thing. All actors should feel good about their work. So what happens in rehearsal is just what happens in rehearsal.[45]

Akalaitis considers herself, with good reason, a collaborative director. She believes that she was very well prepared for this production coming into rehearsal, but because the play is so long, "very big," and her production was technically complex, she thinks she didn't have quite enough time. The rehearsal process itself, structured without breaks for her because there was simply so much to do, "was killing." She was not consciously influenced by any literary critics or previous productions. Considering the startling originality of her *Cymbeline*, I would say she has more right to that claim than perhaps any other director in this project.

The Play in Production

COLLIDING HISTORICITIES: A POSTMODERN *CYMBELINE*

When the audience entered the Public's Newman Theater with its proscenium stage, in the summer of 1989, they saw red curtains across the front of the stage and heard the sounds of a violent thunderstorm.[46] The curtains were lit from below, almost as if by gas footlights, and the first scene took place on the small forestage in front of it, much the way scenes on the Victorian stage were played in front of act curtains. The two gentlemen entered from behind the split in the curtain center stage and spoke with British accents, holding black umbrellas. Their speech and gestures were clearly mannered, their faces almost dark. They stood close together, speaking conspiritorially. Akalaitis was invoking not just the Victorian time period but its theatrical conventions as well, a choice that historicized current theatrical conventions.

This became even more apparent once the curtain opened to reveal a set created partially through twentieth-century technology, designed by George Tsypin. Fog suffused the stage. Large blue-gray columns with hints of moss suggested the palace. But a number of the columns rotated, and in later scenes created different settings. Trees, rocks, and rich vegetation were projected in a shifting and somewhat abstract design on the backdrop, imaging a deep green magical forest. There was a bridge upstage left, and sometimes, images of Stonehenge appeared. An approximately 2-foot-wide, 1.5-foot-high shallow trough ran in a straight line from upstage to downstage. Sided by rocks, its shallow basin was often filled with water, which sometimes steamed. At other points, oceanlike projections made it appear to foam. A similar but more faint pattern of projections also sometimes lit the backdrop, adding to the air of fantasy.

A family of figures was seen dimly moving in the dark, and they left the stage mysteriously just before the queen rushed in. While the lighting and scenery were created by contemporary technology, heavy melodramatic organ music played over the transition. Unlike a cinematic approach now often adopted for swift scene changes, blackouts punctuated many shifts, although some of the scene changes were executed in view of the audience. At another point later in the play, the king was seated on an elevated throne. The throne was whisked offstage quickly on a horizontal plane a few feet above the stage floor, the king flying through the air.

4: ONCE UPON A TIME 227

Then servants moved off by hand the stairs that had elevated the throne. At several junctures in the production, conventions of both centuries were present at the same time, effectively framing one another. Amy Green wrote of the production:

> The production depicted nineteenth-century, Shakespearean melodrama as only a contemporary imagination, fluent in the imagery of late-twentieth-century American culture, could conceive it. Its beauty lay in the way it seemed to exist, paradoxically, in at least three simultaneous theatrical time zones. Ever-present were Elizabethan language and dramaturgy, gushingly romantic Victorian characters and situations, and an aggressively fast-paced and electronically modulated production style.[47]

While claiming never to have read a word of postmodern theory, Akalaitis created a postmodern aesthetic. In the theater, a postmodern aesthetic can encompass a range of approaches, including a pastiche of incongruous elements, a mixing of "high" art and pop culture, a presentation or quotation of character rather than a representation of supposedly realistic human behavior. It seeks to reveal that the interpretive and representational values of unity, coherence, continuity, and closure are not universal, but founded in a modernist worldview that often excludes disruptive and marginal elements of both art and society. Postmodernism is political in its revelation of the supposedly universal as relative, and its questioning of a conservative social order that needs universal values in order to preserve itself. A postmodern aesthetic results in, as Elinor Fuchs writes in praise of this production, "multiple expressivity. This mode of understanding shapes her work—its look, sound, movement, casting, choice of material—and results in a knowable aesthetic that is not realistic, not essentially modernist, but treats all of these as parts of an available vocabulary."[48] The practice of creating unusual juxtapositions and thereby framing the construction of colliding elements formed the basis of Akalaitis's approach to *Cymbeline.*

Akalaitis apparently does not subscribe to any particular relationship between the actor and the audience, although she does encourage actors to share their work generously with the audience.[49] More in line with Victorian than avant-garde practices, the characters did not speak to individuals in the audience or even, with a couple of nominal exceptions, clearly address the audience as a whole. Occasionally characters spoke their lines facing front, but they were still ostensibly speaking to one another, even though their bodies were displayed more fully to the audience than to their scene partners. Although Akalaitis has said acting needs to be contemporary, here she seemed to be playing with Victorian acting practices, thereby relativizing notions of theater and performance. She did not, for instance, create preshow activity, which she often does as a way of educating her audience and preparing them for the show.[50] With a more contemporary awareness, however, she had the actors speak in a range of accents, a more accurate reflection of the potential diversity among both the actors and the characters than a standardized diction would depict. Although certain motifs characterize Akalaitis's work, she seems in many ways free from any absolutes about how any play should be performed. Despite her disavowal of theory, her direction of actors does show evidence of a deconstructivist approach—that is, she is not seeking to replicate recognizable human behavior onstage in order to create the illusion of a unified character/human being. Instead, she is interested in actors creating theatrical moments that may resonate with an audience but the meanings of which will not be tied to an illusion of "reality."

THE VICTORIAN HEROINE

As the second scene of the play began, the evil queen (Joan MacIntosh) stood center stage, her arms outstretched in a recognizably melodramatic pose, Posthumus (Jeffrey Nordling) on her right and Imogen (Joan Cusack) on her left in perfect symmetry. Imogen wore a long, shimmery light-colored gown with a simple round neckline, her shoulders wrapped in a red shawl. As one might expect for a Victorian fantasy, this scene in Akalaitis's production was more chaste than in Gaines's. Imogen and Posthumus first came together in an embrace, which ended with them holding hands. In many ways, the hands became the focus of their touch, whether he was kissing hers, or she was rocking lightly against their clasped hands, as if their hands kept their bodies too far apart. But they did kiss once before he left. Imogen was serious when, as the perfect suffering heroine, she imagined Posthumus courting someone else after her own death. Such a characterization revealed a masculine ideal driving Victorian constructions of gender and also relativized both historical and contemporary notions of romance.

Cusack declaimed her lines in a large, husky voice, using large dramatic gestures as well. At one point she gasped deeply because the pain was so sharp, but despite the Victorian playing

A composite publicity shot of JoAnne Akalaitis's *Cymbeline* showing Imogen (Joan Cusack) and Posthumus (Jeffrey Nordling) in the foreground, with the Queen (Joan MacIntosh), King (George Bartenieff), and Tranio (Peter Francis) off to the left. Photo: Martha Swope.

style, Cusack seemed to be quoting the convention rather than the character. By contrast, Nordling performed in a more typically realistic style. When I asked Akalaitis about the contrast, she remarked that whereas Cusack had performed in the way she envisioned the role, Nordling did not follow her directions in this area. His resistance both in terms of interpreting and performing the character compromised Akalaitis's vision of the play.

When the king (George Bartenieff) entered, Imogen and Posthumus turned and watched his approach. Posthumus came up behind her and pulled her back into his embrace, typifying Victorian stereotypes concerning the gendered roles for protector and protected, which prompted examination of historical ways in which gender roles are constructed. Cymbeline grabbed Imogen's forearms and snatched her way from her husband's embrace. Imogen pulled toward Posthumus after he left, dragging her father behind her until he twisted her arm and forced her to knees. He released her arm and she crouched with her head down while he spoke. Although she raised her head to defy him, she remained on the ground for much of the scene and shrank when he raised his arm to strike her. She also shrank when the queen tried to touch her later in the scene. Imogen was fiery, but her fire was contained within the frame of a submissive, victimized daughter, which in some ways served to heighten the rarity of her strength for her historical time period. Her independence for her (Victorian) gender, which in a contemporary setting or realistic acting style might have been taken for granted, was thereby highlighted.

THE VILLAIN'S SEDUCTION

Dark in coloring, Michael Cumpsty's Iachimo nearly twirled his mustache, his performance suggesting a caricature of Robert Goulet.[51] The contrast was especially marked since Nordling was fair and blond. The columns in this scene appeared to be plastered with Italian art, nudes and partial nudes, but the images from the palace scene were still partially visible to the audience. No world was discrete in its scenic representation, at once accenting and connecting the disparate worlds of *Cymbeline*. Iachimo appeared at the beginning of this scene nude with his back to the audience. He picked up his robe, hanging near him, put it on, and turned around. Already he had established his confidence in and comfort with his body. Dressed predominantly in brown and tan clothes, more plain than his somewhat flamboyantly dressed companions, Posthumus seemed out of place. His manners were also less sophisticated. Reflecting a late-twentieth-century awareness of the negative effects of misogyny on men as well as women, Posthumus fell prey to the misogyny and male bonding of his environment, intimidated into his wager. The other gentlemen leaned dramatically toward Posthumus and stared at him as Iachimo taunted him. At the first mention of the ring, they froze in tableau. This staging portrayed the pressure against Posthumus, criticizing such dictates of behavior for men, while also distancing the audience from that pressure through its use of nineteenth-century conventions, conventions also used by the avant-garde precisely because they seem unnatural to contemporary audiences.

The temptation scene was set appropriately with a long table in between Imogen and Iachimo and fully exploited the melodramatic possibilities of staging their interaction. Soon after an unsuccessful foray and retreat, he took her hand and jumped up on the table, gradually driving her backward as he advanced. She did not resist him this time, upset and sighing. When he reached the end of the table he knelt, his face near hers to talk again about lips (l. 105). She softened and leaned toward him, but turned away on her response line, "My lord, I fear, / Has forgot Britain" (ll. 112–13). She was portraying the innocent, suffering Victorian heroine in distress and thereby framing both Victorian and contemporary seduction rituals and how strongly nineteenth-century culture prescribed behavior in heterosexual relationships according to gender. It also prompted consideration of the historically constructed nature of sexual fantasy.

Iachimo jumped down off the table to begin his next seduction attempt. He moved behind her and let his hand glide over her back, which startled her, but she did not move away. The idea of revenge was clearly foreign to her, but she began considering it. She was almost looking to Iachimo for guidance. Although Imogen seemed to be considering Iachimo's proposition, Akalaitis claims that she and the actors were clear that Imogen never gives in to him. Perhaps Akalaitis wanted to convey that in her innocence, she was listening and responding to his words, but so naive that she never considered the need to be on guard. Her natural receptiveness provided encouragement to Iachimo and heightened the apparent possibility of capitulation without ever compromising her true intent. But if the audience slipped out of such a Victorian mindset, it might easily read Imogen's responses as signs of genuine temptation.

As one might expect in a Victorian romance, the intimacy Iachimo did achieve was markedly more subtle than in Gaines's Renaissance-dressed but essentially contemporary fairy tale. Soon after this moment of inclination toward Iachimo, Imogen became angry, pushed him away, got up, and yelled for Pisanio. Ever the villain, Iachimo began to stalk her across the stage. Backing away, she put a chair between them, but then finally stopped and stood her ground when defending Posthumus's honor (l. 146). When threatening him with telling the king, she physically advanced toward him. Finally beaten, he dropped again to his knees, but when he moved toward her, she backed away. She no longer trusted him, and although she pretended to accept his apology, she was clearly still angry, overacting the role of polite hostess while agitatedly playing with her bracelet. Once again, Imogen's strength became more apparent within the frame of conventionalized submissiveness. The two poles of her responses commented on each other and also prompted consideration of the interplay between social conditioning and individual choice.

A DARK AND STORMY NIGHT

The trunk scene shared with Gaines's production a sexual but appropriately modest approach. It became a dark and stormy night, with servants moving through the dark holding candelabras, the two burning flames creating a Gothic image of fiery eyes glowing in the dark. Imogen's bedroom had a fireplace with a candelabra on the mantel. She kissed the bracelet Posthumus had given her before she settled down to sleep. The sheets and her gown were silver, and her bed was steel and spare, green electric bulbs on the posts. It was reminiscent of a Victorian anatomy table.[52] Imogen was to become the unwitting object of Iachimo's investigation.

When Iachimo came out of the trunk in black pants and a black vest, but wearing no shirt and barefoot, the lights went even more red and the curtains billowed. The visual effect was both purgatorial and sexual—an appropriate combination for this production. Both the English Victorian and contemporary American Puritan roots that bind sex with sin converged in these images, prompting a consideration of our greater self-awareness concerning the cultural construction of sexual fantasy. But for Akalaitis, this image was also appropriate since she believes Iachimo is dangerous because he is evil. As in Gaines's production, he tried to kiss Imogen, but virtuous even in sleep, the Victorian heroine turned over uneasily and prevented him. He found the mole, as Godinez's Iachimo did, by moving to above her head and lifting the neckline of her nightgown. A conventional villain, he showed no self-awareness of his violation and blew out the candles before returning to the trunk.

INTO THE WOODS

Although Imogen was angry with Cloten, no significant change suggested her awareness of a private versus public space or her experience of violation. After all, she was not literally raped. Visual violation and sexual harassment were not clearly defined issues for the Victorians. Cusack played Imogen's response to the chance of meeting her lover with enormous girlish excitement. Reminding the audience again of differences in technology within different historical eras, Imogen and Pisanio rode to Milford Haven on an antique bicycle and scooter. Initially blissful but becoming impatient and petulant, she dismounted and dropped her bicycle on the ground. During much of this scene Imogen was on her knees but insistent that Pisanio kill her, strong in her submissiveness to her husband's will. Her submissiveness was slightly sexualized as well, for as she directed his sword toward her heart (3.4.79), she began to unbutton her dress.[53] When she finally accepted Pisanio's plan, the audience saw how it hurt for her to lose her hair, historicizing the Victorian universality of long hair on women as well as contemporary diversity in women's coiffures. At the end of the scene, she had not yet changed into men's clothes, and her lines about how courageously she would fulfill this role were cut (3.4.182–85). She was sitting on the ground alone, looking rather disconsolate, the end of the first half. Akalaitis wanted to accentuate her bravery by showing the daunting road ahead of her.

True to Victorians' predominant fantasy of the savage, the two brothers, played by a black and a Hispanic actor, were depicted as Native American Indians. Critics took Akalaitis to task for the racially blind casting, which included casting Cloten with an African American actor. If Cloten is a different ethnicity than white, they argued, then the queen must share his ethnicity. They also complained that Imogen could not possibly mistake Cloten's black body for Posthumus's white one. But while admitting a number of incongruities in the play itself, they criticized this casting choice as if it were applied to a realistic production of a nineteenth-century "well-made" play. Harry Newman, former executive director of the Non-traditional Casting Project, supported Akalaitis's choices,[54] and nine years later, a *New York Times* critic would finally understand a similar choice made by Andrei Serban: "Inclusiveness is certainly the watchword for the casting, which in faithful Public Theater tradition is aggressively multiethnic . . . yet given the nature of fantasy, [the racially blind casting is] not all that jarring. In fact, the racially blind decisions are not only a reflection of the play's implicit message, but are also a link to our world and the myriad ways in which families are created in contemporary society, a world of intermarriage and stepparents and test-tube babies and adoption."[55] The racially blind casting was consistent with Akalaitis's postmodern approach.

Within the context of the audience's awareness of racial prejudice, Imogen's sudden weakness seemed caused by her disillusionment with the society that had labeled her gentle brothers as "savage."[56] They sang Glass's composition at Fidele's funeral quite beautifully, a moment that staged a number of competing stereotypes and histories. Gentle, tender, and capable of harmonizing beautifully in a simple but not easily rendered song, their performance deconstructed the Victorian conception of a savage, who would certainly not be capable of such artistic achievement, even if he were noble. In its ethereal, lyrical, haunting movement, the New Age-type music was also completely foreign to the signature musical styles of the Victorian era, the Native American Indian, and Victorian ideas about Native American Indian, African, or Hispanic American cultures. In other words, their song disrupted any possible expectation the audience might have had. In highlighting the actors' voices and artistic achievement, particularly since they faced front and delivered their song ostensibly to the audience, Akalaitis drew the spectators' attention to the individual talents of the actors and her own artistic choices as a director for that moment. In fact, the text stipulates that they do not sing, but Akalaitis cut that line so she could insert a song here. Following a postmodern alternating sequence and mix of conventions, the production went back into its Victorian mode in the next scene.

THE VILLAIN'S TEMPORARY TRIUMPH

The scene where Iachimo convinces Posthumus of his wife's infidelity was more melodramatic than in Gaines's production. When Iachimo returned to Italy, Posthumus was sitting in Iachimo's chair and Iachimo entered as Posthumus had the first time. Iachimo began slowly circling Posthumus, who became increasingly uncomfortable. When he dramatically displayed the bracelet by raising his arm, Posthumus rose to his feet and crossed to Iachimo. Iachimo often faced front during this scene, aware of his performance and almost bragging to the audience, but at this point he drove Posthumus back across the stage to the chair. Posthumus turned away, and the other men stared at him. He became aware of his public shame. Iachimo took his chair back. Posthumus's final monologue was performed in dark blue light. He cried at the beginning of the speech, genuinely heartbroken, although by the time he was searching for "the woman's part" (l. 172), anger took over. Later, he touched his head as if he were distracted or almost mad, then moved back to tears, but hated feeling the pain and fought it with anger again. The speech was never comic, but it was framed at the end with melodramatic organ music, which served to criticize its self-indulgence and extremity.

Not as heroic as Gaines's Posthumus, he stabbed Iachimo and ran out. When Posthumus was asleep in prison, Jupiter appeared as a young boy on a dark, swinging eagle. The scene did not provide the powerful affirmation of Gaines's production. But the figures who had appeared mysteriously in the first scene, and were in the background around the edges of scene changes, became Posthumus's family. In Akalaitis's vision, however, in the rest of the production they represented Tennyson's family. She worked from a picture of the family, and felt it was a beautiful image, to have them there as witnesses, as ghosts. Unfortunately, however, their presence remained a mystery and apparently confused the audience, at least those who sought to identify them and understand their purpose.[57]

AND THEY LIVED HAPPILY EVER AFTER (?)

No dramatic transition clearly marked the prison from the final scene. As in Gaines's production, a number of the revelations were played broadly for comedy. Imogen was standing, listening impassively until she saw Iachimo's face. Her anger rekindled, bringing her to life. Consistent with the actors' performances so far, Posthumus's grief was portrayed realistically while Iachimo's confession appeared insincere. He was not the villain who converted but the unregenerate hypocrite who would die and go to hell. When Posthumus reacted to Imogen as if she were a servant, he slapped her and threw her from him but thoughtlessly, clearly distraught. I suspect this rather sympathetic staging of the violence was the actor's rather than Akalaitis's conception. When Imogen returned to him, she embraced him, and he returned her embrace. They knelt to receive Cymbeline's blessing. In an interesting twist, the soothsayer was a young Indian woman, an allusion to British colonial imperialism—on which the English Victorians and late-twentieth-century Americans have different views.[58] Elinor Fuchs writes, "When she spoke in the final scene, prophesying the success of the union between Rome and Britain, 'which shines here in the West,' we realized that Akalaitis had deftly framed the imperial 'deal' of the play in the ironic perspective of British colonialism. It was a brilliant stroke of self-conscious 'Orientalism,' an extra turn of the political knife, to conflate prophet and colonized and to gender the colonial subject female."[59] Her appearance provided yet another opportunity for the audience to consider the distance between the playworld and their own.

Again reflecting a more conservative sexual ethic, at the end of the production Imogen and Posthumus were holding hands. Posthumus touched her cheek, and she looked down, modest but pleased. This couple would also probably live happily ever after, but their happiness was qualified by its life in an earlier time. What a Victorian woman considered a romantic and happy marriage would not necessarily satisfy a late-twentieth-century woman. Expectations women now carry concerning sex relations and marriage were historicized by their Victorian counterpart and vice versa.

THE COST OF PLAYING WITH SHAKESPEARE

Akalaitis's production produced a stark polarization of criticism. The daily newspaper critics despised it, while theater magazine and academic critics, those who read its postmodern aesthetic, praised it. In December of 1989, *American Theatre* ran a series of articles on the production entitled, "*Cymbeline* and Its Critics: A Case Study." Primary contributors Elinor Fuchs and James Leverett reproved the establishment critics, who in New York were all conservative men, for damning a daring, intelligent, and innovative production. Fuchs reported that the show developed an "underground following," some believing that "a major new American Shakespeare talent had emerged."[60]

Discussing the production's detractors, Leverett wrote: "What offended me so deeply about the reviews of *Cymbeline* was not the way they were negative, a risk all artists run just by being artists, but *how* they were negative. These violent, vituperatively dismissive reactions comprised but another chapter in a long history of abusive, willfully uncomprehending rejection of artists who are responsible for so much of the life in New York Theatre, and to a great extent in American Theatre, during the last quarter-century." While admitting that the play was complex, the critics then "turned on Akalaitis for engaging its complexity."[61] Although Frank Rich complimented Akalaitis, saying she possessed a "not inconsiderable intelligence," he remarked that she wasted it on "the most reckless entry in the Shakespeare Festival's Marathon," creating "a travesty of *Cymbeline*." Rich commented that unlike James Lapine's recent direction of a magical *Winter's Tale,* Akalaitis failed to "knit . . . together" the complicated plot. "Ms. Akalaitis, by contrast, levels everything to the low common denominator of her campy evocation of Victorian melodrama."[62] Writing for the *New York Post,* Clive Barnes was even more scathing: "But there is a gorgeously autumnal mood to 'Cymbeline,' which Akalaitis so thoroughly misses—making everything she can and a few things she can't into a farrago of fun—that one scarcely knows how to discuss a misreading so ignorant as to be effectively beneath consideration."[63] Howard Kissel for the New York *Daily News* criticized the production for not making the plot clear, not developing the play's themes, and not staging believable characters.[64] What the conservative critics demanded—unity, coherence, seriousness, sincere acting, suspension of disbelief—were the very elements her aesthetic put into play and thereby made relative. Fuchs believed that it was precisely Akalaitis's application of this aesthetic to Shakespeare that got her into so much trouble.[65] Unfortunately, her "failure" to produce a conventional production more in line with American expectations of Shakespeare caused an unwarranted critical backlash. When an employee of the Public asked me what I thought of the production when I was there reviewing photographs, I told him I enjoyed it and did not understand why the critics were so vicious. He agreed with me, adding, "I think it was ahead of its time."

My interview with Akalaitis was the shortest, and done via phone despite my request for one in person. Interviewed extensively, Akalaitis "think[s] one master-interview would be fine for the papers. It could . . . be revised a bit every three years."[66] Now in her sixties, she is not as interested in garnering yet more press for her work, and hopes to be directing less in the future: "In some way, I'm more emotionally involved as I get older. It's not easier; it's harder. It's like someone took you into an alley and beat you up to direct a play. . . . I tend to do these plays that hurt you. I tend to do these plays where you suffer a lot. And I do suffer." Sometimes, especially intense plays give her nightmares.[67] However, she is not merely attracted to emotionally difficult pieces dealing with serious themes. Akalaitis believes that theater artists have "a special responsibility at least to try to put work into a political or social context."[68] In a 1990 interview, she said, "I don't know how you can do theatre now without dealing with . . . everything. With this epidemic [AIDS], with all this violence, with all these people being shot on the streets of New York, with this global ecological nightmare that is descending on us minute by minute. It's not that you have to do plays about it. But it simply has to be there."[69]

Robert Brustein has criticized her for a radical feminist ideology that regards all of history as the story of how women have been victimized and brutalized by men.[70] But Akalaitis does research the productions she directs and is interested in the particularities of different historical eras.[71] Although she is clearly interested in a number of different contemporary issues, her feminist way of life informs a vision of the plays especially attuned to the fate of women.

Barbara Gaines is at the opposite end of the spectrum, at least in terms of conscious intent. She is especially attuned to whatever human dynamics she finds in the plays, with only the barest of nods to history and an explicit rejection of politicizing meaning. But her consciousness, influenced inevitably by living as a woman in this society, certainly prompts her to make some production choices that many would view as feminist.

Although finding a permanent home for her theater and developing an international reputation were big dreams for Gaines, in 1993 she reported, "[M]y biggest dream is still to make the company's ticket prices compatible with those for a movie."[72] Accessibility and identification for the audience are the primary forces driving her work. And in those areas, she has been extremely successful. If not politically savvy, her Shakespeare productions are compelling. Gaines has popularized Shakespeare's plays by making them contemporary and working primarily within psychological if not theatrical realism. Akalaitis, at least in this production, relativized her audience's conceptions of romance, fantasy, gender, heterosexual relationships, and performance, making them aware of other histories. These directors cater to different audiences, offering insights to their respective constituents. For a nation of audiences as diverse as America, we need this kind of range in directors of Shakespeare.

Epilogue

WOMEN DIRECTORS OF SHAKESPEARE ON PROMINENT AMERICAN stages still constitute a tiny minority of artistic direction in the American theater. It is hardly surprising, then, that many of these women have worked together, or at least for the same institutions. Wolpe's company grew out of her association with Packer's. O'Brien has not only worked as a text coach for Adams but has also directed at People's Light, as has Wolpe. Both Bensussen and O'Brien have also directed at the North Carolina Shakespeare Festival. Both Bensussen and Akalaitis have worked at the New York Shakespeare Festival. For this rare yet diverse breed, it is a small world.

But certainly many women are directing Shakespeare in lower-profile venues, particularly at academic institutions. When I directed my first full-length Shakespeare play, *The Taming of the Shrew,* for a local theater, I was particularly blessed with a talented and well-trained actor to play Kate, Jennifer Alison. I was able to communicate a framework of interpretation to her and let her find specific choices that she could powerfully embody. However, I was not so lucky with the actor playing Petruchio. He was visually perfect, and he threatened and wooed well, but he was not nearly as well-trained or sensitive to the nuances of the text as the woman lead. And since this was a low-budget, community theater, a number of unfortunate technical disasters diverted my attention near the end of rehearsals, so I could not do as much fine-tuning as I wished. My desire not to alienate the audience of a small company dependent on the box office for its survival also led me to qualify but generally support the comic ending. My experience was similar to the women I interviewed: various elements both helped and hindered the embodiment of my vision of the play. Yet, also like many of them, I did find ways to put theory, or at least a feminist viewpoint, effectively into practice. More recently, I have directed *Measure for Measure* and *Romeo and Juliet* at MacMurray College. Although I still struggled, for instance, with how to give violence a range of values in *Romeo and Juliet,* my knowledge of other productions and particularly the work of these women definitely influenced both my vision and production choices without robbing me of the opportunity to make "original" choices quite different from theirs. H. R. Coursen claims that, unlike the exchange that developed in the 1970s, currently there's almost an insurmountable divide between scholarship and practice, which he generally considers a good thing: "Most directors are shrewd enough to read a script and translate it onto their stage without academic intervention. Not many of us can translate what we have to say about a play into an action that works on stage. Current criticism of the plays—and little of it *deals* with the plays—is really relevant to the plays as dramatic vehicles."[1] While academic theory and theatrical practice ultimately have different purposes and methods, I believe there *can* be fruitful interaction between them.

In an attempt to counteract the typically masculine emphasis on product, a number of other feminist performance studies have focused on the process by which women directors work. This book has considered process, but focused more on performance choices. Future studies might consider following the entire trajectory of a director's work. Attending design meetings as well as rehearsals, and then viewing the performance multiple times, would form the ideal basis for studying women directors at work. The limitation of this, of course, is that the intensive attention to one such director prohibits much comparative work, and to make a book marketable, one would have to choose high-profile directors who have already been written about extensively in other venues. Academic journals might be interested in substantive articles on talented but lesser-known directors. But such an approach would provide valuable information, and a diversity of approaches will allow us to form a multifaceted composite of women directors in the theater.

Perhaps one of the most difficult challenges facing theater historians is determining audience reception. While many feminist performance critics (myself included) talk about the kinds of cultural work in which performances potentially engage, one wonders how deep and far-reaching the impact on spectators truly is. The result of surveys, which I have used in the past, is that they are not often answered, and when they are, the authors are often academic spectators, who hardly form normative responses. In these instances, directors are often "preaching to the choir," as

Bensussen says. The same is going to be true for postshow discussions, because those more highly trained in literary or theatrical cultures are the ones most likely to feel comfortable speaking publicly at such an event. Going with a class of students is another possibility, and yet they, too, form a distinct segment of the audience population unlike the majority of spectators. And some responses are subconscious, or surface much later, after time for reflection and growth. But perhaps searching for a normative or even median audience response is itself a futile endeavor, and all one can hope to accomplish is to assemble a collection of opinions from various audience subcultures. This, too, needs to be explored further in future work.

My conclusions about the women I have studied are clearly the result of my own reading, which is structured by my avowed feminist lens and other biases of which I am not always aware. The most significant thing I learned in my journey from a scholar viewing the women's work, to an interviewer hearing their words, to a practitioner working in the trenches myself, is that meaning is far less stable than I had originally thought, the gap between directorial intention and audience reception not only occasionally wide but quite differently constructed by individual viewers. Olivia's line to Viola sums up most audience members' unconscious responses to meaning in performance: "I would you were as I would have you be" (3.1.144). The disjuncture between directorial vision and various audience members' perceptions reminds us that our undersight and oversight are often the products of our previous readings and/or viewings and our present Will.

Notes

Introduction

1. For an insightful study of this topic, see Carol Chillington Rutter, *Enter the Body: Women and Representation on Shakespeare's Stage* (London: Routledge, 2001).
2. Clifford Geertz, "Thick Description: Toward an Interpretive Theory of Culture," in *The Interpretation of Cultures* (New York: Basic Books, 1973), 3–22.
3. Barbara Hodgdon, "Replicating Richard: Body Doubles, Body Politics," *Theatre Journal* 50 (May 1998): 208; Rutter, *Enter the Body*, xiii.
4. Ellen Donkin and Susan Clement, eds., introduction to *Upstaging Big Daddy: Directing Theater as if Gender and Race Matter* (Ann Arbor: University of Michigan Press, 1993), 2.
5. Unfortunately, there are no women of color in this group and only Lisa Wolpe is openly lesbian. My sense is that few women who are of color and/or lesbian are attracted to directing Shakespeare.
6. Marco de Marinis, "'A Faithful Betrayal of Performance': Notes on the Use of Video in Theatre," trans. Glyn Jones, *New Theatre Quarterly* 1 (November 1985): 387.
7. Ibid., 386.
8. Charlotte Canning, *Feminist Theaters in the USA: Staging Women's Experience* (New York: Routledge, 1996), 17–18. The second part of this quote is her paraphrase of Susan Armitage, "The Next Step," in "Women's Oral History Two," special issue, *Frontiers* 7, no. 1 (1983): 4.
9. See Marinis, "A Faithful Betrayal," 383.
10. Misha Berson, "Women at the Helm: In Leadership Posts Once Reserved for Men, They're Challenging Our Assumptions about Sex and Power," in *A Sourcebook of Feminist Theatre and Performance: On and Beyond the Stage*, ed. Carol Martin (London: Routledge, 1996), 67.
11. Elizabeth Schaefer, *Ms-Directing Shakespeare: Women Direct Shakespeare* (London: The Women's Press, 1998), 12.
12. Lizbeth Goodman, *Feminist Stages: Interviews with Women in Contemporary British Theatre* (Amsterdam: Harwood Academic Publishers, 1996), 296–97.
13. Ibid., 297.
14. Linda Hart, "Motherhood According to Karen Finley: *The Theory of Total Blame*," in *Sourcebook of Feminist Theatre* (see note 10), 111.
15. Lizbeth Goodman, *Contemporary Feminist Theatres: To Each Her Own* (London: Routledge, 1993), 218.

16. Geraldine Harris, *Staging Femininities: Performance and Performativity* (Manchester: Manchester University Press, 1999), 6, 21, 177–89.
17. Richard Schechner, "TDR Comment: Post Post-Structuralism?" *TDR* 44 (fall 2000): 4–7.
18. Richard Schechner, "TDR Comment: Mainstream Theatre and Performance Studies," *TDR* 44 (summer 2000): 4–6.
19. Donkin and Clement, introduction to *Upstaging Big Daddy*, 1.
20. Ibid., 2.
21. Tilda Swinton, "Subverting Images of the Female," interview by Lizbeth Goodman, *New Theatre Quarterly* 6 (August 1990): 222.
22. Lorraine Helms, "Acts of Resistance: The Feminist Player," in *The Weyward Sisters: Shakespeare and Feminist Politics* (Cambridge: Blackwell, 1994), 102–56.
23. Rutter, *Enter the Body*, xv.
24. Penny Gay, *As She Likes It: Shakespeare's Unruly Women* (London: Routledge, 1994), 3.
25. Laurence Senelick, ed., introduction to *Gender in Performance: The Presentation of Difference in the Performing Arts* (Hanover, N.H.: University Press of New England, 1992), xii. See also Faye E. Dudden, *Women in the American Theatre: Actresses and Audiences 1790–1870* (New Haven: Yale University Press, 1994), 4. Dudden traces the development within the nineteenth-century American theater from women's opportunities to transform the construction of their gender onstage toward their objectification as sexual objects.
26. Lesley Ferris, "The Female Self and Performance: The Case of *The First Actress*," in *Theatre and Feminist Aesthetics*, eds. Karen Louise Laughlin and Catherine Schuler (Madison, N.J.: Fairleigh Dickinson University Press, 1995), 247–52.
27. Jill Dolan, *The Feminist Spectator as Critic* (Ann Arbor: University of Michigan Research Press, 1988), 101.
28. Barbara Freedman, "Frame-up: Feminism, Psychoanalysis, Theatre," in *Feminist Theatre and Theory*, ed. Helene Keyssar (New York: St. Martin's Press, 1996), 93–97.
29. Peggy Phelan, "Feminist Theory, Poststructuralism, and Performance," in *Sourcebook of Feminist Theatre* (see note 10), 178–79.
30. Jill Dolan, *Presence and Desire: Essays on Gender, Sexuality, Performance* (Ann Arbor: University of Michigan Press, 1993), 1.
31. Dolan, *Feminist Spectator*, 54.
32. Dudden insightfully writes about the "attenuation of self" probably experienced by women performing in nineteenth-century "Leg Shows": "[A]lthough humans are all inherent objects, we suffer to the extent that we are *only* objects" (*Women in the American Theatre*, 180).
33. Anthony Dawson, "Performance and Participation: Desdemona, Foucault, and the Actor's Body," in *Shakespeare, Theory, and Performance*, ed. James C. Bulman (New York: Routledge, 1996), 31–32.
34. Anna Cutler, "Abstract Body Language: Documenting Women's Bodies in Theatre," *New Theatre Quarterly* 14 (May 1998): 115.
35. Including the self in performance is the defining characteristic of a number of feminist approaches Goodman examines ("Women's Alternative Shakespeares and Women's Alternatives to Shakespeare in Contemporary British Theater," in *Cross-Cultural Performances: Differences in Women's Re-Visions of Shakespeare*, ed. Marianne Novy [Chicago: University of Illinois Press, 1993], 224).

36. Barbara Hodgdon, *The Shakespeare Trade: Performances and Appropriations* (Philadelphia: University of Pennsylvania Press, 1998), 31.
37. Ibid.
38. Ibid., 33.
39. Ibid., 38.
40. Dolan, *Presence and Desire,* 113.
41. Peter Holland, *English Shakespeares: Shakespeare on the English Stage in the 1990s* (Cambridge: Cambridge University Press, 1997), 20, 19.
42. Sarah Werner, *Shakespeare and Feminist Performance: Ideology Onstage* (London: Routledge, 2001), 42.
43. W. B. Worthen, *Shakespeare and the Authority of Performance* (Cambridge: Cambridge University Press, 1997), 27.
44. Ibid., 26.
45. Harris, *Staging Femininities,* 171–72.
46. Susan Bassnett, introduction to "The Changing Status of Women in Theatre," in *The Routledge Reader in Gender and Performance,* ed. Lizbeth Goodman (New York: Routledge, 1998), 87–91.
47. Misha Berson, "Women at the Helm," 61–78, esp. 61, 69. See also Robert Trussell, "Directing Women: The MO Rep Will Join Other Regional Theaters in Giving Females More Chances to Lead Productions," *Kansas City Star,* 7 October 1999, Metropolitan edition, sec. E. *American Theatre* ran a "Women in Theatre" issue in September of 1998 wherein playwright Tina Howe reports, "[T]he theatre is still largely a male bastion. You can count the number of important female critics and artistic directors on one hand" (29).
48. Marianne Novy, *Transforming Shakespeare: Contemporary Women's Re-Visions in Literature and Performance* (New York: St. Martin's Press), 8.
49. Holland, *English Shakespeares,* xiii.
50. Jeffrey Mason, *Performing America: Cultural Nationalism in American Theater,* eds. Jeffrey D. Mason and J. Ellen Gainor (Ann Arbor: University of Michigan Press, 1999), 1.
51. Felicia Londré with Kimberly L. Janczuk, "A Guide to American Shakespeare Companies and Festivals with Academic Affiliations," in *Teaching Shakespeare Through Performance,* ed. Milla Cozart Riggio (New York: Modern Language Association, 1999), 435.
52. For a discussion of Shakespeare's institutionalization in the United States, see Michael D. Bristol, *Shakespeare's America, America's Shakespeare* (New York: Routledge, 1990). For a discussion of *Shakespeare in Love*'s popularity, see Werner, *Shakespeare and Feminist Performance,* 8–19.
53. Mel Gussow, "Shakespeare as Catalyst for Brainstorming Actors," *New York Times,* 10 June 1996, sec. C.
54. Robert Brustein, "A Theatrical Declaration of Independence," in *Reimagining American Theatre* (Chicago: Ivan R. Dee, 1991), 240–48.
55. Robert Brustein, "How to 'Serve' Shakespeare," in *Reimagining American Theatre,* 204.
56. Holland, *English Shakespeares,* 161. He later remarks about Michael Bogdanov's videotaped experiments with inner-city Birmingham residents. Capturing one man quietly speaking Caliban's "This island's mine" monologue in front of a building site "was a powerful affirmation of the subversive potential of *The Tempest,* denying the government's belief in the divine right of Toryism to appropriate Shakespeare for its version of English culture" (254).
57. J. Ellen Gainor, introduction to *Performing America* (see note 50), 15.

Part 1. The Directors

1. Schafer, *Ms-Directing Shakespeare,* 11.
2. Rutter, *Enter the Body,* xvi.
3. I was a dramaturg intern at the Huntington Theatre Company in Boston from 1995–96 under Koszyn's guidance. I admire her creativity and intelligence.
4. Unless otherwise noted, all quotes and paraphrases come from Jayme Koszyn, interview by author, tape recording, 15 June 1997, New Haven, Conn., and Jayme Koszyn, telephone interview by author, tape recording, 30 August 1997.
5. She noted this was not true for the production at the Huntington Theatre she had just finished working on.
6. Priscilla Flood writes: "The old saw is true: women simply do not objectify the male body the way men do the female body. That doesn't mean we take any less pleasure in watching the opposite sex. We love to look at men. But a man seeing a desirable woman walking down the street can easily imagine her undressed and available to him. He needs no response from her to continue his fantasy or even get an erection. A woman's fantasy, on the other hand, revolves around who the man is, how he fits into the world, how he might relate to her; she doesn't make that automatic mental leap into bed. For a woman, the big payoff in street flirtation is simply a look, some communication between her and the man who's caught her eye." "Body Parts," *Esquire,* June 1981, 35–43, quoted in John Marshall Townsend, *What Women Want—What Men Want: Why the Sexes Still See Love and Commitment So Differently* (Oxford: Oxford University Press, 1998), 17.
7. John Berger, *Ways of Seeing* (London: BBC and Penguin, 1972), 54.
8. The archive is maintained and developed by a group of people in the department known as the Shakespeare Project. The archive houses collections of materials from the Folger, Huntington, British, and other university libraries. It contains digital images of books housed in these libraries with links to texts, artwork, and film. The archive is not available to the public but can be used via terminals at the libraries themselves.
9. For further discussion of this, see her article "The Dramaturgy and the Irrational" on serving as the dramaturg for a production of *Iphigenia* in *Dramaturgy in American Theater: A Source Book,* where the sacrifice of the title character was mirrored in the firing of an actor (Susan Jonas, ed. [Fort Worth, Texas: Harcourt Brace College, 1996], 276–82).
10. This quote comes from a single sheet without title, author, or date produced by LAWSC for promotional purposes. It was probably written by Wolpe in 1997.
11. LAWSC Web site, http://www.lawsc.net/lawsclwr.htm; California Shakespeare Festival website for their 1997 artistic staff, www.via.net/~csf/1997/Company/Wolpe.htm (accessed 18 December 1998; site now discontinued).
12. Lisa Wolpe, phone interview by author, tape recording, 16–17 August 1998. All quotes and paraphrases come from this interview unless otherwise noted.
13. Robert Koehler, "*Romeo and Juliet* Are Cross-Dressed Lovers in New Staging," *Los Angeles Times,* 14 March 1993, Valley edition, Calendar.
14. For a fuller description of this theory, see Kristin Linklater, *Freeing the Natural Voice* (New York: Drama Book Publishers, 1976) and *Freeing Shakespeare's Voice* (New York: Theatre Communications Group, 1992).

15. Greg Spring, "All-Woman *Othello* Explores What Men Feel: L.A. Women's Shakespeare Company Finds Deeper Levels, Social Inflections in Bard's Domestic Tragedy," review of *Othello*, as performed by LAWSC, West Los Angeles, Calif., *Back Stage West*, 2 June 1994. *Back Stage West* is the West Coast version of *Back Stage*, a weekly paper primarily produced for the casting industry, the stage version of *Variety* and *Hollywood Reporter*. It also runs feature articles and reviews. A couple of years ago it bought out the well-respected *Drama-Logue*, also a casting industry weekly paper. Most of the reviews on LAWSC were sent to me by the theater.

16. Natsuko Ohama, *Muse of Fire*, prod. and dir. Lisa Wolpe and Sandy Shepherd, 12 min., 1993, videocassette.

17. Vsevolod Meyerhold and Eugenio Barba worked with a similar concept, "pre-acting." However, unlike Meyerhold and Barba, transcending gender is a step in the process for Wolpe that leads ultimately to a realistic performance.

18. Elias Stimac, review of *Othello*, as performed by LAWSC, West Los Angeles, Calif., *Drama-Logue*, 9–15 June 1994.

19. Rob Kendt, "The Theatre Makers," *Back Stage West*, 6–11 July 1995.

20. Philip Brandes, "*Richard III* Puts Twist on Exploring Soul's Dark Side," review of *Richard III*, as performed by the LAWSC, Culver City, Calif., *Los Angeles Times*, 22 March 1996.

21. Paul Birchall, review of *A Midsummer Night's Dream*, as performed by the LAWSC, Culver City, Calif., *Back Stage West*, 7–14 May 1998. This show was highlighted as the Critic's Pick.

22. Lisa Wolpe as quoted in Debbi K. Swanson, "Women Take a Stab at *Richard III*," review of *Richard III*, as performed by the LAWSC, Culver City, Calif., *The Outlook*, 16 March 1996. *The Outlook* is an evening daily paper that comes out of Santa Monica and carries a stage news section. Swanson is a freelance reviewer for several local Los Angeles papers and frequently reviews LAWSC.

23. Robert Hofler, "Pulling the Switch: Actresses Revel in the Power—If Not the Glory—of Playing Men," *Back Stage*, 17–23 September 1993.

24. Tony Tran, "Her Kingdom for a Horse: All-female Version of *Richard III* Proves Revelatory," review of *Richard III*, as performed by the LAWSC, Culver City, Calif., *Los Angeles View*, 29 March–4 April 1996, Theater, 44.

25. Martha Nakagawa, "Shakespeare Lovers, Rejoice!" review of *Hamlet*, as performed by the LAWSC, Culver City, Calif., *The Rafu Shimpo: Los Angeles Japanese Daily News*, 26 April 1995. Despite this paper's general attempt to show that Asians can compete successfully with Caucasians (and an Asian woman was double cast with Wolpe for the title role), I think the criticism is still valid, especially since it is confirmed by other critics without race-specific agendas.

26. Madeleine Shaner, "*Richard III* Done Splendidly with All-Woman Cast," review of *Richard III*, as performed by the LAWSC, Culver City, Calif., *Park Labrea News*, 4 April 1996. This show was highlighted as Best Bet. Shaner is another freelance reviewer of Los Angeles local papers who follows the LAWSC.

27. Lisa Wolpe, interview and e-mail message to author, 17 November 2003.

28. Ibid.

29. Ibid.

30. Helen Epstein, *The Companies She Keeps: Tina Packer Builds a Theatre* (Cambridge: Plunkett Lake Press, 1985), 13.

31. Shakespeare and Company Web site, http://www.shakespeare.org/home/tina.html.
32. Epstein, *Companies She Keeps*, 16–26.
33. Tina Packer as quoted in Constance Gorfinkle, "Scene and Heard: Shakespeare Director at Home in London, Lenox or Foxboro," *Foxboro (Mass.) Patriot Ledger*, 14 September 1996, Saturday ROP edition, Features.
34. John Gielgud with John Miller, *Acting Shakespeare* (New York: Charles Scribner's Sons, 1991), 35. Also see Gussow, "Shakespeare as Catalyst," sec. C.
35. Helen Hayes as quoted in Lawrence Malkin, "In Lenox They Are 'Dropping in' on the Bard of Avon: Shakespeare and Company in Lenox, MA," *Smithsonian*, November 1991, 137.
36. www.shakespeare.org/home/tina.html.
37. Tina Packer as quoted in Malkin, "Dropping in," 138.
38. Dennis Krausnick as quoted in John Morrish, "The [Shakespeare and Company] Camp's the Thing," *Daily Telegraph*, 17 August 1996, Telegraph Magazine, 33.
39. Tina Packer as quoted in Epstein, *The Companies She Keeps*, 38.
40. Patti Hartigan, "Here, They're Not Merely Players: Actors Run Shakespeare and Company," *Boston Globe*, 21 August 1994, city edition, Arts and Film.
41. Morrish, "Camp's the Thing."
42. Gorfinkle, "Scene and Heard."
43. Malkin, "Dropping in," 138.
44. Tina Packer, interview by author, tape recording, Cambridge, Mass., 24 October and 14 November 1997. All quotes and paraphrases of Packer's ideas come from these interviews unless otherwise noted.
45. Ed Siegel, "Shakespeare in Good Company: Dropping in on Packer's Method," *Boston Globe*, 22 September 1996, city edition, sec. N.
46. Ibid.
47. In all fairness, most of the staff was open and accepting. I doubt many other participants in the program felt as I did.
48. Karen Campbell, "A Celebration of Theater Works by Women," *Boston Globe*, 20 February 2000, third edition, sec. M.
49. Ed Siegel, "Mute the Minimalism, Revise the Revisionism: In the Berkshire Hills, the Arts Can Come in Peaks and Valleys," *Boston Globe*, 29 August 1995, city edition, Living.
50. Ed Siegel, "Packer's *Richard III* Considers the Women," review of *Richard III*, as performed by Shakespeare and Company, Lenox, Mass., *Boston Globe*, 15 July 1999, city edition, sec. E.
51. This quote comes from a page of directors' notes entitled "Producing Shakespeare in 1991: Guiding Assumptions," photocopy, Guilford College, Greensboro, N.C.
52. Ellen O'Brien, interview by author, tape recording, Greensboro, N.C., 10 October 1997. All quotations and paraphrases of O'Brien's ideas will come from this interview unless otherwise noted.
53. *The People's Light and Theatre Company: 20 Years 1974–1994*, 2, 4, 29. This booklet is publicity material that does not list a date or publisher.
54. The current mission statement from their Web site is slightly different, though similar in spirit. See http://www.peopleslight.org/2003–2004/43-mission.html.
55. The quoted mission statement and basic operating tenets are on a single sheet of People's Light letterhead, which Abby gave to me at the conclusion of our interview.

56. Abigail Adams, interview by author, tape recording, Malvern, Pa., 10 June 1997. All quotes and paraphrases of Adams come from this interview unless otherwise noted.

57. *People's Light and Theatre,* 17.

58. http://www.peopleslight.org/2003-2004/44-history.html.

59. The last quote comes from the interview, but the previous material comes from a bio sent to me from People's Light.

60. http://www.peopleslight.org/2003-2004/44-history.html.

61. The author of this quote is not cited. It appears in Felicia Hardison Londré, "North Carolina Shakespeare Festival," in *Shakespeare Companies and Festivals: An International Guide,* eds. Ron Engle, Felicia Hardison Londré, and Daniel J. Watermeier (Westport, Conn.: Greenwood Press, 1994), 256.

62. Londré, "North Carolina Shakespeare Festival," 256.

63. As quoted in Londré, "NCSF," 257.

64. Adams also told me that the very conservative right in and around Malvern had criticized People's Light for its productions of other plays but accepted, for instance, a magician and a potential rapist in *The Tempest* without protest. When they did *Twelfth Night* for high school audiences, however, there were some irate letters about Toby's drinking.

65. Londré, "NCSF," 258.

66. Norman Hines Jr., "NCSF's *Twelfth Night* Lives up to Past History of Excellence," review of *Twelfth Night, Asheboro (N.C.) Courier-Tribune,* n.d. [circa late August 1996].

67. This term was actually not used in the interview but occurs in *People's Light and Theater,* 19.

68. This information was in the bio sent to me from Emerson College.

69. Melia Bensussen, interview by author, tape recording, Princeton, N.J., 11 June 1997. All quotes and paraphrases of Bensussen come from this interview unless otherwise noted.

70. Daniel J. Watermeier and Felicia Hardison Londré, "Oregon Shakespeare Festival," in *Shakespeare Companies and Festivals* (see note 61), 275–81.

71. Christopher Reynolds, "Room and Bard," *Los Angeles Times,* 13 July 1997, home edition, sec. L; Steven Winn, "Much Ado about Ashland: Director Henry Woronicz Toys with Tradition," *San Francisco Chronicle,* 13 March 1994, Sunday edition, Sunday Datebook; Paul L. Knight as quoted in Reynolds, "Room and Bard."

72. Reynolds, "Room and Bard."

73. J. D. Brown, "Ashland: Oregon's Stage-Struck Town," *New Orleans Times-Picayune,* 11 June 1995, sec. E.

74. Veronica Gould Stoddart, "Shakespeare Settings, Scene One: Oregon's Famous Festival," *Chicago Sun-Times,* 25 April 1999, late sports final edition, Travel.

75. Winn, "Much Ado."

76. Shirley Patton, quoted in "1935–1995: We're Still in Love with the Future . . . and our Past Proves It," *Oregon Shakespeare Festival* 2 (1995): 87. This article is a collection of staff member contributions and anonymous narrative.

77. Winn, "Much Ado."

78. Rebecca Morris, "Actor Has New Festival Role: Director," *Seattle Times,* 5 March 1992, final edition, sec. C.

79. Misha Berson, "Growing Pains: Under Its New Director, Ashland's Popular Theater Festival Gets a Mild Makeover," *Seattle Times,* 3 March 1994, final edition, sec. E.

80. Patton, quoted in "1935–1995," 91.
81. Henry Woronicz, quoted in "1935–1995," 88.
82. Misha Berson, "Spirit of Change Infuses Shakespeare Festival," *Seattle Times*, 23 June 1996, final edition, sec. M. Based on her reviews of the shows and my own visit to OSF in 1998, I differ in my conclusions somewhat from Berson, who believes that Appel is more progressive than I do.
83. Ben Brantley, "Reporter's Notebook: A Lesson to New York on Grace in Theater," *New York Times*, 1 October 1997, late edition, sec. E.
84. Stoddart, "Shakespeare Settings."
85. Kathy Claussen, e-mail message to author, 29 January 2001. Claussen is on the administrative staff at OSF.
86. Watermeier and Londré, "Oregon Shakespeare Festival," 284.
87. Winn, "Much Ado."
88. Clifford Terry, "Shaking Up Shakespeare: Barbara Gaines Takes on the Bard," *Chicago Tribune*, 28 November 1993, final edition, Arts.
89. "ANUW Fall Event with Barbara Gaines," *Association of Northwestern University Women Newsletter*, fall 2000, http://www.northwestern.edu/anuw/newsletters/winter01_newsletter.html#autumn.
90. Judith Newmark, "Shakespeare Takes the Windy City by Storm," *St. Louis Post-Dispatch*, 9 January 2000, five-star lift edition, sec. C.
91. Terry, "Shaking Up Shakespeare."
92. Barbara Gaines, interview by author, tape recording, Chicago, Ill., 11 November 1997. All quotes or paraphrases of Gaines are taken from this interview unless otherwise noted.
93. Richard Christiansen as quoted in Terry, "Shaking up Shakespeare."
94. Hedy Weiss, "Running the Gamut with Shakespeare Repertory," *Chicago Sun-Times*, 2 February 1992, five-star sports final edition, Show; Jean A. Williams, "*Richard III* Lacks Firepower," review of *Richard III*, Chicago, Ill., *Chicago Sun-Times*, 22 April 1996, Features; Richard Christiansen, "Shakespeare's *Shrew* Tamed for the '90s," review of *The Taming of the Shrew*, Chicago, Ill., *Chicago Tribune*, 2 December 1993, north sports final edition, News.
95. "ANUW Fall Event."
96. "Chicago Mayor Richard M. Daley Declares Shakespeare Repertory Theater Day," *Folio* [Shakespeare Repertory newsletter], autumn 1997: 2.
97. Chicago Shakespeare Theater Web site, http://www.chicagoshakes.com/about.html.
98. Barbara Gaines as quoted in Terry, "Shaking Up Shakespeare."
99. Ibid.
100. Ibid.
101. Barbara Gaines as quoted in Penelope Mesic, "Into the Woods; Murders and Nightmares, Romance and Rustic Comedy—Shakespeare's at His Best in the Great Outdoors: Chicago's Shakespeare Repertory's First Outdoor Production," *Chicago* 43 (August 1994).
102. Hedy Weiss, "Love at First Fight: Barbara Gaines Passionately Tames the *Shrew*," *Chicago Sun-Times*, 1 December 1993, late sports final edition, sec. 2.
103. Barbara Gaines as quoted in ibid.
104. Barbara Gaines as quoted in Terry, "Shaking up Shakespeare."
105. Gaines's discussion of the Folio technique can be found in ibid.
106. Weiss, "Running the Gamut."
107. Pauline Johnson, *Feminism as Radical Humanism* (Boulder, Colo.: Westview Press, 1994).

108. Rebecca Daniels, *Women Stage Directors Speak: Exploring the Influence of Gender on Their Work* (Jefferson, N.C:. McFarland and Co., 1996), 150. One-third of the directors she interviewed defined themselves as humanist rather than feminist, though Daniels remarks, "they firmly believe [the universal human experience] can and must be presented through the experiences of women as well as men" (156).

109. Terry, "Shaking Up Shakespeare."

110. Hedy Weiss, "Pierless: Chicago Shakespeare Theater Opens Its New Navy Pier Home with *Antony and Cleopatra*," *Chicago Sun-Times,* 17 October 1999, late sports final edition, sec. E.

111. Ellen Domke, "Bard's Elegant New Home on Navy Pier: Shakespeare Theater Opening Draws Applause," *Chicago Sun-Times,* 24 October 1999, late sports final edition, News.

112. Terry, "Shaking up Shakespeare."

113. Criss Henderson as quoted in Newmark, "Shakespeare Takes Windy City."

114. Newmark, "Shakespeare Takes Windy City"; *Folio,* autumn 1997; "About the Theater," http://www.chicagoshakes.com/about.html.

115. The penultimate sentence is drawn from my interview with Gaines, and the last sentence is a paraphrase of material found in Terry, "Shaking Up Shakespeare."

116. Stu Feller, "Fine Acting, Brilliant Directing Make *Cymbeline* Grand Theater Spectacle," review of *Cymbeline,* Chicago, Ill., *GNW,* 25 October 1989.

117. Mike Steele, "Feminist Provocateurs of Their Eras: Director Feels 'Sisterhood' with Playwright Aphra Behn," *Minneapolis Star Tribune,* 10 June 1994, metro edition, sec. E.

118. Patrick Pacheco, "'I'm not avant-garde': JoAnne Akalaitis, Joseph Papp's Heir, Faces the Biggest Challenge of Her Career: Getting the Public into New York's Public Theater," *Los Angeles Times,* 15 November 1992, home edition, Calendar; Nancy Hass, "A Cerebral Modernist Whose Revolution Rolls On," *New York Times,* 24 January 1999, late edition, sec. 2; Jeff Daniel, "A Different Direction," *St. Louis Post-Dispatch,* 16 June 1998, five-star lift edition, Everyday Magazine, sec. D; Nelson Pressley, "Director Bearing Greek Gifts: JoAnne Akalaitis Puts a New Face on the Classics," *Washington Post,* 27 March 1999, final edition, sec. C; Deborah Saivetz, *An Event in Space: JoAnne Akalaitis in Rehearsal* (Hanover, N.H.: Smith and Kraus, 2000), xvii-xviii, 138–40; Amy S. Green, *The Revisionist Stage: American Directors Reinvent the Classics* (Cambridge: University of Cambridge Press, 1994), 90; Bard College Web site, http://www.bard.edu/academics/faculty/.

119. Joseph Papp as quoted in Alex Witchel, "Papp Names Akalaitis to Step in as Shakespeare Festival Head," *New York Times,* 21 August 1991, late edition, sec. C.

120. Peter Ziesler as quoted in Allan Parachini, "Joseph Papp Steps down at N.Y. Shakespeare Festival: In Ill Health and Distraught over the Death of His Son, the 70-Year-Old Founder Names JoAnne Akalaitis Artistic Director," *Los Angeles Times,* 22 August 1991, home edition, sec. F.

121. As quoted in Pacheco, "Biggest Challenge," Calendar.

122. JoAnne Akalaitis and Molly Smith as quoted in Pressley, "Director Bearing Greek Gifts."

123. Witchel, "Papp Names Akalaitis."

124. JoAnne Akalaitis as quoted in Frank Rich, "Opening a Window at a Theater Gone Stale," *New York Times,* 21 March 1993, late edition, sec. 2.

125. Pacheco, "Biggest Challenge," Calendar.
126. JoAnne Akalaitis as quoted in Saivetz, Event in Space, 190.
127. JoAnne Akalaitis as quoted in Pressley, "Director Bearing Greek Gifts."
128. "JoAnne Akalaitis, interviewed by Jonathan Kalb," Theater 15 (spring 1984): 13.
129. JoAnne Akalaitis as quoted in Hass, "Cerebral Modernist."
130. Hass, "Cerebral Modernist." For a further description of her application of encephalitis-type movements to acting, see Saivetz, Event in Space, 134.
131. JoAnne Akalaitis as quoted in Pacheco, "Biggest Challenge," Calendar.
132. JoAnne Akalaitis as quoted in Pressley, "Director Bearing Greek Gifts."
133. Ibid.
134. Saivetz, Event in Space, xx-xi.
135. JoAnne Akalaitis, telephone interview by author, tape recording, 8 June 1997. All further quotes or paraphrases of Akalaitis are from this interview unless otherwise noted. Part of my question preceding this response was, "You're known for your free hand with texts."
136. Saivetz, Event in Space, xviii.
137. "JoAnne Akalaitis," 12. See note 128, above.
138. Witchel, "Papp names Akalaitis"; Ron Engle, "New York Shakespeare Festival," in Shakespeare Companies and Festivals (see note 61), 237.
139. Quoted in Engle, "NYSF," 237. The sentence structure in the original suggests that this is from the charter, but the author is not explicitly cited.
140. Ibid.
141. Ibid., 238-39.
142. Ibid., 239.
143. Michael Pye, "Is There Life after Joe Public? Joe Papp Was the Toughest Act in New York Theatre: Michael Pye Meets the Woman Who Must Follow It," London Independent, 24 November 1991, Sunday Review.
144. Vincent Canby, "Does Shakespeare Really Need B12 Shots?" New York Times, 14 June 1998, sec. 2.
145. Witchel, "Papp Names Akalaitis"; Saivetz, Event in Space, 114. Engle cites the 1990-91 budget at $15 million.
146. Sylvie Drake, "An Appreciation: Age of Aquarius Comes to an End—Hair Producer Joseph Papp Was a Cocky, Gutsy Brooklynite Who Virtually Changed the Face of the American Theater," Los Angeles Times, 1 November 1991, home edition, sec. F.
147. Jordan Shapiro, fax to author, 9 February 2001. Shapiro works in the General Management Department at NYSF.
148. JoAnne Akalaitis as quoted in Presley, "Biggest Challenge."
149. Saivetz takes Rich to task for his inaccurate and "mean-spirited" article (Event in Space, 112-14).
150. Rich, "Opening a Window."

Chapter 1. Destruction Wrought by Domestic Violence

1. Ronald Knowles, "Carnival and Death in Romeo and Juliet," in Shakespeare and Carnival after Bakhtin, ed. Ronald Knowles (New York: Macmillan Press, 1998), 37.
2. Ibid., 58.

3. Lawrence Danson, *Shakespeare's Dramatic Genres* (Oxford: Oxford University Press), 122.

4. Susan Snyder, "Ideology and Feud in *Romeo and Juliet*," *Shakespeare Survey* 49 (1996): 92–93. Snyder goes on to argue that their temporary escape from one ideology is only effected through the temporary ascendency of a different one, Friar Lawrence's "Christian agenda of reconciling the two warring houses" (93). But their love broke the division between their households before Friar Lawrence ever instituted his plan.

5. Lloyd Davis, "'Death-Marked Love': Desire and Presence in *Romeo and Juliet*," *Shakespeare Survey* 49 (1996): 60.

6. Snyder, "Ideology and Feud," 92.

7. The connection between sexuality and death in this play has been noted by many literary critics. See, for example, Bill Carroll, "'We Were Born to Die': *Romeo and Juliet*," *Shakespeare Quarterly* 15 (spring 1981): 54–71; Davis, "Death-Marked Love," 57–67; and Valerie Traub, *Desire and Anxiety: Circulations of Sexuality in Shakespeare's Drama* (New York: Routledge, 1992), 64. For feminist critics who have noted the play's construction of a specifically masculine violent sexuality, see Madelon Gohlke, "'I Wooed Thee with My Sword': Shakespeare's Tragic Paradigms," in *The Woman's Part: Feminist Criticism of Shakespeare*, eds. Carolyn Ruth Swift Lenz and Gayle Greene (Urbana: University of Illinois Press), 150–70, esp. 152–53; Marianne Novy, *Love's Argument: Gender Relations in Shakespeare* (Chapel Hill: University of North Carolina Press, 1984), 100; Carol Thomas Neely, *Broken Nuptials in Shakespeare's Plays* (New Haven: Yale University Press, 1985), 146; Snyder, "Ideology and the Feud," 87–96, esp. 92; Robert Appelbaum, "'Standing to the Wall': The Pressures of Masculinity in *Romeo and Juliet*," *Shakespeare Quarterly* 48 (1997): 251–72, esp. 256–57, 261.

8. J. D. Martinez, "The Fallacy of Contextual Analysis As a Means of Evaluating Dramatized Violence," in *Theatre Symposium: Theatre and Violence*, vol. 7 (Tuscaloosa: Southeastern Theatre Conference and University of Alabama Press, 1999), 76–85.

9. Townsend, *What Women Want*, 154–55.

10. Ibid., 264.

11. Janice A. Radway, *Reading the Romance: Women, Patriarchy, and Popular Literature* (Chapel Hill: University of North Carolina Press, 1984), 76.

12. Joan Ozark Holmer, "The Poetics of Paradox: Shakespeare's Versus Zeffirelli's Cultures of Violence," *Shakespeare Survey* 49 (1996): 170.

13. Radway, *Reading the Romance*, 139.

14. Laura L. O'Toole, "Subcultural Theory of Rape Revisited," in *Gender Violence: Interdisciplinary Perspectives*, eds. Laura L. O' Toole and Jessica R. Schiffman (New York: New York University Press, 1997): 215–22.

15. Edwin Schur, "Sexual Coercion in American Life," in *Gender Violence*, 80–91.

16. Townsend may be partially correct when he argues that men's biologically instinctive need to assure their paternity prompts men's violent efforts to control women's sexualities (*What Women Want*, 180–82).

17. I am deliberately bypassing the arguments surrounding sadomasochism because that raises a different set of issues which, although important, are beyond the scope of this study.

18. I have read approximately ninety reviews of 1990s productions, most of which were American.

19. Robert Trussell wrote both articles for *Kansas City Star.* The interview article, "Perceptions of Their Passion: The Relationship between Romeo and Juliet Is at the Heart of the Bard's Most Tragic Tale of Love," appeared in the 21 June 1996, Metropolitan edition. His review article, "Love in a Culture of Violence: This *Romeo and Juliet* Is a Bittersweet Triumph," appeared in the 29 June 1996 Metropolitan edition, sec. E.

20. J. Wynn Rousuck, "*Romeo* Cast with a Twist: Actor's Prowess in Five Roles Makes Center Stage's Production of Shakespeare's Play Stand out in the Crowd," review of *Romeo and Juliet*, Baltimore, Md., *Baltimore Sun*, 7 February 1997, final edition, sec. E.

21. Productions focusing on the playworld's violence are more common abroad. See, for instance, Jackie Bourke, "Men in Tights Are Back on the Road!" 20 January 1998, *Irish Times*, city edition; Georgina Brown, "Death in Verona: *Romeo and Juliet*—Barbican Pit," review of *Romeo and Juliet*, as performed by the RSC, *London Independent*, 8 January 1990; Audrey Stanley, "The 1994 Shanghai International Shakespeare Festival," review of *Romeo and Juliet*, as performed by the Nuremberg Young People's Theater, Shanghai, *Shakespeare Quarterly* 47 (spring 1996): 79–80; Hal Miller, "Two Versions of *Romeo and Juliet* in Vienna," review of *Romeo and Juliet*, as performed by Pralipe (the other production was performed by the Burg Theater ensemble), Vienna, *Shakespeare Bulletin* 13 (summer 1995): 34. The only American production I saw reviewed that focused on the playworld's violence was directed by Cuban-born René Buch and reviewed by an academic (Alan Armstrong, review of *Romeo and Juliet*, Ashland, Ore., *Shakespeare Bulletin* 15 [spring 1997]: 33–34).

22. Bristol, *Shakespeare's America*, 3–4.

23. Felicia Hardison Londré, introduction to "*Romeo and Juliet*" in *Shakespeare Around the Globe: A Guide to Notable Postwar Revivals*, ed. Samuel L. Leiter (New York: Greenwood Press, 1986), 625–26.

24. See Barbara Hodgdon, "William Shakespeare's *Romeo + Juliet:* Everything's Nice in America?" *Shakespeare Survey* 52 (1999): 88–98.

25. Michael Pursell, "Artifice and Authenticity in Zeffirelli's *Romeo and Juliet*," *Literature-Film Quarterly* 14 (1986), 174.

26. Holmer, "The Poetics of Paradox," 163–79.

27. All paraphrases and quotes of Jayme Koszyn unless otherwise noted come from one of my two interviews with her: Interview by author, tape recording, New Haven, Conn., 15 June 97 and phone interview by author, tape recording, 30 August 1997.

28. Patricia Nealon, "3 Indicted in MIT Student's Death," *Boston Globe*, 14 October 1992, city edition, Metro/Region section.

29. Howard Manly and Victoria Benning, "200 March to Protest MIT Student's Death," *Boston Globe*, 25 September 1992, city edition, Metro/Region section.

30. In Brook's production, Goneril (Irene Worth), wearing leather, is kneeling on the ground, thighs spread, contemplating her suicide. Her hands twist her garment over her thighs. Then she begins to rock, the movement gradually growing in intensity. She rotates her hips and torso wildly and then flings herself against a rock with a cry, showing the connection in her between sex and violence.

31. She had probably also seen at least Zeffirelli's *Romeo and Juliet*, but exposure, unconscious influence, and conscious influence are all separate paths

that may or may not lead to artistic choices. Since it is nearly impossible to measure the first two, the latter is the focus of this study.

32. From NWA's "Appetite 4 Destruction," Ace Lyrics Web site, http://www.acelyrics.com/index.html?lyrics/nwa.html.

33. All observations are based on a video of the 21 November 1992 performance.

34. See Elias Stimac, review of *Hamlet*, as performed by the LAWSC, Culver City, Calif., *Drama-Logue*, 4–11 May 1995; Rachel Fischer, review of *Othello*, as performed by the LAWSC, West Los Angeles, Calif., *Back Stage West*, 16–22 June 1994.

35. Lisa Wolpe, phone interview by author, tape recording, 16–17 August 1998. All quotes and paraphrases come from this interview unless otherwise noted. See J. R. Clark (review of *Richard III*, as performed by the LAWSC, Culver City, Calif., *Drama-Logue*, 21–27 March 1996), who attributes the weak fights to lack of rehearsal time; and Shaner (*Richard III*), who attributes the problem to the use of cardboard swords, though in an earlier article (review of *Richard III*, as performed by the LAWSC, Culver City, Calif., *ShowCase Entertainment Magazine*, Night Life section, 29 March 1996), she claimed that the women were not convincing as lethal warriors. By contrast, Tony Tran found the fight scenes in this production "vivid" and "rousing" ("Her Kingdom for a Horse" [see section on the directors, note 24]). My own perspective from watching the fight between Romeo and Tybalt is that Wolpe is fully committed to the violence, but Erin Erlich (who played Tybalt) could not quite keep up with her.

36. Patricia R. Schroeder, "Locked Behind the Proscenium: Feminist Strategies in *Getting Out* and *My Sister in This House*," in *Feminist Theatre and Theory* (see introduction, note 28), 155–67.

37. A particularly interesting use of nudity occurred in a production in the Netherlands, directed by Ivo van Hove. It appeared as part of Theater Festival 1999 in Amsterdam. Verona was portrayed as a prison, and when Capulet first presented his daughter to Paris, "the young girl was lifted up by the neck to kiss her future husband, and in the course of the dialogue, Juliet's father unbuttoned Juliet's top to display her breasts like merchandise." This staging would have been strongly resonant for any audience members familiar with Amsterdam's red light district, where the prostitutes pose in storefront windows for their customers. However, both lovers "made a topless confession of their new love" during the balcony scene, their attraction to one another both sensual and innocent, though their connection was "earthly rather than cosmic" (Ton Hoenselaars, review of *Romeo and Juliet*, Amsterdam, *Shakespeare Bulletin* 18 [winter 2000]: 37). Juliet is more vulnerable here than Romeo, but the combination of these two moments reinforces the distinction between willing bodily revelation motivated by genuine attraction and coercive exposure motivated by patriarchal domination or economic imperative. See also Felicia Hardison Londré, review of *Romeo and Juliet*, directed by Denis Llorca, as performed by the Treteau du Midi, Carcassonne, France, in *Shakespeare around the Globe* (see note 23), 648; review of *Romeo and Juliet*, directed by Horst Seide, Wuppertal, West Germany, in *Shakespeare around the Globe*, 651. These productions occurred in the late seventies and emphasized both the couple's youthfulness and ardent desire for each other.

38. Barry Kyle's production also portrayed Capulet's sexual attraction to his daughter. See Miranda Johnson-Haddad, "Shakespeare Performed: The Shake-

speare Theatre, 1993-4," review of *Romeo and Juliet*, as performed by The Shakespeare Theatre Company, Washington, D.C., *Shakespeare Quarterly* 46 (spring 1995): 86–90, esp. 89.

39. All citations are from the Arden editions of the plays.

40. Although it can be argued that Paris's pilgrimage to Juliet's tomb signals that he is actually in love with her, Koszyn saw Romeo and Juliet as largely separate from the rest of the culture.

41. A number of directors have included some element of clown work in their productions of *Romeo and Juliet*, though all of these were abroad and most did not cast their protagonists in this mode. See Hal Miller, "Two Versions of *Romeo and Juliet* in Vienna," 33; Marvin Carlson, "Beier's *Romeo and Juliet* in Düsseldorf," review of *Romeo and Juliet*, Düsseldorf, Germany, *Western European Stages* 7, no. 1 (1995): 77; John Rockwell, "A Festival of Theater Reaches 30 in Berlin," Berlin, *New York Times*, 8 May 1993, Arts; and Susana Powell, "Shakespeare at the Pub Theatre Network," review of *Romeo and Juliet*, directed by Alex Chisholm, as performed by the Sound and Fury, London, *Shakespeare Bulletin* 13 (winter 1995): 22–23. This last production in London was billed as a circus *Romeo and Juliet* and used clowns extensively, which the reviewer found limiting. Wolpe recognizes the difference between the clown and the fool but talked about them almost interchangeably in this instance.

42. Koehler, "*Romeo and Juliet.*"

43. Ibid.

44. Charles H. Shattuck, *Shakespeare on the American Stage: From the Hallams to Edwin Booth* (Washington, D.C.: Shakespeare Folger Library, 1976), 1: 93. Also see Lisa Merrill, *When Romeo Was a Woman: Charlotte Cushman and Her Circle of Female Spectators* (Ann Arbor: University of Michigan Press, 2001).

45. All observations about the production are taken from a collection of scenes on video provided to the author by Lisa Wolpe.

46. Gionnota, *A Muse of Fire.*

47. A lesbian scholar, Susan Clark, who worked as a dramaturg for the Company of Women, informed me of her knowledge concerning audience responses among lesbians.

48. See also Koehler, *Romeo and Juliet.*

49. Laurence Senelick, introduction to *Gender in Performance: The Presentation of Difference in the Performing Arts* (Hanover, N.H.: University Press of New England, 1992), xii.

50. Schneider, *Explicit Body*, 20.

51. I did not ask her about this specifically, though I did ask about whether she thought sex and violence were related to each other in the play. This response occurred when I had asked her about whether she tended to portray Shakespeare's women characters as strong or victimized. Because she portrayed them as victims, I asked if this view was fueled by her ability to portray women's strengths in their embodiment of male roles.

52. Zeffirelli first directed the play for the Old Vic Theatre Company in 1960, reviving it for the Teatro Romano in Verona in 1964. His work with the play culminated in the 1968 motion picture. Peter Brook produced the play at Stratford-upon-Avon in 1947, a production trying to create the atmosphere depicted in the line, "These hot days is the mad blood stirring"—which to Brook implicated both the civil violence and Romeo and Juliet's passionate love (Londré, introduction to "*Romeo and Juliet*," 626) .

53. Don Shirley, "The Two Dueling 'Juliets': One Conventional, One Not," review of *Romeo and Juliet*, as performed by the LAWSC, Hollywood, Calif., and A Noise Within, Glendale, Calif., *Los Angeles Times*, 23 March 1993, home edition, Calendar.

54. Fran Bennett, *Muse of Fire*.

55. Other productions portraying this kind of ending were René Buch's at the Oregon Shakespeare Festival (see note 21) and Adrian Noble's for the RSC in Stratford-upon-Avon (as reviewed by George L. Geckle, *Shakespeare Bulletin* 14 [winter 1996]: 126–27).

56. Canning, *Feminist Theaters*, 178.

57. Dolan, *Feminist Spectator*, 106.

58. Ibid., 49.

59. Ibid., 103–17.

60. Jill Dolan, "Practicing Cultural Disruptions: Gay and Lesbian Representation and Sexuality," in *Critical Theory and Performance*, eds. Janelle G. Reinelt and Joseph R. Roach (Ann Arbor: University of Michigan Press, 1992), 272.

61. Larry Jonas, review of *Romeo and Juliet*, as performed by LAWSC, Hollywood, Calif., *Drama-Logue*, n.d.

62. Judith Lewis, "Sex Repeal: When Roles Shed Their Chromosomes," review of *Romeo and Juliet*, as performed by LAWSC, Hollywood, Calif., *LA Weekly*, n.d.

63. Shirley, "The Two Dueling 'Juliets'."

64. Ibid.

65. Lewis, "Sex Repeal."

66. John Timpane, review of *Romeo and Juliet*, Madison, N.J., *Shakespeare Bulletin* 18 (spring 2000): 12–13.

67. This quote appeared in the program notes and was written by Joachim Lux, the chief dramaturg on the production. It is quoted in Wilhelm Hortmann, *Shakespeare on the German Stage: The Twentieth Century* (Cambridge: Cambridge University Press, 1998), 461.

68. Ibid., 471.

69. Sarah Hemming, "*Romeo* Without a Ray of Romance—Sarah Hemming Catches a Bleak, Brutal Portrayal of Shakespeare's Tragedy at the Barbican," review of *Romeo and Juliet*, London, *London Financial Times*, 5 November 1994, Arts.

70. Carlson, "*Romeo and Juliet*," 77–78.

71. Hortmann, *German Stage*, 470.

72. Carlson, "*Romeo and Juliet*," 79–80.

73. Hortmann, *German Stage*, 470–71. See also Hemming's review cited above.

74. Bristol, *America's Shakespeare*, 5.

Chapter 2. "How do poor people live?"

1. Sir Arthur Quiller-Couch, introduction to *Measure for Measure*, by William Shakespeare, ed. Quiller-Couch and J. Dover Wilson (Cambridge: Cambridge University Press, 1922), xxx; Charlotte Lennox, *Shakespear Illustrated* (London, 1753), 1: 32; Una Mary Ellis-Fermor, *The Jacobean Drama: An Inter-*

pretation (London: Methuen, 1936), 262; Anna Jameson, *Shakespeare's Heroines: Characteristics of Women, Moral, Political, and Historical* (London: G. Bell, 1913), 66. I first found these early references in Marcia Riefer, "'Instruments of Some More Mightier Member': The Constriction of Female Power in *Measure for Measure,*" *Shakespeare Quarterly* 35 (spring 1984): 157.

2. Neely, *Broken Nuptials,* 93, 98.

3. Maurice Hunt, "Comfort in *Measure for Measure,*" *SEL: Studies in English Literature 1500–1900* 27 (spring 1987): 219. For another critic who sees Isabella as cruel, see Carolyn Brown, "Erotic Religious Flagellation in Shakespeare's *Measure for Measure,*" *English Literary Renaissance* 16 (winter 1986): 139. She also describes her sexual purity as "a sham," the mixture of cruelty and sexual repression creating a sadomasochistic sexuality for Isabella and Angelo.

4. Susan Moore, "Virtue and Power in *Measure for Measure,*" *English Studies* 63 (August 1982): 314.

5. Riefer, "Instruments," 158. See also Mario Digangi, "Pleasure and Danger: Measuring Female Sexuality in *Measure for Measure,*" *ELH* 60 (fall 1993): 589–609.

6. Linda Macfarlane, "Heads You Win Tails I Lose," *Critical Survey* 5, no. 1 (1993): 80.

7. Kathleen McLuskie, "The Patriarchal Bard: Feminist Criticism and Shakespeare: *King Lear* and *Measure for Measure,*" in *Political Shakespeare: New Essays in Cultural Materialism,* eds. Jonathan Dollimore and Alan Sinfield (Ithaca: Cornell University Press, 1985), 88–108; Riefer, "Instruments," 157–69.

8. Jonathan Dollimore, "Transgression and Surveillance in *Measure for Measure*" in *Political Shakespeare,* 82–83. See also Macfarlane, "Heads You Win," 79.

9. Barbara Baines, "Assaying the Power of Chastity in *Measure for Measure,*" *SEL: Studies in English Literature 1500–1900* 30 (1990): 288.

10. Sonia Massai, "Stage over Study: Charles Marowitz, Edward Bond, and Recent Materialist Approaches to Shakespeare," *New Theatre Quarterly* 15 (August 1999): 247–55.

11. Macfarlane, "Heads I Win," 78.

12. Jan Kott, "The Kott-Marowitz Dialogues: *Measure for Measure,*" *New Theatre Quarterly* 10 (May 1994): 160, 162.

13. David McCandless, "'I'll Pray to Increase Your Bondage': Power and Punishment in *Measure for Measure,*" in *Shakespearean Power and Punishment,* ed. Gillian Murray Kendall (Madison, N.J.: Fairleigh Dickinson University Press, 1998), 99–100.

14. See Ralph Berry, "*Measure for Measure* on the Contemporary Stage," *Humanities Association Review* 28 (1977): 241–44.

15. Anne Barton, program note, *Measure for Measure,* directed by David Giles, Stratford, Ontario (1969), quoted in Berry, "*Measure for Measure,*" 242.

16. Carol Rutter et al., *Clamorous Voices: Shakespeare's Women Today* (New York: Routledge, 1989), 40–51; esp. 40–41, 50–51.

17. Michael D. Friedman, "'O, let him marry her!': Matrimony and Recompense in *Measure for Measure,*" *Shakespeare Quarterly* 46 (winter 1995): 68–78. Friedman suggests a contemporary staging the essence of which is having onlookers throw dirt at Isabella during the final scene and the duke clean off her

dress when he proposes. I still think it unlikely that a contemporary audience would grasp the Elizabethan cultural resonances without the help of program notes.

18. Herbert R. Coursen, Jr., "Shakespeare in Maine: Summer, 1971," *Shakespeare Quarterly* 22 (autumn 1971): 392.

19. For productions (or reviewers) who generally portrayed Isabella as a prude, see Clive Barnes, "Papp's Park *Measure* Doesn't Measure Up," review of *Measure for Measure,* directed by Joseph Papp, New York, *New York Post,* 2 July 1985 in *New York Theatre Critics' Reviews* 46 (2 September 1985): 217–18; Charles Spencer, "The Arts: Dispiriting Plod through the RSC's Theatrical No-Man's-Land," review of *Measure for Measure,* directed by Michael Boyd, as performed by the RSC, Stratford-upon-Avon, *London Daily Telegraph,* 4 May 1998; Janet Savin, review of *Measure for Measure,* directed by Carlo Cecchi, as performed by the Teatro Garibaldi company, Paris, *Shakespeare Bulletin* 18 (winter 2000): 41–42; Nanette Jaynes, review of *Measure for Measure,* directed by Tim Ocel, Atlanta, Ga., *Shakespeare Bulletin* 17 (fall 1999): 23–24. The "frumpy" comment can be found in Owen Brady, review of *Measure for Measure,* directed by Michael Bogdanov, Stratford, Ontario, *Theatre Journal* 37 (December 1985): 506–8.

20. David Nice, review of *Measure for Measure,* directed by David Thacker, London, *Plays and Players,* July 1987, 28–29.

21. Nelson Pressley, "Bard's Last Comedy Still Relevant Today: *Measure for Measure* Remains a Hit," review of *Measure for Measure,* directed by Michael Kahn, Washington, D.C., *Washington Times,* 18 June 1996, final edition.

22. Michael Friedman, "Prostitution and the Feminist Appropriation of *Measure for Measure* on the Stage," *Shakespeare Bulletin* 15 (spring 1997): 14–17.

23. Ibid., 17.

24. Because the actor playing Angelo was uncomfortable with this, she did not push it, but was able to stage this with Lisa Wolpe playing the role in the LAWSC production.

25. Tina Packer, interview by author, tape recording, Cambridge, Mass., 24 October and 14 November 1997. All quotes and paraphrases of Packer's ideas come from these interviews unless otherwise noted.

26. G. L. Horton, review of *Measure for Measure,* Lenox, Mass., as performed by Shakespeare and Company, *AisleSay: The Theatre Magazine of the Net,* http://www.stagepage.info/reviews/measure.html.

27. Packer as quoted in Siegel, "Shakespeare in Good Company."

28. Ed Siegel, "Full-Bawdied *Measure* Comes East," review of *Measure for Measure,* as performed by Shakespeare and Company, Foxboro, Mass., *Boston Globe,* 12 September 1996, city edition, sec. E.

29. Michael Hattaway, "Fleshing His Will in the Spoil of Her Honour: Desire, Misogyny, and the Perils of Chivalry," *Shakespeare Survey* 46 (1994): 122, 121–22.

30. All observations concerning the production are from my notes as an audience member of the 26 September 1996 performance.

31. Jessica Slights and Michael Morgan Holmes, "Isabella's Order: Religious Acts and Personal Desires in *Measure for Measure,*" *Studies in Philology* 95 (summer 1998): 282.

32. Epstein, *Companies,* 68.

33. Slights and Holmes, "Isabella's Order," 274, 263–92.

34. In 3.1.142–46, she tells Claudio she will pray for his death, and in 4.3.119, upon hearing from the duke that Angelo executed Claudio despite his promise, she says she will pluck out Angelo's eyes.

35. The first quote comes from Zerbe's own notes and the second comes from my interview with O'Brien, tape recording, Greensboro, N.C., 10 October 1997. All paraphrases and quotes of O'Brien come from this interview unless otherwise noted.

36. Abe D. Jones Jr., "Students Stage Shakespeare's *Measure for Measure* with Contemporary Setting, Context," review of *Measure for Measure*, Guilford College, Greensboro, N.C., *Greensboro News and Record,* 5 April 1991.

37. Ellen O'Brien and Jack Zerbe, "Director's Notes," photocopy, Guilford College, Greensboro N.C., 1991.

38. Ibid. The "however perverse" in reference to the nunnery is Zerbe's interpretation rather than O'Brien's.

39. Ibid.

40. Ibid.

41. Goodman, *Feminist Theatre,* 234.

42. "Director's Notes."

43. I spoke with Zerbe briefly right after interviewing O'Brien.

44. Jones, review, 13.

45. Epstein, *Companies,* 16.

46. Ibid., 100–101.

47. For an interesting, theoretically informed and practice-based discussion of a postmodern, though not specifically feminist, approach to acting Shakespeare, see Ellen J. O'Brien, "Civil Wars in the Rehearsal Room: Conflicting Theories in Collaborative Praxis," in *Shakespeare and the Twentieth Century: The Selected Proceedings of the International Shakespeare Association World Congress, Los Angeles, 1996,* eds. Jonathan Bate, Jill L. Levenson, Dieter Mehl (Newark: University of Delaware Press, 1998): 125–36.

Chapter 3. Whose Gender Is It Anyway?

1. Among literary critics, she is seen as celebrating plurality (Catherine Belsey, "Disrupting Sexual Difference: Meaning and Gender in the Comedies," *Alternative Shakespeares,* ed. John Drakakis [London: Methuen, 1985]: 166–90), feminine flexibility and responsiveness (Paula S. Berggren, "The Woman's Part: Female Sexuality as Power in Shakespeare's Plays," *The Woman's Part* [see chapter 1, note 7], 17–34), gender deconstruction (Christina Malcolmson, "'What You Will': Social Mobility and Gender in *Twelfth Night*," in *The Matter of Difference: Materialist Feminist Criticism of Shakespeare,* ed. Valerie Wayne [Ithaca: Cornell University Press, 1991]: 29–57), psychological androgyny (Robert Kimbrough, "Androgyny Seen through Shakespeare's Disguise," *Shakespeare Quarterly* 33 [spring 1982]: 17–33), and sexual androgyny (Casey Charles, "Gender Trouble in *Twelfth Night*," *Theatre Journal* 49 [May 1997]: 121–41; Joseph Pequigney, "The Two Antonios and Same-Sex Love in *Twelfth Night* and *The Merchant of Venice*," *English Literary Renaissance* 22.2 [spring 1992]: 201–21; Traub, *Desire and Anxiety,* 113–32; Thad Jenkins Logan, "*Twelfth Night:* The Limits of Festivity," *SEL: Studies in English Literature*

1500–1900 22 [1982]: 223–38), although Logan is less than celebratory when regarding her chaotic erotic experiences.

2. See Logan, "The Limits of Festivity," 230–38; David Schalkwyk, "'She Never Told Her Love,': Embodiment, Textuality, and Silence in Shakespeare's Sonnets and Plays," *Shakespeare Quarterly* 45 (winter 1994): 399–407; Jean Howard, "Crossdressing, the Theatre, and Gender Struggle in Early Modern England," *Shakespeare Quarterly* 39 (winter 1988): 430–33.

3. Neely, *Broken Nuptials,* 56; Belsey, "Disrupting Sexual Difference," 185–88.

4. In "Twins and Travesties: Gender, Dependency, and Sexual Availability in *Twelfth Night*" (in *Erotic Politics: Desire on the Renaissance Stage,* ed. Susan Zimmerman [New York: Routledge, 1992]), Lisa Jardine argues that in the early modern period, the dependency and availability of the servant eroticized him or her. Howard ("Crossdressing") sees Viola as rewarded for being the good woman, the feminine bourgeois subject who has interiorized her gender difference and accepted subordinate access to economic and cultural power. In a more positive approach, Malcolmson argues that Viola's assumption of a male role proves that men and women are not essentially different. In fact, Viola's and Maria's social ambitions are rewarded because they are primarily motivated by love, whereas Malvolio's are condemned because they are motivated by selfishness. She further argues that although this value system still demands that women love their husbands submissively, at least women can use their intelligence and wit, traditionally considered gentlemen's characteristics, to improve their social stations.

5. For literary critics, see, for example, Michael Shapiro, *Gender in Play on the Shakespearean Stage: Boy Heroines and Female Pages* (Ann Arbor: University of Michigan Press, 1994), 155–56; Ann Barton, introduction to *Twelfth Night,* in *The Riverside Shakespeare,* 2nd ed., (Boston: Houghton Mifflin, 1997), 440; Howard, "Crossdressing," 432–33.

6. Bill Alexander et al., *RSC Directors' Shakespeare: Approaches to* Twelfth Night, ed. Michael Billington (London: Walter Books Limited, 1990), 38–39, 55.

7. The only reference to Viola's passivity I found was in Dorothy and Wayne Cook, review of *Twelfth Night,* New Haven, Conn., *Shakespeare Bulletin* 13 (spring 1995): 11. Even here she was viewed as merely more passive than Olivia.

8. For productions portraying the women characters as sexual subjects, see, for example, Everett Evans, "*Twelfth Night* at Miller an Uneven Effort," review of *Twelfth Night,* directed by Sidney Berger, Houston, Texas, *Houston Chronicle,* 4 August 1999, 2-star edition, Houston sec.; Jane Collins, review of *Twelfth Night,* directed by Terence O'Brien, Garrison, N.Y., *Shakespeare Bulletin* 17 (fall 1999): 9–10; Steven Winn, "An Enchanting *Night*: California Shakespeare Full of Lustrous Acting," directed by Joe Vincent, Orinda, Calif., *San Francisco Chronicle,* 17 August 1996, final edition, sec. E. For productions oversexualizing the women characters, see Bill Mar, "*Twelfth Night* Walks Line between Comedy, Melancholy," directed by Penny Metropulos, as performed by the Acting Company, Beverly, Mass., *Boston Globe,* 1 May 1999, city edition, sec. C, where Maria is described as dissolving into "nonstop eye-rolling lasciviousness." See also Steven Winn, "San Jose Shakespeare with a Latin Twist: Rep's *Twelfth Night* Daring but Uneven," review of *Twelfth Night,* directed by Michael Butler, San Jose, Calif., *San Francisco Chronicle,* 14 December 1998, final edition, sec. D, where Olivia takes a bite out of a chair, "catches her prey on a tabletop and grinds her pelvis into Viola." The latter may be an

attempt to avoid dealing seriously with the homoerotic implications of the scene.

9. Harry Keyishian, "Shakespeare Abroad: Europe and Asia," review of *Twelfth Night,* directed by Eva Bergman, Stockholm, Sweden, *Shakespeare Bulletin* 12 (winter 1994): 35.

10. See Todd Everett, "Not Half Bard: Cal Lutheran University's Production Successfully Captures Shakespeare's Sense of Humor," review of *Twelfth Night,* directed by Michael J. Arndt, Thousand Oaks, Calif., *Los Angeles Times,* 10 May 1990, Ventura county edition, sec. J ("[K. Jill] Sorgen's portrayal is so witty and self-sufficient, in fact, that one might wonder why her Viola is attracted to Justin Lorber's rather thick Orsino. Perhaps good looks, wealth and a title were enough in those days"); Laurie Winer, "*Twelfth Night* Is a Ladies Night," review of *Twelfth Night,* directed by Will Roberson, Shakespeare Festival, West Los Angeles, Calif., *Los Angeles Times,* 4 July 1994, home edition, sec. F ("When [Viola and Olivia] discuss the nature of love, it is a conversation of equals. Their chemistry points up a weakness in the play: the men are not worthy suitors"); Bill Mar, "An Amusing but Stodgy *Twelfth Night,*" review of *Twelfth Night,* directed by Rick Lombardo, Newton Highlands, Mass., *Boston Globe,* 22 March 1999, city edition, sec. C ("Viola's chilling vow that she would die for Orsino [what does she see in the twit, aside from the fact he speaks gorgeous poetry?], suggest[s] an undercurrent of menace").

11. Mar, "*Twelfth Night,*" Beverly, Mass.

12. Declan Donnellan as quoted in Ralph Berry, *On Directing Shakespeare: Interviews with Contemporary Directors* (London: Hamish Hamilton, 1989), 191.

13. Billington et al., *Approaches to* Twelfth Night, 73.

14. Ibid., 2.

15. Ibid., 73–74.

16. See, for example, Miranda Johnson-Haddad, review of *Twelfth Night,* directed by Daniel Fish, Washington, D.C., *Shakespeare Bulletin* 17 (spring 1999): 15–16; Mar, "*Twelfth Night,*" Beverly, Mass.; Charles Spencer, "The Arts: Splashing out on Doom and Gloom," review of *Twelfth Night,* directed by David Pountney, Nottingham, England, *London Daily Telegraph,* 13 February 1995; William C. Boles, review of *Twelfth Night,* directed by Ian Judge, as performed by the RSC, Stratford-upon-Avon, *Theatre Journal* 47 (May 1995): 302–3.

17. Peter Holland, however, thinks some recent RSC productions have been altogether too cheery (*English Shakespeares,* 81–84, 191–94).

18. Trevor Nunn and Michael Kahn as quoted in Berry, *On Directing Shakespeare,* 65 and 96, respectively; Billington et al., *RSC Directors' Shakespeare,* xvii; Stanley Wells, *Royal Shakespeare: Four Major Productions at Stratford-upon-Avon* (Manchester: Manchester University Press, 1977), 44.

19. Miranda Johnson-Haddad, review of *Twelfth Night,* directed by Lisa Wolpe, as performed by the LAWSC, Los Angeles, Calif., *Shakespeare Bulletin* 18 (fall 2000): 31–32.

20. Colby H. Kullman, "Mississippi's Southern Festival Theatre," directed by Cindy Gold, review of *Twelfth Night,* Oxford, Miss., *Shakespeare Bulletin* 13 (fall 1995): 26.

21. Howard rests her argument on this view: "Moreover, and this is the key point, from the time Viola meets Orsino in 1.4, there is no doubt in the audience's mind of her heterosexual sexual orientation" (431).

22. For women-directed productions in this group, see Meredith Alexander, "Gender as Drag: A Director's Approach to *Twelfth Night*," in *Interpretive Essays: Shakespeare and Britten at Iowa* (Iowa City: University of Iowa, 1991), 9–10; D. J. R. Bruckner, "Sex and Low Humor beyond Shakespeare's," review of *Twelfth Night*, directed by K. G. Wilson, as performed by the Kings County Shakespeare Company, Brooklyn, *New York Times*, 13 August 1995, late edition, sec. C; Nelson Pressley, "*Twelfth*: Clever Production Has Number of Flaws: Genders Are Bent Way Out of Shape," review of *Twelfth Night*, directed by Delia Taylor, as performed by the Washington Shakespeare Company, Arlington, Va., *Washington Times*, 24 April 1997, final edition, sec. C; Ed Siegel, "Smart, Spirited *Twelfth Night* Shakespeare and Company Offers an Engaging Spin on the Classic," review of *Twelfth Night*, directed by Eleanor Holdridge, as performed by Shakespeare and Company, Lenox, Mass., *Boston Globe*, 12 July 2000, sec. C.

23. Abigail Adams, interview by author, tape recording, Malvern, Pa., 10 June 1997. All paraphrases and quotes of Adams are taken from this interview unless otherwise noted.

24. Abigail Adams, "Director's Notes: Power, Sex, Class, and Shipwrecks," in *North Carolina Shakespeare Festival Quarto* (summer 1996), 3.

25. Ibid.

26. Abby Adams as quoted in "Classic Brothers Grimm Takes Stage at People's Light," *Wayne (Pa.) Suburban Advertiser*, 22 November 1995.

27. All observations concerning the production were taken from my notes of the 28 September 1996 performance or my subsequent study of the promptbook at the North Carolina Shakespeare Festival administrative offices in High Point, N.C.

28. Wolpe's LAWSC production also used live musicians onstage but integrated them into the playworld more fully. After playing in the revelry scene at Olivia's in 2.3, they appeared in the next scene at Orsino's "looking bedraggled and hung over" (Haddad, review of *Twelfth Night*, Los Angeles, 31). See also Kullman's review of Cindy Gold's production, where a harpist onstage underscored Orsino's vanity by playing appropriate background music whenever he spoke (27).

29. Tony Brown, "Hilarity That Touches the Heart," review of *Twelfth Night*, High Point, N.C., *Charlotte (N.C.) Observer*, 20 August 1996, sec. E.

30. For an example of the traditional interpretation, see C. L. Barber, *Shakespeare's Festive Comedy: A Study of Dramatic Form and Its Relation to Social Custom* (Cleveland: World Publishing Co., 1963), 246.

31. Elin Diamond, *Unmaking Mimesis: Essays on Gender, Sexuality, Performance* (Ann Arbor: University of Michigan Press, 1993), 50, 144, 150.

32. Janet Price and Margrit Shildrick, "Openings on the Body: A Critical Introduction," in *Feminist Theory and the Body: A Reader*, eds. Janet Price and Margrit Shildrick (Routledge: New York, 1999), 8, 12. My application of this theory is a little broader, for they argue that "differential forms of embodiment . . . can found normative boundaries" (9).

33. Senelick, introduction to *Gender in Performance*, ix, xi.

34. Dolan, *Feminist Spectator*, 103–6; Sue-Ellen Case, "Gender as Play: Simone Benmussa's *The Singular Life of Albert Nobbs*," *Women & Performance Journal* 2 1 (winter 1984): 24.

35. Diamond, *Unmaking Mimesis*, 45–46, 48.

36. Susan Melrose, "'What do women want (in theatre)?'" in *The Routledge Reader of Gender and Performance* (see Introduction, note 46), 133–35.

37. T. H. McCulloh, "First-rate *Twelfth Night* at UCI," review of *Twelfth Night,* directed by Eli Simon, Irvine, Calif., *Los Angeles Times,* 30 April 1998, Orange county edition, sec. F.

38. Benedict Nightingale, "Illyria Put off Balance," review of *Twelfth Night,* directed by Adrian Noble, as performed by the RSC, Stratford-upon-Avon, *London Times,* 27 November 1997, Features.

39. Charles, "Gender Trouble," 136. Charles suggests that the text executes the divide between gender paradigms and the moment's truth, but I believe such a deconstruction happens in the theatre only when supported by a passionately engaged Viola.

40. Shapiro, *Gender in Play,* 146–47. See also his section on *Twelfth Night,* where he argues that Shakespeare dramatized Olivia's deepening passion and the emotional entanglement between the characters more than other playwrights handling similar situations (151–54).

41. Brown, "Hilarity That Touches the Heart." All reviews of this production are photocopies from the theater.

42. Ibid. Some reviewers apparently thought Adams had a dark view of the play, perhaps as a result of a sentence in her director's notes: "Shipwrecks, emotional and otherwise, are clearly the path to illuminating *Twelfth Night* this time." But Adams confirmed that my sense of the fanciful, inviting environment was what she intended.

43. Leslie Mizell, review of *Twelfth Night,* High Point, N.C., *Greensboro (N.C.) Triad Style,* 21 August 1996.

44. Increasing revelation of Olivia's body through her costume was also a feature in a number of other productions: Steven Winn, "*Twelfth Night* Rings a Southern Belle: San Francisco Shakespeare Festival Production in San Jose," review of *Twelfth Night,* directed by Dan Chumley, San Jose, Calif., *San Francisco Chronicle,* 23 August 1993, sec. E; Ted Merwin, review of *Twelfth Night,* directed by Nicolas Hytner, New York, *Theatre Journal* 51 (May 1999): 191–92; Helen Deese, review of *Twelfth Night,* directed by David Chambers, Costa Mesa, Calif., *Shakespeare Bulletin* 10 (1992): 31; and Haddad, review of *Twelfth Night,* D.C., 15–16.

45. Abe D. Jones Jr., "*Twelfth Night* Reveals Charm, Humor," review of *Twelfth Night,* High Point, N.C., *Greensboro (N.C.) News and Record,* 19 August 1996, sec. B.

46. Eve Oakley, "*Twelfth Night* Opens NCSF Season in Fine Fashion," review of *Twelfth Night,* High Point, NC, *ESP: Entertainment Sports and Previews,* 28 August–3 September 1996.

47. For an argument to the contrary, see Novy, *Love's Argument,* 36, and Shapiro, *Gender in Play,* 162–63.

48. Melia Bensussen, interview by author, tape recording, Princeton, N.J., 11 June 1997. All quotes and paraphrases of Bensussen come from this interview unless otherwise noted.

49. A sense of dissatisfaction, uncertainty, and confusion underlined the ending of Ariane Mnouchkine's 1982 production (David Bradby and David Williams, *Directors' Theatre* [New York: St. Martin's Press, 1988], 106).

50. Melia Bensussen, "From the Director," in *Oregon Shakespeare Festival* 1 (1995): 2–4.

51. Similarly, Penny Metropulos's production portrayed Toby as "more of a gruff bully than a jovial drunkard" (Mar, review of *Twelfth Night,* Beverly, Mass.). Four male-directed productions also painted him bleakly. See Spencer, "Doom and Gloom" ("Campbell Morrison plays Sir Toby as a violent, crotch-groping alcoholic," although Kate Bassett, reviewing the same production, described him as reeling "in plimsolls like a boozing schoolboy, or an expatriate on some Greek island refusing to grow up" [Kate Bassett, "Sixties Midsummer Madness," review of *Twelfth Night,* directed by David Pountney, Nottingham, England, *London Times,* 15 February 1995, Features]); Deese, review of *Twelfth Night,* 32; Justin Shaltz, review of *Twelfth Night,* directed by Michael Pennington, as performed by the English Shakespeare Company, Chicago, Ill., *Shakespeare Bulletin* 10 (summer 1992): 28; and Gerald Nachman, "The Bard Meets Big Easy: Berkeley Rep Gives *Twelfth Night* a Louisiana Setting," review of *Twelfth Night,* directed by Richard E. T. Wright, Berkeley, Calif., *San Francisco Chronicle,* 25 September 1990, final edition, sec. E.

52. All observations of the production are taken from my viewing of the video of the 17 February 1995 performance, or review of the promptbook, unless otherwise noted.

53. "About the Production," *Oregon Shakespeare Festival* 1 (1995): 2.

54. Robert Hurwitt, "Triumph of Laughter and Art," review of *Twelfth Night,* Ashland, Ore., *San Francisco Examiner,* 20 June 1995, sec. B.

55. Alan Armstrong, "Shakespeare in Ashland, 1995: The Sixtieth Anniversary Season," review of *Twelfth Night,* Ashland, Ore., *Shakespeare Bulletin* 14 (spring 1996): 30.

56. Felicia Hardison Londré, review of *Twelfth Night, Theatre Journal* 47 (October 1995): 414.

57. Bensussen remembers it being her upper arm. The promptbook records that he tickles her but does not specify where.

58. Daniel Fish's production in Washington, D.C., created a similar moment. All the men entered bare-chested to lie down and sleep. Viola entered shortly afterward, fully clothed. She and Orsino looked at each other with deep longing while the other men stirred to watch them. Reviewer Haddad remarks, however, that the moment was vaguely homoerotic, so it did not have the same focus as Bensussen's idea (Haddad, review of *Twelfth Night,* D.C.).

59. Most of the material on the subject is officially off the record, so I am revealing only what protects Bensussen's confidence.

60. Cindy Gold's production portrayed a similar interpretation (Kullman, review of *Twelfth Night*).

61. Promptbook for *Twelfth Night,* 1995, OSF Archive, Ashland, Ore., 41.

62. Promptbook, 43. The note reads "Remember her class!"

63. As is true for studying the earlier production, occasionally there are discrepancies between when and what blocking happens according to the promptbook and what I see in my notes, probably the result of subtle shifts from night to night or some developments the actors made later in the run. But the changes are minor. I am generally creating a fusion of the two in my descriptions, which is a better representation of the range of performances than either could give alone.

64. Londré, review of *Twelfth Night,* 414.

65. Promptbook, 123.

66. Ibid., 145.

67. Armstrong, review of *Twelfth Night*, 30. Robert Miller, "*Twelfth Night* a Worthy Tribute to Founder Angus Bowmer," review of *Twelfth Night*, Ashland, Ore., *Ashland (Ore.) Daily Tidings*, 27 February 1995.

68. Armstrong, review of *Twelfth Night*, 29.

69. Tom W. Kelly, "Oregon Shakespeare Festival: Fabulous Performances—But Not the Only Show in Town," review of *Twelfth Night*, Ashland, Ore., *San Francisco Bay Times*, 18 May 1995; Nancy Golden, review of *Twelfth Night*, Ashland, Ore., *Lithiagraph*, June 1995, 8; Alison Baker, review of *Twelfth Night*, Ashland, Ore., *Jefferson Monthly*, April 1995, 34.

70. Londré, review of *Twelfth Night*, 416.

71. Justin Shaltz, review of *Twelfth Night*, directed by Karin Coonrod, Chicago, Ill., *Shakespeare Bulletin* 19 (fall 2001): 25.

72. Ibid., 24–25.

73. See H. R. Coursen, *Shakespeare: The Two Traditions* (Madison, N.J.: Fairleigh Dickinson University Press, 1999), 66–76.

74. Shaltz, review of *Twelfth Night*, 24–25.

Chpater 4. Once Upon a Time

1. Roger Warren, *Shakespeare in Performance: Cymbeline* (Manchester: Manchester University Press, 1989), 2.

2. Adrian Noble as quoted in Andrea Stevens, "Comparing Notes on Shakespeare Only for the Brave," *New York Times*, 31 May 1998, late edition, sec. 2.

3. David Bergeron, "Sexuality in *Cymbeline*," *Essays in Literature* 10 (fall 1983): 156–68.

4. Clara Claiborne Park, "As We Like It: How a Girl Can Be Smart and Still Popular," in *The Woman's Part*, 107; Neely, *Broken Nuptials*, 180–81; Ann Thompson, "Person and Office: The Case of Imogen, Princess of Britain," in *Literature and Nationalism*, eds. Vincent Newey and Ann Thompson (Savage, Md.: Barnes and Noble Books, 1991), 84–86; Karen Bamford, "Imogen's Wounded Chastity," *Essays in Theatre/Etudes Theatrales* 12 (November 1993): 56; Susanne Collier, "Cutting to the Heart of the Matter: Stabbing the Woman in *Philaster* and *Cymbeline*," in *Shakespearean Power and Punishment*, 39–58.

5. Bamford, "Chastity," 51–61; Neely, *Broken Nuptials*, 181–82.

6. Although both Bamford and Neely address this in passing, it is most fully developed by Collier, who also discusses Imogen's loss of power.

7. For the former comparison, see Constance Jordan, "Contract and Conscience in *Cymbeline*," *Renaissance Drama* n.s. 25 (1994): 38–41; Lawrence Danson, "'The Catastrophe Is a Nuptial': The Space of Masculine Desire in *Othello*, *Cymbeline*, and *The Winter's Tale*," *Shakespeare Survey* 46 (1993): 75. For the latter comparison, see Bamford, "Chastity," 54; Arthur Kirsch, *Shakespeare and the Experience of Love* (Cambridge: Cambridge University Press, 1981), 154–59. For both, see James E. Siemon, "Noble Virtue in *Cymbeline*," *Shakespeare Survey* 29 (1976): 51–61, though his focus is on Posthumus's likeness with as well as difference from Cloten; Thompson, "Person and Office," 83–84.

8. Berggren, "Female Sexuality," 28.

9. Neely, *Broken Nuptials*, 183–84.

10. Warren in particular notes that Posthumus's similarity to Cloten is never seen in production (*Cymbeline*, 8), though it has appeared very occasionally. A recent production doubled the two characters and staged Posthumus's transformation into Cloten when the actor put on a black hat. See Dorothea Kehler, "*Cymbeline* at the San Diego Old Globe," review of *Cymbeline*, directed by Daniel Sullivan, San Diego, Calif., *Shakespeare Newsletter* 49 (fall 1999): 79.

11. This last comment was made by Vincent Canby when discussing Adrian Noble's production touring in New York ("Does Shakespeare Really Need B12 Shots?" sec. 2 [see The Directors, note 144]). A number of other reviewers noted Joanne Pearce's Imogen's passion and strength in Noble's production, for example, Ben Brantley, "Trying to Broaden the Appeal of Shakespeare, Even at His Least Digestible," review of *Cymbeline*, directed by Adrian Noble, as performed by the RSC, New York, *New York Times,* 5 June 1998, late edition, sec. E; and Nelson Pressley, "Spirited and Exotic *Cymbeline*," review of *Cymbeline*, directed by Adrian Noble, as performed by the RSC, Washington, D.C., *Washington Times,* 26 June 1998, final edition, sec. C. For other reviews of Imogen as strong, or least "spunky," see Nancy Churnin, "*Cymbeline* Is Worth the Trip: The San Diego Rep's Production of This Rarely Done Shakespearean Work Is 3½ Hours Well Spent," review of *Cymbeline*, directed by Douglas Jacobs, San Diego, Calif., *Los Angeles Times* 12 November 1990, sec. F; Nelson Pressley, "*Cymbeline* Is Impish, Engaging Version of Shakespeare," review of *Cymbeline*, directed by Joe Banno, as performed by the Washington Shakespeare Company, Washington, D.C., *Washington Times,* 17 December 1996, final edition, sec. C; and Skip Ascheim, "This *Cymbeline* Falls Short of Magic," review of *Cymbeline*, directed by Mark Lamos, Hartford, Conn., *Boston Globe,* 26 November 1997, city edition, sec. E. The review citing Imogen's passivity was of a student-directed and -acted production: Patty S. Derrick, review of *Cymbeline*, Pittsburgh, Pa., *Shakespeare Bulletin* 10 (winter 1992): 26.

12. For a literary argument that suggests Imogen's complicity in Iachimo's "rape that is not a rape," see Bamford, "Chastity," 53–54. Warren notes the strangeness of Imogen tempted by Iachimo, which appeared in Elijah Moshisky's 1982 production for the BBC (*Cymbeline*, 69). See also Owen E. Brady's review of Robin Phillips's Stratford Festival production (review of *Cymbeline*, Stratford, Ontario, *Theatre Journal* 39 [March 1987]: 104).

13. For a review of a production that portrays Imogen with "sweet virginal bliss" and in general focuses on "the historical ideal of female purity," see Gerald Nachman, "A Shakespeare Curiosity in Berkeley Festival's Last Show at John Hinkel Park Is an Odd Choice," review of *Cymbeline*, directed by Laird Williamson, Berkeley, Calif., *San Francisco Chronicle,* 7 August 1990, final edition, sec. E.

14. Kott, "Dialogues," 163.

15. Danson, "Masculine Desire," 69–79; esp. 79.

16. See, for example, Churnin, "*Cymbeline* Is Worth the Trip"; Helen Deese, review of *Cymbeline*, directed by Daniel Sullivan, San Diego, Calif., *Shakespeare Bulletin* 17 (fall 1999): 41; Robert Smallwood, "Shakespeare Performances in England, 1996–7," review of *Cymbeline*, directed by Adrian Noble, as performed by the RSC, Stratford-upon-Avon, *Shakespeare Survey* 51 (1998): 230.

17. Justin Shaltz, review of *Cymbeline*, directed by Calvin MacLean, Bloomington, Ill., *Shakespeare Bulletin* 13 (fall 1995): 28.

18. Warren, *Cymbeline*, 91.

19. Barbara Gaines, interview by author, tape recording, Chicago, Ill., 11 November 1997. All paraphrases and quotes of Gaines come from this interview unless otherwise noted.
20. Hedy Weiss, "Barbara Gaines Casts New Light on *Cymbeline,*" *Chicago Sun-Times,* 15 October 1989.
21. The conflation of critics and scholars is Gaines's.
22. Sid Smith, "Culture Shock: Shakespeare Repertory Rethinks *Othello* by making Moorish Prince the Star," *Chicago Tribune,* 15 October 1995, Chicagoland final edition, sec. C.
23. Weiss, "New Light."
24. All observations concerning the production are taken from my viewing of the video of a 1989 performance.
25. Similar kinds of framing devices are not uncommon. See, for example, Peter Marks, "Fairy-Tale Plottings of a British Royal Family," review of *Cymbeline,* directed by Andrei Serban, New York, *New York Times,* 17 August 1998, late edition, sec. E; and Kehler, *Cymbeline,* 79. For a fuller discussion of framing devices for *Cymbeline* and Gaines's and Akalaitis's productions in particular, see Pam Holland Seeman, "Magicians, Storytellers and Framing Devices: *Cymbeline* in Production," *Text and Presentation* 13 (1992): 59–64, though she incorrectly interprets Akalaitis's ghosts as the director's attempt to give added unity and coherence to the production.
26. A similar technique was used in Daniel Sullivan's production. See Kehler, "*Cymbeline,*" 80.
27. Lawrence Bommer, "Revival of '89 *Cymbeline* Recaptures Most of the Magic," review of *Cymbeline,* Chicago, Ill., *Chicago Tribune,* 7 October 1993, Du Page sports final edition, sec. Tempo.
28. Albert Williams, review of *Cymbeline,* Chicago, Ill., *Reader,* 27 October 1989.
29. Paul Faberson, "*Cymbeline* Is a Brilliant Show in All Possible Ways," review of *Cymbeline,* Chicago, Ill., *Skyline,* 26 October 1989.
30. A similar moment of restraint appeared in Scot Whitney's production. See Michael W. Shurgot, review of *Cymbeline,* Olympia, Wash., *Shakespeare Bulletin* 14 (spring 1996): 25.
31. Ibid.
32. Wells, "Shakespeare Performances," 140.
33. Warren, *Cymbeline,* 50, 123.
34. An exception is Danny Scheie's production for Shakespeare Santa Cruz in the summer 2000 where Iachimo goes to war in the nude (Steven Winn, "Bard with a Buzz: Shakespeare Santa Cruz's Frantic *Cymbeline* Marks Giddy Return of Danny Scheie," review of *Cymbeline,* Santa Cruz, Calif., *San Francisco Chronicle,* 29 July 2000, final edition, sec. E). But Scheie is gay and not infrequently uses male nudity in his productions.
35. Faberson, "*Cymbeline* Is a Brilliant Show."
36. Tom Simpson, "A Rare *Cymbeline,*" review of *Cymbeline,* Chicago, Ill., *Chicago Maroon,* 31 October 1989.
37. Bommer, "Revival."
38. Simpson, "Rare *Cymbeline.*"
39. Hedy Weiss, review of *Cymbeline,* Chicago, Ill., *Chicago Sun-Times,* 20 October 1989.
40. Collier, "Cutting to the Heart," 39.
41. JoAnne Akalaitis, telephone interview by author, tape recording, 8 June

1997. All further quotes or paraphrases of Akalaitis are from this interview unless otherwise noted.

42. Pressley, "Director Bearing Greek Gifts."
43. Ibid.
44. Green, *Revisionist Stage*, 91.
45. For a different opinion, see John Gielgud, who reports that he has found it "practically impossible to be disliked on the stage. But I had no such problem when I came to Angelo in *Measure for Measure*. I did not have to worry whether he was sympathetic or not: he cannot be anything but a despicable character" (*Acting Shakespeare*, 69).
46. All observations concerning the production are derived from my notes of viewing a video of the June 23, 1989 performance and several promptbooks at the New York Public Library of the Performing Arts unless otherwise noted. The thunderstorm detail I found in Green, *Revisionist Stage*, 93.
47. Ibid.
48. Elinor Fuchs, "Misunderstanding Postmodernism," *American Theatre*, December 1989, 31.
49. Saivetz, *Event in Space*, 194.
50. "JoAnne Akalaitis," 12 (see part 1, The Directors, note 128).
51. John Beaufort, "Update of Bard's *Cymbeline* Is Riddled with Incongruities," review of *Cymbeline*, New York, *Christian Science Monitor*, 16 June 1989, 11.
52. Nancy Graves, "Did Frank Rich Really Look?" *American Theatre*, December 1989, 29.
53. A similar staging occurred in Shepard Sobel's production, though the reviewer writes somewhat ambiguously that Imogen "bares her breast for the sword without the posturing sentimentality of her lines in the text." Nina daVinci Nichols, review of *Cymbeline*, New York, *Shakespeare Bulletin* 14 (fall 1996): 16. For further discussion of the sexual politics of this scene particularly for Jacobean and nineteenth-century audiences, see Collier, "Cutting to the Heart."
54. Harry Newman, "Far from an Affront," *American Theatre*, December 1989, 31.
55. Marks, "Fairy-Tale Plottings."
56. Fuchs, "Misunderstanding Postmodernism," 29.
57. Pam Holland, "*Cymbeline* in Production," 63.
58. Certainly even within these two groups there are widely ranging opinions, but the cultural and historical disjuncture between the stage world and the audience presents the strongest contrast.
59. Fuchs, "Misunderstanding Postmodernism," 29.
60. Ibid., 24.
61. James Leverett, "Why Did Reviewers Turn so Savage?" *American Theatre*, December 1989, 25.
62. Frank Rich, "Fantasy *Cymbeline* Set Long after Shakespeare," review of *Cymbeline*, New York, *New York Times*, 1 June 1989, late edition, sec. C.
63. Clive Barnes, "Travesty of Shakespeare," review of *Cymbeline*, New York, *New York Post*, 1 June 1989.
64. Howard Kissel, "Shakespeare as Victorian Sideshow," review of *Cymbeline*, New York, *Daily News*, 1 June 1989.
65. Fuchs, "Misunderstanding Postmodernism," 30.
66. Pye, "Is There Life after Joe Public?" 28.

67. Joanne Akalaitis as quoted in Pressley, "Director Bearing Greek Gifts."
68. "Joanne Akalaitis," 9.
69. Saivetz, *Event in Space,* 137.
70. Robert Brustein, review of *Woyzeck,* New York, *New Republic,* 4 January 1993, 27.
71. See Pressley, "Director Bearing Gifts"; Daniel, "A Different Direction" (see The Directors, note 118); "JoAnne Akalaitis" (see The Directors, note 128), 10.
72. Weiss, "Love at First Fight."

Epilogue

1. Coursen, *Shakespeare: The Two Traditions,* 38. For a fuller discussion of the relationship between scholarship and practice, see the section in his introduction entitled, "The Academic and the Director," 38–43.

Bibliography

INTRODUCTION: GENERAL BACKGROUND

Adelman, Janet. *Suffocating Mothers: Fantasies of Maternal Origin in Shakespeare's Plays:* Hamlet *to* The Tempest. New York: Routledge, 1992.
Alternative Shakespeares. Ed. John Drakakis. London: Methuen, 1985.
In Another Country: Feminist Perspectives on Renaissance Drama. Eds. Dorothea Kehler and Susan Baker. London: Scarecrow Press, 1991.
Aston, Elaine. *Feminist Theatre Practice: A Handbook.* New York: Routledge, 1999.
Auerbach, Erich. *Mimesis: The Representation of Reality in Western Literature.* Trans. Willard R. Trask. Princeton: Princeton University Press, 1953.
Austin, Gayle. *Feminist Theories for Dramatic Criticism.* Ann Arbor: University of Michigan Press, 1990.
Bamber, Linda. *Comic Women and Tragic Men: A Study of Gender and Genre in Shakespeare.* Stanford: Stanford University Press, 1982.
Barber, C. L. *Shakespeare's Festive Comedy: A Study of Dramatic Form and Its Relation to Social Custom.* Cleveland: World Publishing Co., 1963.
Bartow, Arthur. *The Director's Voice: Twenty One Interviews.* New York: Theatre Communications Group, 1988.
Bassnett, Susan. Introduction to "The Changing Status of Women in Theatre." In *The Routledge Reader in Gender and Performance.* Ed. Lizbeth Goodman. New York: Routledge, 1998.
Belsey, Catherine. "Constructing the Subject, Deconstructing the Text." In *Feminist Criticism and Social Change,* 43–64.
———. "Disrupting Sexual Difference: Meaning and Gender in the Comedies." In *Alternative Shakespeares,* 166–90.
———. *The Subject of Tragedy: Identity and Difference in Renaissance Drama.* New York: Routledge, 1985.
Benjamin, Jessica. "A Desire of One's Own: Psychoanalytic Feminism and Intersubjective Space." In *Feminist Studies: Critical Studies,* 78–101.
Benmussa, Simone, and Hélène Cixous. *Benmussa Directs.* Dallas: River Run Press, 1979.
Bennett, Susan. *Performing Nostalgia: Shifting Shakespeare and the Contemporary Past.* London: Routledge, 1996.
Berger, Harry, Jr. *Imaginary Audition: Shakespeare on Stage and Page.* Berkeley: University of California Press, 1989.

Berger, John. *Ways of Seeing*. London: BBC and Penguin, 1972.

Berggren, Paula S. "The Woman's Part: Female Sexuality and Power in Shakespeare's Plays." In *The Woman's Part*, 17–34.

Berry, Cicely. *The Actor and the Text*. Rev. ed. New York: Applause Books, 1992.

Berry, Cicely, Kristin Linklater, and Patsy Rodenburg. "Shakespeare, Feminism, and Voice: Responses to Sarah Werner." *New Theatre Quarterly* 13 (February 1997): 48–52.

Berry, Ralph. *On Directing Shakespeare: Interviews with Contemporary Directors*. London: Hamish Hamilton, 1989.

Berson, Misha. "Women at the Helm: In Leadership Posts Once Reserved for Men, They're Challenging Our Assumptions about Sex and Power." In *A Sourcebook of Feminist Theatre*, 61–78.

Bradby, David, and David Williams. *Directors' Theatre*. New York: St. Martin's Press, 1988.

Brecht, Bertolt. *Brecht on Theatre*. Ed. and trans. John Willett. New York: Hill and Wang, 1964.

Bristol, Michael D. *Shakespeare's America, America's Shakespeare*. London: Routledge, 1990.

Brunner, Cornelia. "Roberta Sklar: Toward Creating a Women's Theatre." *TDR* 24 (1980): 23–40.

Brustein, Robert. "A Theatrical Declaration of Independence." In *Reimagining American Theatre*. Chicago: Ivan R. Dee, 1991, 240–48.

Buzacott, Martin. *The Death of the Actor: Shakespeare on Page and Stage*. New York: Routledge, 1991.

Canning, Charlotte. *Feminist Theaters in the USA: Staging Women's Experience*. New York: Routledge, 1996.

Case, Sue Ellen. *Feminism and Theatre*. New York: Methuen, 1988.

———. "Gender as Play: Simone Benmussa's *The Singular Life of Albert Nobbs*," *Women & Performance Journal* 2 1 (winter 1984): 21–24.

Case, Sue Ellen and Jeanie Forte. "From Formalism to Feminism." *Theater* 16 (spring 1985): 62–65.

Changing Subjects: The Making of Feminist Literary Criticism. Eds. Gayle Greene and Coppelia Kahn. New York: Routledge, 1993.

Chodorow, Nancy. *The Reproduction of Mothering: Psychoanalysis and the Sociology of Gender*. Berkeley: University of California Press, 1978.

Cohen, Walter. "Political Criticism of Shakespeare." *Shakespeare Reproduced: The Text in History and Ideology*. New York: Methuen, 1987.

Coleman, Beth. "Just Mask: Beth Coleman Talks with Elizabeth LeCompte and Kate Valk." *ArtForum* 21 (May 1993): 83–86.

Colson, Marvin. *Theories of the Theatre: A Historical and Critical Survey from the Greeks to the Present*. Ithaca: Cornell University Press, 1984.

In Contact with the Gods?: Directors Talk Theatre. Eds. Maria M. Delgado and Paul Heritage. Manchester: Manchester University Press, 1996.

Cook, Judith. *Women in Shakespeare*. London: Harrap, 1980.

Coursen, H. R. *Reading Shakespeare on Stage*. Newark: University of Delaware Press, 1995.

———. *Shakespeare: The Two Traditions.* Madison, N.J.: Fairleigh Dickinson University Press, 1999.

Critical Theory and Performance. Eds. Janelle G. Reinelt and Joseph R. Roach. Ann Arbor: University of Michigan Press, 1992.

Cross-Cultural Performance: Differences in Women's Re-Visions of Shakespeare. Ed. Marianne Novy. Urbana: University of Illinois Press, 1993.

Curb, Rosemary. "Re/cognition, Re/presentation, Re/creation in Woman-Conscious Drama: The Seer, The Seen, The Scene, The Obscene." *Theatre Journal* 37 (October 1985): 302–16.

Cutler, Anna. "Abstract Body Language: Documenting Women's Bodies in Theatre." *New Theatre Quarterly* 14 (May 1998): 111–18.

Daniels, Rebecca. *Women Stage Directors Speak: Exploring the Influence of Gender on Their Work.* Jefferson, N.C.: McFarland and Co., 1996.

Danson, Lawrence. *Shakespeare's Dramatic Genres.* Oxford: Oxford University Press, 2000.

Dash, Irene. *Women's Worlds in Shakespeare's Plays.* Newark: University of Delaware Press, 1997.

———. *Wooing, Wedding, and Power: Women in Shakespeare's Plays.* New York: Columbia University Press, 1981.

David, Richard. *Shakespeare in the Theater.* Cambridge: Cambridge University Press, 1985.

Davis, Tracy C. "*Extremities* and *Masterpieces:* A Feminist Paradigm of Art and Politics." In *Feminist Theatre and Theory,* 137–56.

Dawson, Anthony. "Performance and Participation: Desdemona, Foucault, and the Actor's Body." In *Shakespeare, Theory, and Performance,* 29–45.

Dessen, Alan. *Elizabethan Stage Conventions and Modern Interpreters.* Cambridge: Cambridge University Press, 1984.

Diamond, Elin. "Brechtian Theory/Feminist Theory: Toward a Gestic Feminist Criticism." *TDR* 32 (spring 1988): 82–95.

———. "Mimesis, Mimicry, and the 'True-Real'." *Modern Drama* 32 (March 1989): 59–72.

———. *Unmaking Mimesis: Essays on Feminism and Theater.* New York: Routledge, 1997.

The Director and the Stage: From Naturalism to Grotowski. Ed. Edward Braun. New York: Holmes and Meier, 1982.

Directors on Directing. Eds. Toby Cole and Helen Chinoy. Rev. ed. Indianapolis: Bobbs Merrill, 1963.

Dolan, Jill. "Fathom Languages: Feminist Performance, Pedagogy, and Practice." In *Sourcebook of Feminist Theatre,* 1–20.

———. *The Feminist Spectator As Critic.* Ann Arbor: University of Michigan Research Press, 1988.

———. "Gender Impersonation Onstage: Destroying or Maintaining the Mirror of Gender Roles." *Women & Performance Journal* 4 2 (1985): 5–11.

———. "Practicing Cultural Disruptions: Gay and Lesbian Representation and Sexuality." In *Critical Theory and Performance,* 263–75.

———. *Presence and Desire: Essays on Gender, Sexuality, Performance.* Ann Arbor: University of Michigan Press, 1993.

Dollimore, Jonathan. *Radical Tragedy: Religion, Ideology and Power in the Drama of Shakespeare and His Contemporaries.* 2nd ed. Durham: Duke University Press, 1993.
Donkin, Ellen and Susan Clement. Introduction to *Upstaging Big Daddy.*
———. "Subverting the Text." In *Upstaging Big Daddy,* 89.
Dudden, Faye E. *Women in the American Theatre: Actresses and Audiences 1790–1870.* New Haven: Yale University Press, 1994.
Dunbar, Roxanne. "Female Liberation as the Basis for Social Revolution." In *Sisterhood Is Powerful,* edited by Robin Morgan, 477–92. New York: Vintage, 1970.
Dusinberre, Juliet. *Shakespeare and the Nature of Women.* 2nd ed. New York: St. Martin's Press, 1996.
Ebert, Teresa L. "The 'Difference' of Postmodern Feminism." *College English* 53 (December 1991): 886–904.
Eisenstein, Zillah. *The Radical Future of Liberal Feminism.* New York: Longman, 1981.
(En)Gendering Knowledge: Feminists in Academe. Eds. Joan E. Hartman and Ellen Messer-Davidow. Knoxville: University of Tennessee Press, 1991.
Feminist Criticism and Social Change: Sex, Class and Race in Literature and Culture. Eds. Judith Newton and Deborah Rosenfelt. New York: Methuen, 1988.
Feminist Studies/Critical Studies. Ed. Theresa de Lauretis. Bloomington: Indiana University Press, 1986.
Feminist Theatre and Theory. Ed. Helene Keyssar. New York: St. Martin's Press, 1996.
Ferris, Lesley. *Acting Women: Images of Women in Theatre.* New York: New York University Press, 1989.
———. "The Female Self and Performance: The Case of *The First Actress.*" In *Theatre and Feminist Aesthetics,* 242–57.
Firestone, Shulamith. *The Dialectic of Sex.* New York: Bantam, 1971.
Forte, Jeanie. "Realism, Narrative and the Feminist Playwrights: A Problem of Reception." In *Feminist Theatre and Theory,* 19–34.
Forte, Jeanie, and Christine Sumption. "Encountering *Dora:* Putting Theory into Practice." In *Upstaging Big Daddy,* 37–52.
Freedman, Barbara. "Frame-up: Feminism, Psychoanalysis, Theatre." In *Feminist Theatre and Theory,* 78–108.
French, Marilyn. *Shakespeare's Division of Experience.* New York: Summit Books, 1981.
Furse, Anna. "Bleeding, Sweating, Crying and Jumping: Blood Group—Women's Experimental Theatre." *Performance Research* 5, 1 (2000): 16–31.
Gajowski, Evelyn. *The Art of Loving: Female Subjectivity and Male Discursive Traditions in Shakespeare's Tragedies.* Newark: University of Delaware Press, 1992.
Gainor, J. Ellen. Introduction to *Performing America: Cultural Nationalism in American Theater.* Eds. Jeffrey D. Mason and J. Ellen Gainor. Ann Arbor: University of Michigan Press, 1999.
Gallop, Jane. *The Daughter's Seduction: Feminism and Psychoanalysis.* Ithaca: Cornell University Press, 1982.

Gay, Penny. *As She Likes It: Shakespeare's Unruly Women*. New York: Routledge, 1994.
Geertz, Clifford. "Thick Description: Toward an Interpretive Theory of Culture." In *The Interpretation of Cultures*, 3–22. New York: Basic Books, 1973.
Gielgud, John with John Miller. *Acting Shakespeare*. New York: Charles Scribner's Sons, 1991.
Gold, Sylviane. "The Possession of Julie Taymor." *American Theatre*, September 1998, 20–25.
Goldman, Michael. *The Actor's Freedom: Toward a Theory of Drama*. New York: Viking Press, 1975.
Goodman, Lizbeth. *Contemporary Feminist Theaters: To Each Her Own*. London: Routledge, 1993.
———. *Feminist Stages: Interviews with Women in Contemporary British Theatre*. Amsterdam, The Netherlands: Harwood Academic Publishers, 1996.
Gur, Andrew. *Playgoing in Shakespeare's London*. Cambridge: Cambridge University Press, 1987.
Harris, Geraldine. *Staging Femininities: Performance and Performativity*. Manchester: Manchester University Press, 1999.
Hart, Linda. "Motherhood According to Karen Finley: The Theory of Total Blame." In *Sourcebook of Feminist Theatre*, 108–19.
Helms, Lorraine. "Acts of Resistance: The Feminist Player." In *The Weyward Sisters: Shakespeare and Feminist Politics*. 102–56. Cambridge, Mass.: Blackwell, 1994.
Hodgdon, Barbara. "Replicating Richard: Body Doubles, Body Politics." *Theatre Journal* 50 (1998): 207–25.
———. *The Shakespeare Trade: Performances and Appropriations*. Philadelphia: University of Pennsylvania Press, 1998.
———. "*William Shakespeare's Romeo + Juliet*: Everything's Nice in America?" *Shakespeare Survey* 52 (1999): 88–98.
Holland, Peter. *English Shakespeares: Shakespeare on the English Stage in the 1990s*. Cambridge: Cambridge University Press, 1997.
Hortmann, Wilhelm. *Shakespeare on the German Stage: The Twentieth Century*. New York: Cambridge University Press, 1998.
Howard, Jean E. "Crossdressing, The Theatre, and Gender Struggle in Early Modern England." *Shakespeare Quarterly* 39 (winter 1988): 418–40.
———. *The Stage and Social Struggle in Early Modern England*. New York: Routledge, 1994.
Howard, Jean, and Phyllis Rackin. Introduction to *Engendering a Nation: A Feminist Account of Shakespeare's English Histories*. New York: Routledge, 1997.
Jaggar, Alison. *Feminist Politics and Human Nature*. Sussex: Harvester Press, 1983.
Jardine, Lisa. *Still Harping on Daughters: Women and Drama in the Age of Shakespeare*. Sussex, N.J.: The Harvester Press, 1983.
Johnson, Pauline. *Feminism as Radical Humanism*. Boulder, Colo.: Westview Press, 1994.

Kahn, Coppélia. *Man's Estate: Masculine Identity in Shakespeare.* Berkeley: University of Calif. Press, 1981.

———. *Roman Shakespeare: Warriors, Wounds, and Women. Feminist Readings of Shakespeare.* New York: Routledge, 1997.

Kaplan, Ann E. *Women and Film: Both Sides of the Camera.* New York: Methuen, 1983.

Kennedy, Dennis. *Foreign Shakespeare: Contemporary Performance.* New York: Cambridge University Press, 1993.

———. *Looking at Shakespeare: A Visual History of Twentieth-Century Performance.* Cambridge: Cambridge University Press, 1995.

Keyssar, Helene. "Drama and the Dialogic Imagination: *The Heidi Chronicles* and *Fefu and Her Friends.*" In *Feminist Theatre and Theory,* 109–36.

———. Introduction to *Feminist Theatre and Theory.*

Kimura, Doreen. "Sex Differences in the Brain." *Scientific American,* September 1992, 118–25.

Kirsch, Arthur. *Shakespeare and the Experience of Love.* Cambridge: Cambridge University Press, 1981.

Koszyn, Jayme. "The Dramaturgy and the Irrational." In *Dramaturgy in American Theater: A Source Book,* edited by Susan Jonas, 276–82. Fort Worth, Tex.: Harcourt Brace College, 1996.

Kristeva, Julia. "Woman Can Never Be Defined." In *New French Feminisms,* 137–41.

Kruger, Loren. "The Dis-Play's the Thing: Gender and Public Sphere in Contemporary British Theatre." In *Feminist Theatre and Theory,* 49–77.

Laughlin, Karen. Introduction to *Theatre and Feminist Aesthetics.*

de Lauretis, Theresa. *Alice Doesn't: Feminism, Semiotics, Cinema.* Bloomington: Indiana University Press, 1984.

———. *Technologies of Gender: Essays on Theory, Film, and Fiction.* Bloomington: Indiana University Press, 1987.

Linklater, Kristin. *Freeing the Natural Voice.* New York: Drama Book Publishers, 1976.

———. *Freeing Shakespeare's Voice.* New York: Theatre Communications Group, 1992.

Lomax, Marion. *Stage Images and Traditions: Shakespeare to Ford.* Cambridge: Cambridge University Press, 1987.

Londré, Felicia, with Kimberly L. Janczuk. "A Guide to American Shakespeare Companies and Festivals with Academic Affiliations." In *Teaching Shakespeare through Performance,* edited by Milla Cozart Riggio, 435–41. New York: Modern Language Association, 1999.

———. "North Carolina Shakespeare Festival." In *Shakespeare Companies and Festivals,* 255–59.

Londré, Felicia, and Daniel J. Watermeier. "Oregon Shakespeare Festival." In *Shakespeare Companies and Festivals,* 275–87.

Lurie, Susan. *Unsettled Subjects.* Durham, N.C.: Duke University Press, 1997.

Malpede, Karen. "Rebeccah: Rehearsal Notes." In *Women in American Theatre,* 311–15.

Manfull, Helen. *In Other Words: Women Directors Speak.* Lyme, N.H..: Smith and Kraus, 1997.

de Marinis, Marco. "'A Faithful Betrayal of Performance': Notes on the Use of Video in Theatre." Trans. Glyn Jones. *New Theatre Quarterly* 1 (November 1985): 387.

Marowitz, Charles. *Recycling Shakespeare.* New York: Applause Theatre Book Publishers, 1991.

Martinez, J. D. "The Fallacy of Contextual Analysis As a Means of Evaluating Dramatized Violence." In *Theatre Symposium: Theatre and Violence,* edited by John W. Frick, 76–85. Vol. 7. Tuscaloosa: Southeastern Theatre Conference and University of Alabama Press, 1999.

Mason, Jeffrey. Introduction to *Performing America.*

The Matter of Difference: Materialist Feminist Criticism of Shakespeare. Ed. Valerie Wayne. Ithaca: Cornell University Press, 1991.

Mayne, Judith. "Feminist Film Theory and Women at the Movies." *Profession 87* [MLA annual for 1987]: 14–19.

Mazer, Cary. "Shakespeare, the Reviewer, and the Theatre Historian." *Shakespeare Quarterly* 36 (1985): 648–61.

McDonald, Joyce Green. "Women and Theatrical Authority: Deborah Warner's *Titus Andronicus.*" In *Women's Re-Visions of Shakespeare,* 185–205.

McGuire, Philip. *Speechless Dialect: Shakespeare's Open Silences.* Berkeley: University of California Press, 1985.

McLuskie, Kathleen. "'Nay, faith, let me not play a woman, I have a beard coming': Women in Shakespeare's Plays." *Critical Survey* 4, 2 (1992): 114–23.

"Megan Terry Interviewed by Dinah L. Leavitt." In *Women in American Theatre,* 285–92.

Merrill, Lisa. *When Romeo Was a Woman: Charlotte Cushman and Her Circle of Female Spectators.* Ann Arbor: University of Michigan Press, 2001.

Miller, Nancy K. *Getting Personal: Feminist Occasions and Other Autobiographical Acts.* New York: Routledge, 1991.

Moi, Toril. *Sexual/Textual Politics: Feminist Literary Theory.* London: Routledge, 1985.

Mulvey, Laura. "Visual Pleasure and Narrative Cinema." In *After Modernism: Rethinking Representation,* edited by Brian Willis, 361–73. New York: The New Museum of Contemporary Art, 1984.

Neely, Carol Thomas. *Broken Nuptials in Shakespeare's Plays.* New Haven: Yale University Press, 1985.

———. "Constructing the Subject: Feminist Practice and the New Renaissance Discourse." *ELR* 18, 1 (1988): 5–18.

New French Feminisms. Eds. Elaine Marks and Isabelle de Courtivron. New York: Schocken Books, 1981.

Notable Women in American Theatre. Eds. Alice M. Robinson et al. New York: Greenwood Press, 1989.

Novy, Marianne. "Demythologizing Shakespeare." *Women's Studies* 9 (1981): 17–27.

———. *Love's Argument: Gender Relations in Shakespeare.* Chapel Hill: University of North Carolina Press, 1984.

O'Brien, Ellen. "Civil Wars in the Rehearsal Room: Conflicting Theories in Collaborative Praxis." In *Shakespeare and the Twentieth Century: The Selected Proceedings of the International Shakespeare Association World Congress, Los Angeles, 1996,* edited by Jonathan Bate, Jill L. Levenson, and Dieter Mehl, 125–36. Newark: University of Delaware Press, 1998.

The Performance of Power: Theatrical Discourse and Politics. Eds. Sue-Ellen Case and Janelle Reinelt. Iowa City: University of Iowa Press, 1991.

Performing America: Cultural Nationalism in American Theatre. Eds. Jeffrey Mason and J. Ellen Gainor. Ann Arbor: University of Michigan Press, 1999.

Performing Feminisms: Critical Theory and Theatre. Ed. Sue-Ellen Case. Baltimore: John Hopkins University Press, 1990.

Phelan, Peggy. *Unmarked: The Politics of Performance.* London: Routledge, 1993.

Players of Shakespeare. 3 vols. Cambridge: Cambridge University Press, 1985, 1988, 1993.

Political Shakespeare: New Essays in Cultural Materialism. Eds. Jonathan Dollimore and Alan Sinfield. Ithaca: Cornell University Press, 1985.

Porter, Laurin R. "Shakespeare's 'Sisters': Desdemona, Juliet, and Constance Ledbelly in *Goodnight Desdemona (Good Morning Juliet).*" Drama 38 (1995): 362–77.

Price, Janet, and Margrit Shildrick. "Openings on the Body: A Critical Introduction." In *Feminist Theory and the Body: A Reader.* Eds. Janet Price and Margrit Shildrick. Routledge: New York, 1999.

Primus, Francesca. "Women's Theatres around Town: Feminist or Contemporary?" *Back Stage,* 6 December 1985.

Pursell, Michael. "Artifice and Authenticity in Zeffirelli's *Romeo and Juliet.*" *Literature-Film Quarterly* 14, 4 (1986): 173–78.

Radway, Janice A. *Reading the Romance: Women, Patriarchy, and Popular Literature.* Chapel Hill, N.C.: University of North Carolina Press, 1984.

Rea, Charlotte. "Women for Women." In *Sourcebook of Feminist Theatre and Performance,* 31–41.

Reinelt, Janelle. "Beyond Brecht: Britain's New Feminist Drama." In *Feminist Theatre and Theory,* 35–48.

———. "Feminist Theory and the Problems of Performance." *Modern Drama* 32 (March 1989): 48–57.

Routledge Reader in Gender and Performance. Ed. Lizbeth Goodman. New York: Routledge, 1998.

Rubin, Gayle. "The Traffic in Women: Notes on the 'Political Economy' of Sex." In *Toward an Anthropology of Women,* edited by Rayna Reiter, 157–210. New York: Monthly Review Press, 1978.

Rutter, Carol, et al. *Clamorous Voices: Shakespeare's Women Today.* New York: Routledge, 1989.

Rutter, Carol Chillington. *Enter the Body: Women and Representation on Shakespeare's Stage.* London: Routledge, 2001.

Schafer, Elizabeth. *Ms-Directing Shakespeare: Women Direct Shakespeare.* London: The Women's Press, 1998.

Schechner, Richard. *Performance Theory.* New York: Routledge, 1988.

———. "TDR Comment: Mainstream Theatre and Performance Studies." *TDR* 44 (summer 2000): 4–6.

———. "TDR Comment: Post Post-Structuralism?" *TDR* 44 (fall 2000): 4–7.

Schneider, Rebecca. *The Explicit Body in Performance.* New York: Routledge, 1997.

Schroeder, Patricia R. "Locked behind the Proscenium: Feminist Strategies in *Getting Out* and *My Sister in This House.*" In *Feminist Theatre and Theory,* 155–67.

Scolnicov, Hanna. *Woman's Theatrical Space.* Cambridge: Cambridge University Press, 1994.

Senelick, Laurence. Introduction to *Gender in Performance: The Presentation of Difference in the Performing Arts.* Ed. Laurence Senelick. Hanover, N.H.: University Press of New England, 1992.

Shakespeare Around the Globe: A Guide to Notable Postwar Revivals. Ed. Samuel L. Leiter. New York: Greenwood Press, 1986.

Shakespeare Companies and Festivals: An International Guide. Eds. Ron Engle, Felicia Hardison Londré, and Daniel J. Watermeier. Westport, Conn.: Greenwood Press, 1994.

Shakespeare and Gender: A History. Eds. Deborah Barker and Ivo Kamps. London: Verso, 1995.

Shakespeare and the New Europe. Eds. Michael Hattaway, Boika Sokolova, and Derek Roper. Sheffield, England: Sheffield Academic Press, 1994.

Shakespearean Power and Punishment. Ed. Gillian Murray Kendall. Madison, N.J.: Fairleigh Dickinson University Press, 1998.

Shakespeare and the Sense of Performance: Essays in the Tradition of Performance Criticism in Honor of Bernard Beckerman. Eds. Marvin and Ruth Thompson. Newark: University of Delaware Press, 1989.

Shakespeare, Theory, and Performance. Ed. James C. Bulman. New York: Routledge, 1996.

Shapiro, Michael. *Gender in Play on the Shakespearean Stage: Boy Heroines and Female Pages.* Ann Arbor: University of Michigan Press, 1994.

Shattuck, Charles H. *Shakespeare on the American Stage: From the Hallams to Edwin Booth.* 2 vols. Washington, D.C.: Shakespeare Folger Library, 1976.

Silverman, Kaja. *The Acoustic Mirror: The Female Voice in Psychoanalysis and Cinema.* Bloomington: Indiana University Press, 1988.

Smith, Bruce R. *Shakespeare and Masculinity.* Oxford: Oxford University Press, 2000.

Solomon, Alisa. *Re-Dressing the Canon: Essays on Theatre and Gender.* New York: Routledge, 1997.

Sourcebook of Feminist Theatre and Performance: On and beyond the Stage. Ed. Carol Martin. London: Routledge, 1996.

Styan, J. L. *Drama, Stage and Audience.* Cambridge: Cambridge University Press, 1977.

———. *The Shakespeare Revolution: Criticism and Performance in the Twentieth Century.* Cambridge: Cambridge University Press, 1977.

Sullivan, Esther Beth. "Women, Woman, and the Subject of Feminism: Feminist Directions." In *Upstaging Big Daddy,* 11–34.

Swift, Carolyn R. and Natalie B. Strong. "Toward a Feminist Renaissance: Woman-Centering Shakespeare's Tragedy." In *Women's Re-Visions of Shakespeare*, 212–26.

Switon, Tilda. "Subverting Images of the Female." Interview by Lizbeth Goodman. *New Theatre Quarterly* 6 (August 1990): 215–28.

Theatre and Feminist Aesthetics. Eds. Karen Laughlin and Catherine Schuler. Madison, N.J.: Fairleigh Dickinson University Press, 1995.

Thompson, Ann. Series editor's preface to *Roman Shakespeare* by Coppélia Kahn. New York: Routledge, 1997.

———. "Shakespeare and Sexuality." *Shakespeare Survey* 46 (1994): 1–8.

Townsend, John Marshall. *What Women Want—What Men Want: Why the Sexes Still See Love and Commitment so Differently*. Oxford: Oxford University Press, 1998.

Transforming Shakespeare: Contemporary Women's Re-Visions in Literature and Performance. Ed. Marianne Novy. New York: St. Martin's Press, 1999.

Traub, Valerie. *Desire and Anxiety: Circulations of Sexuality in Shakespeare's Drama*. New York: Routledge, 1992.

Trussell, Robert. "Directing Women: The MO Rep Will Join Other Regional Theaters in Giving Females More Chances to Lead Productions." *Kansas City Star*, 7 October 1999.

Upstaging Big Daddy: Directing Theatre as if Gender and Race Matter. Eds. Ellen Donkin and Susan Clement. Ann Arbor: University of Michigan Press, 1993.

Venables, Clare. "The Woman Director in the Theatre." *Theatre Quarterly* 10, 38 (1980): 3–7.

Wells, Stanley. *Royal Shakespeare: Four Major Productions at Stratford-upon-Avon*. Manchester: Manchester University Press, 1977.

Werner, Sarah. "Performing Shakespeare: Voice Training and a Feminist Actor." *New Theatre Quarterly* 12 (August 1996): 249–58.

———. *Shakespeare and Feminist Performance: Ideology Onstage*. London: Routledge, 2001.

Wiles, Timothy J. *The Theatre Event: Modern Theories of Performance*. Chicago: University of Chicago Press, 1980.

Willis, Ellen. "Radical Feminism and Feminist Radicalism." In *The '60s without Apology*, edited by Sohnya Sayres et al., 91–118. Minneapolis: University of Minnesota Press, 1984.

The Woman's Part: Feminist Criticism of Shakespeare. Eds. Carolyn Ruth Swift Lenz, Gayle Greene, and Carol Thomas Neely. Chicago: University of Illinois Press, 1980.

Women in American Theatre: Careers, Images, Movements. Eds. Helen Krich Chinoy and Linda Walsh Jenkins. New York: Crown Publisher, Inc., 1981.

Women and Theatre: Calling the Shots. Ed. Susan Todd. London: Faber and Faber, 1984.

Women in Theatre: Compassion and Hope. Ed. Karen Malpede. New York: Limelight Editions, 1983.

Women's Re-Visions of Shakespeare. Ed. Marianne Novy. Chicago: University of Illinois Press, 1990.

Worthen, W. B. "Deeper Meanings and Theatrical Technique: The Rhetoric of Performance Criticism." *Shakespeare Quarterly* 40 (winter 1989): 441–55.

———. *The Idea of the Actor: Drama and the Ethics of Performance.* Princeton: Princeton University Press, 1984.

———. *Shakespeare and the Authority of Performance.* Cambridge: Cambridge University Press, 1997.

THE INTERVIEWS

Adams, Abigail. Interview by author. Tape recording. Malvern, Pa., 10 June 1997.

Akalaitis, JoAnne. Phone interview by author. Tape recording. 8 June 1997.

Bensussen, Melia. Interview by author. Tape recording. Princeton, N.J., 11 June 1997.

Gaines, Barbara. Interview by author. Tape recording. Chicago, Ill., 11 November 1997.

Koszyn, Jayme. Interview by author. Tape recording. New Haven, Conn., 15 June 1997.

———. Phone interview by author. Tape recording. 30 August 1997.

O'Brien, Ellen. Interview by author. Tape recording. Greensboro, N.C., 10 October 1997.

Packer, Tina. Interview by author. Tape recording. Cambridge, Mass., 24 October 1997.

———. Interview by author. Tape recording. Cambridge, Mass., 14 November 1997.

Wolpe, Lisa. Phone interview by author. Tape recording. 16–17 August 1998.

CHAPTER 1: *ROMEO AND JULIET*

Literary Criticism

Appelbaum, Robert. "'Standing to the Wall': The Pressures of Masculinity in *Romeo and Juliet*." *Shakespeare Quarterly* 48 (1997): 251–72.

Brown, Carolyn. "Juliet's Taming of Romeo." *Studies in English Literature* 36 (1996): 333–53.

Carroll, William. "'We Were Born to Die': *Romeo and Juliet*." *Shakespeare Quarterly* 15 (spring 1981): 54–71.

Davis, Lloyd. "'Death-Marked Love': Desire and Presence in *Romeo and Juliet*." *Shakespeare Survey* 49 (1996): 57–67.

Gohlke, Madelon. "'I Wooed Thee with My Sword': Shakespeare's Tragic Paradigms." In *The Woman's Part*, 150–70.

Holmer, Joan Ozark. "The Poetics of Paradox: Shakespeare's Versus Zeffirelli's Cultures of Violence." *Shakespeare Survey* 49 (1996): 163–79.

Kahn, Coppélia. "Coming of Age in Verona." In *The Woman's Part*, 171–93.

Knowles, Ronald. "Carnival and Death in *Romeo and Juliet.*" In *Shakespeare and Carnival after Bakhtin,* edited by Ronald Knowles, 36–60. New York: Macmillan Press, 1998.

Levenson, Jill. "The Definition of Love: Shakespeare's Phrasing in *Romeo and Juliet.*" *Shakespeare Studies* 15 (1982): 21–36.

Moisan, Thomas. "'O any thing of nothing first create!': Gender and Patriarchy and the Tragedy of *Romeo and Juliet.*" In *In Another Country,* 113–36.

Romeo and Juliet: Critical Essays. Ed. John Andrews. New York: Garland Press, 1993.

Snyder, Susan. "Ideology and Feud in *Romeo and Juliet.*" *Shakespeare Survey* 49 (1996): 87–96.

Recent Production History

Armstrong, Alan. Review of *Romeo and Juliet,* directed by René Buch. Ashland, Ore. *Shakespeare Bulletin* 15 (spring 1997): 33–34.

Barker, Felix. Review of *Romeo and Juliet,* directed by Declan Donnellan. New Shakespeare Company. London. *Plays and Players,* August 1986, 20–21.

Brady, Owen. Review of *Romeo and Juliet,* directed by John Dewes. Stratford, Ontario. *Theatre Journal* 37 (March 1985): 111–13.

———. Review of *Romeo and Juliet,* directed by Richard Monette. Stratford, Ontario. *Theatre Journal* 45 (May 1993): 242–45.

Carlson, Marvin. "Beier's *Romeo and Juliet* in Dusseldorf." Review of *Romeo and Juliet,* directed by Karin Beier. Dusseldorf, Germany. *Western European Stages* 7, 1 (1995): 77–80.

Coe, Robert. Review of *Romeo and Juliet,* directed by Bill Rauch. The Cornerstone Theater Company. Fort Gibson, Mississippi. *American Theatre,* May 1989, 14–21, 52–57.

Cook, Dorothy, and Wayne Cook. Review of *Romeo and Juliet,* directed by Mark Lamos. The Hartford Stage Company. Hartford, Conn. *Shakespeare Bulletin* 14 (spring 1996): 11–12.

Flachmann, Michael. Review of *Romeo and Juliet,* directed by Des McAnuff. La Jolla, Calif. *Shakespeare Quarterly* 35 (spring 1984): 105–7.

Frye, Rinda. Review of *Romeo and Juliet,* directed by John Jory. Louisville, Kentucky. *Theatre Journal* 47 (March 1995): 126–28.

Geckle, George L. Review of *Romeo and Juliet,* directed by Adrian Noble. RSC. Stratford-upon-Avon. *Shakespeare Bulletin* 14 (winter 1996): 126–27.

Hoenselaars, Ton. Review of *Romeo and Juliet,* directed by Ivo van Hove. Amsterdam. *Shakespeare Bulletin* 18 (winter 2000): 37–38.

Hurren, Kenneth. Review of *Romeo and Juliet,* directed by Michael Bogdanov. RSC. Stratford-upon-Avon. *Plays and Players,* June 1986, 24–25.

Jackson, Russell. "Shakespeare Performed: Shakespeare at Stratford-upon-Avon 1995–96." Review of *Romeo and Juliet,* directed by Adrian Noble. RSC. Stratford-upon-Avon. *Shakespeare Quarterly* 47 (1996): 319–26.

Johnson-Haddad, Miranda. "Shakespeare Performed: The Shakespeare Theatre, 1993–4." Review of *Romeo and Juliet,* directed by Jay Goede. The Shakespeare Company. Washington, D.C. *Shakespeare Quarterly* 46 (1995): 82–90.

Londré, Felicia Hardison. Introduction to *"Romeo and Juliet."* In *Shakespeare Around the Globe,* 625–31.

———. Review of *Romeo and Juliet,* directed by Denis Llorca. Carcassonne, France. In *Shakespeare around the Globe,* 648.

———. Review of *Romeo and Juliet,* directed by Horst Seide. Wuppertal, West Germany. In *Shakespeare around the Globe,* 650–51.

Mento, Joan. Review of *Romeo and Juliet,* directed by Andrea Haring. Shakespeare and Company. Lenox, Mass. *Shakespeare Bulletin* 14 (spring 1996): 11–12.

Miller, Hal. "Shakespeare Abroad: Two Versions of Romeo and Juliet in Vienna." Reviews of *Romeo and Juliet,* directed by Karlheinz Hackl and Rahim Burhan. Vienna, Austria. *Shakespeare Bulletin* 13 (summer 1995): 33–34.

Powell, Susana. "Shakespeare at the Public Theatre Network." Review of *Romeo and Juliet,* directed by Alex Chisholm. Sound and Fury. London. *Shakespeare Bulletin* 13 (winter 1995): 22–23.

Roper, David. Review of *Romeo and Juliet,* directed by Kenneth Branaugh. Hammersmith, England. *Plays and Players,* October 1986, 23.

———. Review of *Romeo and Juliet,* directed by John Caird. RSC/Nat West Touring Production. Stratford-upon-Avon. *Plays and Players,* June 1984, 27–28.

Rutherford, Malcolm. "Of Inspiration and Effort." Review of *Romeo and Juliet,* directed by Sir Peter Hall. RSC. London. *Encounter* 24 (April 1990): 74–75.

Shaltz, Justin. Review of *Romeo and Juliet,* directed by Diana Leblanc. Stratford, Ontario. *Shakespeare Bulletin* 16 (winter 1998): 41–42.

Shurbanov, Alexander and Boika Sokolova. "From the Unlove of *Romeo and Juliet* to *Hamlet* without the Prince: The Shakespearean Mirror Held up to the Fortunes of the New Bulgaria." In *Shakespeare and the New Europe,* 24–53.

Smidt, Kristian. Review of *Romeo and Juliet,* directed by Pål Løkkeberg. Oslo, Norway. *Shakespeare Quarterly* 37 (spring 1986): 111–14.

Stanley, Audrey. "The 1994 Shanghai International Shakespeare Festival." Review of *Romeo and Juliet,* directed by Roft Johannsmeier. Nuremberg Young People's Theater. Shanghai, China. *Shakespeare Quarterly* 47 (spring 1996): 79–80.

Timpane, John. Review of *Romeo and Juliet,* directed by Bonnie J. Monte. Madison, N.J. *Shakespeare Bulletin* 18 (spring 2000): 12–13.

Director's Work: Lisa Wolpe

Birchall, Paul. Review of *A Midsummer Night's Dream,* directed by Lisa Wolpe. Los Angeles Women's Shakespeare Company. Culver City, Calif. *Back Stage West,* 7–14 May 1998.

Brandes, Philip. "Theater Beat: *Richard III* Puts Twist on Exploring Soul's Dark Side." Review of *Richard III,* directed by Maureen Shea. LAWSC. Culver City, Calif. *Los Angeles Times,* 22 March 1996, home edition, sec. F.

Clark, J. R. Review of *Richard III,* directed by Maureen Shea. LAWSC. Culver City, Calif. *Drama-Logue,* 21–27 March 1996.

Fisher, Rachel. Review of *Othello,* directed by Lisa Wolpe. LAWSC. West Los Angeles, Calif. *Back Stage West,* 16–22 June 1994.

Foley, Kathleen F. "An All-Female *Othello* at Odyssey." Review of *Othello,* directed by Lisa Wolpe. LAWSC. Los Angeles, Calif. *Los Angeles Times,* 9 June 1994, home edition, sec. F.

———. "Theater Beat: Effective Female Ensemble in *Hamlet.*" Review of *Hamlet,* directed by Lisa Wolpe and Natsuko Ohama. LAWSC. Culver City, Calif. *Los Angeles Times,* 28 April 1995, home edition, sec. F.

Foster, Daniel R. "Palm Latitudes: The Biz: Shaking up Shakespeare." *Los Angeles Times,* 20 March 1994, home edition, Magazine.

Haithman, Diane. "It's Women's Turn to Be or Not to Be." Review of *Hamlet,* directed by Lisa Wolpe and Natsuko Ohama. LAWSC. Culver City, Calif. *Los Angeles Times,* 22 April 1995, sec. F.

Hofler, Robert. "Pulling the Switch: Actresses Revel in the Power—If Not the Glory—of Playing Men." *Back Stage,* 17 September 1993.

Horowitz, Lisa D. Review of *Richard III,* directed by Maureen Shea. LAWSC. Culver City, Calif. *Newton (Mass.) Daily Variety,* 25 March 1996.

Johnson-Haddad, Miranda. Review of *Twelfth Night.* LAWSC. Los Angeles. *Shakespeare Bulletin* 18 (fall 2000): 31–32.

Jonas, Larry. Review of *Romeo and Juliet,* directed by Lisa Wolpe and Erica Bilder. LAWSC. Hollywood, Calif. *Drama-Logue,* n.d.

Kendt, Rob. "The Theatre Makers." *Back Stage West,* 6–12 July 1995.

Koehler, Robert. "*Romeo and Juliet* Are Cross-Dressed Lovers in New Staging." Review of *Romeo and Juliet,* directed by Lisa Wolpe and Erica Bilder. LAWSC. Hollywood, Calif. *Los Angeles Times,* 14 March 1993, valley edition, Calendar.

Lewis, Judith. "Sex Repeal: When Roles Shed Their Chromosomes." Review of Romeo and Juliet, directed by Lisa Wolpe and Erica Bilder. LAWSC. Hollywood, Calif. *LA Weekly,* n.d.

Los Angeles Women's Shakespeare Company. *A Muse of Fire.* Produced and directed by Lisa Wolpe and Sandy Shepherd. 12 min. 1993. Videocassette.

Loynd, Ray. Review of *King Lear,* directed by Scott Rogers. New Women's Repertory Company. Santa Monica, Calif. *Los Angeles Times,* 4 October 1991, home edition, sec. F.

Nakagawa, Martha. "Shakespeare Lovers, Rejoice!" Review of *Hamlet,* directed by Lisa Wolpe and Natsuko Ohama. LAWSC. Culver City, Calif. *The Rafu Shimpo: Los Angeles Japanese Daily News,* 26 April 1995.

Shaner, Madelyn. Review of *Richard III,* directed by Maureen Shea. LAWSC. Culver City, Calif. *ShowCase Entertainment Magazine,* Night Life section, 29 March 1996.

———. "*Richard III* Done Splendidly with All-Woman Cast." Review of *Richard III,* directed by Maureen Shea. LAWSC. Culver City, Calif. *Park Labrea News,* 4 April 1996.

Shirley, Don. "The Two Dueling 'Juliets': One Conventional, One Not." Reviews of *Romeo and Juliet,* directed by Lisa Wolpe and Erica Bilder for LAWSC, Hollywood, Calif.; and by Art Manke for A Noise Within, Glendale, Calif. *Los Angeles Times,* 23 March 1993, home edition, sec. F.

Spring, Greg. "All-Woman *Othello* Explores What Men Feel: L.A. Women's Shakespeare Company Finds Deeper Levels, Social Inflections in Bard's Domestic Tragedy." Review of *Othello*, directed by Lisa Wolpe. LAWSC. West Los Angeles, Calif. *Back Stage West,* 2 June 1994, 5.

Stimac, Elias. Review of *Othello,* directed by Lisa Wolpe. LAWSC. West Los Angeles, Calif. *Drama-Logue,* 9–15 June 1994.

Swanson, Debbi K. "Women Take a Stab at *Richard III.*" Review of *Richard III,* directed by Maureen Shea. LAWSC. Culver City, Calif. *The Outlook,* 16 March 1996.

Tran, Tony. "Her Kingdom for Horse: All-female Version of *Richard III* Proves Revelatory." Review of *Richard III,* directed by Maureen Shea. LAWSC. Culver City, Calif. *Los Angeles View,* 29 March–4 April 1996, 44.

Wolpe, Lisa, Robin Payne, and Nassira Nicola. Interview with Mark Burnheimer. "Women's Theater Troupe Gender-Twists Shakespeare." CNN, Atlanta, GA. 14 April 1996. Transcript #1330–9.

Chapter 2: *Measure for Measure*

Literary Criticism

Baines, Barbara. "Assaying the Power of Chastity in *Measure for Measure.*" *SEL: Studies in English Literature 1500–1900* 30, 2 (1990): 283–301.

Brown, Carolyn. "Erotic Religious Flagellation in Shakespeare's *Measure for Measure.*" *English Literary Renaissance* 16 (winter 1986): 139–65.

Carlson, Susan. "'Fond Fathers' and Sweet Sisters: Alternative Sexualities in *Measure for Measure.*" *Essays in Literature* 16 (spring 1989): 13–31.

Charney, Maurice. "'To Catch a Saint': Sexual Reciprocities in *Measure for Measure.*" *Shakespeare Bulletin* 2, 1 (1983): 13–16.

Desai, Rupin W. "Freudian Undertones in the Isabella-Angelo Relationship of *Measure for Measure.*" *Psychoanalytic Review* 64 (1977): 487–94.

Desmet, Christy. "'Neither Maid, Widow, nor Wife': Rhetoric of the Woman Controversy in *Measure for Measure* and *The Duchess of Malfi.*" In *In Another Country,* 71–92.

Digangi, Mario. "Pleasure and Danger: Measuring Female Sexuality in *Measure for Measure.*" *ELH* 60 (fall 1993): 589–609.

Dollimore, Jonathan. "Transgression and Surveillance in *Measure for Measure.*" In *Political Shakespeare,* 72–87.

Ellis-Fermor, Una Mary. *The Jacobean Drama: An Interpretation.* London: Methuen, 1936.

Friedman, Michael D. "'O, let him marry her!': Matrimony and Recompense in *Measure for Measure.*" *Shakespeare Quarterly* 46 (winter 1995): 68–78.

Geckle, George L., Ed. *Twentieth-Century Interpretations of Measure for Measure.* Englewood Cliffs, N.J.: Prentice-Hall, 1970.

Hattaway, Michael. "Fleshing His Will in the Spoil of Her Honor: Desire, Misogyny, and the Perils of Chivalry." *Shakespeare Survey* 46 (1994): 121–35.

Hawkins, Harriet. "'The Devil's Party': Virtues and Vices in *Measure for Measure.*" *Shakespeare Survey* 31 (1978): 105–13.
Howard, Jean. "*Measure for Measure* and the Restraints of Convention." *Essays in Literature* 10 (1983): 149–58.
Huebert, Ronald. "Taking the Measure of Manliness." *Dalhousie Review* 63 (spring 1983): 125–34.
Hunt, Maurice. "Comfort in *Measure for Measure.*" *SEL: Studies in English Literature 1500–1900* 27 (spring 1987): 213–32.
Jameson, Anna. *Shakespeare's Heroines: Characteristics of Women, Moral, Political, and Historical.* London: G. Bell, 1913.
Knoppers, Laura Lunger. "(En)gendering Shame: *Measure for Measure* and the Spectacles of Power." *English Literary Renaissance* 23 (autumn 1993): 450–71.
Kott, Jan, and Charles Marowitz. "The Kott-Marowitz Dialogues: *Measure for Measure.*" *New Theatre Quarterly* 10 (May 1994): 157–66.
Lennox, Charlotte. *Shakespear Illustrated.* 2 vols. London: 1753.
MacDonald, Ronald. "*Measure for Measure:* The Flesh Made Word." *SEL: Studies in English Literature 1500–1900* 30 (spring 1990): 265–82.
Macfarlane, Linda. "Heads You Win Tails I Lose." *Critical Survey* 5, 1 (1993): 77–82.
McCandless, David. "'I'll Pray to Increase Your Bondage': Power and Punishment in *Measure for Measure.*" In *Shakespearean Power and Punishment,* 89–112.
McLuskie, Kathleen. "The Patriarchal Bard: Feminist Criticism and Shakespeare: *King Lear* and *Measure for Measure.*" In *Political Shakespeare,* 88–108.
Moore, Susan. "Virtue and Power in *Measure for Measure.*" *English Studies* 63 (August 1982): 308–17.
Quiller-Couch, Sir Arthur. Introduction to *Measure for Measure.* Eds. Sir Arthur Quiller-Couch and J. Dover Wilson. Cambridge: Cambridge University Press, 1922.
Riefer, Marcia. "'Instruments of Some More Mightier Member': The Constriction of Female Power in *Measure for Measure.*" *Shakespeare Quarterly* 35 (spring 1984): 157–69.
Rose, Jacqueline. "Sexuality in the Reading of Shakespeare: *Hamlet* and *Measure for Measure.*" In *Alternative Shakespeares,* 95–118.
Slights, Jessica, and Michael Morgan Holmes. "Isabella's Order: Religious Acts and Personal Desires in *Measure for Measure.*" *Studies in Philology* 95 (summer 1998): 263–92.

Recent Production History

Andresen, Martha. Review of *Measure for Measure,* directed by Robert Egan. Center Theatre Group. Los Angeles. *Shakespeare Quarterly* 37 (winter 1986): 506–8.
Bock, Judith. Review of *Measure for Measure,* directed by Joel Fink. Boulder, Colo. *Theatre Journal* 44 (March 1992): 118–19.

Brady, Owen. Review of *Measure for Measure,* directed by Michael Bogdanov. Stratford, Ontario. *Theater Journal* 37 (December 1985): 506–8.

Friedman, Michael. "Prostitution and Feminist Appropriation of *Measure for Measure* on the Stage." *Shakespeare Bulletin* 15 (spring 1997): 14–17.

Galenbeck, Susan. Review of *Measure for Measure,* directed by Paul Bettis. Ames, Iowa. *Theatre Journal* 36 (March 1984): 115–16.

Gordon, Giles. Review of *Measure for Measure,* directed by Adrian Noble. RSC. London. *Plays and Players,* July 1984, 33.

Jaynes, Nanette. Review of *Measure for Measure,* directed by Tim Ocel. Atlanta, Ga. *Shakespeare Bulletin* 17 (fall 1999): 23–24.

Massai, Sonia. "Stage over Study: Charles Marowitz, Edward Bond, and Recent Materialist Approaches to Shakespeare." *New Theatre Quarterly* 15 (1999): 247–55.

"*Measure for Measure.*" *New York Theater Critics Reviews* 46 (September 2, 1985): 215–19.

Nice, David. Review of *Measure for Measure,* directed by David Thacker. London. *Plays and Players,* July 1987, 28–29.

Roberts, Peter. Review of *Measure for Measure,* directed by Adrian Noble. RSC. Stratford-upon-Avon. *Plays and Players* 362 (November 1983): 21–22.

Savin, Janet. Review of *Measure for Measure,* directed by Carlo Cecchi. Teatro Garibaldi Company. Paris. *Shakespeare Bulletin* 18 (winter 2000): 41–42.

Shrimpton, Nicholas. "Shakespeare Performances in Stratford-upon-Avon and London, 1983–4." Review of *Measure for Measure,* directed by Adrian Noble. RSC. Stratford-upon-Avon. *Shakespeare Survey* 38 (1985): 201–4.

Vaughan, Virginia M. Review of *Measure for Measure,* directed by Andrei Belgrader. Cambridge, Mass. *Theatre Journal* 36 (October 1984): 406–7.

Director's Work: Tina Packer

Byrne, Terry. "Shakespeare and Company's Production Measures Up." Review of *Measure for Measure,* directed by Tina Packer. Shakespeare and Company. Foxboro, Mass. *Boston Herald,* 29 September 1996, first edition, Entertainment.

Campbell, Karen. "A Celebration of Theater Works by Women." *Boston Globe,* 20 February 2000, third edition, sec. M.

Clay, Carolyn. "After the Fall: Arthur Miller and *Measure for Measure* in the Berkshires." Review of *Measure for Measure,* directed by Tina Packer. Shakespeare and Company. Lenox, Mass. *Boston Phoenix,* 26 July 1996, sec. 3.

Duckett, Richard. "Lively Tina Packer Is a 'Woman of Will.'" *Worcester (Mass.) Sunday Telegram,* 7 July 1996, Datebook.

Dunning, Jennifer. "*Twelfth Night* Staged in Prospect Park." Review of *Twelfth Night,* directed by Tina Packer. Shakespeare and Company. Brooklyn, N.Y. *New York Times,* 11 July 1982, late city final edition, sec. 1, part 2.

Epstein, Helen. *The Companies She Keeps: Tina Packer Builds a Theater.* Cambridge, Mass: Plunkett Lake Press, 1985.

Fanger, Iris. "Playing Bare Bard for Good *Measure.*" Review of *Measure for Measure,* directed by Tina Packer. Shakespeare and Company. Foxboro, Mass. *Boston Herald,* 13 September 1996, sec. S.

Gorfinkle, Constance. "Scene and Heard: Shakespeare Director at Home in London, Lenox or Foxboro." *Foxboro (Mass.) Patriot Ledger,* 14 September 1996, ROP edition, Features.

Gussow, Mel. "Outdoor *Antony.*" Review of *Antony and Cleopatra,* directed by Tina Packer. Shakespeare and Company. Lenox, Mass. *New York Times,* 24 July 1986, sec. C.

———. "The Play's the Thing, for Directors, Too." *New York Times,* 15 May 1996, late city edition, sec. C.

Hartigan, Patti. "Here, They're Not Merely Players: Actors Run Shakespeare and Company." *Boston Globe,* 21 August 1994, city edition, Arts and Film.

———. "Women Rediscovered Their Voices: Tackling Shakespeare from a Female Point of View." *Boston Globe,* 2 August 1992, city edition, sec. B.

Horton, G. L. Review of *Measure for Measure,* directed by Tina Packer. Shakespeare and Company. Lenox, Mass. *AisleSay: The Theatre Magazine of the Net.* http://www.stagepage.info/reviews/measure.html.

Lehman, Jon. "A Skillfully Measured Production in Foxboro: Sexual Politics and Slapstick Comedy." Review of *Measure for Measure,* directed by Tina Packer. Shakespeare and Company. Foxboro, Mass. *Foxboro (Mass.) Patriot Ledger,* 17 September 1996, ROP edition, Features.

Malkin, Lawrence. "In Lenox They Are 'Dropping in' on the Bard of Avon: Shakespeare and Company in Lenox, Mass." *Smithsonian,* November 1991, 134–44.

Moore, Margo J. "*Measure for Measure* Timely Political Commentary." Review of *Measure for Measure,* directed by Tina Packer. Shakespeare and Company. Foxboro, Mass. *Milford (Mass.) Country Gazette,* 20 September 1996, Entertainment.

Morrish, John. "The Camp's the Thing." *Daily Telegraph,* 17 August 1996, Telegraph Magazine.

Perkins, Carol. "Strong Direction, Relevance Boost *Measure for Measure.*" Review of *Measure for Measure,* directed by Tina Packer. Shakespeare and Company. Lenox, Mass. *Pittsfield (Mass.) Gazette,* 5 July 1996, sec. A.

Siegel, Ed. "Full-Bawdied *Measure* Comes East." Review of *Measure for Measure,* directed by Tina Packer. Shakespeare and Company. Foxboro, Mass. *Boston Globe,* 12 September 1996, city edition, sec. E.

———. "Mute the Minimalism, Revise the Revisionism: In the Berkshire Hills, the Arts Can Come in Peaks and Valleys." *Boston Globe,* 29 August 1995, city edition, Living.

———. "Packer's *Richard III* Considers the Women." Review of *Richard III,* directed by Tina Packer. Shakespeare and Company. Lenox, Mass. *Boston Globe,* 15 July 1999, city edition, sec. E.

———. "Shakespeare in Good Company: Dropping in on Packer's Method." *Boston Globe,* 22 September 1996, city edition, sec. N.

———. "A Wealth of Women's Roles in Various Stages." Review of *Much Ado about Nothing,* directed by Tina Packer. Shakespeare and Company. Lenox, Mass. *Boston Globe,* 27 July 1995, city edition, Living.

Director's Work: Ellen O'Brien

Barhnill, Anne. "Aristophanes' Updated *Birds* Is Amusing Spoof." Review of *The Birds*, by Aristophanes, directed by Ellen O'Brien. Greensboro, N.C. *Greensboro (N.C.) News and Record*, 11 November 1996, sec. B.
Brown, Chris. "Desdemona and Juliet Get Rave Reviews." Review of *Goodnight Desdemona (good morning Juliet)*, by Ann-Marie MacDonald, directed by Ellen O'Brien. Greensboro, N.C. *The Guilfordian*, 19 November 1999.
"The Devil's Gateway Set." *Greensboro News and Record*, 8 February 1998.
"Flighty Fun at Guilford's Production of *The Birds*." Review of *The Birds*, by Aristophanes, directed by Ellen O'Brien. Greensboro, N.C. *Carolina Peacemaker*, 17–23 October 1996.
Jones, Abe D. "Students Stage Shakespeare's *Measure for Measure* with Contemporary Setting, Context." Review of *Measure for Measure*, directed by Ellen O'Brien. Greensboro, N.C. *Greensboro (N.C.) News and Record*, 5 April 1991.
———. "Two Share Direction of Guilford College Production." *Greensboro (N.C.) News and Record*, 28 March 1991.
Jones, Tina P. "Four Actors Take You Way Back to the Future." Review of *On the Verge*, By Eric Overmyer, directed by Ellen O'Brien. Greensboro, N.C. *Greensboro (N.C.) News and Record*, 2 April 1992, sec. D.
"*Trojan Women* No Light Fair." *Greensboro (N.C.) News and Record*, 27 March 1994, sec. B.

CHAPTER 3: *TWELFTH NIGHT*

Literary Criticism

Barton, Ann. Introduction to *Twelfth Night*. In *The Riverside Shakespeare*. 2nd ed. Boston: Houghton Mifflin, 1997.
Charles, Casey. "Gender Trouble in *Twelfth Night*." *Theatre Journal* 49 (May 1997): 121–41.
Freedman, Barbara. "Separation and Fusion in *Twelfth Night*." In *Psychoanalytic Approaches to Literature and Film*, edited by Maurice Charney and Joseph Reppen, 96–119. Rutherford, N.J.: Fairleigh Dickinson University Press, 1987.
Jardine, Lisa. "Twins and Travesties: Gender, Dependency, and Sexual Availability in *Twelfth Night*." In *Erotic Politics: Desire on the Renaissance Stage*, ed. Susan Zimmerman, 27–38. New York: Routledge, 1992.
Kimbrough, Robert. "Androgyny Seen through Disguise." *Shakespeare Quarterly* 33 (spring 1982): 17–33.
Logan, Thad Jenkins. "*Twelfth Night:* The Limits of Festivity." *SEL: Studies in English Literature 1500–1900* 22 (1982): 223–38.
Malcolmson, Christina. "'What You Will': Social Mobility and Gender in *Twelfth Night*." In *The Matter of Difference*, 29–57.

Pequigney, Joseph. "The Two Antonios and Same-Sex Love in *Twelfth Night* and *The Merchant of Venice.*" *English Literary Renaissance* 22 (spring 1992): 201–21.
Rose, Mary Beth. *The Expense of Spirit: Love and Sexuality in English Renaissance Drama.* Ithaca: Cornell University Press, 1988.
Schalkwyk, David. "'She never told her love': Embodiment, Textuality, and Silence in Shakespeare's Sonnets and Plays." *Shakespeare Quarterly* 45 (winter 1994): 381–407.

Recent Production History

Alexander, Meredith. "Gender As Drag: A Director's Approach to *Twelfth Night.*" In *Shakespeare and Britten at Iowa: Interpretive Essay,* 9–10. Iowa City: University of Iowa, 1991.
Armstrong, Alan. Review of *Twelfth Night,* directed by Pat Patton. The Oregon Shakespeare Festival Company. Portland, Ore. *Shakespeare Bulletin* 12 (spring 1994): 31.
Bartlett, Neil. "Underneath Our Clothes." *American Theatre,* July/August 1992, 44–45.
Berry, Ralph. "*Measure for Measure* on the Contemporary Stage." *Humanities Association Review* 28 (1977): 241–44.
Boles, William. Review of *Twelfth Night,* directed by Ian Judge. RSC. Stratford-upon-Avon. *Theatre Journal* 47 (May 1995): 302–3.
Brady, Owen. Review of *Twelfth Night,* directed by Bernard Hopkins. Stratford, Ontario. *Theatre Journal* 44 (May 1992): 237–39.
Clayton, Thomas. Review of *Twelfth Night,* directed by Liviu Ciulei. Minneapolis. *Shakespeare Quarterly* 36 (autumn 1985): 353–59.
Collins, Jane. Review of *Twelfth Night,* directed by Terence O'Brien. Garrison, N.Y. *Shakespeare Bulletin* 17 (fall 1999): 9–10.
Cook, Dorothy, and Wayne Cook. Review of *Twelfth Night,* directed by Mark Rucker. New Haven, Conn. *Shakespeare Bulletin* 13 (spring 1995): 11.
Coursen, Herbert R., Jr. "Shakespeare in Maine: Summer, 1971." *Shakespeare Quarterly* 22 (autumn 1971): 392.
Deese, Helen. Review of *Twelfth Night,* Directed by David Chambers. Costa Mesa, Calif. *Shakespeare Bulletin* 10 (1992): 30–32.
Evans, Gareth Lloyd. Review of *Twelfth Night,* directed by John Caird. RSC. Stratford-upon-Avon. *Drama* 150 (winter 1983): 46–47.
Farmer, Patrick. Review of *Twelfth Night,* directed by John Caird. RSC. Stratford-upon-Avon. *Theatre Journal* 36 (March 1984): 113–14.
Johnson-Haddad, Miranda. Review of *Twelfth Night,* directed by Daniel Fish. Washington, D.C. *Shakespeare Bulletin* 17.2 (spring 1999): 15–16.
Keyishian, Harry. "Shakespeare Abroad: Europe and Asia." Review of *Twelfth Night,* directed by Eva Bergman. Stockholm, Sweden. *Shakespeare Bulletin* 12 (winter 1994): 35–36.
Kullman, Colby H. "Mississippi's Southern Festival Theatre." Review of *Twelfth Night,* directed by Cindy Gold. Oxford, Miss. *Shakespeare Bulletin* 13 (fall 1995): 26–27.

Lukacs, Barbara Ann. Review of *Twelfth Night,* directed by Bonnie J. Monte. Madison, N.J. *Shakespeare Bulletin* 10 (winter 1992): 23–24.

Merwin, Ted. Review of *Twelfth Night,* directed by Nicholas Hytner. New York. *Theatre Journal* 51 (May 1999): 191–92.

Miller, Judith G. Review of *Twelfth Night,* directed by Ariane Mnouchkine. Avignon, France. *Theatre Journal* 35 (March 1983): 114–16.

Morley, Sheridan. Review of *Twelfth Night,* directed by John Caird. RSC. London. *Plays and Players,* October 1984, 25.

O'Connor, Garry. Review of *Twelfth Night,* directed by Bill Alexander. RSC. Stratford-upon-Avon. *Plays and Players,* September 1987, 16–17.

Shaltz, Justin. Review of *Twelfth Night,* directed by Karin Coonrod. Chicago, Ill. *Shakespeare Bulletin* 19 (fall 2001): 24–25.

———. Review of *Twelfth Night,* directed by Michael Pennington. English Shakespeare Company. Chicago, Ill. *Shakespeare Bulletin* 10 (summer 1992): 27–28.

"*Twelfth Night.*" *New York Theater Critics Reviews* 47 (September 22, 1986): 200–204.

"*Twelfth Night.*" *New York Theater Critics Reviews* 50 (October 2, 1989): 216–23.

Vick, Susan. Review of *Twelfth Night,* directed by Marc Lamos. Hartford Stage Company. Hartford, Conn. *Theatre Journal* 38 (May 1986): 229–30.

Vineberg, Steve. Review of *Twelfth Night,* directed by Robin Phillips. Stratford Festival Young Company. Stratford, Ontario. *Theatre Journal* 41 (October 1989): 400.

Director's Work: Abigail Adams

Adams, Abigail. "Director's Notes: Power, Sex, Class, and Shipwrecks." In *North Carolina Shakespeare Festival Quarto* (summer 1996), 3.

Alex, Christina. "Four Generations of Women at People's Light and Theater." Review of *My Mother Said I Never Should,* by Charlotte Keatley, directed by Abigail Adams. Malvern, Pa. *Main Line (Pa.) Life,* 26 October 1995.

Brown, Tony. "Hilarity That Touches the Heart." Review of *the Twelfth Night,* directed by Abigail Adams. North Carolina Shakespeare Festival Company. High Point, N.C. *Charlotte (N.C.) Observer,* 20 August 1996, sec. E.

"Classic Brothers Grimm Tales Staged at People's Light." Review of *Grimm Tales,* adapted by Carol Ann Duffy, directed by Abigail Adams. Malvern, Penn. *Wayne (Pa.) Suburban Advertiser,* 22 November 1995.

Gant-Hill, Cathy. "At Festival, Stage Gives Characters Added Vitality." *Greensboro (N.C.) News and Record,* 15 August 1996, sec. D.

Hines, Norman Jr. "NCSF's *Twelfth Night* Lives up to Past History of Excellence." Review of *Twelfth Night,* directed by Abigail Adams. NCSF Company. High Point, N.C. *Asheboro (N.C.) Courier-Tribune,* n.d.

Irwin, Leo. "Desperate Lives on the Frontier." Review of *Abundance,* by Beth Henley, directed by Abigail Adams. Malvern, Pa. *West Chester (Pa.) Daily Local News,* 2 May 1997.

Jones, Abe D. Jr. "*Twelfth Night* Reveals Charm, Humor." Review of *Twelfth Night*, directed by Abigail Adams. NCSF Company. High Point, North Carolina. *Greensboro (N.C.) News and Record*, 19 August 1996, sec. B.

Mizell, Leslie. Review of *Twelfth Night*, directed by Abigail Adams. NCSF Company. High Point, N.C. *Triad Style*, 21 August 1996.

Oakley, Eve. "*Twelfth Night* Opens NCSF Season in Fine Fashion." Review of *Twelfth Night*, directed by Abigail Adams. NCSF Company. High Point, N.C. *ESP: Entertainment Sports and Previews*, 28 August-3 September 1996.

The People's Light and Theatre Company: 20 Years 1974–1994. N.p., n.d.

White, Laurie. "*Twelfth Night* Delivers Darker Version of the Play." Review of *Twelfth Night*, directed by Abigail Adams. NCSF Company. High Point, N.C. *High Point (N.C.) Enterprise*, 19 August 1996, sec. B.

Director's Work: Melia Bensussen

"About the Production." In *Oregon Shakespeare Festival* 1 (1995): 2.

Armstrong, Alan. "Shakespeare in Ashland, 1995: The Sixtieth Anniversary Season." Review of *Twelfth Night*. Oregon Shakespeare Festival Company. Ashland, Ore. *Shakespeare Bulletin* 14 (spring 1996): 29–30.

Baker, Alison. Review of *Twelfth Night*, directed by Melia Bensussen. OSF Company. Ashland, Ore. *Jefferson Monthly*, April 1995, 34.

Beaufort, John. "Emotion Weights Lorca's *Blood Wedding*." Review of *Blood Wedding*. New York. *Christian Science Monitor*, 28 May 1992, The Arts.

Bensussen, Melia. "From the Director." In *Oregon Shakespeare Festival* 1 (1995): 2–4.

Berson, Misha. "Shakespeare in Spring—Ashland's Venerable Festival Celebrates a Very Special Birthday with a Bit of Bard—and More." Review of *Twelfth Night*, directed by Melia Bensussen. OSF Company. Ashland, Ore. *Seattle Times*, 5 March 1995, final edition, sec. M.

Campbell, Jackie. "*A Dybbuk* a Gothic Horror Wrapped in Rabbinical Garb." Review of *A Dybbuk*, by S. Ansky, adapted by Tony Kushner, directed by Melia Bensussen. Denver Center Theatre Company. Denver. *Rocky Mountain News*, 25 January 1996, local edition, sec. F.

Dillard-Rosen, Sandra. "Messages Overpower Deep, Dark *Marisol*." Review of *Marisol*, by Jose Rivera, directed by Melia Bensussen. *Denver Post*, 2 May 1995, 2nd edition, sec. E.

Evett, Marianne. "*Lughnasa*'s View of Human Foibles Popular." Review of *Dancing at Lughnasa*, by Brian Friel, directed by Melia Bensussen. Cleveland, Ohio. *Plain Dealer*, 2 October 1994, sec. J.

Golden, Nancy. Review of *Twelfth Night*, directed by Melia Bensussen. OSF Company. Ashland, Ore. *Lithiagraph*, June 1995, 8.

Gussow, Mel. "Five Southern Bridesmaids with Gossip to Share." Review of *Five Women Wearing the Same Dress*, by Alan Ball, directed by Melia Bensussen. Manhattan Class Company. New York. *New York Times*, 18 February 1993, late edition, sec. C.

———. "A Sexual Cover-Up in *New Anatomies*." Review of *New Anatomies*, by Timberlake Wertenbaker, directed by Melia Bensussen. Compass Theater

Company. New York. *New York Times,* 22 February 1990, late edition, sec. C.

Hampton, Wilborn. "Freud, Jung, and Sabina: Analysis of a Triangle." Review of *Sabina,* by Willy Holtzman directed by Melia Bensussen. Primary Stages Company. New York. *New York Times,* 23 March 1996, late edition, sec. 1.

Kelly, Tom W. "Oregon Shakespeare Festival: Fabulous Performances—But Not the Only Show in Town." Review of *Twelfth Night,* directed by Melia Bensussen. OSF Company. Ashland, Ore. *San Francisco Bay Times,* 18 May 1995.

Londré, Felicia Harrison. Review of *Twelfth Night.* OSF Company. Ashland, Ore. *Theatre Journal* 47 (October 1995): 414–16.

Mannion, Kristina. Review of *Twelfth Night.* OSF Company. Ashland, Ore. *Back Stage West,* 13 April 1995.

Miller, Robert. "*Twelfth Night* A Worthy Tribute to Founder Angus Bowmer." Review of *Twelfth Night,* directed by Melia Bensussen. OSF Company. Ashland, Ore. *Ashland Daily Tidings,* 27 February 1995.

Nelson, Helene. "*Twelfth Night* Falls Flat, But Ashland Still Delights." Review of *Twelfth Night,* directed by Melia Bensussen. OSF Company. Ashland, Ore. *McMinville (Ore.) News-Register,* 28 December 1995.

Sheward, David. "Tony Sails Off into *Sunset.*" *Back Stage,* 9 June 1995.

Syna, Sy. Review of *Camp Paradox,* by Barbara Graham. New York. *Back Stage,* 13 November 1992.

———. Review of *Love Lemmings,* by Joe DiPeitro, directed by Melia Bensussen. New York. *Back Stage,* 21 June 1991.

Trussell, Robert. "Success of Festival Hasn't Left Its Organizer Complacent." *Kansas City Star,* 2 July 1995, metropolitan edition, Arts.

Chapter 4: *Cymbeline*

Literary Criticism

Bamford, Karen. "Imogen's Wounded Chastity." *Essays in Theater/Etude Theatrales* 12 (November 1993): 51–61.

Bergeron, David. "Sexuality in *Cymbeline.*" *Essays in Literature* 10 (fall 1983): 156–68.

Collier, Susanne. "Cutting to the Heart of the Matter: Stabbing the Woman in *Philaster* and *Cymbeline.*" In *Shakespearean Power and Punishment,* 39–58.

Danson, Lawrence. "'The Catastrophe Is a Nuptial': The Space of Masculine Desire in *Othello, Cymbeline,* and *The Winter's Tale.*" *Shakespeare Survey* 46 (1993): 69–79.

Frey, Charles. "'O Sacred, Shadowy, Cold, and Constant Queen': Shakespeare's Imperiled and Chastening Daughters of Romance." In *The Woman's Part,* 295–313.

Jacobs, Henry E. "Rewriting Shakespeare: The Framing of *Cymbeline.*" *Renaissance Papers* (1983): 79–87.

Jordan, Constance. "Contract and Conscience in *Cymbeline.*" *Renaissance Drama* n.s. 25 (1994): 33–58.

Siemon, James Edward. "Noble Virtue in *Cymbeline*." *Shakespeare Survey* 29 (1976): 51–61.

Skura, Meredith. "Interpreting Posthumus' Dream from above and below: Families, Psychoanalysts, and Literary Critics." In *Representing Shakespeare: New Psychoanalytic Essays*, edited by Murray Schwartz and Coppélia Kahn, 203–16. Baltimore: John Hopkins University Press, 1980.

Thompson, Ann. "Person and Office: The Case of Imogen, Princess of Britain." In *Literature and Nationalism*, edited by Vincent Newey and Ann Thompson, 76–87. Savage, Md.: Barnes and Noble Books, 1991.

Recent Production History

Armstrong, Alan. Review of *Cymbeline*, directed by Henry Woronicz. OSF Company. Ashland, Ore. *Shakespeare Bulletin* 12 (1994): 31–32.

Brady, Owen. Review of *Cymbeline*, directed by Robin Phillips. Stratford, Ontario. *Theatre Journal* 39 (March 1987): 103–4.

Collins, Jane. Review of *Cymbeline*, directed by Andrei Serban. New York. *Shakespeare Bulletin* 16 (fall 1998): 8–9.

Cook, Dorothy, and Wayne Cook. Review of *Cymbeline*, directed by Mark Lamos. Hartford Stage Company. Hartford, Conn. *Shakespeare Bulletin* 16 (spring 1998): 20–21.

Crowl, Samuel. Review of *Cymbeline*, directed by Adrian Noble. RSC. Stratford-upon-Avon. *Shakespeare Bulletin* 16 (winter 1998): 12–13.

Deese, Helen. Review of *Cymbeline*, directed by Daniel Sullivan. San Diego, Calif. *Shakespeare Bulletin* 17 (fall 1999): 40–41.

Derrick, Patty S. Review of *Cymbeline*, directed by Jay Scott Chipman. Pittsburgh, Pa. *Shakespeare Bulletin* 10 (winter 1992): 26.

French, William. Review of *Cymbeline*, directed by Don Baker. Lexington, Va. *Theater Review* 37 (May 1985): 227–28.

Kehler, Dorothea. "*Cymbeline* at the San Diego Old Globe." Review of *Cymbeline*, directed by Daniel Sullivan. San Diego, Calif. *Shakespeare Newsletter* 49 (fall 1999): 79.

Nichols, Nina daVinci. Review of *Cymbeline*, directed by Shepard Sobel. Pearl Theatre Company, Inc. New York. *Shakespeare Bulletin* 14 (fall 1996): 16.

Seeman, Pam Holland. "Magicians, Storytellers and Framing Devices: *Cymbeline* in Production." *Text and Presentation: Journal of the Comparative Drama Conference* 13 (1992): 59–64.

Shaltz, Justin. Review of *Cymbeline*, directed by Calvin MacLean. Bloomington, Ill. *Shakespeare Bulletin* 13 (fall 1995): 28.

Shurgot, Michael W. Review of *Cymbeline*, directed by Scot Whitney. Harlequin Productions. Olympia, Wash. *Shakespeare Bulletin* 14 (spring 1996): 25.

Smallwood, Robert. "Shakespeare Performances in England, 1996–7." Review of *Cymbeline*, directed by Adrian Noble. RSC. Stratford-upon-Avon. *Shakespeare Survey* 51 (1998): 219–55.

Warren, Roger. *Cymbeline*. Shakespeare in Performance. Manchester: Manchester University Press, 1989.

Wells, Stanley. "Shakespeare Performances in England, 1987–8." Reviews of *Cymbeline*, directed by Sir Peter Hall, London, and Bill Alexander, RSC, Stratford-upon-Avon. *Shakespeare Survey* 42 (1989): 129–48.

Wilcocks, Dick. Review of *Cymbeline*, directed by Graham Murray, Greg Hersov, James Maxwell, and Caspar Wrede. Manchester, England. *Plays and Players*, November 1984, 30.

Director's Work: Barbara Gaines

"ANUW fall Event with Barbara Gaines." *Association of Northwestern University Women Newsletter*, fall 2000. www.northwestern.edu/anuw/newsletters/winter01newsletter.html#autumn.

Bommer, Lawrence. "Revival of '89 *Cymbeline* Recaptures Most of the Magic." Review of *Cymbeline*, directed by Barbara Gaines. Chicago. *Chicago Tribune*, 7 October 1993, Du Page sports final edition, Tempo.

Christiansen, Richard. "This *Measure for Measure* Ranks with Best of Repertory's Work." Review of *Measure for Measure*, directed by Barbara Gaines. Chicago. *Chicago Tribune*, 24 February 1994, News.

———. "Shakespeare's *Shrew* Tamed for '90s." Review of *The Taming of the Shrew*, directed by Barbara Gaines. Chicago. *Chicago Tribune*, 2 December 1993, north sports final edition, News.

———. "Top 10 Productions." *Chicago Tribune*, 31 December 1989, Arts.

———. "Unforgettable: Shakespeare Repertory Presents *Hamlet* at Its Best." Review of *Hamlet*, directed by Barbara Gaines. Chicago. *Chicago Tribune*, 22 October 1996, north sports final edition, Tempo.

Domke, Ellen. "Bard's Elegant New Home on Navy Pier: Shakespeare Theater Opening Draws Applause." *Chicago Sun-Times*, 24 October 1999, late sports final edition, News.

Faberson, Paul. "*Cymbeline* Is a Brilliant Show in All Possible Ways." Review of *Cymbeline*, directed by Barbara Gaines. Chicago. *Skyline*, 26 October 1989.

Feller, Stu. "Fine Acting, Brilliant Directing Make *Cymbeline* Grand Theater Spectacle." Review of *Cymbeline*, directed by Barbara Gaines. Chicago. *GNW*, 25 October 1989.

Mesic, Penelope. "Into the Woods: Murders and Nightmares, Romance and Rustic Comedy—Shakespeare's at His Best in the Great Outdoors: Shakespeare Repertory's First Outdoor Production." *Chicago*, August 1994.

Newmark, Judith. "Shakespeare Takes the Windy City by Storm." *St. Louis Post-Dispatch*, 9 January 2000, five-star lift edition, sec. C.

Pixler, Joe. "Shakespeare Rep Offers Startling *Measure*." Review of *Measure for Measure*, directed by Barbara Gaines. Chicago. *Chicago Sun-Times*, 18 February 1994, late sports final edition, Weekend Plus.

Shaltz, Justin. Review of *Measure for Measure*, directed by Barbara Gaines. Chicago. *Shakespeare Bulletin* 12 (spring 1994): 24–25.

Simpson, Tom. "A Rare *Cymbeline*." Review of *Cymbeline*, directed by Barbara Gaines. Chicago. *Chicago Maroon*, 31 October 1989.

Smith, Sid. "Culture Shock: Shakespeare Repertory Rethinks *Othello* by Making Moorish Prince the Star." Review of *Othello,* directed by Barbara Gaines. Chicago. *Chicago Tribune,* 15 October 1995, final edition, Arts.
Terry, Clifford. "Shaking up Shakespeare: Barbara Gaines Takes on the Bard." *Chicago Tribune,* 28 November 1993, Arts.
Weiss, Hedy. "Barbara Gaines Casts New Light on *Cymbeline.*" *Chicago Sun-Times,* 15 October 1989.
———. "Love at First Fight: Barbara Gaines Passionately Tames the *Shrew.*" Review of *The Taming of the Shrew,* directed by Barbara Gaines. Chicago. *Chicago Sun-Times,* 1 December 1993, late sports final edition, sec. 2.
———. "Peerless but not Pierless: Chicago Shakespeare Theater Opens Its New Home with *Antony and Cleopatra.*" *Chicago Sun-Times,* 17 October 1999, late sports final edition, Show.
———. Review of *Cymbeline,* directed by Barbara Gaines. Chicago. *Chicago Sun-Times,* 20 October 1989.
———. "Running the Gamut with Shakespeare Repertory." *Chicago Sun-Times,* 2 February 1992, five star sports final edition, Show.
———. "Strong Acting, Simple Style Keep *Winter's Tale* Warm." Review of *The Winter's Tale,* directed by Barbara Gaines. Chicago. *Chicago Sun-Times,* 31 October 1994, late sports final edition, News.
———. "Vivid *Cymbeline* Brings the Bard to Popular Peak." Review of *Cymbeline,* directed by Barbara Gaines. Chicago. *Chicago Sun-Times,* 30 September 1993, final edition, sec. 2.
Williams, Jean A. "*Richard III* Lacks Firepower." Review of *Richard III,* directed by Barbara Gaines. Chicago. *Chicago Sun-Times,* 22 April 1996, Features.

Director's Work: JoAnne Akalaitis

Akalaitis, JoAnne. "Meeting Beckett." *TDR* 34 (fall 1990): 11–12.
Barnes, Clive. "Travesty of Shakespeare." Review of *Cymbeline,* directed by JoAnne Akalaitis. New York. *New York Post,* 1 June 1989.
Beaufort, John. "Update of Bard's *Cymbeline* Is Riddled with Incongruities." Review of *Cymbeline,* directed by JoAnne Akalaitis. New York. *Christian Science Monitor,* 16 June 1989.
Bly, Mark. "JoAnne Akalaitis's *Leon and Lena (and Lenz):* A Log from the Dramaturg." *Theater* 12 (winter 1989/spring 1990): 81–95.
Brustein, Robert. Review of *The Tempest,* directed by JoAnne Akalaitis. New York. *New Republic,* 10 July 1989, 28–30.
———. Review of *Woyzeck,* directed by JoAnne Akalaitis. New York. *New Republic,* 4–11 January 1993, 27–28.
Breslauer, January. "Ellis Island with Palms." Review of *Green Card,* directed by JoAnne Akalaitis. Los Angeles. *Theater* 18 (winter 1986-7): 91–93.
Carlson, Susan. "Cannibalizing and Carnivaling: Reviving Aphra Behn's *The Rover.*" Review of *The Rover,* by Aphra Behn, directed by JoAnne Akalaitis. Minneapolis, Minn. *Theatre Journal* 47 (December 1995): 517–39.
"*Cymbeline* and Its Critics: A Case Study." *American Theatre,* December 1989, 24–31, 63–65.

Daniel, Jeff. "A Different Direction." *St. Louis Post-Dispatch,* 16 June 1998, five-star lift edition, *Everyday Magazine,* sec. D.

Feldberg, Robert. Review of *'Tis Pity She's a Whore,* directed by JoAnne Akalaitis. New York. *Hackensack (N.J.) Record,* 6 April 1992, sec. B.

Fuchs, Elinor. "Misunderstanding Postmodernism." Review of *Cymbeline,* directed by JoAnne Akalaitis. New York. *American Theatre,* December 1989, 24, 26–31.

Graves, Nancy. "Did Frank Rich Really Look?" *American Theatre,* December 1989, 29.

Hass, Nancy. "A Cerebral Modernist Whose Revolution Rolls On." *New York Times,* 24 January 1999, late edition, sec. 2.

Hodgson, Moira. Review of *Cymbeline,* directed by JoAnne Akalaitis. New York. *Nation,* 3 July 1989, 29–30.

"JoAnne Akalaitis, interviewed by Jonathan Kalb." *Theater* 15 (spring 1984): 6–13.

Kissel, Howard. "Shakespeare as Victorian Sideshow." Review of *Cymbeline,* directed by JoAnne Akalaitis. New York. *Daily News,* 1 June 1989.

Leverett, James. "Why Did the Reviewers Turn so Savage?" *American Theatre,* December 1989, 25, 63–65.

Newman, Harry. "Far from an Affront." *American Theatre,* December 1989, 31.

Pacheco, Patrick. "'I'm Not Avant-garde': JoAnne Akalaitis, Joseph Papp's Heir, Faces the Biggest Challenge of Her Career: Getting the Public into New York's Public Theater." *Los Angeles Times,* 15 November 1992, home edition, Calendar.

Presley, Nelson. "Director Bearing Greek Gifts: JoAnne Akalaitis Puts a New Face on the Classics." *Washington Post,* 27 March 1999, final edition, sec. C.

Pye, Michael. "Is There Life after Joe Public? Joe Papp Was the Toughest Act in New York Theatre: Michael Pye Meets the Woman Who Must Follow It." *London Independent,* 24 November 1991, Sunday Review.

Rich, Frank. "Opening a Window at a Theater Gone Stale." *New York Times,* 21 March 1993, late edition, sec. 2.

———. Review of *Henry IV,* Parts 1 and 2, directed by JoAnne Akalaitis. New York. *New York Times,* 28 February 1991, late edition, sec. C.

Saivetz, Deborah. *An Event in Space: JoAnne Akalaitis in Rehearsal.* Hanover, N.H.: Smith and Kraus, 2000.

Witchel, Alex. "Papp Names Akalaitis to Step in as Shakespeare Festival Head." *New York Times,* 21 August 1991, late edition, sec. C.

Index

Page numbers in italics refer to illustration pages.

Abhorson, 135
Acting, style of, 20–21, 46–48, 53–54, 79–80, 186–88; direct address, 119, 139, 214; mix of styles, 223, 227–28; presentational, 116–17, 172, 175, 190–92, 216, 223; representational, 98, 212, 221, 229; theory of, 23, 43–44, 50, 52–53, 79–80, 142–43, 154, 163; Victorian, 226, 227–29. *See also* conventions, of theatrical realism
Adams, Abigail, 14, 30, 60–65, 70–71, 167, 168–85; comparison to Bensussen, 185–86, 204–5
Akalaitis, JoAnne, 14, 31, 77–81, 224–38, 239
Akimoto, Bonnie (Olivia), 70, *197, 201*
Alexander, Bill, 165, 221
Alexander, LeWan (Orsino), 70, 195
Alison, Jennifer (Kate), 239
All's Well That Ends Well, 76
Andonyadis, Nephelie, 152–53
Andrew, 173–74, 177, 183, 191–92, *191,* 200
Angelo, 55, 128–62, *136, 156, 158*
Angelos, Eureka, 46
Antonio, 168
Appel, Libby, 69
Ariel, 135
Armstrong, Alan, 102, 199, 202
Arviragus, 83
Ashcroft, Peggy (Juliet), 91
Asprey, Jason (Claudio), 141
As You like It, 139, 185
Authority: of Capulet, 107, 109; in culture, 98; of duke (spiritual), 147; Malvolio's lack of, 202; of Olivia, 196, 199; in rehearsal, 37, 47; of text, 43, 101, 123, 148, 166, 171; of women directors, 127; anti-authoritarianism, 134
Avant-garde, 12, 14, 19, 22, 31, 115, 163, 227, 230
Aylward, Peter (Posthumus), 214, 217

Bacon, Wallace, 71, 72
Baines, Barbara, 129
Barnes, Clive, 237
Barnes, Rosalie, 93
Bartenieff, George (Cymbeline), 229
Barton, John, 52, 95, 131, 167
Beaumont, Karen (Escalus), 140; (Provost), 141
Beckett, Samuel, 78
Beier, Karin, 125–26
Benmussa, Simone, 175
Bennett, Fran (Nurse), 121, 122
Bennett, Susan, 22, 27
Bensussen, Melia, 14, 30, 65–67, 83, 185–205, 239, 240–41; comparison to Gaines, 212
Berger, John, 39
Bergeron, David, 207
Bergman, Eva, 166
Berry, Cicely, 29
Berson, Misha, 16
Bilder, Erica, 41, 110–11, 113
Body, the, 35, 51, 52, 53, 174; class and, 151, 153; cross-dressing and, 173, 194; cross- gender casting and, 112; female, 20–25, 37, 49, 115, 130–32, 145; of Juliet, 105, 109; as site of inscription, 24, 158, 175;

297

Body (*continued*)
   male, 43–44, 230. *See also* nudity; sexuality
Bogdanov, Michael, 75
Bommer, Laurence, 215, 223
Bowmer, Angus L., 68
Brantley, Ben, 69
Brecht, Bertolt, 23–24, 123, 134, 137, 154, 163
Breuer, Lee, 78
Bristol, Michael, 91, 127
Brook, Peter, 75–76, 95, 116
Brooks, Stuart, 62
Brown, Tony, 173, 180
Brustein, Robert, 93, 238
Bryce, Philip (the duke), 140
Burrows, Allyn (Angelo), *136,* 140; (Provost), 141

Caird, John, 166
Caliban, 135
Canning, Charlotte, 16
Capulet 40, 99, 102, *107,* 111, 112, *121;* abusiveness of, 41, 94, 106–10; in Beier's production, 126; in Monte's production, 125; tyranny of, 42, 115, 116, 121
Case, Sue-Ellen, 20, 175
Casting, 40–41, 42, 49, 54–55, 58, 67; cross-gender, 41–42, 43–49, 96–98, 111–12, 115–16, 120, 122–25, 140, 168 (*see also* cross-dressing); double casting, 135, 137, 145; non-traditional 62–63, 67, 69–70, 79, 111, 233
Chapman, Raymond L. (Sebastian), 194
Charles, Casey, 177
Chicago Shakespeare Theater, 72, 75–77
Chodorow, Nancy, 89
Class, 30, 58, 66, 80, 92, 133–34, 138, 141–42; inequities of and sex relations, 165, 176–77, 184, 195, 260 n. 4; related to character motivations, 169, 196–98; tensions among classes, 150–55, 171, 190; upward mobility and, 185
Claudio, 137, 141, 142–43, 147, 157–59, *159*

Claudius, 56
Clement, Susan, 20
Cloten, 80, 207, 216, 225, 233
Collaboration, 41, 47, 54, 61, 66, 70, 78, 212–13, 225; actor's reception of, 70, 213; as LAWSC ethic, 116–17; with another director, 42–43, 57–58, 110–11
Company of Women, 43, 47, 111, 114–15, 118
Conventions, of theater, 13, 25, 31; of character depiction, 46, 138; of costume, 216; highlighting of, 167–68, 190–93, 203, 226–27; juxtaposing for postmodern aesthetic, 226–28, 230, 234, 238; of theatrical realism, 20, 98, 104, 105, 138–40, 166, 190, 238. *See also* acting, style of
conventions for heroine, 216; created by actor/character, 167–68; for Duke, 140–41; gender reversal and, 192–93; highlighting sexuality, 24, 38, 137, 138, 145, 155, 215–16; for Iachimo, 219, 232; for Imogen, 215–16, 218, 228; for Juliet, 101, 104; for Lady Capulet, 110; for Olivia, 179, 181, 195, 199; for Paris, 108; for Prince, 99; for Viola/Cesario, 173, 193
Coonrod, Karin, 203
Corzatte, Clayton (Feste), 191
Costume, 35, 58, 64, 93, 170, 203, 224, 230; connection to class, 153, 215–16;
Coursen, Herbert, 132, 240
Cross-dressing, 13, 30, 47, 55, 63, 97–98, 164, 166, 173, 193–94. *See also* casting, cross- gender; costume; gender
Culshaw, Robert, 76
Cumpsty, Michael (Iachimo), 230
Curran, Leigh (Capulet), 121
Cusack, Joan (Imogen), 228, 232
Cushman, Charlotte (Romeo), 111
Cutler, Anna, 23
Cymbeline, 13, 14, 72, 78, 206–37; recent stage history of, 208–9
Cymbeline, 217, 222–23, 226, 227–28, *229,* 230

INDEX 299

Daley, Richard M., 72
Danson, Lawrence, 208–9
Davis, Lloyd, 87
deChatelet, Ted (Sebastian), 182
DeSandre, Eileen (Maria), 200
Diamond, Elin, 174, 175
Dodson, Lisa, 77; (Imogen), 214, 215, 217, *219, 220*
Dolan, Jill, 20–22, 44, 123, 175
Dollimore, Jonathan, 129
Donaldson, Peter, 40
Doniger, Wendy, 210
Donkin, Ellen, 19
Donnellan, Declan, 166
Drake, Sylvie, 82
Ducrocq, Caroline (Lady Capulet), 120
Duke, 128–62, *162*

Ebner, Caroline (Juliet), 126
Editing, textual, 36–39, 43, 55–56, 59, 64–65, 66, 80, 213
Edwards, Gale, 23–24
Engle, Ron, 82
Epstein, Johnny (Falstaff), 140
Erlich, Erin (Tybalt), 113
Escalus, 135, 140

Falstaff, 140
Femininity: essentialization of, 170; feminine qualities, 44, 56, 193; feminizing, 87; when playing men, 115–16, 173
Ferris, Leslie, 21
Feste, 167, 168, 172, 180, *182*, 191, 192, 194, 203
Fichandler, Zelda, 74
Fight Choreography, 41, 88, 100, 106–8, 114–15, 191–92
Finley, Karen, 17
Freedman, Barbara, 21
Friar Lawrence, 89, 95, 108–9
Friedman, Michael, 132–33
Fuchs, Elinor, 235, 236, 237

Gaines, Barbara, 14, 30, 71–77, 209–23; comparison to Akalaitis, 224–25, 235, 238
Gainor, J. Ellen, 29
Galati, Frank, 223

Gaskill, William, 221
Gay, Penny, 20
Geertz, Clifford, 13
Gender, 13, 21, 37, 42, 44–49, 67, 80, 94; and class, 151; construction of, 25, 30, 243 n. 5; cross-dressing and, 165, 170, 193–94; cross-gender casting and, 112, 116, 124; deconstruction/destabilization of, 123, 160, 177, 179–80, 189, 193; oppressive codes of, 140, 188; performativity of, 174–75, 179, 188, 193, 196; raising issues of for audience, 31, 42, 57, 155; in relationship to sexual attraction, 164, 176–77, 185–86, 188, 201; reversal of traditional roles, 104, 173, 175; Victorian codes for, 229, 231. *See also* casting, cross-gender; costume; cross-dressing
Genre, 13–14, 30, 64; of comedy, 30, 164, 239; of fairytale, 210, 216, 218–19, 223; of romance, 206, 211. *See also* marriage, at end of comedy
Giannota, Donya (Juliet), 111, *119, 121*, 124
Gielgud, John, 50, (Romeo and Mercutio), 91
Gilligan, Carol, 43
Glass, Philip, 78, 213, 234
Godinez, Henry (Iachimo), 217, *219, 220*
Gold, Cindy, 167
Goldblum, Jeff, 188
Goodman, Lizbeth, 17
Goring, Marius (Angelo), 133
Goya, Francisco, 126
Green, Amy, 227
Gregory, *97*
Grotowski, Jerzy, 78
Guidarius, 83

Hall, Peter, 75, 76, 167, 221
Hamlet, 46, 72, 75, 79
Hamlet, 46, 56
Hands, Terry, 165, 166–67
Harris, Geraldine, 18, 27
Hart, Linda, 17
Hattaway, Michael, 137

Hayes, Helen, 50; award, 36
Helms, Lorraine, 19
Henderson, Criss, 76
Henley, Beth, 204
Henry IV, 80, 140
Henry V, 59, 71
Henry V, 118
Hickle-Edwards, Allan (Toby), 182
Hodgdon, Barbara, 7, 23–24
Hoffman, Dustin, 52–53
Holland, Peter, 26, 28
Holmer, Joan Ozark, 89
Holmes, Michael Morgan, 146
Homosexuality, 46, 48, 63, 99, 118; bisexuality, 141, 184, 199; characters, orientation of, 168, 179–80, 186, 195; staged, audience response to, 112, 123, 202–3
Hortmann, Wilhelm, 126
Houghton, Lucius (Andrew), 173
Hynek, Robin (Juliet in *Measure for Measure*), 141; (Provost), 141

Iachimo, 207, 210–11, 216, 217–22, *219, 220,* 225, 230–32, 234–35
Iago, 211–12
Imogen, 77, 83, 206–37, *219, 220, 229*
Isabella, 55, 128–62, *136, 156, 158, 159, 162;* comparison to Imogen, 208

Jaques, 139
Jones, Abe, 161–62
Jonson-Haddad, Miranda, 167
Juliet, 40, 41, 89, 94–127, *103, 107, 119, 121,* 128; comparison to Imogen, 206
Juliet in *Measure for Measure*, 141, 142, 147

Kamtman, Michael (Feste), 172
Kate, 55, 73, 239
Keatley, Charlotte, 204
Kincaid, Mark (Orsino), 175
Kincaid, Tess Malis (Olivia), 177
King Lear, 47, 72, 95, 115
King Lear, 47
Knowles, Ronald, 87
Koszyn, Jayme, 14, 30, 36–41, 92–110, 127; comparison to Beier, 126; comparison to Monte, 125; comparison to Wolpe, 112–13, 115–16, 118, 121, 122
Kott, Jan, 130, 208
Krausnick, Dennis, 51
Kushner, Tony, 180

Lady Capulet, 94, 101, 106–8, 109, 110, 120–21
Lady Macbeth, 53–54
Lapine, James, 236
LAWSC, 41, 43–49, 97–98, 110–11, 133
Leavis, F. R., 52
Leverett, James, 236
Lévi-Strauss, Claude, 186
Levitt, Bruce, 90
Lewis, Irene, 16, 90
Light Design: for Akalaitis, 80; for *Cymbeline,* 213, 214–15, 218, 219, 222, 223, 226, 232, 234; for *Measure for Measure,* 137, 139, 147; for *Romeo and Juliet,* 103; for *Twelfth Night,* 172, 173, 179, 184, 189
Linklater, Kristin, 43, 44, 51
Londré, Felicia Hardison, 69, 91, 199, 202, 204
Lucio, *136,* 139, 142, 149, 155
Luhrmann, Baz, 91, 120
Luscombe, Christopher, 68

Mabou Mines, 78, 79
Macfarlane, Linda, 130
MacIntosh, Joan (the Queen), 228
Maleczech, Ruth, 78
Malvolio, 64, 65, 168, 171, 172–73, 177, 190, 192–93, 200, 201, 203
Maria, 165, 166–67, 171, 182–83, 188, 200, 203–4
Mariana, 134–35, 147–49, 160–61
Marowitz, Charles, 130–31
Marriage, 104–5, 108, 119, 129, 130–31, 147, 206; duke's use of power for, 146, 159–61; at end of comedy, 30, 164, 202, 205; historical conceptions of, 236; problems with, 77, 166, 185, 188, 201–2; repressive effects of, 165, 207; success of, 199, 211
Martinez, J. D., 88
Marx, Bill, 166

Masculinity, 45, 88, 103, 112, 192, 240; cross-dressing and, 173–74, 186–88, 193–94; when women play men, 44, 115–16
Mason, Jeffrey, 28
Massai, Sonia, 129–30
McCandless, David, 130
McHugh, Shon, 93
McLuskie, Kathleen, 129
McNally, Terence, 69
Measure for Measure, 11–12, 13, 14, 55, 58, 128–62, 239–40; comparison to *Romeo and Juliet* and *Twelfth Night,* 164; comparison to *Cymbeline,* 208; stage history, 130–33, 160
Merchant of Venice, 77, 82, 214
Mercutio 39, 40, 89, 100–101, 113–14, 126
Method, the, 29, 51, 52, 114, 154. *See also* acting, style of, representational
Metropulos, Penny, 166
Michelangelo, 135
Midsummer Night's Dream, 43, 46
Miller, Jonathan, 131
Misogyny, 31, 66, 137, 210–11, 225, 230. *See also* patriarchy; sexism
Mistress Overdone, 135, 137, 139, 155
MIT, 40–41, 93, 96
Montague, 110, 122
Monte, Bonnie J., 125
Mountford, Diane (Paris), 122
Multiculturalism, 48, 49
Multiracial, 42, 233. *See also* race
Mulvey, Laura, 123
Murphy, Mark (Andrew), 191

NCSF (North Carolina Shakespeare Festival), 57, 62–65, 66, 239
Newman, Harry, 233
Newmark, Judith, 76
Noble, Adrian, 131, 176, 206
Nordli, Robin Goodrin, 70, 186, *187, 191,* 195, *197,* 200, *201*
Nordling, Jeffrey (Posthumus), 228
Novy, Marianne, 28
Nudity, 38–39, 49, 63, 105, 115, 120, 126, 145, 221, 254 n. 37
Nunn, Trevor, 75, 176

Nurse 39, 94, 101, 102, 106–8, 109, 113, 121–22
NYSF (New York Shakespeare Festival), 65, 78, 79, 239

Objectification, 22–24, 38–39, 81, 104, 188, 245 n. 6; complicated audience viewpoint resists, 126; in *Cymbeline,* 207; prompted by costume,155, 215–16, 243 nn. 25 and 32; prompted by stage action, 138. *See also* sexuality, sexualization of women onstage
O'Brien, Ellen 14, 30–31, 64, 149–63, 239
O'Connor, Paul Vincent (Malvolio), 190
Ohama, Natsuko, 44
Olivia, 64, 70, 165–204, *178, 181, 182, 197, 201,* 241
Olivier, Laurence, 52–53, (Romeo and Mercutio), 91
Orsino, 64, 70, 165–203
OSF (Oregon Shakespeare Festival), 67–71, 185, 189
Othello, 45, 80, 211–12
Othello, 212
O'Toole, Laura, 89

Packer, Tina, 12, 14, 40, 43, 44, 47, 49–56, 59, 133–49, 239; comparison to O'Brien, 152, 153, 160, 162–63
Papp, Joseph, 78–79, 81–82, 224
Paris, 100, 101, 108–9, 122
Patriarchy: and class, 153; in plays 39–40, 65, 66–67, 87, 122, 129, 169; in set, 116; in society 56, 60, 65, 89, 116, 160; supportive of sex and violence, 96, 126. *See also* sexism and misogyny
Patton, Shirley, 68
Pennington, Michael, 75
People's Light and Theatre Company, 14, 42, 57, 60–62, 239
Petruchio, 58, 73, 75, 239
Pfeiffer, Michelle, 188
Phallus, 43–44
Phelan, Peggy, 21
Phillips, Robin, 209
Pisanio, 207, 209, 210, *229,* 233

Pompey, 134, 139
Posthumus 77, 206–37, *229*
Presley, Elvis, imitation of, 203
Prince, 98–99, 122, 126
Prostitution, 137, 139, 141–42, 154–55, 218
Provost, 141, 153
Public Theater, 79, 82–83, 224, 226, 233, 237

Queen, the, 83, 207, 216–17, 224, 226, 228, *229*, 230

Race, 58, 69–70, 74, 80, 92, 233–34. See also casting, nontraditional; multiracial
Radway, Janice, 89
Rap: NWA, 96; Gangsta, 96
Rape, 88–89, 128, 132, 133, 139; judicial/social consequences of, 148; psychic, 207, 209, 232; staging of, 38, 135, 144–45
Reeves, Saskia (Isabella), 132
Rehearsal, 41, 44, 45, 48, 53–54, 57–59
Representation, 20, 24–25, 29, 38, 55, 88, 105, 112, 139–40, 154, 202, 227
Rich, Frank, 83–84, 236–37
Richard III, 46–47, 48
Richard III, 46–47
Riefer, Marcia, 129
Ritual: and coming out, 101; and stylization, 105; and violence, 93, 96, 100
Robertson, Dennis (Toby), 102
Robinson, Diane (Mercutio), 113
Romeo, 89, 94–127, *103*
Romeo and Juliet, 13, 14, 40–41, 42, 43, 44, 90, 93–127, 239–40; comparison to *Measure for Measure,* 128, 135, 164; comparison to *Twelfth Night,* 164; recent stage history, 90–92
Rosalind, 112
RSC (Royal Shakespeare Company): actors of, 68, 76; book on, 165; directors of, 23, 75, 95, 131, 165, 188, 221; trainers for, 29, 71
Rubin, Gayle, 175
Rubio, Lydia, 189

Rutter, Carol Chillington, 20, 35
Rylance, Mark, 75

Sacks, Oliver, 80
Saivetz, Deborah, 80
Sampson, 89, *97*
Schaefer, Elizabeth, 16, 27
Schneider, Rebecca, 115
Schroeder, Patricia, 98
Schur, Edwin, 89
Scott, George C., 82
Sebastian, 166, 168, 182, 184, 193, 194, 201, 202, 204
Senelick, Laurence, 21, 115
Serban, Andrei, 233
Set Design: for *Cymbeline,* 212, 213–15, 219, 222, 226–27, 230, 232; for *Measure for Measure,* 137–38, 152–54; for *Romeo and Juliet,* 64, 93, 116, 125; for *Twelfth Night,* 169–70, 172, 173, 189–90, 202; use of scrim, 98, 101, 102, 106
Sexism: in plays, 66, 74; reverse sexism, 81, 118; in reviewers, 132. See also misogyny; patriarchy
Sexuality, 19, 21–24, 30–31, 42, 48, 55, 67, 81; of Angelo, 143–46; in *Cymbeline,* 207–9, 225; demonization of, 151; healthy vs. warped, 106; of Imogen, 206, 208, 228–32, 236; intercourse as rite of passage, 104, 120; of Isabella, 128–33, 135, 144–47, 208; of Juliet, 104–5, 118–20, 122, 125–26; of Maria, 182–83, 200; of Olivia, 179–82, 196–99; sexualization of women on stage, 38–39, 49, 130, 133, 155, 208; sexual possessiveness of Capulet, 106–7; spirituality and, 134–35, 146; of Viola, 176, 179, 195. See also body; subjectivity, sexual; violence, connection with sex
Shakespeare and Company, 12, 40, 42, 50–56
Shakespeare Interactive Archive, 40
Shaltz, Justin, 203
Shank, Alison (Maria), 182
Shapiro, Michael, 179
Shaw, George Bernard, 207

Shea, Maureen, 47
Shirley, Don, 120
Shylock, 82
Siegel, Ed, 137
Simon, Eli, 176
Sissons, Neil, 137
Slights, Jessica, 146
Smith, Graham (Malvolio), 172–73
Smith, Molly, 79
Smith, Sid, 211
Spirituality, 63, 79, 131, 135, 141, 142–49, 151, 158–59; of Barbara Gaines, 210; in *Cymbeline*, 209, 210. *See also* sexuality, spirituality and
Stanislavsky, 20, 23, 137, 163
Stereotype(s), 36, 44, 46, 47, 49, 124, 206–7, 234
Stevenson, Juliet (Isabella), 131
Subjectivity, female, 12–14, 22, 25, 31, 39; of Imogen, 207, 217, 224–25, 231–34; of Isabella, 151, 160–61; of Juliet, 104, 109, 120; in *Measure for Measure*, 128–35; sexual subjectivity, 19, 87, 125, 170, 176, 179, 183, 186, 204–5, 216–17; of Viola, 173, 186. *See also* sexuality

Taming of the Shrew, 23–24, 55, 59, 73, 75, 80, 210, 239
Tennyson, Alfred Lord, 224, 235
Timon of Athens, 75
Timpane, John, 125
Toby, 166–67, 171, 177, 182–83, 188, 192, 200, 203
Townsend, John Marshall, 88
Troius and Cressida, 71
Tsypin, George, 226
Tucker, Patrick, 71
Twelfth Night, 13, 14, 75, 164–204, 212; comparison to *Measure for Measure* and *Romeo and Juliet*, 163, 168; stage history, 165–68
Tybalt, 95, 98–99, 100, 102, 106, 112, 113, 115–16

Venables, Clare, 17
Victimization, 35, 38–39, 42, 96, 207, 238
Vinkler, Greg, 77
Viola, 164–204, *178, 181, 182, 187, 191, 197, 201,* 241
Violence, 42, 92–93, 98–99, 122, 134, 237, 240; domestic, 30, 40–41, 88, 93–94, 106–10, 116, 120–21, 127, 184, 207, 222, 235; connection with sex, 88–92, 96–97, 99–101, 112–15, 118, 126, 128, 134, 145, 157–58; sources of, 145, 147
Vogel, Paula, 69

Warner, Deborah, 16
Warren, Roger, 206
Warrilow, David, 78
Watermeier, Daniel, 69
Watson, Walton (Provost), 141
Weapon(s), 43, 96, 100, 102, 113–14, 117, 173, 175, 192. *See also* fight choreography
Weiss, Hedy, 73, 74, 210, 212, 223
Wells, Stanley, 221
Wentworth, Scott, 75
West Side Story, 91–92
Whitney, John O., 50
Wiggins, Michael (Orsino), 166
Wilson, Walter (Lucio), *136*
Winn, Steven, 68
Winter's Tale, 223
Wold, Kristin (Isabella), *136*
Wolfe, George C., 82
Wolpe, Lisa, 14, 30, 41–49, 97–98, 110–27, *113, 114, 119,* 133, 167, 239
Women's Ensemble, 123
Woods, Mark, 62
Woronicz, Henry, 68–69, 70
Worthen, W. B., 7, 26

Zeffirelli, Franco, 91, 116
Zeisler, Peter, 79
Zerbe, Jack, 57–58, 59, 150–52, 158, 160, 161